IT IS FINISHED

365 Days of
Good News

TULLIAN
TCHIVIDJIAN

WITH NICK LANNON

transforming lives together

IT IS FINISHED
Published by David C Cook
4050 Lee Vance View
Colorado Springs, CO 80918 U.S.A.

David C Cook Distribution Canada
55 Woodslee Avenue, Paris, Ontario, Canada N3L 3E5

David C Cook U.K., Kingsway Communications
Eastbourne, East Sussex BN23 6NT, England

The graphic circle C logo is a registered trademark of David C Cook.

The website addresses noted throughout this book are
offered as a resource to you. These websites are not intended in any way to be or imply an
endorsement on the part of David C Cook, nor do we vouch for their content.

Unless otherwise noted, all Scripture quotations are taken from the Holy Bible, New International
Version®, NIV®. Copyright © 1973, 2011 by Biblica, Inc.™ Used by permission of Zondervan. All
rights reserved worldwide. www.zondervan.com. Scripture quotations marked ESV are taken from
The Holy Bible, English Standard Version® (ESV®), copyright © 2001 by Crossway, a publishing
ministry of Good News Publishers. Used by permission. All rights reserved; NASB are taken from
the New American Standard Bible®, Copyright © 1960, 1995 by The Lockman Foundation.
Used by permission. (www.lockman.org.); NRSV are taken from the New Revised Standard
Version Bible, copyright 1989, Division of Christian Education of the National Council of the
Churches of Christ in the United States of America. Used by permission. All rights reserved.
The author has added italics to Scripture quotations for emphasis.

Every effort has been made to trace copyright owners of material included
in this book. We apologize for any omissions or errors.

ISBN 978-1-62953-321-6

The Team: Alex Field, Jared C. Wilson, Amy Konyndyk,
Leigh Westin, Tiffany Thomas, Karen Athen
Cover Design: Nick Lee
Cover Photo: Shutterstock

Printed in the United States of America

In 1738, literary giant Samuel Johnson wrote in his diary: "O Lord, enable me … to redeem the time which I have spent in sloth." Nineteen years later, he wrote, "Almighty God, enable me to shake off sloth, and to redeem the time misspent in idleness and sin, by a diligent application of the days yet remaining." Every few years thereafter, he wrote some variation of this prayer, finally culminating in 1775, when he wrote, "When I look back upon resolutions of improvement and amendment, which have year after year been made and broken, … why do I yet try to resolve again? I try because reformation is necessary, and despair is criminal."

Johnson is describing all human life.

We start every new year thinking, *This is the year!* We resolve to turn over a new leaf—and this time we're serious. We promise ourselves that we're going to quit bad habits and start good ones. We're going to get in shape, eat better, waste less time, and be more content, disciplined, and intentional. We're going to be better husbands, wives, fathers, mothers. We're going to pray more, serve more, plan more, give more, read more, and memorize more Bible verses. We're going to finally be all that we can be. No more messing around.

And then, twelve months later, we realize we've fallen short—again.

What I'm most deeply grateful for is that God's love for us, approval of us, and commitment to us does not ride on our resolve but on Jesus's resolve for us. The gospel is the good news announcing Jesus's infallible devotion to us despite our inconsistent devotion to Him. The gospel is not a command to hang on to Jesus; it's a promise that no matter how weak and unsuccessful our faith and efforts may be, God is always holding on to us.

As this new year gets under way, take comfort knowing that we are weak and He is strong—that even as our love for Jesus falls short, Jesus's love for us is eternal.

Happy New Year!

Have you ever found yourself writing and rewriting an email? Or do you procrastinate making a phone call? The recipient almost inevitably becomes a proxy for the law because you fear his or her judgment. We put people in this role with alarming ease.

Having this sense of law is universal. The apostle Paul claims that it is written on each person's heart. Even those who don't believe in God tend to struggle with self-recrimination and self-hatred as much as believers. No one is free of guilt, for the law is not subject to belief in it. Some of us even compound our sense of guilt by heaping judgment upon judgment, intoxicated by the voice of "not-enoughness" until we have effectively usurped the role of the only One who is actually qualified to pass a sentence.

But against this tumult of law comes God's grace. Grace is the gift that comes with no strings attached. It is one-way love and is what makes the good news so good, the "once for all" proclamation that "there is now no condemnation for those who are in Christ Jesus" (Rom. 8:1).

The gospel of grace announces that Jesus came to acquit the guilty. Christ came to satisfy the deep judgment against us once and for all so we could be free from God's judgment as well as the judgment of others and ourselves. He came to give rest to our efforts at trying to handle judgment on our own. The gospel declares that our guilt has been atoned for, so we don't need to live under the burden of trying to own the judgment we feel. In Christ, the ultimate demand has been met. The internal voice that says, *Do this and live!* gets out-shouted by the external voice that says, "It is finished!"

The grace of God always prevails. When we finally come to the end of ourselves, there it will be. There He will be. Just as He will be the next time we come to the end of ourselves, and the time after that, and the time after that.

My friend Dr. Rod Rosenbladt told me the story of how he'd wrecked his car when he was sixteen years old after he and his friends had been drinking.

Following the accident, Rod called his dad, and the first thing his dad asked him was, "Are you all right?" Rod said yes. Then he confessed to his father that he was drunk. Rod was naturally terrified about how his father might respond. Later that night after Rod had made it home, he wept and wept in his father's study. He was embarrassed, ashamed. At the end of the ordeal, his father asked him this question: "How about tomorrow we go and get you a new car?"

Rod now says that he became a Christian in that moment. God's grace became real to him in that moment of forgiveness and mercy. Now nearly seventy, Rod has since spent his life as a spokesman for the theology of grace. Rod's father's grace didn't turn Rod into a drunk—it made him love his father and the Lord he served.

Now let me ask you: What would you like to say to Rod's dad? Rod says that every time he tells that story in public, there are always people in the audience who get angry. They say, "Your dad let you get away with that? He didn't punish you at all? What a great opportunity for your dad to teach you responsibility!" Rod always chuckles when he hears that response and says, "Do you think I didn't know what I had done? Do you think it wasn't the most painful moment of my whole life up to that point? I was ashamed; I was scared. My father spoke grace to me in a moment when I knew I deserved wrath … and I came alive."

Isn't that the nature of grace? We know that we deserve punishment and then, when we receive mercy instead, we discover grace. Romans 5:8 reads, "While we were still sinners, Christ died for us." God gives forgiveness and imputes righteousness to us even though we are sinful and while we were His enemies (vv. 6, 8, 10). Our offenses are infinitely greater than a sixteen-year-old getting drunk and wrecking his car, yet God's grace is greater still.

After the Florida Gators football team won the National Championship in 2007, coach Urban Meyer was on top of the world. Later he would describe that time by saying, "Building takes passion and energy. Maintenance is awful. It's nothing but fatigue. Once you reach the top, maintaining that beast is awful." One commentator described him as "a man running for a finish line that doesn't exist." Soon the chest pains started, and then they started getting worse. A few hours after the Gators' winning streak finally came to an end in 2009, Urban was found on the floor of his house, unable to move or speak. He had come to a breaking point. Soon he would resign, come back, and resign again.

Urban Meyer's story may be a bit extreme, but maybe you can relate. Maybe you had demanding parents for whom nothing was ever good enough. Maybe you have a demanding spouse who only notices your failures. No one can live under the burden of perfection forever. It may work for a while, but sooner or later, we hit the wall. Meyer hit the floor.

He had fallen victim to a vicious form of "performancism." He had become a slave to his record, where the points scored on the field were more than just his team's accomplishments—they were the measure of his personal worth and identity.

The law is God's scorecard, and it is His first word. But thankfully, it's not the last. The last word is the one that comes straight from the mouth of Jesus Himself, who said, "For God did not send his Son into the world to condemn the world, but to save the world through him" (John 3:17).

If you're a Christian, here's the good news: who you really are has nothing to do with you—how much you can accomplish, who you can become, your behavior, your strengths, your weaknesses, your sordid past, your family background, your education, your looks, and so on. Your identity is firmly anchored in Christ's accomplishment, not yours; His strength, not yours; His performance, not yours; His victory, not yours.

In 2011, Robert Downey Jr. received the 25th American Cinematheque Award, a prize given to "an extraordinary artist in the entertainment industry, who is fully engaged in his or her work." A big deal, in other words. Downey was allowed to choose who would present him with the award, and he made a bold decision. He selected his onetime costar Mel Gibson to do the honors.

Downey's invitation came to Mel when Gibson was pariah numero uno in Tinseltown.

Of course, Downey was no stranger to being ostracized. In the 1990s, he became something of a punch line himself as someone notoriously unable to kick an addiction to drugs and alcohol. Here's what he said after Gibson introduced him:

> I asked Mel to present this award to me for a reason. Because when I couldn't get sober, he told me not to give up hope and he urged me to find my faith … and most importantly, he said that if I accepted responsibility for my wrongdoings and if I embraced that part of my soul that was ugly—"hugging the cactus" he calls it … my life would take on new meaning. And I did and it worked. All he asked in return was that someday I help the next guy in some small way. It's reasonable to assume that at the time he didn't imagine the next guy would be him.… I humbly ask that you join me … in forgiving my friend his trespasses, offering him the same clean slate you have me, and allowing him to continue his great and ongoing contribution to our collective art without shame.

To advocate for Mel in such a public manner meant putting Downey's own reputation on the line. It was a self-sacrificial and even reckless move. There was no evident gain for Downey. No, his defense of the indefensible was the uncoerced act of a heart that's been touched by one-way love.

Of course, this episode is not a one-to-one analogy for the gospel—no story could be. But it's a vivid illustration of the reality that there is not even a hint of exchange in God's grace. No suggestion of payback or paying it forward. There are no strings attached. Grace is pure gift.

It is one-way love.

Have you ever heard people say that even if they believed in God, they wouldn't like Him? Some people, it seems, almost need God not to exist, in order to make their perception of the world make sense.

Many people are like this. They've considered the state that the world is in and have concluded, if there is a God, He's a God they don't want to have anything to do with. The reason? They haven't made the jump that Paul makes in the beginning of Romans 1. They know about the descriptions of God and Jesus, but they can't comprehend that God in Jesus would be *for them.*

For too many, Jesus is some idealized figure representing some impersonal deity. When we think like that, the gospel just seems like some kind of religious slogan. But in the Bible we discover that the message we call the gospel actually unites us to the real Jesus Christ. So Jesus is Himself the gospel—not just because He is God, but because He is God *for us!* He is the incarnation of God's movement *toward* His sinful people. It is Jesus through whom we have received grace.

Jesus is God's movement toward us, even as we run away. Jesus is the giver of grace and the way through which grace is granted. And this grace, resident in and embodied by Jesus Christ, is the power of God for salvation. Jesus is something much better than *a* savior—He's *your Savior.*

Paul is writing Romans to a church he didn't found. They didn't know him. In the same way, Jesus proclaimed—and, in fact, *was*—a message to a world that didn't know Him. John 1:10 says that even "though the world was made through him, the world did not recognize him." God's message of grace is always a message to a people who are strangers to Him.

Paul wrote to tell the Romans the same thing that Jesus Christ came to tell—and *be* for—the world: you can't do this on your own. But take heart. God has a Son, and this Son is a Savior. Your Savior.

The Jesus that Paul proclaims to you is the gospel, and even better, He's the gospel for you.

Noah is often presented to us as the first character in the Bible really worthy of emulation. Scripture, though, says that the Lord decided to blot man out because "every inclination of the thoughts of the human heart was only evil all the time" (v. 5). Look at all the superlatives: *every* inclination, *only* evil, *all* the time! That kind of language doesn't leave a lot of room for exceptions … not even for Noah.

So how do we get from "I will wipe mankind, whom I have created, from the face of the earth … for I am grieved that I have made them" (v. 7) to "Noah was a righteous man" (v. 9)? We get from here to there—from sin to righteousness—by the glory of verse 8, which highlights God's initiating grace: "But Noah found favor in the eyes of the Lord."

Some read this and make it sound as if God is scouring the earth to find someone—anyone—who is righteous. And then one day, while searching high and low, God sees Noah and breathes a divine sigh of relief. "Phew! At least there's one." But that's not what it says.

Favor here is the same word that is translated elsewhere as "grace." In other words, as is the case with all of us who know God, it was God who found us—we didn't find God. We are where we are today not because we found grace but because grace found us.

It took the grace of God to move Noah from the ranks of the unrighteous to the ranks of the redeemed. Noah's righteousness is not a precondition for his receiving favor (though we are wired to read it this way). His righteousness *is a result of his having already received favor*.

The gospel is not a story of God meeting sinners halfway. The news is so much better than that. The gospel is that God gives favor to those who don't deserve it. Sinners—Noah and the rest of us—are recipients of a preemptive love that changes everything, breathing new life into us with the power to carry us from unrighteousness to righteousness without an ounce of help.

When I was sixteen, my parents kicked me out of the house. It got to the point where my lifestyle had become so disruptive to the rest of the household that they were left with no choice but to painfully say, "We love you, but you can't live under our roof."

A couple years after they kicked me out and after losing yet another of my many dead-end jobs, I asked my dad for money. It's the only reason I ever called. Without asking me anything, he gave me a signed blank check, and said, "Take whatever you need. This should hold you over until you can find another job." He didn't probe into why I lost my job or yell at me for doing so. He didn't give me a limit. I remember not only taking that check and writing it out for much more than I needed, but also sneaking into my parents' house on numerous occasions and stealing more checks. I had mastered forging my dad's signature and even went six months without a job because I had all the money I "needed." I completely took advantage of his kindness—and he knew it!

Years later, he told me that he saw the results of all those checks being cashed but decided not to say anything about it. It didn't happen immediately, but that demonstration of unconditional grace was the beginning of God doing a miraculous work in my heart and life. My dad's literal "turning the other cheek" gave me a picture of God's unconditional love that I couldn't shake.

Now, I'm not saying this is the pattern every time for every child in every situation. What I've given is a snapshot of one thing my father did at a very particular time for a very particular reason. My parents handled me differently in a variety of situations. But on this occasion, knowing me the way only a father can know his son, my dad did something I'm sure was scary for him. And God used it.

Steve Brown wrote, "Children will run from law, and they'll run from grace. The ones who run from law never come back. But the ones who run from grace always come back. Grace draws its own back home." I ran from grace. It drew me home.

It was a staple of Jewish literature around the time of Christ to run down a sort of history of sin, always laying it at the feet of Gentile idolaters. In other words, for first-century Jews there was a distinct dividing line between "us" and "them." We do the same thing today, both in our literature and in our lives. In fact, we base our entire personal universes on "us" and "them."

We may not be perfect, we say to ourselves, *but at least we spend more time with our children than "they" do. We may have our issues, but at least we're not throwing all our money away on jewelry like "they" do. We may be broken sinners, but at least we've found a good church and are regularly attending, unlike "them."* As long as we're not like "them," we think we're okay.

Into this very familiar pattern of bashing "them" for causing all of the world's problems, Paul throws a haymaker. Every "they" in chapter one becomes "you" in chapter two!

For instance, Paul transitions from "Although they knew God, they neither glorified him as God nor gave thanks to him, but their thinking became futile and their foolish hearts were darkened. Although they claimed to be wise, they became fools" (Rom. 1:21–22) to "You, therefore, have no excuse, you who pass judgment on someone else" (Rom. 2:1).

And down comes the tragic hammer of the law: we *are* "they." This is bad news. It's perhaps the worst of news: you're far worse off than you think. "They" can't be blamed for any of your problems. You are the problem. You always have been. Ouch.

But this story, as painfully as it begins, always ends with good news: by the life and sacrifice of Jesus Christ, God brings life out of death and righteousness out of sin. In fact, Jesus puts Himself in the "them" category, taking the blame for all that's wrong in the world. He identifies with "them," which means He is identifying with you, that you might be identified with *Him.* In the gospel, God has eradicated our moralistic categories and declared bad people good by the virtue of His Son.

We may sometimes shift blame for our problems from ourselves. You know what I mean: "It's not me; it's him [or her or this or that]." That's why James can seem incredulous.

Many of us have been told our whole lives that we can do and be anything we want—in short, that we're wonderful and just have to overcome these outside obstacles frustrating our inner awesomeness and limitless potential. So when confronted with James's words—that *we're* the problem—we recoil. His words are offensive, but they're also true.

James hits us hard by revealing that relational breakdown has nothing to do with anything outside of us—it has everything to do with what's going on inside of us. When we don't have what we want, we'll kill for it. When I'm not getting from you what I think I need, I'll fight you. Once James puts it into words, it couldn't be more obvious: our main problem in life is ourselves. Cartoonist Walt Kelly put it most lyrically: "We have met the enemy and he is us."

The Bible is God's single story of great sinners in need of and being met by a great Savior. We set time apart for God through prayer and Bible reading, for example, because it is in those places where God reminds us again and again that things between us are forever fixed. They are the rendezvous points where God declares to us concretely that the debt has been paid, the ledger put away, and that, in Christ, everything we need we already possess. This convincing assurance produces humility, because we realize that our needs are fulfilled. We don't have to worry about ourselves anymore. This, in turn, allows us to stop looking out for what we think we need and liberates us to love our neighbor by looking out for what *they* need. The vertical relationship is secure, freeing us to think about the horizontal ones—about others. What comes next is a peace we could not attain on our own.

Once we are convinced that we have everything we need in Christ and that His saving work is finished, our faith is stoked once more, and love—concern for others that overshadows a concern for ourselves—blossoms.

In 2013, Riley Cooper, a wide receiver for the Philadelphia Eagles, used a racial slur (*the* racial slur) during a confrontation at a concert while claiming that he wanted to fight all of the African Americans there. (Cooper is white.) The entire tirade was caught on video.

Cooper apologized, immediately and profusely, but what's really interesting is not the quality of Cooper's apology but the reaction of Cooper's teammates *to* the apology.

Two very different reactions from two different teammates (both African American) illustrate very powerfully some famous words of Jesus that those who are forgiven much, love much.

The first reaction to Cooper's apology came from his quarterback, Michael Vick, the quarterback who spent nearly two years in prison for running a dog-fighting ring. Vick said, "As a team we understood because we all make mistakes in life.... But [it's] easy to forgive him."

On the other end of the spectrum is LeSean McCoy, the Eagles' star running back: "I forgive him. We've been friends for a long time. But in a situation like this you really find out about someone.... I can't really respect someone like that." (McCoy has since come to publicly regret these comments.)

Notice that where Vick said "we," McCoy said "I." Michael Vick put himself in a category with Riley Cooper. While McCoy sought to distance himself from a former friend, Vick put himself next to the accused. The difference between Vick and McCoy? Twenty-one months in a federal penitentiary and a deep knowledge of what it feels like to need forgiveness.

To the extent that we ignore (or run from) our own sinfulness, we will be unable to care for other sinners. We will be unable to extend forgiveness to others until we are honest about the extent to which we are forgiven. Ungracious people are those who haven't come to grips with their own dire, daily need for grace. The most forgiving people are those who are coming to daily, deeper terms with their own need for forgiveness.

In 2012, the *Telegraph* (UK) published an email sent by retired Royal Navy officer Nick Crews to his children. It quickly became a viral sensation. The letter lists, in remarkably colorful language, all the misery that they had put their parents through, from failed marriages and careers to poor finances and fears about their grandchildren's well-being. The final paragraph is particularly vicious.

> I can now tell you that I for one, and I sense Mum feels the same, have had enough of being forced to live through the never-ending bad dream of our children's underachievement and domestic ineptitudes.... I am bitterly, bitterly disappointed.

Wow. Many parents, though, can probably relate. But do you think that the letter had the effect Mr. Crews intended? Absolutely not! The letter may have succeeded in scaring the kids straight for a spell, but fear of further berating would be the driving factor, not the genuine desire to fly right.

What's much more likely is that the children were so hurt that they struck back at their father by releasing his letter to the media so that he might be humiliated by the public. Which is precisely what happened. His email backfired. Instead of bringing his children closer, it pushed them further away. This is an echo of what the apostle Paul meant when he wrote that "the law was brought in so that the trespass might increase" (v. 20).

We make a big mistake when we conclude that the law is the answer to bad behavior. In fact, the law alone stirs up more of such behavior. People get worse, not better, when you lay down the law. To be sure, the Spirit does use both God's law and God's gospel in our sanctification. But the law and the gospel do very different things. The law reveals sin but is powerless to remove it. It points to righteousness but can't produce it. It shows us what godliness is, but it cannot make us godly. As Martin Luther said, "Sin is not canceled by lawful living, for no person is able to live up to the Law. Nothing can take away sin except the grace of God." The law apart from the gospel can only crush; it cannot cure.

When the Ghostbusters are called into the mayor's office, they're asked to describe what might happen if the character Gozer is unleashed on the world. They try to describe it: "A disaster of biblical proportions.... Fire and brimstone coming down from the skies! Rivers and seas boiling! Forty years of darkness! Earthquakes, volcanoes ... The dead rising from the grave! Human sacrifice, dogs and cats living together ... mass hysteria!" Billy Bob Thornton does about the same thing in *Armageddon*, when he's asked what will happen if an asteroid the size of Texas were to hit the earth. "Half the world's population will be incinerated by the heat blast, and the rest will freeze to death from nuclear winter. Basically the worst parts of the Bible."

But given what we see, not just in Hollywood movies but in newspaper headlines every day, doesn't it seem like it's the worst parts of the Bible—such as what's described in Luke 21—that we're living through now ... and that the best parts are merely part of some hopeful future?

There is good news: Jesus is aware of what life is like. He is the ultimate tell-it-like-it-is guy. No sugarcoating from Jesus. No power of positive thinking. He knows this life is hard. That's why He came. The worst parts of the Bible are the ones that describe a world waiting and aching for a Savior. As Tom Petty said, "The waiting is the hardest part."

But in the end, while waiting is the hardest part, it opens the door to the best part. We have a God who comes to us and doesn't ask us to go to Him. And so, we wait. We wait for the world to not be the way it is anymore. We wait for ourselves to not be the way we are anymore. In the midst of our waiting, a Savior comes, and comes to us. He's a Savior who knows what the waiting has been like, who knows that the waiting is the hardest part. All we have to do, and all we can do, is wait. He'll do the work. And when He comes, "stand up and lift up your heads, because your redemption is drawing near" (v. 28).

The scribes and Pharisees catch a woman in the act of adultery and drag her before Jesus. They tell Jesus of her infraction and remind Him that the law of Moses says such women should be stoned. Then they issue a challenge: "What do you say?" (v. 5). They're trying to trick Jesus into admitting what they suspect: that He's soft on the law.

Boy, were they wrong.

Confronted by this test, Jesus bends down and writes in the sand with His finger. We aren't told what He writes, but whatever He wrote, the function of His writing is clear: it serves to reveal the sin of those gathered.

Far from being soft on the law, Jesus shows just how high the bar really is. How do we know? Because the scribes and Pharisees respond the same way that all of us respond when we are confronted with the depth of God's inflexible demands—they scattered.

When Jesus and the woman are left alone and she acknowledges that no one remains to condemn her, Jesus speaks His final word to her: "Neither do I condemn you. Go now and leave your life of sin" (v. 11). This is where the story gets misunderstood.

"Aha!" we cry. "See! Jesus tells her to shape up. He leaves her with an exhortation." But look at the order of Jesus's words: *First*, he tells the woman that He does not condemn her. *Only then* does He instruct her to sin no more. He does not make His love conditional on her behavior.

Our Savior does so much better than that.

Jesus creates new life in the woman by loving her unconditionally. By forgiving her profound shame, He impacts her profoundly. By refusing to condemn her, He sets her free to do what she has no doubt already pledged to do on her own: leave her old life behind.

Like the adulteress, we are all caught in the act—discovered in a shameful breach of God's law. Though no one on earth can throw the first stone, God can. And He did. The wonder of all wonders is that the rock of condemnation we justly deserved was hurled by the Father onto the Son. The lawmaker became the law keeper and died for you and me—the lawbreakers—so we might be declared law keepers too, all by the grace of Jesus.

I'll never forget telling my dad that Kim, my then-fiancée (now my wife), was pregnant.

We summoned the courage to go over to my parents' house the day after we found out—Mother's Day, believe it or not. After some awkward small talk, I asked my father if we could speak to him alone. Almost as soon as I began talking, I burst into tears. "Kim's pregnant." Kim started bawling too. Next thing I knew, he was embracing both of us, me with one arm, her with the other, while we wept. He held us for ten minutes. He could see how overwhelmed we were. I can still hear his voice telling us, "It's okay. We love you. It's going to be okay. This child is going to be a blessing."

The whole situation was wrapped in grace. I deserved his reproach and disapproval—premarital sex resulting in unexpected pregnancy is no father's dream for his child—yet his gracious response assured me that he not only wasn't crushed, but that his love for me was stronger than ever. When I told him (through many tears) how sorry I was for letting him down, he simply hushed me by hugging me tighter and saying over and over again, "It's okay. I love you. It's okay. I love you." At that moment in the driveway, when I rightly deserved my dad's disappointment, he assured me of his delight. Even now it is hard to put into words the emotional relief I felt. *Lifesaving* is not too strong a word. I thank God with every fiber of my being that He put me in a family where I was surrounded by such one-way love.

This act of grace served as a powerful reflection of that one true act of grace. My dad treated me in a way that was analogous to how God treats you and me. My dad may not be God, but like many fathers, he plays a similar role in my life—someone in authority who showed me love in the midst of deserved judgment. And like that one true act of grace, my father's forgiveness and love changed me forever.

One of the most common objections grace-addicted people hear is, "Okay, I get it. Can we move on now? Can we hear something different already?" The truth is, we never ever outgrow our need to hear the gospel.

According to Paul, real love is impossible without faith (Gal. 5:6). Faith is vertical (it's upward)—it's trusting that everything I need and long for I already have because of what Jesus has accomplished for me. Love, on the other hand, is horizontal (it's outward)—because Jesus has done everything for me (faith), I can now do everything for you without needing you to do anything for me (love).

You could put it this way: love is faith worked out by us for our neighbor horizontally; faith is love worked into us from God vertically. The implication, of course, is that love is absent to the degree that faith is missing. If I'm not trusting that everything I need in Christ I already possess (lack of faith), then I will be looking to take from you rather than to give to you (lack of love). I'll be concentrating on what I need, not on what you need. I'll be looking out for me, not you.

So if we ever hope to "love our neighbor as ourselves," which is precisely what God's law calls for, it will depend on faith. And faith, according to Paul, depends on hearing the gospel—over and over and over again. God stokes faith through the gospel's proclamation, and since our faith needs constant stoking, proclamation of the gospel needs to be constant. As long as love is always needed, faith must be fueled, and the only fuel for faith is the gospel.

In short: only the gospel's proclamation activates faith, and then only faith activates love.

If the world is ever going to experience the kind of reformation we long for, Christians are going to have to understand we are not called to say many different things about many different subjects but rather the same thing in different ways about every subject. We don't graduate from the gospel, and we shouldn't tire of it. It can and does apply to everything.

Just as we never outgrow our need for the gospel, we never outgrow our need to hear it.

We're all exhausted.

The fact is, real life is long on law and short on grace—demands never stop, failures pile up, and fears set in. Life requires many things from us—successful careers, stable marriages, well-behaved children, a certain quality of life. When life gets hard, the hardworking work harder. Is it any wonder we're all so weary? Anyone living inside the guilt, anxiety, stress, strain, and uncertainty of daily life knows from instinct and hard experience that the weight of life is heavy. We are all in need of some relief.

But there's another reason we're so tired: we're trying to save ourselves.

Every single one of us is plagued by "performancism." Performancism is the mind-set that equates our identity and value directly with our performance. Performancism sees achievement not as something we do or don't do but as something we are or aren't. How we look, how intelligent we are, how our kids turn out, what people think of us—these things are synonymous with our worth. In the world of performancism, success equals life and failure equals death.

In other words, we're exhausted because we're trying to rescue ourselves from a meaningless existence by what we do. We're weary because we feel the burden to create our own validation.

But broken people cannot fix brokenness. We need divine intervention. We need validation, but we can't muster it ourselves. What an amazing thing, then, that the holy God of the universe, who set the standard for validation higher than we could ever reach, reaches down to us and proclaims over messy sinners who can't ever get their own act together, "Justified!"

As long as we are seeking our worth in anything and everything but the gospel of God's grace, we will keep seeking and keep wearing ourselves out in the process. But in Christ's finished work is ultimate and eternal validation. And ultimate and eternal rest.

In the 2014 Sochi Olympics, Jeremy Abbott, the American men's singles ice-skating champion, fell spectacularly on his first jump in the short program. It was, however, a fall that viewers could see coming a mile away. He fell during the same program in the team competition and looked nervous beyond belief before he got on the ice.

He got credit for a gutsy performance in finishing his program, which included several more difficult jumps. The commentators expressed surprise that he could skate so well after such an embarrassing fall. But really, it ought to have been expected. Once the possibility of Olympic glory was gone, Abbott clearly felt a freedom that he hadn't felt before. There was no longer any reason to be nervous. He skated with a verve that wouldn't have been possible had his shortcomings not been so obviously exposed to the world.

It is when we can look ourselves in the mirror and be honest about what we see—failings, sins, and shortcomings—that we can begin to live our lives with some measure of freedom. As long as we look in that mirror and tell ourselves that glory is possible, we'll be like Jeremy Abbott before the fall—a nervous wreck. We'll be terrified of exposure, of failure, of being outed as frauds.

Once we face our flaws, we find that our freedom is even better than Abbott's. Our errors, our embarrassing falls, and our public disgraces have been given to a substitute. His perfect score has been given to us. We now live secure in the knowledge that when the Judge regards us, He sees only His blameless Son, Jesus Christ. The next time Jeremy Abbott skates that program, that fall will likely surface in his memory. He might worry about it and hope it doesn't happen again. Fortunately, our falls can never come back to us. They were nailed to a cross two thousand years ago.

We have all gone crashing to the ice too many times to keep telling ourselves that our quest for glory is ongoing. It's over. We've failed. But now we're free. We can live our lives without trying to fool anyone into thinking that we don't need saving. We do, and desperately.

Out on parole after nineteen years in prison, *Les Misérables* protagonist Jean Valjean is denied shelter at several respectable establishments because his passport identifies him as a former convict. He is finally taken in by the kindly bishop, Monseigneur Bienvenu. Valjean repays his host by stealing the church's silver. When Valjean is dragged back to the bishop's house by the police, Bienvenu not only validates Valjean's lie that the silver was a gift but chastises him for forgetting the candlesticks! Jean Valjean is utterly confounded. When he deserved imprisonment, he received mercy. Actually, more than mercy. Mercy would involve simply dropping the charges, but the bishop goes further—he actually rewards Valjean for his transgression! Bienvenu acts, in other words, in the polar opposite way than what would be expected of him. He is not wise or responsible. He treats Valjean recklessly, overruling what the law—literally standing in front of him—demands. He takes a major risk and blesses this criminal who has shown no ability to act in a nonshameful way.

His love has everything to do with the sacrifice of the one doing the loving rather than the merit of the beloved.

This is another way to go, thanks be to God—the way of grace as opposed to law. This one moment of grace changes Valjean in a way that a lifetime of punishment never could. In fact, his heroic, self-sacrificing actions in the rest of the novel flow directly from the word he hears from the bishop, which is the word of the gospel.

Listen closely: The law exposes Valjean (and us), while grace exonerates him. The law accuses; grace acquits. The law can break a hard heart, but only grace can heal one. Which is precisely what happens to Valjean. He may be a fictional character, but our response to his predicament is not fictional. The tears come because each one of us is dying to be treated this way.

And the glorious truth is that Jesus Christ died so we would.

One of my all-time favorite moments in television history happened on *Seinfeld*, when Elaine comes into Jerry's apartment after just having *another* frustrating interaction with someone. I don't remember if it was the "low talker" or the "sidler" or what, but she comes in flustered, declaring, "I hate people!" And without missing a beat, Jerry looks up from what he's doing and says, "They're the worst."

This frustration is a universal human experience. The level of dislike I can generate toward someone who cuts me off in traffic is very disturbing to me. I may usually be Dr. Jekyll, but my inner Mr. Hyde is always lying in wait.

So Jesus's "new command" (v. 34) is already starting to cause a problem for me. "Love one another." Like, always? Even the clown in the Lexus convertible who didn't even look before careening over into my lane? But then, Jesus isn't finished. "*As I have loved you*, so you must love one another" (v. 34). So it's not enough to love people in our self-satisfying, when-we-feel-like-it human way; we have to love as Jesus loves us! This is a reality check that Jesus is giving to the people He's talking to.

Yet God's Word is creative. Jesus continues, "By this everyone will know that you are my disciples, if you love one another" (v. 35). Miraculously, you find yourself loving and being loved. Now, we might admit freely that we love because Jesus first loved us, but we don't love because we owe it to Him or because He told us to. We love because love for us *brings out love for one another*. We are loved by the Jesus who loved the people who weren't good enough. We are loved by the Jesus who loved the people who came up short. We are loved by the Jesus who planted His love in our hearts.

The good news of the gospel is that Jesus did not wait until we were loving before He loved us; He didn't even wait till we asked Him to love us before He loved us—He loved us in our unloveliness. And His love *for* us births love *in* us, which bleeds love through us to those around us.

"You should be like the Good Samaritan." If you grew up in church, you probably heard this a thousand times. But this misses the main point of the story.

If Jesus had been asked, "How should we treat our neighbors?" and had responded with that story, perhaps "be like the Good Samaritan" would be an acceptable interpretation. Instead, Jesus was asked, "What must I do to inherit eternal life?" (Mark 10:17). He is asked this vertical question (a question about a person's relationship to God) before the horizontal one ("Who is my neighbor?"). This parable must, therefore, be interpreted vertically first.

Instead of telling this parable to help us learn a moralistic lesson about being nice to people, Jesus is showing us how far from being like the Good Samaritan—and how much like the priest and Levite—we actually are. Jesus's parable aims to destroy our efforts to justify ourselves, to find a class of people we can call neighbors that we actually do love. Jesus brings the hammer of the law ("Be perfect …") down on our self-justifying work.

In a rich irony, we move from being identified with the priest and the Levite—never perfectly loving our best friends as ourselves, much less our enemies—to being identified with the traveler in desperate need of salvation. Jesus intends the parable itself to leave us beaten and bloodied, lying in a ditch, like the man in the story. We are the needy, unable to do anything to help ourselves. We are the broken, beaten up by life, robbed of hope.

But then Jesus comes. Casting the Samaritan—considered an enemy by the average Jew—as the hero of the story is a reminder that Jesus has identified with those far from God to bring them near, that He has "become sin" to cancel sin's debt.

Unlike the priest and Levite, Jesus doesn't avoid us. He crosses the street, from heaven to earth, comes into our mess, and gets His hands dirty. At great cost to Himself on the cross, He heals our wounds, covers our nakedness, and loves us with a no-strings-attached love. He brings us to the Father and promises that His help is not simply a onetime gift—rather, it's a gift that will forever cover future charges we incur.

Jesus is the Good Samaritan.

One night, as I was putting my daughter to bed, I asked her, "Honey, how do you think God feels about you?" Her immediate response was, "Disappointed." After some probing, I realized that she wasn't feeling convicted about any particular sin; she simply sees God as Someone whose feelings toward her are basically unhappy ones. She knows that God is perfect and that she is imperfect. She understands that God is holy and that she is sinful, and so it only makes sense to her that God is perpetually displeased with her.

I scrambled in my mind for an illustration that might help an eleven-year-old grasp the liberating power of Christ's imputed righteousness.

I said, "Imagine some stranger—let's call him Steven—comes walking down our street right about the time Mommy is making dinner. He walks up our driveway, through our front door without knocking, into our kitchen, looks at Mommy, and asks, 'What's for dinner?' Now, you and I both know that Mommy is hospitable. But a complete stranger walking into our house would freak her out. She'd probably say something like, 'Who are you? And if you don't turn around and leave right now, I'm going to call the police.'"

I continued, "Now imagine that same stranger comes walking down our street around dinnertime *with your older brother*. The two of them together walk up our driveway, through the front door, and into our kitchen. Your brother looks at Mommy with his arm around his friend and says, 'Mom, this is my friend Steven. Can he stay for dinner?' Her response would be totally different, wouldn't it? She would say something like, 'Nice to meet you, Steven. Of course you can have dinner with us.' Then she'd get another place setting and treat Steven like a son at our table. Why? Because he was with *our* son."

Many Christians think that God is perpetually disappointed with them. But because of what Jesus did for us on the cross, God sees us as friends and children, not as enemies and strangers. God is a good Father, and because we're with Jesus, God's affection for us is unchanging and His approval of us is forever.

How often have you heard the gospel equated with a positive change in a believer's life? "I used to _____, but then I met Jesus and now I'm _____." It may be unintentional, but we make a serious mistake when we reduce the good news to its results—such as patience, sobriety, and compassion—in the lives of those who have heard it. These are beautiful developments, and belief in the gospel does produce such fruit. But the results should not be confused with the gospel itself.

Well-meaning Christians sometimes adopt a narrative of improvement that becomes a functional law for them through which they filter their experiences. The narrative can be as simple as "I was worse, but now I am better," or as arbitrary as "I used to have a difficult relationship with my mother, but now it's much easier." Soon we wed our faith to these narratives, and when an experience or feeling doesn't fit—for example, when we have a sudden outburst of anger at someone we thought we had forgiven—it disturbs our security or causes us to doubt.

If the narrative we've adopted says that our lives have to get better in order for our relationships with God to be legitimate, we twist the gospel into a moral improvement scheme.

God is not interested in what you think you should be or how you should feel. He is not interested in the narrative you construct for yourself or that others construct for you. He may even use suffering to deconstruct that narrative. Rather, He is interested in *you*, the you who suffers, the you who inflicts suffering on others, the you who hides, the you who has bad days (and good ones). And He meets you where you are. Jesus is not the man at the top of the stairs; He is the man at the bottom, the friend of sinners, the Savior of those in need of one. Which is all of us, all of the time.

I used to think that the simple good news of Christianity was just for non-Christians. Jesus came to save sinners, but once someone became saved, I figured they'd move on to the advanced material. I saw the gospel as Christianity 101 and the rest of the Christian life as graduate-level courses. But I've come to realize that the gospel isn't the first step in a stairway of truths but more like the hub in a wheel of truth. Once God rescues sinners, He doesn't give them something else to think about or do, He simply gives them more gospel, grace upon grace. All good theology is an exposition of the gospel.

It seems to me that there are two challenges Christians face day after day in this broken world: First, we need to understand theologically that the gospel doesn't just ignite the Christian life, but it's also the fuel that keeps Christians going and growing every day. The second challenge, which is much harder for me than the first, is to understand how this actually works.

I address the second challenge by regularly asking myself questions such as: Because Jesus secured my pardon and absorbed the Father's wrath on my behalf so "there is now no condemnation for those who are in Christ Jesus" (Rom. 8:1), how does that impact my longing for approval, my tendency to be controlling, and my fear of the unknown?

Where exactly am I experiencing agitation, impatience, unease, anxiety? Why is it there? What's it really about? I try to identify where my restlessness is rooted, because that's where a confrontation with the gospel is needed. Whatever deficiency lies at the deepest root of our restlessness—no matter how big or small, whether it's life-gripping or comparatively trivial—the missing component is something very specific that Christ has already secured for restless sinners like you and me.

The gospel is like a skeleton key this way, fitting into every sin and fear I have, applying to them all. The finished work of Christ satisfies my deepest daily needs, so I can experience the liberating power of the gospel every day and in every way.

If you've ever watched a sports postgame press conference, you know there's one thing that you never hear, even from a dominant winning team: "I don't think we can do any better. That was it. That was perfect." No. Instead, players always say something like, "We played great, but there's always room for improvement." "We could play better defense." "We missed some open shots." And you know what? They're right. They could play better defense. They could make every single one of their shots. There is always room for improvement. And that, I believe, that room for improvement, is the distance between God and humanity.

God is perfect. "In him there is no darkness at all" (1 John 1:5). Interestingly, we don't need the Bible to tell us that. We know it intuitively. Remember that famous line from the old priest in *Rudy*? "Son," says the priest, "I have only come up with two hard, incontrovertible facts: there is a God, and I'm not Him."

Who can argue with this? We think to ourselves, *Nobody's perfect. Perfection is an unattainable goal!* And yet, we strive. Boy, do we strive.

We understand, inherently, that if we're not perfect, if we have darkness in us, we can't be in relationship with a perfect God. But the old priest's self-awareness is uncommon. We say, "I'm not him," with our lips, but our hearts desire the God role more than any other. That's why we get to work on attaining perfection, all the while admitting that it's impossible.

So if perfection is unattainable (which we know in our heads) but required (which we know in our hearts), how can there be good news? The good news is that our perfection has been won for us—and gifted to us—rather than required from us. Or better, it has been required and then gifted. The law requires our own perfection; the gospel gifts us God's own perfection. There's no better news than that.

John Fitzgerald Page was voted Gawker.com's 2007 "Worst Person in the World" for an exchange he had with a woman on a dating website. Here's a bit of what he wrote to her when she turned down his invitation:

> So next time you meet a guy of my caliber, instead of trying to turn it around, just get to the gym! I will even give you one free training session, so you don't blow it with the next 8.9 on Hot or Not, Ivy League grad, Mensa member, can bench/squat/leg press over 1200 lbs., has had lunch with the secretary of defense, has an MBA from the top school in the country, ... drives a Beemer convertible, has been in 14 major motion pictures, was in Jezebel's Best dressed, etc. Oh, that is right, there aren't any more of those!

In the face of rejection, poor John defended himself. He listed his achievements, his attributes, and accolades—some of which are, on the surface, impressive. John's problem isn't his résumé; it's what he thinks about his résumé. He used it to justify his existence, leaning on it for righteousness, and therefore love.

We all do this. We're just typically slick enough to keep it more private than John did.

Paul also had plenty to be proud of. His pedigree, his track record, his religious standing were all impeccable. If he had wanted to justify his existence, he would have had a solid basis on which to do so—the first-century Jewish equivalent of blue-blood, Ivy League, Fortune 500 status. But Paul understands this still falls short of the righteousness needed: "But whatever were gains to me I now consider loss for the sake of Christ ... for whose sake I have lost all things ... that I may gain Christ and be found in him, not having a righteousness of my own ... but that which is through faith in Christ—the righteousness that comes from God on the basis of faith" (vv. 7–9).

Our identity is anchored in Christ's accomplishment, not our own; Christ's strength, not ours; Christ's pedigree and track record, not ours; Christ's victory, not ours. Who we really are has nothing to do with us at all—rather, it has everything to do with what Jesus has done for us.

No one in the Bible is more of a repeat offender than the apostle Peter. His consistent ineptitude is almost comical, or at least it would be were he not also the one who Jesus appointed to be His chief representative.

Peter lived with Jesus for three and a half years, witnessed many miracles, and heard His teaching. He had given up everything for the Lord he deeply loved (Matt. 19:27), and he loved his Savior more than he had ever loved anyone. And yet, his track record was abysmal.

He sank when Jesus told him to walk on water. Jesus called him Satan when Peter tried to persuade Jesus that He wouldn't have to die. He fell asleep three times in Gethsemane, despite Jesus asking him to keep watch. Jesus rebuked him for drawing and using his sword at Christ's arrest. He denied knowing Jesus three times on the night He was tried.

Apart from his being the first to acknowledge that Jesus was the Christ, the Son of God, almost everything he did in the Gospels ended in a correction, a rebuke, or just simple failure. Yet he is designated "the rock." Why?

It is no coincidence that Peter was both the weakest and the one who recognized who Jesus was. He could recognize the Savior, because he knew how much he needed one. His faith was directly tied to his failure. As one writer accurately put it, "The great and merciful surprise is that we come to God not by doing it right but by doing it wrong!"

This is proved by one of the most comforting passages in the Bible. When the women find the young man minding the empty tomb on Easter morning, he gives them a message, which names Peter specifically, who must have feared that his relationship with Jesus was over. That disciple who had seemingly done all in his power to ruin his relationship with Christ, and who had, only a few days before, denied even knowing Him at all, was still going to receive a kept promise: "There you will see him, just as he told you" (Mark 16:7).

Though Peter was an ultimate promise breaker, as are we, Jesus was and ever will be the ultimate promise keeper.

If you've had small children, you've had to spend a lot of time differentiating between things in your house. You know, there are things that you can put in your mouth and things that you can't or shouldn't. Basically, in our house, we've broken down all of God's creation into two categories: clean and yucky. On the table? Clean. On the floor? Yucky. On the counter? Clean. In the trash can? Yucky. In the refrigerator? Clean. In the toilet? Well, you can see how it works.

But this exercise is more common than you would think. It's not simply reserved for the raising of children. You and I are always trying to discern the clean from the yucky, between what's allowed and not allowed. Christians spend a lot of time doing this kind of separation with sin. Gambling is a sin. Or maybe it's not. It probably depends on who's doing it, where they're doing it, how much they're doing it for. Lying is a sin. Or maybe it's not. Depends on what you're lying about, whose feelings you might be protecting, how uncomfortable the truth might be. We like to find the loopholes for ourselves and tighten them up for others.

In any event, we all spend a lot of energy a lot of the time separating the good from the bad, and we do it all with a scary amount of self-interest and ignorance.

When an "unclean" spirit asks if Jesus has come to destroy him, the answer is basically yes. Jesus rebukes the spirit, saying, "Be quiet, and come out of him!" (v. 25 NASB), and with writhing and a shriek, the spirit leaves the man. Mark begins his story of the ministry of Jesus with this kind of battle royal between clean and unclean, something that people living at this time would have been *very* familiar with. We're still familiar with it.

Nobody can sort the clean from the yucky like Jesus can.

Jesus destroys the unclean thing. Jesus is the holiness that destroys unholiness. He's the cleanliness that scrubs away uncleanliness. He's the righteousness that covers unrighteousness. And He can do it in us and for us infinitely better than we could manage it ourselves.

Paul's testimony in Romans 7 demonstrates what we all know to be true about ourselves. Even after God saves us, our thoughts, words, motives, deeds, and affections need the constant cleansing of Christ's blood and forgiveness that comes our way for free. Paul, like us, has been raised from the dead and is now alive to Christ, but remaining sin continues to plague him at every level and in every way.

While it is gloriously true for the Christian that there is nowhere Christ has not arrived by His Spirit, there is a converse and more sobering truth: there is no part of any Christian in this life that is free of sin. Because of the totality of sin's effect, therefore, we never outgrow our need for Christ's finished work on our behalf. We never graduate beyond our desperate need for Christ's righteousness.

The reason this is so important is because we will always be suspicious of grace until we realize our desperate need for it. Our dire need for God's grace doesn't get smaller after God saves us—it actually gets bigger. Christian growth is always growth into grace, not away from it.

Many Christians think that becoming sanctified means that we become stronger and stronger, more and more competent. The truth, however, is that Christian growth and progress involves realizing just how weak and incompetent we continue to be and how strong and competent Jesus is. Spiritual maturity is not marked by our growing, independent fitness; it's marked by our growing dependence on Christ's fitness for us.

Because of human nature, you and I were desperate for God's grace before we were saved. Because of human nature, you and I remain desperate for God's grace even after we're saved.

Thankfully, though our sin reaches far, God's grace reaches infinitely farther.

It's easy to forget that Zacchaeus would have been a double outcast in his time—hated *by the Jews* for collecting taxes for the oppressive Roman Empire and hated *as a Jew* by his Roman employers. It's safe to say, in other words, that Zacchaeus was likely not suffering from an overabundance of friends. Who knows when Zacchaeus had last entertained a guest in his home?

Jesus, out of the large crowd that would have been following Him, picked Zacchaeus and said, "I must stay at your house today." Jesus was compelled to be with Zacchaeus, the sinner.

Perhaps the most powerful thing in this passage, though, is Zacchaeus's response to Jesus once the Savior was in his home. He said, "Look, Lord! Here and now I give half of my possessions to the poor, and if I have cheated anybody out of anything, I will pay back four times the amount" (v. 8). His obedience flowed naturally from him the moment Jesus entered his life. The gospel, God's one-way love for sinners, creates what the law, God's holy standard, can only require. And it creates more!

Zacchaeus went above and beyond the call of duty. No doubt, Zacchaeus had been told many times what the law required, but hadn't moved an inch to follow it. Faced with the power of God's one-way, undeserved love for broken, sinful people, though? Zacchaeus pledged to do more, happily, than the law ever would have asked of him.

What we see here (and in our lives) is that love inspires what the law demands—the law prescribes good works, but only grace can produce them. Gratitude, generosity, honesty, compassion, acts of mercy, and self-sacrifice (all requirements of the law) spring unsummoned from a forgiven heart.

This is how God works on us. He picks us, the least deserving, out of the crowd, insists upon being in a relationship with us, and creates in us a new heart, miraculously capable of pleasing Him.

On at least two occasions in the last year, I've been late for a meeting or an appointment and haven't been able to find my car keys. Certain that either my wife or one of my three children has misplaced them, I've frantically run from room to room blaming someone, anyone, and everyone for misplacing my keys. "Has anyone seen my keys? I'm late for a meeting. Who was playing with my keys? I put them right here on the counter, and now they're gone. They didn't just vanish into thin air! Who picked them up? I'm late."

After the humans in my house can't help me locate the keys, I turn to the animals. Maybe one of our many furry houseguests ate the keys, I think. As if I needed another reason to want these animals out of my house. Now they're eating my keys!

The search drives me crazy. I get flustered, manic, and furious. It's as though my entire life is riding on the whereabouts of these keys. I get angrier and angrier, feel more and more victimized. And right about the time I'm ready to start handing out punishments to my family, I've walked into my bedroom one last time to look, put my hand in my pocket, and found my keys. They'd been there the whole time.

Every time I tell that story, people laugh. And rightfully so. What forgetful moron falls prey to frantically looking for car keys that are in his pocket? Me. That's who. But you know what? You do too.

The truth is, however, that this is the way we Christians typically live—frantically and frustratingly searching for something we already have. The gospel is God's good news announcement that everything we need we already possess in Christ. Because of Jesus's finished work, Christians already have all they need and all they desperately long for and look for in a thousand things infinitely smaller than Jesus.

Through the Holy Spirit, God daily delivers the gospel to forgetful Christians like me, declaring, "The keys are in your pocket."

Contrary to popular assumptions, the Bible isn't about us. All too often, the Bible functions for us like a well: we look into it, but, because of our inherent narcissism, we are only able to see our own reflections.

By looking at the Bible as if it were fundamentally about us, we totally miss the point—like the two disciples on the road to Emmaus. As Luke 24 shows, it's possible to read the Bible, study the Bible, and memorize large portions of the Bible while missing the whole point. It's entirely possible, in other words, to read the stories and miss the big story. In fact, unless we go to the Bible to see Jesus and His work for us, even our devout Bible reading can become fuel for our own narcissistic self-improvement plans.

The Bible is not a record of the blessed good but rather the blessed bad. Far from being a book full of moral heroes to emulate, what we discover is that the so-called heroes in the Bible are not really heroes at all. They fall and fail; they make huge mistakes; they get scared; they're selfish, deceptive, egotistical, and unreliable. The Bible is one long story of God meeting our rebellion with His rescue, our sin with His salvation, our failure with His favor, our guilt with His grace, our badness with His goodness.

So if we read the Bible asking first, "What would Jesus do?" instead of asking, "What has Jesus done?" we'll miss the good news that in itself can set us free.

The overwhelming focus of the Bible is not the work of the redeemed but the work of the Redeemer. This means that the Bible is not a recipe book for Christian living but a revelation book of Jesus who is the answer to our un-Christian living.

There are things worth dying for. The gospel is at the top. Regardless of what others may say or what seems most culturally acceptable, the gospel remains as the power of God to deal with the penalty, power, and (eventually) presence of sin and is therefore worth giving your life to and for.

This is superimportant to remember at a time when so many preachers are calling into question (and even mocking) cardinal doctrines of the Christian faith that brothers and sisters throughout history have literally taken a bullet for, been burned for, lost their children for, and been thrown in prison for. In light of this, I can't help but think of Jude's warning about "ungodly people, who pervert the grace of our God" (v. 4).

Perverting the grace of God is serious business.

Both theological liberalism and theological legalism pervert the grace of our God. Both are equally dangerous because both ignore the gospel. Liberals pervert the grace of God by turning it into God's soft tolerance and refusal to judge anybody for anything. Legalists pervert it by maintaining a suspicious posture toward grace—championing the need to keep it in check and sustaining a "yes grace, but …" position that keeps moralism swirling around in our hearts and churches.

At the root of both theological liberalism and theological legalism is unbelief—failure to believe the gospel of God's grace in all of its glory and "radicality."

Speaking into this failure to believe the gospel, which inevitably leads to a failure to preach the gospel, B. B. Warfield exhorts us with urgent passion and clarity:

> We cannot proclaim to the world that the house is afire—it is a disagreeable thing to say, scarcely to be risked in the presence of those whose interest it is not to believe it. But believe it, and how quickly you rush forth to shout the unpalatable truth! … What care we if it be unpalatable, if it be true? For if it be true, it is urgent.

Christian, believe the gospel, and then preach the gospel. You may lose life and limb, sacrifice reputation and relevance, but the gospel remains God's power to set the captives free. Don't forget it. Don't ignore it. It's worth dying for.

Have you heard of a "players-only meeting"? When a team is performing poorly over an extended stretch of games, a player in a leadership role might call a players-only meeting. No coaches or staff are allowed. The players sit together, clear the air, and attempt to figure out how to return to their winning ways.

One notable college basketball coach once said that "players-only meetings are the most useless thing in sports."

The urge to call a players-only meeting comes from a thought that should be familiar to all of us: "I have a problem, and I am going to solve it." It's ironic that the players exclude from their problem-solving meeting the people who are paid specifically to solve their problems: their coaches.

Many Christians tend to operate in the same way when we have a problem—we plan to solve it, which sounds logical, even laudable. The real problem, though, is that the players are in a blind-leading-the-blind situation.

Coaches are paid to be dispassionate observers, not caught up in who's getting more shots or who makes the most money from endorsements or who has a bonus clause in his contract that he's trying to reach. Teams need this word from outside to help them accurately evaluate the problems they're facing and efficiently determine solutions to those problems.

God has a true word from outside for us. Jesus Christ, God incarnate, crosses the chasm from heaven to earth, even as we fail to bridge it ourselves. Our failure makes us think that we need to do more, try harder, or even call a spiritual players-only meeting. The problem, though, isn't with the chasm. It's us! God's word from the outside, the very thing that we tried to keep out of the meeting, busts down the door and saves us despite ourselves.

Victory can be ours, to be sure. In fact, victory *is* ours. But it is a victory given, not a victory earned. Outside help is required, and has already been given. Thank God for that.

The gospel liberates us to be okay with not being okay. We know we're not okay—though we try very hard to convince ourselves and other people that we're basically fine. The gospel effectively tells us, "Relax. It is finished. The pressure's off."

Because of the gospel, we have nothing to prove or protect. We can stop pretending. We can take off our masks and be real. The gospel frees us from trying to impress people, appease people, or measure up for people. The gospel frees us from the burden of trying to control what other people think about us. It frees us from the miserable, unquenchable pursuit to make something of ourselves by using others.

The gospel frees us from what one writer called "the law of capability"— the law, he said, "that judges us wanting if we are not capable, if we cannot handle it all, if we are not competent to balance our diverse commitments without a slip." The gospel grants us the strength to admit we're weak and needy and restless—knowing that Christ's finished work has proven to be all the strength, fulfillment, and peace we could ever want, and more. Because Jesus is our strength, our weaknesses don't threaten our sense of worth and value. Now we're free to admit our wrongs and weaknesses without feeling as if our flesh is being ripped off our bones.

When we understand that our significance, security, and identity are all anchored in Christ, we don't have to win—we're free to lose. And nothing in this broken world can beat a person who isn't afraid to lose. We'll be free to say crazy, risky, counterintuitive stuff such as, "To live is Christ and to die is gain!"

Real, pure, unadulterated freedom happens when the resources of the gospel crush any sense of need to secure for ourselves anything beyond what Christ has already secured for us.

This verse speaks to the first desire of all of us: The desire to be someone. To be something. To make a name for ourselves.

On the interstate in Arkansas, there's a very interesting sight. At least, there was the last time I was there, several years ago. When approaching Hope, Arkansas, the little town where Bill Clinton is from, there's a sign by the side of the road that is difficult to read. As you get closer, you can finally make out what it says: "Hope, Arkansas, home of President Bill Clinton." And you can also tell why it was so hard to read. It is so riddled with bullet holes that the words are almost completely illegible.

Wouldn't it be nice if your hometown thought it worthy of putting a sign up for you? Welcome to Hometown, U.S.A., home of [your name]. Much like Hope, Arkansas, but without the bullet holes.

But what is 1 Corinthians 13:2 saying? "If I have the gift of prophecy and can fathom all mysteries and all knowledge, and if I have a faith that can move mountains, but do not have love, I am nothing." Now, if there was ever a list of accomplishments that warranted a sign outside your hometown, that's it. But Paul said that even though you might have all those things, if you don't have love, you are nothing. Notice the wording, which is more deeply damaging than simply saying, "You have nothing." He said without love, you *are* nothing.

In order to be someone, in order to make a name for yourself, you must have love! Love makes you who you are. The love that God had for you *created* you, and the love you have for God and others allows you to acknowledge His creation.

In the gospel, we have a love that is given, not required. When we are unloving, Jesus is love incarnate. We are not defined by the love we generate for others; we are defined by the love that Jesus has for us. Your name is on a sign outside Jesus's hometown, and it's written on the rolls of eternity.

To conclude, as many people do, that suffering people have somehow heaped up trouble for themselves on the Cosmic Registry and that God is doling out the misery in direct proportion would be more than mistaken; it would be cruel. The humorist Jack Handey perceptively parodied such ideas in his *Saturday Night Live*–featured book *Deep Thoughts*:

> If a kid asks where rain comes from, I think a cute thing to tell him is "God is crying." And if he asks why God is crying, another cute thing to tell him is "Probably because of something you did."

It's funny—but not really. The truth is that while we laugh at something as silly as Handey's "deep thought," most of us are naturally governed by this kind of thinking regarding God.

So while no one can deny that our actions have consequences—that if you put your finger in a light socket, you will "reap" a shock—we do God and ourselves a disservice when we turn His sovereign ways into a kind of karma.

The truth is, when you and I insist on that all-too-comfortable paradigm of cosmic score-keeping, we're no longer talking about Christianity. In fact, what we reveal is that we've unwittingly adopted a Westernized form of Hinduism. If you are a bad person and things are going well for you, it is only a matter of time before karma catches up with you and you get yours. If you are a good person, the inverse is true: just be patient and your good deeds will come back to you.

On the opposite end of our natural tendency to moralize life and suffering is the counterintuitive affirmation of Christianity. Christianity affirms that Jesus severed the link between suffering and deserving once for all on Calvary. God put the ledgers away and settled the accounts. The good news of the gospel is *not* that good people get good stuff. It's not that life is cyclical and that "what goes around comes around." Rather, it's that the bad get the best, the worst inherit the wealth, and the slave becomes a son.

Should Christians always be afraid of imperatives in the Bible? Do things that we're told to do always lead to our condemnation? Actually, no. But to understand this, we must say a little bit about how the law works.

Notice that Paul uses Leviticus 18:5 in Galatians 3 and Romans 10 as a summary of the salvation structure of the law: If you keep God's statutes and rules, then you shall live. Here, there is a promise of life linked to the condition of doing the commandments. The "if" and "then" make all the difference. When this conditional tone encounters the sinful human, the outcome is inevitable: "All the world may become accountable to God" (Rom. 3:19 NASB). It is the condition that does the work of condemnation. "Ifs" kill!

Now consider Galatians 5:1. After four chapters of passionate insistence that justification is by faith apart from works of the law, Paul issues a couple of strong imperatives: "It is for freedom that Christ has set us free. Stand firm, [imperative] then, and do not let yourselves [imperative] be burdened again by a yoke of slavery." Are these commandments with conditions? Is there an "if"? No! The command here is precisely to not return to the law. It is an imperative to stand firm in freedom from the law.

Christ is the end of the law, because in the gospel, God unconditionally gives the righteousness that the law demands. So Christ kicks the law out of the conscience by overcoming the law's voice of condemnation.

Freed from the burden and bondage of attempting to use the law to establish our righteousness before God, Christians are free to look to the "imperatives" of Scripture, not as conditions, but as descriptions and directions as they seek to serve their neighbor. Once a person is liberated from the commonsense delusion that keeping the rules makes us right with God and, in faith, believes the counterintuitive reality that being made righteous by God's forgiving and resurrecting word precedes and produces loving action (defined as serving our neighbor), then the justified person is unlocked to love, which is fulfillment of the law.

Have you seen the 2014 version of *RoboCop*? No? Well, believe me, you're not the only one who decided to stay away. One of the few interesting things about the film, though, is its decision to make a foray into a touchy subject—we might say *the* touchy subject: free will.

In the film, the Robosuit is apparently outfitted with a function to trick its wearer into thinking that he's making free decisions, while all the while doing the work for him. Later in the movie, the inevitable happens: RoboCop's human elements begin to override the system's priorities. His free will will be shown to be so strong, in other words, that even fourth-degree burns and a suspiciously flexible cyborg suit can't keep it down.

The RoboCop of this film is yet another paean to human freedom and our ability to overcome any obstacle in our path. All RoboCop must do is set his humanity loose to be all that he can be.

Let me make a dangerous suggestion. The fact that we aren't free is good news, not bad. When we humans exercise our freedom, we turn our world into the spiritual version of the postapocalyptic wasteland of *RoboCop*. We act in our own self-interest, putting the needs of others far behind our own and endeavor to solve our own problems whenever they occur. Disaster results.

The problem is, the extent to which we believe in our freedom is the extent to which we will never acknowledge our need for a Savior.

Jesus, however, didn't come for the free. He came to proclaim release to the captives (Luke 4:18). We aren't free to choose Jesus; He chooses us (John 15:16). This is good news! This is *the* good news. We desperately need the freedom of God's sovereignty precisely because of the bondage of our free will.

The system that overrides us is a gracious one. As we run from God, as we rebel, and as we exert our free will, God leaves the ninety-nine sheep who don't need rescuing to come find us—the lost ones—and gather us up in His arms and carry us home.

How many times have you read the Adam and Eve story and thought to yourself, *Gosh, if only I had been in that garden instead of Adam and Eve. I would have made a better choice.*

Unfortunately, it's too late. The story has already ended, and we've already made our decisions. More unfortunately and specifically, we've already made *Adam's* decision. The proof of this is in the incessant self-salvation projects we engage in. They are evidence that we are not only in Adam—that is, suffering from the results of Adam's sin—but that Adam is in us! We would have made the exact same choice he made.

Adam's sin was in reaching up and trying to be like God. He wanted to decide for himself what was right and wrong. That's the lie the serpent told him, and that's the lie Adam believed—that he would be like God.

Jesus succeeded in every way that Adam failed. The symmetry of the stories is amazing. Where Adam was selfish in a garden (Eden) and brought death into the world, Jesus was selfless in another garden (Gethsemane) and brought life to the world. Adam's failure was that he wanted to be like God. Jesus "did not consider equality with God something to be used to his own advantage" (Phil. 2:6). The Adam story is really about the essence of sin: our substituting ourselves for God. The Jesus story is really about the essence of salvation: God substituting Himself for us.

Adam is not merely a cautionary tale, an example to learn from. Adam was chosen by God as the perfect representative of the human race. Like Adam, when we are presented with the chance to be gods, to decide for ourselves what is right and wrong, we *always* say yes. No, Adam's is not a cautionary tale but more of a prophecy. Adam's story points us to a better man, in a different garden, dealing with another tree. Adam, a selfish man, picked the fruit of a tree, acted disobediently in a garden, and brought death to us all. Jesus, a selfless man, hung on a tree after being obedient in a garden and brought us new life.

When my boys were younger, they would gather all the neighborhood kids to play football in our yard. Every once in a while, a pass would be overthrown, landing in my neighbor's grass. My curmudgeonly neighbor would always come outside and scream at my boys and their friends, threatening to confiscate the ball if it happened again. There were countless times that I wanted to march over to my neighbor and give him a piece of my mind. I never did, though. I would stare him down from time to time but never did I go next door to let him have it. Some would assume I was righteously exercising love, patience, and self-control. But was I?

Only God and I (and soon, you) know the real reason: the potential risk to me was too high. I didn't want to get in trouble. I didn't want him calling the police. I didn't want him filing a complaint against me to our neighborhood association. I didn't want him gossiping about me, leading people in the neighborhood to think less of me. After all, everyone knows I'm a pastor, so I didn't want to tarnish my image. In other words, the very thing that may have on the surface seemed righteous was motivated by something terribly unrighteous—selfishness.

So the apparent righteousness of my deed was destroyed by the motivation that inspired it.

Only when our understanding of "righteousness exceeds that of the scribes and Pharisees" (Matt. 5:20 NRSV) and goes beyond outer conduct will we see the impossibility of achieving our own righteousness and the necessity of receiving Christ's righteousness. There is nothing that sinners hate more than to be told there's nothing they can do, that no matter how hard they try, their best is never good enough. And yet we'll never be free until we give up fighting for a righteousness we can claim as our own. But when we do, Jesus will give us His.

I have an idea: let's all stop trying to fix one another. Instead, why don't we "spur one another on toward love and good deeds" (v. 24) by daily reminding one another, in humble love, of the riches we already possess in Christ. All the good stuff that is ours already in Christ settles at the bottom when we focus on ourselves more than Jesus (after all, Peter only began to sink when he took his eyes off Jesus and focused on his performance).

Theologian John Owen said, "Holiness is nothing but the implanting, writing, and living out of the gospel in our souls." And what is the gospel? Not my work for Jesus, but Jesus's work for me. In other words, holiness happens not by looking at ourselves but by looking at Jesus. Therefore, it takes the loving actions of our Christian brothers and sisters to remind us every day of the gospel—that everything we need and look for in things smaller than Jesus is already ours "in Christ." When this happens, the good stuff rises to the top.

The Puritans used to say that far too many Christians live beneath the level of their privileges. Therefore, I need to be told by those around me that every time I sin, I'm momentarily suffering from an identity crisis—forgetting who I actually belong to, what I really want at my remade core, and all that is already mine in Christ. The only way to deal with remaining sin long-term is to develop a distaste for it in light of the glorious riches we already possess in Christ. I need my real friends to remind me of this—every day. Please tell me again and again that God doesn't love me more when I obey or less when I disobey. Knowing this actually enlarges my heart for God and therefore shrinks my hunger for sin. So don't let me forget it. My life depends on it!

In the summer of 2013, Dwight Howard was the most sought-after free agent in the NBA. He was courted heavily by the Los Angeles Lakers, his team at the time and the team capable of offering him the most money.

The Lakers' star player is Kobe Bryant, a consensus top-ten player of all time, a legendary competitor, and a hater of Dwight Howard. Howard is known as a happy-go-lucky guy, perhaps more interested in having fun and participating in dunk contests than in winning championships. This grates on Bryant. To the sports world, otherworldly competitiveness is a more righteous characteristic (because you can generate it in yourself) than otherworldly talent (because it comes as a gift from the "gods" of DNA).

Kobe Bryant sees Dwight Howard as a waste of otherworldly talent.

As part of the Lakers' pitch to Howard, hoping that he would re-sign with them (and believe me, they were hoping that he would; he is a transcendently talented player), Bryant; future Hall of Fame point guard Steve Nash; head coach, Mike D'Antoni; and general manager, Mitch Kupchak, met with Howard personally. Here is a tweet from ESPN NBA writer Chris Broussard following that meeting (note: D12 is Dwight Howard; 12 is his jersey number): "Sources close to Howard tell me Kobe's reported pitch in Tuesday's meeting about teaching D12 how to win will be a 'complete turn-off' to D12."

Bryant pledged to teach Howard how to win on July 2. On July 5, Howard announced that he would sign a contract with the Houston Rockets. This is hilarious! Kobe Bryant actually thought that telling Dwight Howard that he would "teach him how to win" would make him want to stay!

The law can demand a change of heart, but it cannot force one. As it tries, it's a complete turnoff. The law tends to provoke its opposite.

The gospel, on the other hand, offers the change that the law points to but cannot produce—a heart transplant directly from Jesus Christ to you.

One reason moviegoers enjoy action films so much, I'm convinced, is self-projection. We love stories about lone lawmen such as Clint Eastwood, the guy who is the only thing that stands between the bad guys and total oppression, because we imagine ourselves in that heroic role.

We want to be the hero. It's supercool to be the guy whose bullets never miss and who can't be hit, the guy who can catch the ledge when he's falling off the roof. In real-world terms, we want to be the person who gets the job and keeps it, who can work a full day, help the kids with the homework, and then cook a delicious and nutritious meal. We want to be the person with the right answer, who does the right thing, who accomplishes their goals in the end. We want to bring our own good works to completion. Action-movie heroes, though, are an impossible standard to hold ourselves to. Unlike these mythic superstars, we are not bulletproof. We reach for the ledge as we fall off the roof, but our fingers don't catch.

So even though what we most want in the world is to be Clint Eastwood or Arnold Schwarzenegger or Bruce Willis, crushing the bad guys and rescuing the victims, what we *need* is to be the one in need of rescue. When everything's falling apart around us, we want to think that we've got it under control, that we'll find a way to win in the end. But when everything's falling apart around us, we need to remember there's Someone in control up there, a safety net, Someone to make sure that the ending is the right one.

And as our lives go on, sometimes full of failure and uncertainty, we can find our joy in knowing the real Hero has written a victorious ending to the story, one in which He gets the credit, but we indeed get the rescue.

How can we know that when we come before God's final judgment, His ruling will be "not guilty"? Where does our assurance come from? How can we have peace?

The Bible is plain that God requires moral perfection. Defects, blemishes, or stains, even to the smallest degree, are unacceptable and deserving of God's wrath. And just in case we're deluded enough to think that our Spirit-wrought moral improvement since we became Christians is making the grade, Jesus, in the Sermon on the Mount, intensifies what God's required perfection entails—internal perfection, not just external obedience.

So we need a different answer, a different place in which to put our faith.

True assurance only happens when the God-given, Spirit-wrought gift of faith enables us to believe that we are forever pardoned, that Christ's righteousness is counted as our own, that in Christ, God does not count our sins against us (2 Cor. 5:19). We are justified by grace alone, through faith alone, in Christ alone. God's demand for moral perfection has been satisfied by Christ for us (Matt. 5:17). Therefore, assurance can never be found by looking *in*. It can only happen by faith (looking *up*), believing in Him who was "delivered over to death for our sins and was raised to life for our justification" (Rom. 4:25).

Our assurance is anchored in the love and grace of God expressed in the glorious exchange: our sin for His righteousness. Since our faith is always weak and wavering—the gospel is just so hard to believe!—we need to be reminded of this good news all the time. There must be a clear, continuous, and unqualified pronouncement of the assurance of salvation on the basis of the fullness of the atonement of Christ.

Satan tempts us to find our assurance within, but it does not exist there. Inside, we find only sin. We have a God, however, who replaced our sin with His own righteousness. Rest assured and be at peace. Before God, the righteousness of Christ is all we have. Before God, the righteousness of Christ is all we need.

In James Gunn's low-budget cringe comedy *Super*, Rainn Wilson plays a sad-sack fry cook who loses his wife to a drug dealer and, in response, becomes the Crimson Bolt, a "superhero" who cracks criminals over the head with a lug wrench.

The problem with the Crimson Bolt is the same as the problem with the law of God: there's no wiggle room. Sure, he targets the worst of the worst, cracking child molesters, thieves, and drug dealers with his wrench, but he also goes after lesser violators, such as line cutters. "You don't butt in line! You don't sell drugs! … The rules were set a long time ago! They don't change!" he shouts as he bashes the head of his final victim. And truly, *victim* is the proper word. Because even though the Crimson Bolt is a hero in his own eyes, to the rest of the world he's a violent lunatic, unable to distinguish great offenses from lesser ones, thus leaving a trail of victims in his judgmental wake.

Similarly, we are victims of our own mishandling of God's law.

We like the law when it exposes the sins of others, the "bad" people who enable us to look at ourselves as "better than" the rest of the world. The law is attractive in the same way that the idea of being a superhero is attractive. But we have a problem: the law is *too* good. We think the proper thing for the law to do is to go after bad guys. But it's so proper that it counts us among the bad guys to go after!

Jesus isn't like the Crimson Bolt. He comes not to condemn the bad guys—we're condemned already—but to save them (John 3:17). It is while we are God's enemies (Rom. 5:10) that this unique Superhero comes and, rather than bashing us over the head with more law, instead accepts the cranial wrench-bashing for us.

The good news is only so good because the bad news is so bad. We're the bad guys. You, me, and everyone we know who is "better than" other people. We deserve the Crimson Bolt's wrench. Instead, we get the comforting words of a Savior: "I have not come to call the righteous, but sinners" (Mark 2:17).

What are you building your identity on? Think of it this way: What do you wake up in the middle of the night worrying about? Chances are, it's something similar to the favored-son status that Joseph built his identity on. For us, it's career or kids or our standing in the community.

Joseph's brashness testifies to the fact he had built his identity on being his father's favored son. To be the patriarch's favorite son was a big deal, and Joseph derived his worth from it. It led him to believe he was better than his brothers, and that gave him a sense of significance and pride. As long as he was the favorite, he was somebody. He mattered.

But the story of Joseph doesn't end there. While the bad stuff in his life points out our sin, the good stuff points out our Savior—and how He works to rescue sinners out of slavery and death. Within the story of Joseph, we hear whispers of a new and better Joseph. Over and over again Joseph's story illustrates that life comes out of death. He is sold into slavery, thrown into a pit, and locked away in prison. After all of that, the king puts him in a place of power and honor. He relives the pain of his brothers' betrayal when they come to him for food years later, but uses his new power to save them rather than kill them—assuring them that what they meant for evil, God meant for good. And as a result of his mediation, a world on the brink of death is saved. All of this points us to Jesus.

Years later, another favored Son would be betrayed, sold, and mistreated by His brothers. He, too, would be falsely accused, thrown into captivity—the captivity of the cross—paying the price for sins He did not commit. And in the prison of that cross, He, too, was forsaken—but like Joseph, He didn't stay imprisoned. Like Joseph, Jesus was brought to life out of death and now sits at the right hand of the King, forgiving those who betrayed Him (all of us), and using His power to save rather than kill.

Grace has the power to bind generations together. I was blessed to have experienced the power of one-way love, not just from my parents but from my grandparents as well.

Whenever people learn that I was kicked out of the house at sixteen, they invariably ask how my grandparents responded. What they usually mean is, "How did Billy and Ruth Graham respond to actual sin in their midst?" The truth is, my grandparents never said a single word to me about getting my act together. They never pulled me aside at a family gathering and told me what I needed to do or stop doing, how I was squandering all that my parents had given me, and how my hard-heartedness was hurting others—especially those who loved me most.

For example, I wore earrings back in those days. One in the left, and one in the right. It used to drive my parents nuts. Every time my grandmother Ruth came down to visit, she would bring me a fresh set of earrings to wear! They were always funny. At Christmastime, she would bring me ornament earrings and make me put them in and take a picture. At Thanksgiving, she brought fork and knife earrings, and she took a picture. She made light of it. She would often tell me with a twinkle in her eye that I was her favorite granddaughter. She wasn't making fun of me. She was saying, "This isn't that big of a deal. He's going to grow out of it." It may sound pretty trivial, but it meant the world to me. Everyone else was on my case, and instead of giving me one more thing to rebel against, my grandmother drew me in closer.

Such is the result of one-way love. My grandmother was embodying Proverbs 15:1: "A gentle answer turns away wrath." She was gentle with me, patient, playful, and it had the effect, not of stirring up my adolescent rebellion, but of bringing my guard down, opening my heart to her and my family further. Similarly, Jesus Christ in the gospel does not nag or coerce us into His fold. He woos us.

The urge to pick one aspect of Christ's life—namely, His death—as more important than the others is understandable. We certainly see in the New Testament how everything seems to turn on the cross. We could accurately say that the cross is the crossroads of history, the moment at which our sin was laid on Christ's shoulders and His righteousness was transferred to us. It's easy to see why Christ's death might overshadow anything else about Him. But to talk about "cross-centeredness" as if the death of Christ (His passive obedience) is more important than the life of Christ (His active obedience) is to miss other incredibly important things about Jesus.

The truth is, our redemption depends not only on Christ's substitutionary death, but His substitutionary *life* as well. J. Gresham Machen's last recorded words (sent by telegram to fellow theologian and friend John Murray) were, "I'm so thankful for [the] active obedience of Christ. No hope without it." He understood that apart from Christ's law-fulfilling life, there is *no* righteousness to impute. We are, therefore, left dressed in our own filthy rags.

Murray wrote: "The real use and purpose of the formula (active and passive obedience) is to emphasize the two distinct aspects of our Lord's vicarious obedience. The truth expressed rests upon the recognition that the law of God has both penal sanctions and positive demands. It demands not only the full discharge of its precepts but also the infliction of penalty for all infractions and shortcomings. It is this twofold demand of the law of God which is taken into account when we speak of the active and passive obedience of Christ."

Christ's life, in other words, is just as central to our rescue as His death. As I've said before, we are not saved apart from the law. Rather, we are saved in Christ who perfectly kept the law on our behalf.

So Christ's death is not the center of the gospel any more than Christ's life is the center of the gospel. One without the other fails to bring about redemption. It's much more theologically accurate to say that Christ *Himself* is the center of the gospel. He didn't just die for you; He *lived* for you too.

Often, when a sports team is losing and the game is almost over, their fans will start to head for the exits. Sometimes they want to beat the traffic home, but often they're just disgusted with the way the game is going and can't watch any more. It's interesting to note the human movement: when the team seems sure to lose, the people move away, literally leaving the arena. If a miracle happens, and the team looks as if it might win, they come streaming back.

This is what we humans do. We are desperate to associate with winners and terrified to be associated with losers. This is true in high school cafeterias, high-powered boardrooms, sports arenas, and even in church pews. We want winners around us, and we shield ourselves (politely, of course) from losers.

Jesus moves the other way.

Our Savior would be found coming into the arena as the clock seemed to click to zero on the home team's failure. Jesus showed over and over again that His life's work was to associate with losers. The most common insult sent Christ's way was, "He has gone to be the guest of a sinner" (v. 7). Paul knew the power of Christ's habit. "You see, at just the right time, when we were still powerless, Christ died for the ungodly. Very rarely will anyone die for a righteous person, though for a good person someone might possibly dare to die. But God demonstrates His own love for us in this: While we were still sinners, Christ died for us" (Rom. 5:6–8).

In common parlance: Jesus came for losers. People hardly ever give their all for anyone. But for a real winner, someone might give up something. God, though, shows His love in one special way: While we were losers, He sent His Son for us. While we were at our worst, God gave us His best.

Jesus went repeatedly to the down-and-out. The movement of Jesus's life, death, and resurrection is toward overwhelmed losers like you and me—radically different than what we expect, and radically better than what we deserve.

The comedian Louis C. K. performs a bit in which he suggests that our day and age is marked by an interesting juxtaposition: everything's amazing and nobody's happy. He describes the grousing that people do about airplane travel: "I had to wait on the tarmac for *forty-five minutes*! It was awful!"

"I'm sorry," he retorts, "did you just fly through the sky, sitting in a chair?" He tells of someone who tried to connect to the Wi-Fi on an airplane and was enraged when told that it was out of order. "How could you be so angry," he wonders, "about something you only found out existed thirty seconds ago?"

The reflection is hilarious but also keenly perceptive. But Louis C. K. is wrong about one thing: dissatisfaction is no modern phenomenon. People have always bemoaned the state of the world. The psalmist lives in a time when many are asking for some good. They want God to lift the light of His face upon them. They're just looking for a little good news, a little happiness.

The problem with true happiness—joy—is that it can stay a little bit out of our reach as we chase after it. John D. Rockefeller is said to have responded to a questioner who asked him, "How much money is enough?" with "Just a little bit more."

So where does happiness come from? Back to the psalmist: "You have put gladness in my heart more than when their grain and wine abound" (v. 7 NRSV). The psalmist is making a radical statement here. Things aren't going well, but he has gladness in his heart.

This is Christianity in a nutshell. God works when we are in need. When our quest for glory is falling apart, that's when God is there. True joy is knowing that God comes to us when we're not good enough, when we're ashamed, when we're sick, and when we're exhausted. Grace always runs downhill.

Today as we search for joy, know that God does not await you there. He is with you even now.

Because Jesus was strong for you, you're free to be weak. Because Jesus was "someone," you're free to be no one. Because Jesus was extraordinary, you're free to be ordinary. Because Jesus succeeded for you, you're free to fail. Because Jesus won for you, you're free to lose. When truly considered, these are remarkably powerful words. They mean true freedom for the hearer.

But hold on. Wait a minute. Doesn't this unconditional declaration generate apathy—an "I don't care" posture toward life?

The truth is, the gospel of grace actually empowers risk-taking effort and neighbor-embracing love.

The thing that prevents us from taking great risks is the fear that if we don't succeed, we'll lose out on something we need in order to be happy. And so we live life playing our cards close to the vest—relationally, vocationally, spiritually. We measure our investments carefully because we need a return. We're afraid to give because it might not work out (and we really need it to work out).

In light of the gospel, though, the fear of not knowing whether we'll get a return is replaced by the freedom of knowing we already have everything. Because, in Christ, we already possess everything we need, we're now free to do everything for others without needing them to do anything for us. We can now actively spend our lives giving instead of taking, going to the back instead of getting to the front, sacrificing ourselves for others instead of sacrificing others for ourselves. The gospel alone liberates us to live a life of scandalous generosity, unrestrained sacrifice, uncommon valor, and unbounded courage.

When we don't have anything to lose, we discover something wonderful: we're free to take great risks without fear or reservation.

So what are you going to do now that you don't have to do anything?

In the movie *Collateral*, Jamie Foxx plays the unlucky cab driver taken hostage for a night by Tom Cruise, a contract killer. Early in the film, we learn that driving a cab isn't Foxx's ultimate ambition. What he wants to do is start a company called Island Limos, a limousine service so luxurious and relaxing that "you won't want to get out at the airport." He's driving the cab, he says to a woman he's trying to impress, to get his "Benz" off its lease, to set up the right client list, to make sure everything's perfect.

Later in the film, when everything has begun to fall apart, Cruise needles Foxx about the fact that he's been driving the cab for eight years, unable to pull the trigger on starting his limo company. Foxx gets angrier and angrier, muttering, "It has to be perfect, it has to be perfect" to himself, eventually crashing the taxi into a median and propelling the story toward its bloody climax.

Such is the violent assault that so-called perfection mounts. Perfection stands above the fray of our daily lives and says, "You're not quite ready yet." "You're not good enough yet." Or, "You'll fail unless you improve."

The irony of the pursuit of perfection is that it doesn't inspire—it paralyzes. We imagine that a good, far-off goal is just the thing we need to get us moving. And what goal is further off than Christlikeness? We tell ourselves, "I know I'll never achieve it, but it'll be a good thing to work toward." But it will lead inevitably to stagnation, frustration, and resignation.

The pursuit of perfection is life under the law. "Be perfect" is the law sharpened to its most deadly point. The gospel, however, diverts that point. We all are sitting in our cabs, afraid to get out there and fail. And though we deserve that stinging point of the law, that condemning voice constantly reminding us that we're "not good enough," it instead embeds itself in Christ on the cross.

Perfection can never be achieved, only given. And in the gospel, it has been.

The story of the Tower of Babel makes one thing perfectly clear: none of our best attempts and none of our self-righteous strivings (and that is exactly what they are) can get us up to God. In fact, as the tower builders are making their tower that is supposed to reach the heavens, God has to come down to even see what they're doing. All that work, and they're not even close!

But can't you understand the desire to build the tower in the first place? We are like the tower builders—addicted to a ladder-climbing life. We think that a life of ladder climbing is a life of freedom—free to move at our own pace, up or down depending on our decisions, responsible for our own progress. We climb our ladders for the same reasons that the people of the world built their tower—to make a name for ourselves, to ensure our own legacy, to secure our own value. We love to imagine that we're on a higher rung than someone else, a better father than someone else, a more accomplished follower of Christ than someone else. But ladder climbing actually and inevitably leads to slavery.

But there is good news: our towers of Babel don't remain standing.

God loves us too much to leave us in the hell of unhappiness that comes from trying to do His job. Into the slavish misery of our ladder-defined lives, God condescends. His first act with the builders of the Tower of Babel is an act of judgment. He scatters and disorganizes them, literally. God takes away their faith in themselves, the very misplaced faith that enslaves them. When everyone in the world spoke the same language, God came down in judgment, breaking the world apart. But at just the right time, He descended the ladder again, this time to reconcile that sinful world to Himself. He replaces our ladder with His cross. His final descent was to save us, and to set us free.

God is not at the top of a ladder shouting, "Climb!" He is at the bottom on a cross whispering, "It is finished."

My adolescent rebellion in my early teens had descended into a black hole of disrespect and self-centeredness consuming my entire family. My parents were well-loved in our community, and their friends could see the heartache they were going through with me. I remember two separate instances of people caring enough to ask them for permission to talk with me one-on-one to see if maybe they could get through to me.

My parents' friend picked me up after school, brought me to Burger King, and read me the riot act. "Shape up, man! Snap out of it." Of course, he was 100 percent right. In fact, if he had known the full truth of what I was up to, he would have had every reason to be even harsher. But in the first five minutes of this guy talking to me, I could tell where it was going, and I just tuned out. As far as I was concerned, it was white noise. I could not wait for it to be over and for him to drop me back off at home.

This first friend was the voice of the law. He was articulating the standard that I was falling short of, and he couldn't have been more correct. But that's the curious thing about the law and judgment in general: it can tell us the right thing to do, but it cannot inspire us to do it. In fact, it often creates the opposite reaction of the one that is intended. It certainly did for me. I don't blame the man in question. He was trying to do the right thing. It's just that his methods completely backfired.

About a year and a half later, another family friend took me to lunch and said, "Listen, I know you're going through a tough time. And I just want to tell you that I love you, I'm here for you, and I think God's going to do great things with you. If you ever need anything, call me." That guy—the second guy—is still a friend of mine to this day. He will forever be marked in my personal history as an example of amazing grace.

The law may expose bad behavior, but only grace can win the heart.

The law is a gift from God, and it's a good gift. It graciously shows Christians what God commands in the way of holiness. But nowhere does the Bible say that the law possesses the power to enable us to do what it says. You could put it this way: The law guides, but it does not give. The law shows us what a sanctified life looks like, but it does not have sanctifying power. As this little poem often attributed to John Bunyan memorably puts it:

> Run, John, run, the law commands,
> But gives us neither feet nor hands.
> Far better news the gospel brings:
> It bids us fly and gives us wings.

To say, however, that the law has no power to change us in no way reduces its ongoing role in the life of a Christian. We just have to understand the role that it plays. When we break God's law, it serves us by making us thankful for Jesus and by showing how to love God and others. And when we fail to keep it, the gospel comforts by reminding us that God's approval does not depend on our keeping of the law but Christ's keeping of the law on our behalf. The gospel serves the Christian in every way by reminding us that God's love for us does not get bigger when we're obedient or smaller when we're disobedient. This makes me want to obey Him more, not less!

Charles Spurgeon wrote, "When I thought that God was hard, I found it easy to sin; but when I found God so kind, so good, so overflowing with compassion, I smote upon my breast to think that I could ever have rebelled against One who loved me so, and sought my good."

Therefore, it's the gospel (what Jesus has done) that alone can give God-honoring animation to our obedience. The power to obey comes from being moved and motivated by the completed work of Jesus for us. The fuel to do good flows from what's already been done. So while the law directs us, only the gospel can drive us.

In a 2013 article in *Sports Illustrated*, Austin Murphy wrote about a participation boom in marathons, half marathons, "tough mudders," and other endurance races. His conclusion? It's not that there were more serious runners in the world; it's that less serious runners were coming out for these events in droves.

Here's a quote: "In the decades-long battle between the Penguins [noncompetitive runners] and the sinewy, 45-beats-per-minute-resting-heart-rate, front-of-the-pack Serious Runners, the Penguins have won a decisive victory. They've done this by uncoupling performance from identity: You don't need to be fast to be considered an endurance athlete."

Did you hear that? They've uncoupled performance from identity! Those four words should hang over the door of every church and be emblazoned on the bathroom mirror of every Christian. "Uncoupling performance from identity." The reason that participation in these endurance runs has increased so significantly is that race organizers have successfully convinced the runners that the race isn't really about how well they do. Usually, it's for charity, for community spirit, or just for fun. When people actually believe that their performances aren't going to be judged at the end of the day, they'll jump into the event with both feet.

Christians can uncouple performance from identity. After all, don't we live our lives under a banner that reads "It is finished"? Wasn't that Jesus's final pronouncement from the cross?

Christians can show up to the starting line knowing that the race is already won; we are free to be Penguins, knowing that Christ is our victory. The apostle Paul said that if anyone could have boasted in their godly workout, it was he (vv. 5–6). But he counted all that effort, all that striving, all that competing as rubbish in the face of the glory and perfection of Jesus Christ. He realized that, compared to Christ, he was a Penguin, but that because of Christ's completed work on the cross, he's a champion.

The good news is God's final announcement that our need to compete has been overcome in Christ, and we can forever rest, for His work is complete.

In *Fiddler on the Roof*, Tevye asks his wife, Golde, if she loves him. "Do I what?" she replies. "Do you love me?" he asks again. "Do I love you?" Golde responds. "For twenty-five years I've washed your clothes, cooked your meals, cleaned your house, given you children, milked the cow. After twenty-five years, why talk about love right now?" She ends up saying, "I'm your wife!" And Tevye says, "I know. But, do you love me?"

So we have here a situation where two different ideas of love are being expressed. "Do you love me?" Well, I do all of this stuff, washed your clothes, cooked your meals, cleaned your house, given you children, even milked the cow. What do you think? "But," comes the response, "do you love me?"

Golde, when she thinks of love, thinks of a list of proofs, a list of actions. Tevye finds this list unsatisfactory. He's still worried. He's lived with this woman for twenty-five years, he's seen all the clean laundry and milked cows, and he's still asking about being loved. Tevye's idea of love is something more than Golde's, something deeper, something that can't be quantified on a checklist. To herself she says, "I did the shopping. Check. I love my husband. Check." It doesn't work that way.

Maybe you feel like Tevye. You've been in this relationship with God for many years, and you know He's given you some good gifts, but you'd still like to be sure that He loves you. We also know that our own checklist isn't as well checked off as Golde's. Some of our cows have gone unmilked and some of our clothes have gone unlaundered.

But Jesus chose His words carefully.

Jesus said that those who love Him *will* obey His commandments. Not "you'd better." You will. He's not simply asking you to; He's not just telling you to. He's promising that you *will*. When we worry, and we look up to heaven and ask, like Tevye, "Do you love me?" Jesus says, "Look to the cross. It is proof I love you. And it's the end of your own checklist."

I grew up with the impression that when it comes to the Christian life, justi-fication was step one, sanctification was step two, and that once we arrive at step two, there's no reason to revisit step one. In my experience as a pastor, this is one of the reasons why it seems so new to people that the gospel is not just for non-Christians but for Christians, too. It doesn't just ignite the Christian life; it fuels it as well.

Justification and sanctification are both God's work, and while they can and must be distinguished, the Bible won't let us separate them. Both are gifts of our union with Christ and, within this double blessing, justification is the root of sanctification, and sanctification is the fruit of justification. Moralism happens when we separate the fruit from the root.

When we understand that everything between God and us has been fully and finally made right, that Christians live their lives under a banner that reads, "It is finished," we necessarily turn away from ourselves and turn toward our neighbor. Forever freed from our need to pay God back or secure God's love and acceptance, we are now free to love and serve others. Because of Christ's work, I can now actively spend my life giving instead of taking, going to the back instead of angling for the front, sacrificing myself for others instead of sacrificing others for myself.

So I'm all for effort, fighting sin, and resisting temptation, as long as we understand that it is not our work for God, but God's work for us that has fully and finally set things right between God and sinners. We must always remember that the good works that necessarily flow from faith are not part of a transaction with God—they are for others. The Reformation was launched by (and contained in) the idea that it's not doing good works that makes us right with God. Instead, it's the one to whom righteousness has been given who will do good works.

I've witnessed Romans 8:28 misused more than any other verse. And I know I have been guilty of misusing it myself. Maybe you've heard it thrown out in a small-group setting, maybe in a casual discussion. Inevitably someone has just shared a painful story about what she's going through or has gone through. We don't know what to say—the predicament is a sad one. It goes beyond the normal categories and struggles. It's awkward. We want to help, perhaps, but we also want the moment to end. Or maybe we are just focused on saying the "right" thing.

Make no mistake, in this context, Romans 8:28 can be a bona fide conversation stopper. A spiritual "shut up," if you will. And lest we think only Christians are prone to such insensitivity, the secular translation, "Don't worry. It'll all work out," is no less common. Both are classic minimizations of suffering.

Quick fixes are inevitably attempts to minimize. And so is the offering of "cheer up" platitudes. But whether suffering is approached through the eyes of faith or not, the God of the Bible never reduces or compartmentalizes suffering—ever. The problems of life are large and complex. Pat answers are not only inaccurate but also unkind.

Our big problem requires a big solution. And in the old rugged cross, we have one. Despite our efforts to contain, move past, or silence it, the cross stands tall, resolutely announcing that "in all things God works for the good of those who love him, who have been called according to his purpose" (v. 28). All things, Paul said, even misused Bible verses and the men and women who misuse them. Instead of diminishing our pain, then, these words proclaim the corresponding and overwhelming gratuity of our Redeemer.

In a piece on Hollywood.com about the MTV show *Catfish*, a viewer was interviewed after allegations surfaced that much of the show is staged. "It's more or less obvious that it's just baiting," said Rachel Turnpaugh. "It always ends up being the worst-case scenario anyway." But, the interviewer asks, would Turnpaugh still watch the series knowing there are editing changes? "Absolutely."

Turnpaugh is just like me. She's just like you. When a lie is something that we enjoy or that makes us feel good about ourselves, we are happy, even eager, to believe it.

The same goes for the lie associated with the law. It's a lie that the world tells us, and a lie that we tell ourselves: to get in good with God, we have to be good. "Here's the checklist," the lie goes. "Just do this stuff—and do it right—and you'll be fine." This lie makes us feel good; it makes us think that we have a chance; it makes us think we're in control. Even though it leaves us empty in the end, we always come back for more.

For Christians, though, the truth is so much better than the lie: Jesus Christ has already finished all of the work for you. There's nothing left to be done. Despite this, we find ourselves reverting daily to "to-do-list Christianity," like watching episode after episode of *Catfish*, telling ourselves that we're enjoying it, but feeling curiously unsatisfied.

The good news about Jesus Christ is true news. It's the filet mignon that's been put in front of us with the note "no charge." We don't trust the chef, though. We're terrified that some mistake has been made and the bill will be overwhelming. So we push the plate away and figure we'll forage for our own dinner. We think we'll like it more since we got it for ourselves, and while we're eating it, there is that twinge of satisfaction. But soon, we'll just be hungry again.

Jesus said, "Everyone who drinks this water will be thirsty again, but whoever drinks the water I give them will never thirst. Indeed, the water I give them will become in them a spring of water welling up to eternal life" (vv. 13–14).

Only the gospel—a truth given free of charge—will fully satisfy.

All too often, though we admit that God is in the business of destroying our idols, we forget, that that includes our biggest idol—our own self-sufficiency.

Before Gideon faces the Midianites, God takes his army from thirty-two thousand well-armed fighting men to three hundred who lap like dogs, armed with trumpets and jars of fire. He does this for an explicit reason: He doesn't want any confusion. He wants Gideon and the nation of Israel to know just who it is who has delivered them.

God makes Israel weak so that He might be shown to be strong. God shows Israel their need for a Savior by sending almost the entire army home (v. 3) before answering that need, saying, "With the three hundred men that lapped *I will save you* and give the Midianites into your hands" (v. 7).

God uses His law to show us our need, to strip us down to our bare bones. This hurts. Gideon goes from a well-outfitted army of thirty-two thousand to a group of three hundred dog lappers with trumpets and empty jars. Just when we think we have it all together, the brakes go out on the car, a credit card bounces in public, or your kid pees on your couch.

But our God is the God of resurrections. That's His second job. His first job, announced with His first word, the law, is to destroy us. Or at least, to destroy our idea of an "us" that is not already destroyed. This is God's first work, destroying our idol of self-sufficiency.

There is, though, good news. We're sitting in the middle of the rubble of our lives, wondering how we ended up like this. We're looking at the walls of the Midianites, and all we've got are some trumpets and some jars with a little fire. We're dead. But our God is a God of resurrection, and He has promised to make *all* things new, and that includes you and me. Today! Right now! We are made new! Death has been defeated and life eternal has been won, and it's all been announced before we ever had to do a thing. Jesus did everything so that we need do nothing. It is finished—right now, today, and forever.

When Paul said that, without love, we are a noisy gong or a clanging cymbal, what did he mean? I think he meant an instrument that is not contributing to the beauty of the music. Did you play a musical instrument in school? I did. I remember how one instrument poorly played could ruin a tune. I remember the time a string quartet came to the school to demonstrate the stringed instruments and to encourage students to learn to play. As part of their demonstration, they told us that they were going to play a tune, adding one instrument at a time, and to raise our hand when we recognized it. First, the bass. Then the cello. Then the viola. But it wasn't until the violin began to play the melody that the tune was recognizable.

Do you see what was going on? Each instrument makes its unique contribution to the piece, and taken in sum, it produces beautiful music. This is very similar to what Paul was talking about. One of the main things that each of us wants to accomplish in our lives is to make some kind of contribution to the world. How many times have you heard people say that they "just want to make a difference" or they "just want to give something back"? These people are concerned with their contribution to the world.

And what did Paul have to say about this? You've got it—without love, you contribute nothing. Without love, you are the clanging cymbal or the noisy gong. Not only are you playing alone, making the tune unrecognizable, you're playing out of tune. We are designed to be loving creatures. If we don't have love, we are out of tune!

That's why our lives are out of tune so often. We love less than we ought to. Praise God that Jesus Christ is the whole orchestra. He drowns out our clanging cymbal with the beautiful music of His love. Even better, He gives His loveliness to us, fitting us into the music just as we were created to be.

My mom reminds me of Jesus. Not because she always acts likes Jesus. In fact, she would be the first to admit that, in her attempts to behave the way Jesus behaved, she fails more often than she succeeds. She reminds me of Jesus because she birthed me.

Let me explain.

The very process of giving birth is a beautiful picture of what Jesus Christ has accomplished for sinners like me. In his remarkable book *Jesus Ascended*, author Gerrit Scott Dawson puts it this way:

> A child is conceived through the loving communion of husband and wife. The child grows inside the sheltering womb of the mother. But the child cannot live there forever. He is made for another world, a world of daylight and air, starlight and sky. So in the hours of her labor, the mother offers a new and living way. The way to life as a human being into the world passes through the curtain of her flesh. The curtain must be torn that the child might live and reach the daylight world.... By her pain, the child is born.

This is precisely the way the Bible speaks of Christ's work on the cross. In Isaiah 53, the prophet foretold of a "suffering servant" who would one day bear the sin of many. He told of a "man of sorrows" who would take on Himself the punishment we sinners deserve. It was Christ who accomplished a glorious exchange: His death brings us life. In the same way that we were brought into this world through the pain and suffering of another, we are brought into fellowship with God through the pain and suffering of Christ.

So when I think about my mother, I can't help but think about the suffering she endured to give me life. Her blood, literally, brought me into this world. The way to true, everlasting life passes through the curtain of Christ's flesh. He is the One who passed through the "valley of the shadow of death" so that I might enjoy the "still waters" and "green pastures" that friendship with God brings (Ps. 23).

Joe Paterno was the legendary Penn State football coach who fell from grace due to questions about his response to child-abuse allegations by a former staff member. Just before he died, he bemoaned the sullying of his name, saying, "My name. I have spent my whole life trying to make that name mean something. And now it's gone."

Like Paterno's, our downfalls often come at the very times when we think we're on the way up, when we're finally ready to "make a name for ourselves." There is a theological reason for this: God is in the business of tearing down our idols, and the most precious idol in each of our lives is our own self-sufficiency, the quality of our name.

When someone hears our name, we want them to think of competence, even excellence. As we build the mythology of our name in our mind, we do everything we can to associate it with success. This inevitably leads to a low Christology—when and where we think our name is great, there is no room in the equation, no need, for the One whose "name is above every name." But when we fall or, more accurately, when our true nature is revealed, the name we spent so long cultivating is revealed to be a hollow husk, surrounding a rotten core. It is usually only when we are forced—when our name is gone, as Paterno put it—that we can acknowledge the true state of our humanity.

But the good news is this: our name is not ours to make or break; it is God's to give (Gen. 35:10). And this name, the peace and identity that God gives in Jesus, can never be "gone." It is "written in the Lamb's book of life, the Lamb who was slain from the creation of the world" (Rev. 13:8; Luke 10:20).

Joe Paterno spent his whole life trying to make his name mean something—something other than what our names all mean: desperately in need of a Savior. Praise God that He knows our true names, and sent us just the Savior we needed.

In his funny web series *Comedians in Cars Getting Coffee*, Jerry Seinfeld shared this "parable" with fellow comedian Sarah Silverman:

> This is my reductive story of marriage. It's one line, and it's a wife talking to her husband after a party. She says to him, "I thought it was a wonderful joke and I'm sure everyone else did too." Obviously, he told a horrible, off-color joke that ruined everyone's night. It doesn't matter that he just ruined any chance he's going to have to advance in his company. She's not going to tell him the truth.

"I love that … that sounds like what love is!" responded Silverman.

Now, admittedly, there is some power in calling a thing good when it isn't. A husband can certainly feel buoyed by the support of his wife. In fact, I'm willing to bet that most people would agree with Seinfeld here, at least in principle. When our kids do poorly at a piano recital, we're quick to tell them that they were wonderful. When, at basketball practice, they can neither dribble, pass, nor shoot, we heap on the praise and tell them they're doing a great job. But our God loves us better than this.

When we call a thing something it's not, we're lying. When God does it, He's creating. When God called light out of darkness and separated the waters from the dry land, He spoke a word and these things actually happened. When Jerry's wife tells him that "it was a wonderful joke" and she's "sure everyone else" thought so too, it doesn't change the effect that the joke had on the party or will have on Jerry's career. And unless Jerry's an idiot, he knows that. Jerry might feel better (for a moment), but his state is unchanged.

God's words act differently than human words: Our words can encourage or discourage, build up or put down, buoy or sink. God's words create and destroy. God's first word (the law) destroys us. It cuts us to the quick and ends our lives. God's second word, the gospel, is just as powerful—it makes all things new (Rev. 21:5).

We're very accustomed to the idea of Jesus being the shepherd. In fact, He's the shepherd only two verses after these. But there's a surprise twist in this parable: He's also the door.

Jesus is doing something pretty radical here. He's downplaying His role as leader and playing up His role as Savior. We are so conditioned to thinking of Jesus as our leader that it sometimes becomes easy to sum up Christianity with the well-worn slogan "What would Jesus do?" But in John 10:7–9, Jesus isn't talking about following Him as He does in other places.

We like doors because they're simple. Open or closed. A door can only be one of two things. In a sense, a door is either saying yes or no. It's saying "come in" or "go away."

Jesus's door isn't like that. A life in Christ is a life of forgiveness rather than a life of condemnation, a life of eternal support rather than a life of fear, a life of promise rather than of a life of panic. When Jesus said that He's the door, He promised more than just a way in. He said, "Whoever enters through me will be saved. They will come in *and go out*, and find pasture" (v. 9). So, no worries about getting in, no worries about getting thrown out. This door, Jesus's door, is just standing open.

Paul elaborated on Jesus as door in his second letter to the Corinthians: "For the Son of God, Jesus Christ, who was preached among you by us—by me and Silas and Timothy—was not 'Yes' and 'No,' but in him it has always been 'Yes'" (2 Cor. 1:19). All of the promises God has made are "yes" in Christ. Jesus doesn't say two things, like every other door in your life. Jesus as "door" always says one thing: All you who are weary and heavy laden come in and find rest (Matt. 11:28). You are always welcome here.

Remember the face-melting scene from *Raiders of the Lost Ark*? Do you still watch it through your fingers like I do?

When the beautiful spirits arise from the sands contained within the ark, Indiana Jones knows what's coming: death and destruction (2 Cor. 3:6). The ark held the Ten Commandments, the law given by God to Moses as a reflection of His holiness. Indy knows that the law of God is not something to be trifled with, not something to be controlled.

When we come face-to-face with the law, we see how short of its standard we fall, and we die. This is no exaggeration. We have all come to see ourselves as the sum of our achievements. We say things like, "I am a good father," "I am a college professor," "I am a pastor," or "I am a good Christian." When our spiritual currency is shown to be fraudulent, our lives crash in upon themselves. This is nothing less than a death, and a much more painful death than our literal and physical one because we are cursed to live through it.

The Bible also claims that the law kills, and literally. When Moses brought the law down from the mountain, finding the Israelites worshipping the golden calf, three thousand people died (Exod. 32). Life under and with the law killed the entire first generation of Israelites who had come out of Egypt before the Promised Land was reached (the book of Numbers). Death is the real result of interaction with the law of God.

Too often, we set our sights on self-powered achievements. We don't know that, by doing this, we are willingly placing ourselves in front of the firing squad of the law. We forget that the law melts faces.

Of course, we cannot simply close our eyes to the law "engraved in letters on stone." It is too powerful. We have a better hope than Indiana Jones had though—the hope found in a resurrected Savior who promised to fulfill the law on our behalf, stare its destructive power in the maw, and give His victory to us.

We are addicted to strength. We talk about having a "strong faith." We look up to people whom we believe are "strong Christians," and we aspire to be described as "prayer warriors." We constantly tell the secular world that we're as smart as they are, as cunning, as resourceful, even that we're coming to change their world. Nothing could be more off-putting, or further from gospel truth.

No one comes to mind as quickly for Christians when talking about strength than Samson. Ask any preteen boy who the coolest guy in the Bible is, and he'll probably say Samson.

The story of Samson gives us a hero to aspire to, someone God used to accomplish His powerful purpose, right? In short, the story of Samson is a perfect illustration of the story of the Christian progression—from weakness to strength. Right?

Not so fast.

Samson's life actually helps us come to the realization that our strength *doesn't come from us*.

We think his strength is in his hair (even Samson thought that his strength was in his hair), but before every great deed Samson performed, we read, "The Spirit of the LORD came powerfully upon him" (Judg. 14:6). This is why he can bring down the house at his death. It was never his hair; it was God.

Before he tears a lion apart with his bare hands (14:6), before he kills the thirty men of Ashkelon (14:19), and before he kills a thousand men with the jawbone of a donkey (15:15), the exact same phrase is used: "The Spirit of the LORD came powerfully upon him." The author of Judges is at pains to make it clear that these feats of strength are not Samson's, but God's.

Samson's story shows us a profound truth of Christianity: ours is a progress from strength to weakness, not weakness to strength. It is when Samson is at his weakest that he is most powerfully used. Samson ends his life blind and in chains. He is weak. So are we. God promises, in His Son, to perfect His power in our powerlessness (2 Cor. 12:9). So we can own our weakness. We'll find God's strength in it.

My friend Steve Brown tells a story about a time his daughter Robin found herself in a very difficult literature class that she desperately wanted to get out of.

She sat there on her first day and thought, *If I don't transfer out of this class, I'm going to fail. The other people in this class are much smarter than me. I can't do this.* She came home and with tears in her eyes begged her dad to help her get out of the class so she could take a regular English course. Steve said, "Of course."

So the next day he took her down to the school and went to the head of the English department, who was a Jewish woman and a great teacher. Steve took Robin in to request that the teacher put his daughter into a different English class, and the teacher responded with a shocking suggestion. "What if I promised you an A, no matter what you did in the class? If I gave you an A before you even started, would you be willing to take the class?" Of course, Robin isn't dumb, and agreed. The teacher's final word to her was, "I'm going to give you an A in the class. So now you can go to class."

Later the teacher explained to Steve what she had done. She explained how she took away the threat of a bad grade so that Robin could learn English. Robin ended up making straight As in that class on her own.

That's how God deals with us. Because we are, right now, under the completely sufficient imputed righteousness of Christ, Christians already have an A. The threat of failure, judgment, and condemnation has been removed. We're in—forever! Nothing we do will make our grade better, and nothing we do will make our grade worse. We've been set free.

The gospel isn't simply a set of truths that non-Christians must believe in order to become saved. It's a reality that Christians must daily embrace in order to experience being saved. The gospel not only saves us from the penalty of sin (justification), but it also saves us from the power of sin (sanctification) day after day. Or as John Piper has said, "The cross is not only a past place of objective substitution; it is also a present place of subjective execution." Our daily sin requires God's daily grace—the grace that comes to us through the finished work of Jesus Christ.

Churches, for example, have for years debated whether their worship services ought to be geared toward Christians (to encourage and strengthen them) or non-Christians (to appeal to and win them). But this debate and the struggle over it are misguided. We're asking the wrong questions and making the wrong assumptions. The truth is that our worship services should be geared to sinners in need of God's rescue—and that includes both Christians and non-Christians. Since both groups need His deliverance, both need His gospel.

Christians need the gospel because our hearts are always prone to wander, and we're always tempted to run from God. It takes the power of the gospel to direct us back to our first love. Consciously going to the gospel ought to be a daily reality and experience for us all. It means, as Jerry Bridges reminds us, "preaching the gospel to yourself every day." We have to allow God to remind us every day through His Word of Christ's finished work on behalf of sinners in order to stay convinced that the gospel is relevant.

The difference between living for God and living for anything else is that when we live for anything else, we do so to gain acceptance, but when we live for God, we do so because we are already accepted. Real freedom, the freedom that only the gospel grants, is living for something because we already have favor instead of living for something in order to gain favor.

Near the end of a thirty-two-hundred-meter race at the Ohio Division III girls state high school track meet in 2012, last-place runner Meghan Vogel noticed something strange on the track ahead of her: Arden McMath, the only other runner yet to finish the race, had collapsed on the track with only twenty meters to go. Vogel said that she did what any other runner on the track would have done for her: she picked McMath up and assisted her over the finish line, being careful to finished behind the girl she was carrying. As you might imagine, the two girls became instant celebrities, speaking to media outlets too numerous to count.

"It's been crazy," said Vogel. "It's strange to have people telling me that this was such a powerful act of kindness and using words like 'humanity.' It's weird. When I hear words like that I think of Harriet Tubman and saving people's lives. I don't consider myself a hero. I just did what I knew was right and what I was supposed to do." It's ironic, of course, that Vogel is hearing words like "humanity," because she did something that no human ever does—put herself second.

Humans only ever invoke their humanity when they've done something wrong. When was the last time you heard someone, celebrated for doing a great thing, say, "Well, I *am* human"? Never. Not once. We say, "I'm only human" to apologize for our mistakes. Jeremiah said that the human heart is deceitful above all things and beyond cure. Meghan Vogel should have been hearing about her humanity had she taken the opportunity to pass McMath and avoid finishing last. That's what a human would do. Anything else is a miracle.

A miracle is exactly what happened. Vogel thought of someone else before herself. Martin Luther talked about sin being humanity curved back in on itself, and that redemption in Christ allowed humans to be what they were created to be: full of true humanity, loving their neighbors as themselves.

Third Day has two songs—on the same album—that show that Christians have an amazing ability to hold completely opposing views of the thing we think is the most important thing in the world, and that we do so very comfortably.

The first song, "Take My Life," is a wonderful, gospel-saturated song and a sentiment that almost every Christian would agree with:

> *How many times have I turned away?*
> *The number is the same as the sand on the shore*
> *But every time You've taken me back*
> *And now I pray You do it once more*

We know that we're not perfect—even the most self-righteous would admit that—and we are aware that it is the grace of God that keeps us in the proverbial fold.

The other song, "Did You Mean It?" has a radically different message:

> *Now the time has come to make your promise true*
> *But you sit around after all He's done for you*
> *You need forgiveness, you don't do anything*
> *You didn't mean it*

As much as we like "Take My Life" religion (the gospel), we often find ourselves drawn to "Did You Mean It?" religion (the law). Law and gospel, though, cannot both be God's final word. The gospel triumphs over the law, every time, rescuing us as we are being dragged to our deaths by our inability to perfectly keep the law. When "Did You Mean It?" Christianity is choking you to death, remember that our promises are meaningless next to God's promises and that God is the God of "Take My Life" Christianity, taking our lives onto Himself when we don't have the strength to give them away to Him. He takes them, destroys them, raises them up from the dead, and redeems them.

In his wonderful book *Theology Is for Proclamation*, Gerhard Forde wrote about the fall of mankind:

> Adam and Eve fell into sin. The fall is really not what the word implies at all. It is not a downward plunge to some lower level in the great chain of being, some lower rung on the ladder of morality and freedom. Rather it is an upward rebellion, an invasion of the realm of things "above," the usurping of divine prerogative. To retain traditional language, one would have to resort to an oxymoron and speak of an "upward fall." This, after all, is precisely what the temptation by the serpent in the garden implies: "You will not die ... you will be like God, knowing good and evil" (Genesis 3:4–5). A line had been drawn over which Adam and Eve were not to step. They were not to eat of the tree of knowledge of good and evil. There was a realm "above" which they were to leave to God; if they did not, their death would result. But the tempter insinuated, "Don't believe it for an instant! God is only jealous of the divine preserve! God knows that if you step over the line you will not die but become gods. You have something going for you! You have divine qualities, you have an immortal soul." So the step is taken. It is rebellion, an upward fall.

The temptation for Christians is to think that once God saves us, we move beyond the first "Adamic" impulse to fall upward. The truth is, however, that even after God saves us we continue to fall upward, trying to claim for ourselves the glory that belongs to God alone. John Stott wrote, "Man asserts himself against God and puts himself where only God deserves to be. God sacrifices himself for man and puts himself where only man deserves to be."

The first Adam ventured up into the "realm of things above" and brought death. The second Adam ventured down into the "realm of things below" and brought life. His gift of life is yours today.

The world tells us in a thousand different ways that the bigger we become, the freer we will be. The richer, the more beautiful, and the more powerful we grow, the more security, liberty, and happiness we will experience. And yet, the gospel tells us just the opposite—the smaller we become, the freer we will be.

This may sound at first like bad news, but it could not be better news!

When your meaning, your significance, your security, your protection, your safety are all riding on you, it actually feels like slavery. People seldom "choose" to embezzle money. They feel as though they have to if they are to uphold whatever law they live under. That is, they equate their value with some attribute or ability—what others think of them, how much is in their bank account, their relative stature in their community—and without that attribute or ability, they cease to matter.

This is a burden we were never meant to bear, and yet after the fall, self-reliance became our default mode of operation. You might even call it our inheritance. In our exile from Eden, we naturally tend toward self-reliance.

Fortunately, God does not leave us there. The gospel is for the defeated, not the dominant. In view of God's holiness, we are all losers (Rom. 3:23). We are all sinners. The distinction between winners and losers is irrelevant when no one can claim victory.

Instead, the gospel is for those who have realized that they can't carry the weight of the world on their shoulders. Only when God drives us to the end of ourselves do we begin to see life in the gospel. Another way to say this is that only those who stand in need of a Savior will look for or recognize a Savior. Fortunately, Christianity in its original, most authentic expression understands God chiefly as Savior and human beings chiefly as those in need of being saved.

"I love you" is a phrase of well-known power. The reason that characters in romantic comedies are so worried about saying these three words and about what the repercussions might be is that everyone knows these words have power.

But there's a problem: we don't believe that we can be loved. We acknowledge the words "I love you" have great power, and we swoon when Ryan Gosling says them to Rachel McAdams. But we can't see ourselves in her shoes. In the romantic comedies we've seen, the jock doesn't really fall in love with the girl until she's had her stunning nerd-to-gorgeous makeover. We wish for a similar makeover, and so we work toward it.

God's "I love you" can feel even more evasive than Ryan Gosling's. His standards certainly seem higher. Rachel McAdams never had to turn the other cheek, did she? She didn't have to love with all her heart, soul, mind, and strength, did she? These are the sorts of things we think are required of us for God's "I love you" to apply.

So when someone says, "God loves you," we smirk inside. It feels trite and forced. It feels manipulative. We act as if God's "I love you" has no power, because we have convinced ourselves that God's "I love you" will be revoked if we don't deserve it.

The good news is that God's "I love you" is proclaimed specifically to those who don't deserve it. In other words, we don't need a makeover to be loved by God. God's love is not fake or forced; it is an "I love you" that says, "I forgive you." God's "I love you" is based on the deserving of another. "God demonstrates his own love for us in this: While we were still sinners, Christ died for us" (Rom. 5:8). On the cross, Christ's righteousness was given to us and our sin was laid upon Him. God's "I love you," aimed at His perfect Son, is ours forever.

Remember how Joshua won the battle of Jericho? Actually, that's a trick question: Joshua *didn't* win the battle of Jericho.

Jericho was a hugely fortified city, and God's big plan was to have Joshua's army *walk* around the city for six days. Then on the seventh day, God's people were to walk around the city seven times and conclude with a huge shout. When the walls of Jericho "come tumbling down," it seems as though Joshua's faithfulness (and willingness to follow through on this ridiculous plan) is being rewarded.

We turn this story into nothing more than a moral lesson: if we, like Joshua, have great faith and bravely fight the battles in our lives, we will see our personal walls of sin come tumbling down and enter into the Promised Land of spiritual maturity.

When we read the story of Joshua this way, we demonstrate that we've completely missed the hinge on which this story turns. This whole story hinges on the placement of one verse: "See, I have delivered Jericho into your hands, along with its king and its fighting men" (v. 2). Incredibly, Joshua doesn't even order the people to begin marching around the city until verse seven. God hands Jericho over to Joshua *before* Joshua does what God wants!

God makes His pronouncements at the *beginning*, before any improvement or qualification occurs—before any conditions are met. God decides the outcome of Joshua's battle before anyone straps on a shield or picks up a sword. And He not only decides to deliver unconditionally, He does so single-handedly. No one lifts a finger to dismantle the wall—the promised victory is received, not achieved. Joshua did not even *fight* the battle of Jericho. God did. Joshua and the Israelites simply received the victory God secured.

Of course, this battle points us to another battle that God unconditionally and single-handedly fought for us. We are the ones trapped inside the fortified walls of sin and death—of fear and anxiety and insecurity and self-salvation—and Jesus's "it is finished" shout from the cross alone causes the walls of our self-induced slavery to come tumbling down.

I once heard a woman on the radio telling the story of her family's very public fall from grace. Sara grew up in a privileged family—enormous house, beautiful clothes, expensive cars, and country club memberships. Everything in her life was very prim and proper. But Sara claimed that despite the excess that could be seen from the outside, on the inside, her home environment was one of constraint:

> Rules were very important. Etiquette, very important. And my dad's insane temper could be set off by the slightest offense. When I heard the Porsche rumble up the driveway every day when he came home, I would run into my room and hide. Because maybe today would be the day he found the candy wrapper in the sofa cushion…. It was all just about avoiding awakening the bee's nest.

Sara went on to describe the fateful day when her parents called a family meeting to tell the children that her father had embezzled much of their money from the trust fund of one of his disabled clients. Her father, who was a prominent lawyer, wept on the couch as he confessed his wrongdoing to his children. The guilt-induced suffering became too much to bear. He couldn't live with his wrongdoing any longer. "We're going to have to start over," he said. "We are going to rebuild our lives." Sara then shared how her father was disbarred, how they had to sell their house and cars and move to the other side of town. Her mother went to work. The scandal made headlines. At school, kids teased Sara for being the daughter of a "bank robber." And yet in that death—of security, wealth, achievement, identity, and so on—we find out that new life is born.

Sara said, "My dad was instantly better…. He was happy."

Sara's story is a powerful testimony of how suffering can liberate us, a tangible echo of the theology of the cross. When we experience what it means to take up our cross and follow Jesus, we have all of our supports taken away and feel the burden of our sin, but at the same time, we experience Jesus's taking of our sin upon Himself in His suffering on the cross. Though we die, yet will we live (John 11:25).

What are we to make of this, that law came through Moses and grace and truth came through Jesus? Is the Bible arguing with itself? Are Jesus and Moses having a theological disagreement? Heaven forbid, is the real issue between *God* and Jesus? After all, Moses got the law from God.

That, friends, is the elephant in the room, the thing that none of us really wants to talk about: the fact that the law—the thing that makes us feel so bad—comes from God. It's easy for us to say, "Well, Moses is about law, and Jesus is about grace." It's a little bit weirder, and quite a bit harder, to say that "God is about law, and Jesus is about grace." One reason that it's weird and hard to say that is because it's not quite true.

It's easy to think of God as the judgmental heaven-dweller with the long white beard, the guy who may or may not be throwing lightning bolts at His disobedient creatures. It's easy to forget that He loved us in this way: He sent His Son Jesus to die for us.

Yes, of course, Moses got those stone tablets from God. And the law is glorious. It is God's holy word to His people, showing them how to live. The Ten Commandments, for instance, are bedrock rules to live by. They are good. But that's the problem. They're *too* good. Remember that Paul said the people of Israel could not even look at Moses's face after he'd been inside the Holy of Holies, it was so glorious! But Paul goes on to say, the law is so glorious that it brings only condemnation. These glorious laws, these good and true rules to live life by, given to us by God, threaten to destroy us because of our inability to obey.

Jesus, though, takes the law's condemnation onto Himself, ushering grace and truth into the world, and promises a glory to us now that is not damning but saving.

What is the center of the gospel? Can (or should) the essence of the gospel be distinguished from its implications? Some insist the gospel is just the message of Christ's substitutionary atonement and that anything else is an "entailment" or a "result." But the Bible reveals the essence of the gospel is larger than this.

For instance, in Romans 2:16, Paul says that Christ coming to judge (and put the world to rights) is part of His gospel. And in Acts 13:32 Paul says that the good news includes the fact that, in Christ, the Old Testament promises to Israel are fulfilled. But perhaps the most explicit places where the fullness of the gospel's essence is seen are in Mark 1:14–15 and Luke 16:16, where Jesus defines the gospel as the coming of the kingdom of God that includes the restoration of all things. In other words, the gospel is certainly not less than Christ's atoning work on the cross, but it is more.

As I've come to understand it, the gospel is the good news that God's kingdom has come from heaven to earth in the person of Jesus. This includes all He accomplished by living a perfect life, all He accomplished by His substitutionary death on the cross, and all He accomplished by being raised from the dead.

In other words, Christ's life by itself is not the center of the gospel, the cross by itself is not the center of the gospel, and the resurrection by itself is not the center of the gospel. Any one of these without the other two fails to bring about redemption. In a sense, you could say the gospel has a tricentrality to it. So we don't have to choose between parts of Christ's finished work as being the center of the gospel. It's much more theologically accurate to say that Christ Himself (His life, death, and resurrection) is the center of the gospel.

The gospel, then, is as big and glorious as Jesus Christ Himself.

Do you know the football Mannings? Father Archie was picked second in the NFL draft, sons Peyton and Eli were each picked first. They are the first family of football.

Oh, and one more thing: Archie Manning is the best dad in the world.

As a youngster, Archie always wanted more affection from his father than the man seemed willing to give. Football was the love they shared and the reason that Archie played with such passion. During the summer between his sophomore and junior years at Ole Miss, just when Archie was primed to make the jump from local legend to national superstar, Buddy Manning shot and killed himself in the family home. Archie was the one who found him.

Never able to get the love he wanted from his dad, and never having his dad around to revel in his athletic success, Archie pledged to be there for his kids. Archie put his family ahead of football, and despite a fourteen-season career of more losses than wins, he never came home without the energy to roll around in the yard with his kids.

It's Archie who took the hit from fans when Peyton chose Tennessee over Ole Miss. It's Archie who had the loving heart-to-heart with Eli when he was arrested for public intoxication during his freshman year. It's Archie who helps his oldest son learn to walk again.

I don't know about you, but I feel like Archie Manning's fatherhood puts mine to shame. How long are my kids home from school before I'm frustrated with them? An hour? Five minutes? If they succeed, I'm convinced my kids will do it despite me, not because of me. This is the problem with the comparison game: our heroes cease to inspire and begin to crush.

We must take care how we regard Jesus, too. He is certainly our example. But if that's the only way I regard Him, I obviously will never measure up and will always be spiritually crushed. But regarding Him by His gospel, I don't have to measure up. The pressure is off; He's measured up for me!

I'll never be the father Archie Manning is. But my failing fatherhood was taken up to the cross with Jesus and sacrificed there. I can love my children now, freed from the deadly burden of perfection.

R. Crumb, probably the most famous of the underground comics writers, was the subject of the acclaimed 1994 Terry Zwigoff documentary *Crumb*. Perhaps the most succinct way to describe Crumb's work can be found in the IMDb keywords for that film: weird sex, obsession, and comic books.

Crumb's artwork and storytelling are frequently accused of misogyny, as they often depict women as either grossly deformed (e.g., enormous breasts and legs, but no head), rapaciously evil, or both. Most artists, when accused of harboring such sentiments, attempt to hide behind their role as an artist, much like an actor might seek to distance himself from the unsavory characteristics of a role. Not Crumb.

In the film, Crumb confronts his failings head-on. He names them and, as Martin Luther would have called it, calls a thing what it is. He acknowledges an awful truth: he has a hostility toward women inside of him. He admits that it's evil. He even suggests that it's possible that he ought to be locked up and his pencils taken away. He hopes, though, that by confronting it and revealing that truth about himself, he can be helpful somehow.

Crumb is a fascinating juxtaposition: he's a mild-mannered, artistic, gentle man, and yet he harbors these very angry and hostile ideas inside of him. In other words, he's just like us. He's a whitewashed tomb whose door has been thrown open and its contents poured onto the street. Every single one of us has things, deep, dark things, that we keep stuffed into the corners of our consciousness, terrified that someone might discover them.

How much better is it to do what Crumb does, to face up to our sinfulness, to confess? As Crumb said, it's not the easy way—in fact, it is the way that leads to death—but it is death that leads to resurrection. "If we confess our sins, [God] is faithful and just and will forgive us our sins and purify us from all unrighteousness" (v. 9).

God's grace always, always, *always* comes as a contradiction to what makes natural sense to us—it always comes as a "but," not a "therefore." Here are just a few examples:

> The wages of sin is death, *but* the gift of God is eternal life. (Rom. 6:23)

> We were dead in our trespasses and sin … *but* God made us alive. (Eph. 2)

> By works of the law no flesh will be justified before God … *but* now the righteousness of God has been revealed. (Rom. 3)

The *but* means everything. I've heard it said that *but God* are the two sweetest words in the Bible, and I tend to agree. Grace comes into a situation that is going badly for us (death and condemnation are knocking on our door) and injects a Savior into the equation. It's not fair, but it is sorely needed.

Not long ago, a gentleman approached me after a talk I had delivered and said, "I'm sixty years old and have had great success as a businessman, and I'm here to tell you from experience that grace doesn't work in this world." My immediate response was, "Well maybe it appears that way only because grace isn't from this world."

This quote from Robert Kolb makes the point beautifully:

God promises righteousness and freedom to sinners. That promise contradicts ordinary human expectation. Sinners ought to receive punishment rather than pardon, incarceration rather than freedom. But by the double work of his law and gospel, God teaches sinners to close their eyes to ordinary human expectations and the conclusions of common sense and to open their ears to the promise which offers life and freedom.

The fact that grace isn't from this world is the best kind of news: all this world ever does is put us in shackles. When God crosses the great divide from heaven to earth, from righteousness to sinfulness, He turns the spiritual economy of our business as usual upside down—which is to say, right side up.

We are, without question, a society of doers. Ever since the Enlightenment, we've been told in a thousand different ways that accomplishment precedes acceptance, that achievement precedes approval. And since we all long for affirmation and validation, we set out to prove our worth by working. Unwittingly, Christians in this cultural context have absorbed this mentality and taken it into their relationship with God and their understanding of the Christian life. Even when Jesus was asked in John 6:28, "What must we do to do the works God requires?" He answered, "The work of God is this: to believe in the one he has sent" (v. 29).

What? That's it? There has to be more work for us to do than that!

As it was with Martha in Luke 10, so it is with us: we always feel that we have to be *doing something*. We're totally on her side when she asks Jesus to tell Mary to help her out. We can't sit still. Achieving, not receiving, has become the mark of spiritual maturity. With this in mind, Martin Luther wrote, "To be convinced in our hearts that we have forgiveness of sins and peace with God by grace alone is the hardest thing." The hardest thing to do even as believers in Christ is to simply sit down and receive something, which is why Mike Horton titled one of the chapters in his book *The Gospel-Driven Life*, "Don't Just Do Something, Sit There."

Christians these days are drawn to practical to-do lists rather than to the announcement, "It is finished." People think that they need to hear more than a simple proclamation of Christ's finished work. We want to be told what to do. We want something applicable! It's important to remember, though, that the real application that defines Christians is the application of Christ's work to them, not their work for Christ.

John Piper once asked, "How do you glorify a water fountain? Come thirsty and drink!" Jesus is not glorified by our "doing" things for Him. He is glorified by our resting in and receiving what He's done for us.

Sometimes it seems like all I pray for is peace. Peace in the world, peace in my home, peace at work, peace in my soul. Almost as soon as the words are out of my mouth, though, I worry that they're not going to do any good. None of those places are peaceful! The peace I so desperately need is totally elusive. Where does peace come from, then?

Peace, I think, comes from hope. The hope that this is not the way things were meant to be and that this is not the way they will be forever; that there is a time and place beyond this one where "God will wipe away every tear from their eyes" (Rev. 7:17). In Psalm 121, the psalmist lifts up his eyes to the mountains and wonders where his help comes from. Immediately, though, he answers his own question in verse 2: "My help comes from the LORD, the Maker of heaven and earth."

The psalmist knew what we often forget: help, and therefore peace, must come from another, from outside of us, and from a place up on the hill rather than down in the valley where we reside. The reason we often lack peace is that we believe it is up to us to shape our destinies. But if whatever happens to us is due to our choices and we decide our own fate, then we are surely lost.

If we turn our eyes upward, though, elevating them above the fray that fills our valley and look up to the hills, we can see from whence our help comes. It comes from God, who not only created heaven and earth, but who sent His Son to wage a victorious war on death and damnation. He is, as God the Father, the source of our peace. As God the Spirit, He is the presence of that peace. As God the Son, He is our peace.

Here's how we typically read the David and Goliath story: like David, we can bravely face any challenge. If we have the faith of David, we, too, can cut the heads off of the giants in our lives.

Here's the problem: when we read the story of David and Goliath like this, we are the ones who emerge victorious! All it takes is for us to do what David did. It's a story about the success of David, a success that we can self-ascribe if we do what it takes to become like him.

The David and Goliath story, however, is not primarily about us. It's not even a story that's primarily about David. In fact, if we insist on reading the David and Goliath story and turning it into a narrative exhortation to "be brave" and "be faithful" and "stand up to bullies," it becomes an invitation to slavery. It plays right into our deepest desire—to be our own Savior. And there's nothing more enslaving than self-salvation projects. They never end because they never work.

The story of David and Goliath is meant to point us to the one true hero, the one hero who is perfect at all times. Reading it this way, we are not David in the story. We are the frightened Israelites unable to face our enemies. We need an unlikely intervention. And like the Israelites, we find an unexpected substitute. Saul, the king who stood a head taller than anyone in the kingdom, didn't stand in the gap for his people. The shepherd boy from Bethlehem did.

God uses David's apparent weakness as the means to destroy the giant, and David becomes Israel's champion redeemer so that his victory is credited to them. The Israelites get the credit for winning a battle that they never fought, indeed for a battle in which they didn't lift a finger but instead cowered in weakness and fear.

Years later another underdog, the Good Shepherd from Bethlehem, would stand in the gap for His people. In fear and unbelief we cower, refusing to face our real enemies, hiding behind the patchwork quilts of our own self-salvation projects. But on the cross, it is Jesus's weakness that outmuscles and destroys the giant of sin and death.

I've heard a story several times that perfectly illustrates the profound creative power of God's grace in our lives. I don't know if it really happened (I hope that it did) or if it's just an apocryphal tale, but during the time of the Civil War, before America's slaves were freed, a Northerner went to a slave auction and purchased a young slave girl. As they walked away from the auction, the man turned to the girl and told her, "You're free."

With amazement she responded, "You mean, I'm free to do whatever I want?"

"Yes," he said.

"And to say whatever I want to say?"

"Yes, anything."

"And to be whatever I want to be?"

"Yep."

"And even go wherever I want to go?"

"Yes," he answered with a smile. "You're free to go wherever you'd like."

She looked at him intently and replied, "Then I will go with you."

Some fear that grace-delivered, blood-bought, radical freedom (to do, say, and be whatever we want) will result in loveless license. But as the above story illustrates, redeeming unconditional love alone (not fear, not guilt, not shame) carries the power to compel heartfelt loyalty to the One who bought us.

Notice that the slave girl can't believe her good fortune at first. She interrogates the man who has set her free, seemingly intent on finding the boundaries of her freedom. "He can't mean *totally* free," she seems to be thinking to herself. "Surely I'll cross a line at some point and realize that this release is conditional after all."

The miracle of grace is that the freedom it provides is indeed total. No strings attached. No conditions. No returns, refunds, exchanges, or recalls. We resist the idea at first; it seems impossible. The more we test the boundary though—"what if I do *this*?"—the further God's grace extends to accept us. Though our sin—the lack of faith that leads to such testing—reaches far, His grace reaches farther.

Some Christians use verses that describe how it's going to be at the end of things to justify an escapist theology, approaching this world with a "Why shine the brass on a sinking ship?" attitude. In Matthew's passage, Jesus likens "the coming of the Son of Man" to the time of Noah, when people "knew nothing about what would happen until the flood came and took them all away" (v. 39). Then Jesus gives two brief pictures of the effect of His coming: "Two men will be in the field; one will be taken and the other left. Two women will be grinding with a hand mill; one will be taken and the other left" (vv. 40–41).

These verses have been employed to support the idea that God will one day evacuate, or rapture, all the righteous people, leaving behind an evil world destined for annihilation. Therefore, the thinking goes, Christians should focus exclusively on seeking to rescue lost souls rather than waste time trying to fix things that are broken. This perspective was reflected in a comment I read not long ago from a well-known Bible teacher: "Evangelism is the only reason God's people are still on earth."

But a closer look at the context reveals that in those pictures Jesus gave of men in the field and women at the mill, those "left behind" are the righteous rather than the unrighteous. Like the people in Noah's day who were "swept away," leaving behind Noah and his family to rebuild the world, so the unrighteous are "taken," while the righteous are left behind. Why? Because this world belongs to God, and He's in the process of gaining it all back, not giving it all up.

When it comes to this world's future, God will follow the same pattern He engineered in Noah's day, when He washed away everything that was perverse and wicked but did not obliterate everything. God will not annihilate the cosmos; He'll redeem it. As Randy Alcorn wrote, "We will be the same people made new, and we will live on the same earth made new."

One thing all of this means is that God intends to bring redemption into every arena where sin has brought corruption—and that's everywhere!

In 2013 Florida State's Jameis Winston was the nation's best player and eventual Heisman Trophy winner. Before he won the award, though, he was accused of raping another student.

Heisman voters had a decision to make. How much stock do they put in two words, "with integrity," included in the Heisman's description: "the outstanding college football player whose performance best exhibits the pursuit of excellence with integrity"?

Here's the truth: no one has integrity. With a firm morality clause in place, the Heisman Trust should never give the award. Ever.

It's not hard to imagine Jesus taking a look at the Heisman hopefuls and calling them "whitewashed tombs." In fact, it's the job of a school's PR department to do the whitewashing. And don't think I'm singling out college athletes. We all have PR departments—they're just internal ones. As Chris Rock said, when people meet us, they don't actually meet us. They meet our representative. This representative is the creation of our personal PR department, and we create him or her because we know one thing for sure: the morality clause is a problem for us.

As soon as we make "morality clauses" (as soon as we invoke the law), we exclude the entire human race.

Jesus wanted us to take our focus off the outside ("whitewashed") and put it on the inside ("tombs"). The further in we go, the more corpses we have to wade through. The deeper we go into the human heart, the more people get excluded by our morality clauses. We realize that "there is none righteous; no not one" (v. 10 NASB).

The Jameis Winston story shines a light on a truth of human nature: we are sinners. Every last one of us. Christianity, though, is so much more profound than the Heisman Trust. God isn't looking for someone who can "pursue excellence with integrity." He is in the business of saving sinners. The function of the law—of morality clauses—is to shine light on sin, to expose need. The function of the gospel is to announce that the only truly moral One has come, and He has come to die for the immoral.

In late 2013 Stephen Colbert interviewed David Christian, host of the H2 series *Big History*. The stated goal of the series is to "let us get to know the entire history of the universe." As Colbert joked, "Why not something more ambitious?"

Christian and Colbert began a little bit at loggerheads when Christian suggested that *Big History* is interested in creating a map on which people are to place themselves. "We already have this kind of map," protested Colbert. "It's called the Bible." Christian started implying that his show has some of life's most important answers with statements like, "With a course like this, you can put all this knowledge together. You can see a coherent story of the whole of the past, and it's full of meaning."

When asked about the meaning of life, though, Christian prevaricated for a few moments before listing a series of dates and events, such as the universe appearing 13.8 billion years ago and the subsequent appearance of more complicated organisms. He called it "a wonderful story about how we got to be here." Colbert corrected him: "Those are the events of life; that's not the meaning of life."

As Colbert noted, science might be good for describing life's events. But as Christian's hesitation evinced, science isn't so good at discussing life's *meaning*. Life, in fact, makes no sense without the ability to discuss Genesis 1–3. Without knowledge of a perfect law-giving Creator God, our external actions and internal motivations will remain a mystery to us. Our struggle toward and failure to reach perfection will make no sense.

It's not up to each individual to place themselves on the map; we need to have our location announced to us. The only way we're ever able to understand ourselves—to find meaning in life—is to be given the key to the map.

There is a God. We're not Him, but many wish they were. We rebel against Him. In order to reconcile us to Himself, this God sent His Son to take our just condemnation onto Himself. This is His finished work. Getting used to the idea? That's the meaning of life.

Temptation is a promise that doesn't deliver. When we give in to temptation, we are believing a lie. This may come as a surprise to you, but resisting temptation has more to do with belief than it does with behavior. Every temptation to sin is, at its root, a temptation to disbelieve the gospel.

When we are being tempted, we are being enticed to purchase something we think we need in order to escape the judgment of emptiness. On the surface, the bait might be lust, anger, greed, self-pity, defensiveness, entitlement, revenge, having to win, and so on. But the only reason we take the bait is because we think it will satisfy our deeper hunger for meaning, freedom, validation, respect, empowerment, affection, a sense of identity, worth, and so on.

John Calvin rightly said that "Christians are in perpetual conflict with their own unbelief." So here's the connection between sinning (the fruit of the problem) and unbelief (the root of the problem): our failure to lay aside the sin that so easily entangles is the direct result of our refusal to believe in the rich resources already provided in Christ. We sin, basically, when we're dissatisfied with the all-satisfying Christ.

Failing to believe the gospel leads to slavery because now finding peace, joy, meaning, and satisfaction is up to us. We're on our own. We give in to temptation because we're desperately looking under every rock and behind every tree for something to make us happy, something to save us, something to set us free.

The gospel declares that I don't need to save myself, defend myself, legitimize myself, justify myself, or free myself. The gospel frees me from the obsessive pressure to avoid the judgment of joylessness, the enslaving demand to find happiness. What I need and long for most has come from outside of me in the person of Jesus.

Real freedom in "the hour of temptation" happens only when the resources of the gospel smash any sense of need to secure for myself anything beyond what Christ has already secured for me.

Martin Luther was once approached by a man who enthusiastically announced that he'd recently become a Christian. Wanting desperately to serve the Lord, he asked Luther, "What should I do now?" As if to say, should he become a minister or perhaps a traveling evangelist? A monk, perhaps? Luther asked him, "What is your work now?" "I'm a shoe maker," came the reply. Much to the cobbler's surprise, Luther replied, "Then make a good shoe, and sell it at a fair price."

In becoming a Christian, we don't need to retreat from the vocational calling we already have—nor do we need to justify that calling, whatever it is, in terms of its "spiritual" value or evangelistic usefulness. We simply exercise whatever our calling is with new God-glorifying motives, goals, and standards—and with a renewed commitment to performing our calling with greater excellence. "Whatever you do, work heartily," as Paul said, "as for the Lord" (Col. 3:23 ESV).

One way we reflect our Creator is by being creative right where we are with the talents and gifts He has given us. As Paul wrote, "Each person should remain in the situation they were in when God called them.... Brothers and sisters, each person, as responsible to God, should remain in the situation they were in when God called them" (1 Cor. 7:20, 24). As we do this, we fulfill our God-given mandate to redeem our various stations, giving this world an imperfect preview of the beautification that will be a perfect, universal actuality when Jesus returns to finish what He started.

We make a huge mistake when we define our calling in terms of participation inside the church—nursery work, Sunday school teacher, youth worker, music leader, and so on. Our calling is much bigger than how much time we put into church matters. Calling involves everything we are and everything we do, both inside and, more important, *outside* the church walls.

"Calling," said Os Guinness, "is the truth that God calls us to himself so decisively that everything we are, everything we do, and everything we have is invested with a special devotion, dynamism, and direction."

In early 2014, a television show called *Portlandia* created a funny clip called "Church is an Option." It's a little racy in a couple of spots, so don't go googling it if you're easily offended. Basically, the gist of the sketch is that Father Timothy is trying to "rebrand" his church. He knows that people are looking for peace and tranquillity, and he wants them to know that the church is a place where one can find those things. He starts offering acupuncture sessions, vision boards instead of prayer, and promising to come to you "whenever you want."

It's funny because it's true! Churches actually are trying to get people in the doors in these ways! Churches know that people are looking for peace and tranquillity—who isn't?—and they're trying to position themselves as one of the places people can go to get some of those things in their lives. So we make sure we're next to the spa on people's speed dial.

But the church isn't just one option among many. If peace and tranquillity are what you want, church is the only option. More accurately, Jesus is the only option.

The woman at the well in John 4 came there because she was thirsty. She knew she'd have to come back the next day, and the day after, and so on. Jesus, though, offered her living water, which, if she drank it, meant she will never thirst again. To her credit, the woman said, "Sir, give me this water" (John 4:15).

In the video, Father Timothy puts church on the same list as massage, yoga, acupuncture, exercise, Chinese medicine, therapy, vitamins, and colonics. Those things can be sources of peace, but the religious marketer wants you to know that church is an option too. What Jesus is saying to the woman at the well, though, is that all those other things will leave her thirsty again. The peace and tranquillity that Jesus offers—the atoning sacrifice for sins—will satisfy forever.

When Shadrach, Meshach, and Abednego are threatened with the fiery furnace, the three men say something astounding to the judgmental king: "We have no need to present a defense to you" (v. 16 NRSV). Their powerful truth: God was their defender.

As awesome as the story of Shadrach, Meshach, and Abednego is, it remains only a pale shadow of Christ's story. Ultimately they cannot be our heroes, because they only saved themselves, and this is a highlighted instance of their having received a miraculous sustaining grace for the given moment. It is hard to apply such once-in-a-lifetime needs to the daily struggle of life and sin. So their story is more one of frustration for me than one of inspiration: we know what we're *supposed* to do. But if Nebuchadnezzar had sat us down and told us that our choices were (a) bowing down to an idol or (b) the fiery furnace, let's just say we might not have been as brave as Shadrach, Meshach, and Abednego. In fact, we probably would have folded like origami. In other words, we need a Savior who doesn't just save the faithful. We need a Savior who saves the faithless.

When Shadrach, Meshach, and Abednego went into the fire, they had reason to be confident: they'd done everything right. We haven't. We need the God of Romans 5, who comes to those who are ungodly, to the weak, to the sinners. We need the Christ of 2 Corinthians 5, who became sin though He knew no sin, so that I, a sinner, could become the righteousness of God.

This Christ has come. He has lived and died as one of us; He has taken our sins to the cross and been forsaken by His Father for them. As we crucified Him, He asked His father to forgive us. As we run away from Him, He comes after us. As we disobey Him, He dies for us. Shadrach, Meshach, and Abednego, the faithful, get saved from the fiery furnace, but they point to a greater Savior, an eternal Savior, a Savior who saves sinners.

At a recent birthday party I overheard some kids singing Matthew 7:7. The verse was fine, but the chorus was a problem.

Ask and it will be given to you
Seek and you will find
Knock and the door will be opened to you.

You gotta ask! (clap clap clap)
You gotta seek! (clap clap clap)
You gotta knock! (clap clap clap)

Now, I'm all for helping kids remember Bible verses. If I'd been made to sing songs like this as a child, I'd probably know more of my Bible today. But this song is a particularly egregious example of focusing on the wrong part of the verse and letting law crowd out gospel. Matthew 7:7 is not primarily about what we have to do; it's about what God has promised to do. When we focus on the imperatives of the verse (what we are to do) instead of the indicatives (what is being done, in this case by God), we reflect a self-focused faith. And while the imperatives of Matthew 7:7 are undeniably there, the verse still isn't about asking, seeking, and knocking as much as it is about receiving, finding, and being welcomed. I'd prefer if the chorus went something like this:

He's gonna give! (clap clap clap)
He's gonna show! (clap clap clap)
He's gonna hug! (clap clap clap)

After all, Matthew 7:11 says, "If you, then, though you are evil, know how to give good gifts to your children, how much more will your Father in heaven give good gifts to those who ask him!" This little section is about the gift giver! It's not about what the receiver has to do to get the gift.

We're evil, and even we know how to give good gifts. Our God is gracious, and He has given us the greatest gift of all: His Son, Jesus Christ, who is an answered petition, a revealed treasure, and an open door. Let's sing about that.

There's a growing trend in some churches to offer door prizes to any return-ing visitor. A friend who recently visited a church was promised a ten-dollar Starbucks gift card if he came back the following week.

Isaiah shows us the "door prize" that awaited him when he walked into the house of God—the uncomfortable, wrecking presence of God's glory: "Woe to me!" he cries (v. 5).

In the Bible, the glory of God refers to God's "heaviness," His powerful presence. It's God's prevailing excellence on display, the expansive gravity of all His attributes.

When we come into the presence of God's glory, we are awestruck by His majesty. In this sense, a worship service isn't the place to showcase human talent but the place for God to showcase His divine wonder.

This is in stark contrast to the influence of the consumer world's insistence in the church that the bigger we get and the better we feel about ourselves, the freer we'll become. That's why many worship services have been reduced to little more than motivational, self-help seminars filled with "you can do it" songs and sermons. But what we find in the gospel is just the opposite. The gospel is good news for losers, not winners. It's for those who long to be freed from the slavery of believing that all of their significance, meaning, purpose, and security depend on their ability to "become a better you." The gospel tells us that weakness precedes usefulness—that, in fact, the smaller you get, the freer you will be.

As G. K. Chesterton wrote, "How much larger your life would be if your self could become smaller in it." Nothing makes you more aware of your smallness and life's potential bigness than encountering the glory of almighty God. Christians desperately need to recover a sense of God's size!

Nicholas Wolterstorff is a Christian who taught philosophical theology for many years at Yale. He and his wife have six children, but he lost an adult son who died in a mountain-climbing accident. Wolterstorff chronicled the grief he experienced through his loss in a journal, which he published years later as a book entitled *Lament for a Son*. The book opens with his recollection of the moment the dreaded phone call came:

> The call came at 3:30 on that Sunday afternoon, a bright sunny day. We had just sent his younger brother off to the plane to be with him for the summer. The phone rings, "Hello."
>
> "Mr. Wolterstorff?"
>
> "Yes."
>
> "Is this Eric's father?"
>
> "Yes."
>
> "Mr. Wolterstorff, I must give you some bad news."
>
> "Yes."
>
> "Eric has been climbing in the mountains and has had an accident."
>
> "Yes."
>
> "Eric has had a serious accident."
>
> "Yes, go on."
>
> "Mr. Wolterstorff, I must tell you, Eric is dead. Mr. Wolterstorff, are you there? You must come at once! Mr. Wolterstorff, Eric is dead."
>
> For three seconds I felt the peace of resignation; arms extended, limp son in hand, peacefully offering him to someone—Someone. Then the pain—cold, burning pain.

Wolterstorff's harrowing account explodes the tempting notion that if we only grasped God's will more clearly, if we only knew something we don't know now, the wound would hurt less. But the gospel is not ultimately a defense *from* suffering. Rather, it is the message of God's rescue *through* suffering. The good news is Jesus Himself, the Man of Sorrows, the crucified God who meets us in our grief.

Churches have ruined the word *preach*. Think of the Madonna song "Papa Don't Preach." Madonna has messed up. She's been seeing a guy her father doesn't approve of, and she's gotten pregnant. In her own words, they're "in an awful mess." So she goes to her father, and her one request is that he not preach.

Phrases like, "don't preach at me," or "that movie was so preachy" shine a light on the redefinition of the word. To *preach*, in common parlance, now means "to judge" or "to criticize." When the Madonna of the song goes to her father, she's saying, "I already know that what I did was wrong, so I don't need you to tell me again. I need your help, not a sermon."

And who wouldn't agree with that sentiment? "I need your help, not a sermon." But that's the tragedy: sermons are supposed to help!

The preaching event is supposed to be about the proclamation of the good news. We preach the gospel. Of course, as some will be quick to point out, we preach the law, too (and first!), but our sermons should never be typified by law. People should never walk out of our churches feeling the weight of the law. They should walk out feeling the relief of the gospel.

The church should foster an environment in which Madonna can go to her father and say something like, "Dad, I'm in big trouble. I kept seeing the guy who you told me was bad news, and we messed up. I'm pregnant. I feel terrible. Please preach to me."

A proper sermon, a true proclamation of law and gospel, should convict at the beginning and pardon at the end. We never end with conviction, because it is not we who have been convicted—it is Christ in our place. Perhaps if we can recover the pulpit for the proclamation of the gospel, *preaching* can recover a helpful meaning, a comforting meaning, a true meaning.

"Live for the moment." "Seize the day." "YOLO [you only live once]." I'm sure you're familiar with these mottoes. The kind of thinking behind these phrases makes every moment a pressure-filled "what do I do?" conundrum. For Christians who put the religious gloss on these sentiments, every moment becomes a pressure-filled "what would Jesus do?" scenario.

In Romans 13:11 Paul is talking about a different kind of moment. True, it's a moment on which everything hangs, but it's a moment with a different actor. Paul is talking about the moment in which God saved you.

This is the ultimate moment. And it's not happening today. It's not up to you. It's not a decision you need to make. It's not about what you should do. It's not even about what Jesus would do.

The Lamb of God, Jesus Christ, was chosen and slain before the foundation of the world. That's an eternal moment that had nothing to do with you. When Paul writes that "it is now the moment," he's not telling us that now is the moment for a decision, a choice that will determine the rest of our lives or our eternal destination. He says that it is now the moment for us to "wake from sleep," to have our eyes opened to a truth that has existed since the beginning of time.

Our natural inclination—to spend our days worrying about being in good with God, being a good person, doing the right things so that God will be pleased with us and desire to be in a relationship with us—only causes us to be asleep to the wonderful truth of the gospel: that, in Christ, God chose us even as He was separating the light from the darkness. Today, know that you are chosen by God. Your moment is happening now, has happened before the foundation of the world, and will be happening every day, forever.

Do you watch those restaurant-rescue shows like *Kitchen Nightmares* and *Restaurant: Impossible*?

Both shows star celebrity chefs, Gordon Ramsay and Robert Irvine, respectively, attempting to rehabilitate failing restaurants. When the chefs arrive at the terminally ill establishments, it always looks as if there's no way these places have any chance of success: they owe hundreds of thousands of dollars, their owners are clueless, and the roaches outnumber their customers. By the time the show ends, though, the dining rooms have been remodeled, the kitchens have been reformed, and everyone has been given the tools for success.

But then what? What happens to Metropolis when Superman leaves town? As I'm sure most viewers do, I google the featured restaurants to see whether or not they're still open and usually discover something fascinating. A huge percentage of the restaurants that appear on *Kitchen Nightmares* are now closed, while the same percentage of restaurants that appear on *Restaurant: Impossible* are still open!

What's the difference? Now it's nothing as cut and dried as "Irvine preaches grace" and "Ramsay preaches law." Both men bring the hammer of judgment down early in an episode, shining a light on these restaurants' seamy underbellies. Irvine sometimes yells. Ramsay, though, knows that yelling is his bread and butter. He probably gets paid by the decibel. He seems to go in aiming to humiliate. In this sense, Ramsay is judgment personified: he's out to crush you.

Irvine, on the other hand, seems to come beside his clients in a way that Ramsay never does. Both chefs have to do a lot of family therapy—at least as much as they do pots-and-pans training—but Irvine doesn't steamroll the staff toward relaunch night, even though his timetable is shorter.

Obviously, it's reductive to say that Irvine personifies grace and Ramsay personifies judgment. However, in comparison to Ramsay, Irvine comes across as more graceful than Mother Teresa. Judgment kills, and the results can be seen by surveying the tombstones of all the closed restaurants that Gordon Ramsay leaves in his wake. Grace gives life.

Theologies of glory are approaches to Christianity and life that try in various ways to minimize difficult and painful things or to move past them rather than looking them square in the face and accepting them. Theologies of glory acknowledge the cross, but view it primarily as a means to an end— an unpleasant but necessary step on the way to personal improvement, the transformation of human potential. As Martin Luther put it, the theologian of glory "does not know God hidden in suffering. Therefore he prefers works to suffering, glory to the cross, strength to weakness, wisdom to folly, and, in general, good to evil." The theology of glory is the natural default setting for human beings addicted to control and measurement. This perspective puts us squarely in the driver's seat, after all.

A theology of the cross, in contrast, understands the cross to be the ultimate statement of God's involvement in the world on this side of heaven. A theology of the cross accepts the difficult thing rather than immediately trying to change it or use it. It looks directly into pain and identifies God as "hidden in [the] suffering." Luther actually took things one important step further. He said that God was not only hidden in suffering, but He was *at work* in it.

When you are at the end of your rope—when you no longer have hope within yourself—that is when you run to God for mercy.

The house of religious cards that glory builds collapses when we encounter unforeseen pain and suffering. Suddenly, the mask comes off, and the glory road reaches a dead end. We come to the end of ourselves, to an emotional ruin, to our literal knees, to the place where if we are to find any help or comfort, it must come from somewhere outside of us. Much to our surprise, this is the precise place where the good news of the gospel—that God did for us what we couldn't do for ourselves—finally makes sense. It's only immersed in the reality of bad news that the good news finally sounds good!

The story that fills Judges 19 is probably the most sordid in the entire Bible. A Levite takes a concubine and is eventually welcomed into someone's home as a visitor. In the middle of the night, the men of Gibeah come to the house and demand that the Levite be sent out so that they can have sex with him. Rather than succumb to their demands, the master of the house instead offers them his virgin daughter and his visitor's concubine.

There's not a lot of righteousness to go around in this story. The men of Gibeah are corrupt, sex-addicted murderers. The Levite is a coward at best and a party to rape and murder at worst. The master of the house is himself no saint, offering his own daughter and his welcomed guest. The only person in the story who might be called blameless is the concubine herself.

It is the blamelessness of the concubine that reveals the profundity of the story and points us ahead to the truly blameless Jesus Christ.

Think of it. When death knocks at your door, who's going out? When the time comes and you're caught in a situation that's going bad, to whom do you turn?

The sacrifice of the concubine points us to Jesus's sacrifice. However, where the concubine has to be forced out, Jesus goes out willingly. Where the concubine faced the destructive wrath of a sinful group of men, Jesus faces the destructive wrath of a holy God. Where the concubine's death causes a war (Judg. 20–21), Jesus's death brings abiding peace.

Jesus faces the music of God's wrath toward sin on our behalf. Going into the presence of almighty God will mean our deaths as surely as going out into the courtyard meant the death of that concubine. Jesus stands in our place—not waiting for us to ask Him to but willingly stepping out the front door while we cower in fear. Indeed, while we were yet enemies of God, He died for us.

All of us are worshippers of something. It's that simple. We're created, designed, and wired for worship. To be human is to be a worshipper. The English word *worship* derives from the idea of "worth-ship," meaning that we all serve those things to which we attribute ultimate worth.

Worship is a posture of the heart. It's an attitude of loyalty and trust toward something in our lives that we believe makes life worth living. Thus, we all worship something or someone. This is true whether you consider yourself to be religious or not. Typically, what we worship is our non-negotiable. Should we lose or part with that one thing, it would bring both devastation and hopelessness.

What you choose to worship also depends on what you fear the most. If you fear loneliness, you worship relationships. If you fear not being accepted or esteemed, you worship your social network, the way you look, the car you drive, or the amount of money you make. If you fear insignificance, you end up worshipping your career or your accomplishments.

Behind everything you worship is some fear that, without this person or thing, you'd be lost. Life wouldn't be worth living. Your fears cause you to attribute ultimate worth either to things such as success, reputation, family, relationships, or to God. Either you believe your life would be meaningless without your friends or your career achievement or your children or your possessions or your social status or whatever, or you believe your life wouldn't be worth living without God because you know He alone can provide everything you need (and, in fact, everything you long for)—justification, love, mercy, grace, cleansing, a new beginning, eternal approval and acceptance, righteousness, and rescue.

We're all worshippers—but God is the only reliable object of worship, because nothing and no one extends these things like God does in the person and work of Jesus Christ.

Remember when Lance Armstrong was first accused of using steroids? He went ballistic in his denials, denouncing his accusers and suing them into silence. Many athletes who are accused of cheating do this until the evidence catches up to them. When they're finally caught, their denial turns to evasiveness. "I was injured and just needed to recover." "Everyone was doing it." "I needed to stay competitive."

We are evasive by nature. In the December 8, 2005 issue of the *Telegraph*, a new Israeli law was described. Here's the headline: "Israelis to be allowed euthanasia by machine."

Here's a bit of the article, which describes an incredible example of human evasiveness:

> A special timer will be fitted to a patient's respirator which will sound an alarm 12 hours before turning it off.... Normally, carers would override the alarm and keep the respirator turned on but, if various stringent conditions are met, including the giving of consent by the patient or legal guardian, the alarm would not be overridden.... Parliamentarians reached a solution after discussions with a 58-member panel of medical, religious and philosophical experts. "The point was that it is wrong, under Jewish law, for a person's life to be taken by a person but, for a machine, it is acceptable," a parliamentary spokesman said. "A man would not be able to shorten human life but a machine can."

When we say that "God catches the wise in their craftiness," the way He does it is by continuously raising the bar of requirement until no amount of craftiness can get us over it or around it. We all wreck ourselves on the wall of "be perfect, therefore, as your heavenly Father is perfect."

Thankfully, for us, Jesus steadfastly claimed to come for wrecks: "It is not the healthy who need a doctor, but the sick. I have not come to call the righteous, but sinners" (Mark 2:17).

The Mariah Carey and Whitney Houston song "When You Believe" from
The Prince of Egypt movie sound track is a nice song, but it has terrible lyrics:

> *There can be miracles*
> *When you believe*
> *Though hope is frail*
> *It's hard to kill*
> *Who knows what miracles*
> *You can achieve*
> *When you believe*
> *Somehow you will*
> *You will when you believe*

Allow me to suggest an alternative. There must be miracles, precisely
because we *don't* believe. We, by the word's very definition, don't "achieve"
miracles. They are the astounding direct intervention of God into our world.
In the context of the Exodus story, the written lyrics for "When You Believe"
are all the more ridiculous. The last miracle we can achieve is our own deliverance, our own salvation. In fact, it is our reliance on ourselves and our
achievements that lands us in bondage in the first place!

The Israelites couldn't have thought for a moment that their salvation
was wrought by their own achievements. They'd heard about the burning
bush, they'd seen the plagues, they'd followed pillars of cloud and fire, and
they'd walked across the dry floor of a divided sea.

There were miracles, but not because the people believed. The burning
bush had to convince Moses that he was God's chosen leader for this mission.
The miracle created belief, not the other way around. The same is true of us.
The miracle of God's love—often felt when we are on the run from God—is
a love that comes to us before we deserve it. God's love expects nothing in
return, creates our belief, yet does not depend on our belief.

And so, despite the beauty with which Mariah and Whitney sing it,
know that their message is false, which is good news. Even when we don't
believe, miracles happen, and we are saved. Praise God!

Paul addressed the Christians of the Corinthian church in the most glowing terms possible. He called them "sanctified in Christ Jesus," he said that he gives "thanks to my God always" for them, that they've been "enriched in Him," and that they "are not lacking in any spiritual gift." He finished his description of them by claiming that on the day of the Lord Jesus Christ they will be "blameless" (vv. 2–8 NRSV).

Wouldn't you give anything to be described like that? We feel, unfortunately, that such adjectives just don't apply to us. In just a few sentences, however, Paul did get to some things that sound a lot like us: "It has been reported ... that there are quarrels among you" (v. 11 NRSV). And throughout the letter Paul said things such as, "It is actually reported that there is sexual immorality among you.... And you are arrogant!" (1 Cor. 5:1–2 NRSV), that their bragging is not good, and that they sue and cheat their own brethren. Perhaps now you feel a bit more accurately described.

The key verse for understanding how Paul could call this bunch of bragging, suing, cheating, and fornicating people "blameless" is verse 9: "God is faithful, through whom you were called into fellowship with His Son, Jesus Christ our Lord" (NASB). Notice who is faithful. It's not us! We've already seen that! We could each list a hundred ways we are unfaithful.

But God is faithful, and He has called us into the fellowship of His Son, Jesus Christ our Lord. He has called us. And do you know what He has called us? He has called us sanctified, He has called us saints, He has called us enriched in every way, in all speech and knowledge, and He has called us not lacking in any spiritual gift. He has called us blameless. And in that calling, we are made the thing that He calls us.

Today, in Christ, you are blameless.

Radio psychiatrist Frasier Crane (from the TV show *Frasier*) has had a long, rough day. Finally, when a man steals his waited-for seat at the local coffee shop, Frasier has had enough. Grabbing the man by the collar, he runs him out of the shop, shouting, "What you need is an etiquette lesson!"

Later Frasier chastises himself for allowing his more animal nature to come out. He prefers, he says, to settle his disagreements like an adult, with words and reason. But the newspaper hails him as a sort of folk hero. And to his dismay, people begin to follow his example, giving little etiquette lessons of their own. A caller, whose neighbor used a leaf blower at seven o'clock in the morning, brags about smashing the leaf blower into a tree. Another shoves a pound of rotten shrimp into a rival's air conditioner.

After dozens of callers describe their vigilante exploits, Frasier exclaims that they've gone too far. "I displayed a minor bit of force to just make a point. I didn't go around smashing windows or torching lawns! Where does it end?" His caller replies, "Are you saying that what I did was wrong?" "Of course I am!" shouts Frasier. And the caller responds, "But what you did was okay?" This stops Frasier in his tracks. And then—and this is one of the reasons I really love this show—Frasier realizes what the right thing to do is, and does it. "Come to think of it, what I did was just as wrong. I mean, who am I to draw the line at the acceptable level of force?"

Frasier realizes in that moment what God has provided for all along: righteousness must be complete to be worth anything at all. Any sin, whether more or less socially acceptable, is evidence of a root problem. Anger and murder come from the same place. It is only God who can draw the line, and it is only God who can toe it.

Today, remember that you're worse than you think you are. But remember, also, that God's gift of righteousness to you is greater than you could ever imagine.

When a lot of Christians think about spirituality, they tend to think of it individualistically. Many of us, in other words, think about spirituality exclusively in terms of personal piety and internal devotion. We focus almost entirely on ourselves and our private disciplines of praying, reading the Bible, and so on.

In his letter, however, James made it clear that true spirituality actually takes us away from ourselves and into the messy lives of other people. "If a brother or sister is poorly clothed and lacking in daily food, and one of you says to them, 'Go in peace, be warmed and filled,' without giving them the things needed for the body, what good is that?" (vv. 15–16 ESV). In other words, spirituality is not introverted, it is extroverted. Spirituality doesn't take me deeper into me but sends me away from me.

That's quite different from the way our culture normally thinks about spirituality. Almost everything that is considered spiritual today is private and focuses on the inner life and personal betterment of the individual. One serious consequence of engaging in this type of introspection is that we fail to see the needs of our neighbor and serve them, which is James's definition of *good works*. After all, as Martin Luther said, "God does not need our good works, but our neighbor does."

We were designed to embrace God and others, but instead we are now consumed with ourselves. The gospel causes us to look up to Christ and what He did, and outward to our neighbors and what they need, not inward to ourselves and only what we need. There's nothing about the gospel that fixes my eyes on me. Any version of Christianity, therefore, that encourages you to think mostly about you is detrimental to your faith—whether it's your failures or your successes, your good works or your bad works, your strengths or your weaknesses, your obedience or your disobedience.

The irony, of course, is that you and I are renewed inwardly to the degree that we focus not on inward renewal but upward worship and outward service. The more you see that the gospel isn't about you, the more spiritual *you* will become.

The people of Israel have gathered together and have asked Ezra to bring the book of the law and to read it to them. This is key: they *ask* Ezra to bring the law. But then something interesting happens. After this morning-long church service (v. 3) spent reading the book of the law and worshipping God, all the people had broken down in tears.

This is the way of life. We ask for the law, we hear the law, and we are broken by the law. This relationship with the law is as old as time itself. We think we want it, but as soon as we get it, we are broken by it.

So why do we ask for the law? You would think that we'd want to be free, right? No rules, no restrictions. We ask, though, because we want to see how we measure up. We love a test, as long as we pass. When we hear the true standard, though, the full requirement of God's holy law, it destroys us. Far from showing us how well we're doing, the law shows us just how short we fall. We are exactly like the Israelites in Nehemiah, destroyed by the realization that the law is beyond our ability to obey, and that the only standard is perfection (Matt. 5:48). We fall to our faces, covered in tears. We are wrecked.

Amazingly, Ezra and Nehemiah tell the people not to be grieved, "for the joy of the LORD is your strength," even in this time when they feel so weak, so broken (v. 10 ESV).

The good news of Jesus Christ is that, although the law comes and destroys us, the Son of God comes and resurrects us. Our death is overturned by Christ's death. Our life is created by Christ's life. We hear the law and are brought to tears. We hear the gospel and are moved to joy. In Christ, we who were poor are now rich. We who were captive are now released. We who were blind can now see. We who were oppressed are now free. Because of Jesus, we are made new.

God doesn't budge. He doesn't negotiate. He is stable, consistent. "For I the LORD do not change" (v. 6 ESV). He won't bend to make our lives temporarily better when larger, longer-term issues are at stake.

If you want to live for things that bring only temporary comfort and happiness, there are plenty of things to choose from—just watch the television commercials. Only God can take you beyond that—if you want to go beyond what you could ever become on your own.

God's grace isn't seen in the lessening of His demands toward us. He always has and always will demand perfect obedience. His grace is experienced when we come to realize that His perfect demands for each of us have already been met by Jesus. He lived the life we couldn't live and died the death we should have died.

This rescue doesn't come apart from God's law but rather in the perfect fulfillment of the law through the person of Jesus, who perfectly kept that law. Christianity is the only faith system where God both makes the demands and meets them.

God is more interested in the worker than He is in the work the worker does. He's more interested in you than in what you can accomplish.

All of us need to be continually rescued by God, both from sin's power and presence, and also (once and for all) from its penalty. And one expression of God's amazing grace is that He pursues our rescue even though we cannot do one thing for Him. God doesn't need you and me for anything. In and of Himself, He is already of infinite value and worth. The reason He seeks sinners and saves sinners is that God loves sinners.

Jack Miller, a noted Presbyterian pastor and author in Philadelphia in the last century, often summed up the gospel this way: "Cheer up; you're a lot worse off than you think you are, but in Jesus you're far more loved than you ever could have imagined."

In his 2008 movie, *The Happening*, writer/director M. Night Shyamalan unfolds a freaky plot about an invisible toxin that causes anyone exposed to it to commit suicide. One of the first signs that the unaware victim has breathed in this self-destructing toxin is that they begin walking backward—signaling that every natural instinct to go on living and to fight for survival has been reversed. The victim's default survival mechanism is turned upside down.

This, in a sense, is what needs to happen to us when we think about progress in the Christian life. When breathed in, the radical, unconditional, free grace of God reverses every natural instinct regarding what it means to spiritually survive and thrive. Only the "toxin" of God's grace can reverse the way we typically think about Christian growth.

For a whole host of reasons, when it comes to measuring spiritual growth and progress, our natural instincts revolve almost exclusively around behavioral improvement.

But we need to get over the idea that salvation means earning up credit with God. When Paul says things like, "Work out your salvation" (Phil. 2:12), he does not mean that we are to work *for* our salvation or work up our salvation. He is reminding us, instead, that "progression" in the Christian life is really a matter of applying outwardly what you've already received inwardly, purely by God's grace. You are working out what God has worked *in*. You don't lack for anything in your salvation; the work is done.

This means that real change happens only as we continuously rediscover the gospel. The progress of the Christian life is not our movement toward the goal; it's the movement of the goal on us. Sanctification involves God's attack on our unbelief—our self-centered refusal to believe that God's approval of us in Christ is full and final. It happens as we daily receive and rest in our unconditional justification.

A decade ago, some people were offended when media mogul Ted Turner called Christianity "a religion for losers" (he later expressed regret for that and similar remarks). But the fact is, Ted Turner is exactly right. Christianity is for losers.

For too long, Christians have spent time and energy and money trying our best to convince the world we're cool and that we're winners. And in our world, cool means being just as prominent and prosperous, just as smart and stylish, just as successful and savvy as anybody else. Just look at how Christians swell with pride when a successful athlete or actor or politician professes his faith. It's as if we shout to everyone, "See! This guy has everything, and he's a believer—so Christianity has to be cool." We want to parade these celebrities and their faith before the world.

The gospel, however, is not just for the all-star and the illustrious and the legendary. It's for the loser. It's for the defeated, not the dominant. It's for those who realize they're unable to carry the weight of the world on their shoulders—those who've figured out that they're not gods. It's for people who understand the bankruptcy of life without God. It's for people who recognize that while they're definitely deficient, God is more than sufficient.

Jesus came to show us that the gospel explains success in terms of giving, not taking; self-sacrifice, not self-protection; going to the back, not getting to the front. The gospel shows that we win by losing, we triumph through defeat, we achieve power through service, and we become rich by giving ourselves away.

In fact, in gospel-centered living, we follow Jesus in laying down our lives for those who hate us and hurt us. We spend our lives serving instead of being served and seeking last place, not first. Gospel-centered people are those who love giving up their place for others, not guarding their place from others—because their value and worth is found in Christ, not their position.

Remember today that your value is secure in Jesus.

Some Christians have always thought that the end is basically here now—or that it could be. Because Jesus came, we now have the power to make Isaiah's predictions come true—lions lying down with lambs, children playing with snakes, peace and harmony in all the world. All we have to do is tap in to that power of Christ and make it happen.

I'm sure you've heard people talk this way: "Live in to the kingdom reality!" "Let's become the kingdom of God." There's only one problem with this view. Well, let's say there are seven billion problems with it—every person on the planet.

By making it our job to usher in the kingdom through our actions, we're making the coming of the kingdom contingent on us! In the Genesis song "Land of Confusion," Phil Collins sings, "My generation will put it right. We're not just making promises that we know we'll never keep." Unfortunately, that's an old song, and nothing has been put right. It didn't work for Phil Collins, and it won't work for us.

But it's not up to us. Jesus has come. It's happened. But *something* hasn't happened yet. The final day of the Lord is still coming. The kingdom, as the theologians say, has been *inaugurated*, but it is yet to be *consummated*. For Christians, the day of the Lord is already here and also hasn't come yet.

We know that it's here. Any time someone loves us when we feel unlovable. Any time we find room in our hearts for another. Any time we laugh, and any time we cry, we know that God is at work in this world. But when our hearts ache, when we feel pain deeper than any pain we've ever felt, when we feel the hatred of others, and when we realize our own hatreds, we can hold out hope that the great and terrible day of the Lord is still coming. He will come and clean this place up. And because of the day of the Lord that has already come, we can be assured of our place at God's side when the final day of the Lord arrives.

Years ago, on an episode of *The Amazing Race*, a contestant named Kelly was interviewed. She tells the camera (and therefore millions of people at home) that when she woke up that morning, she read "the love chapter" in the Bible, 1 Corinthians 13. Instead of the word "love," though, she put in her name. "Kelly is patient, Kelly is kind," and so on. She said that she was going to try and be those things to her boyfriend, Ron, that day. Now, *The Amazing Race* can get a little tense, and sometimes team members can get frustrated with one another. At one point, near the end of the day, Kelly got annoyed with Ron and ended up calling him a "redneck piece of trash." And this is in front of the same millions of people she told about reading the love chapter that same morning!

Now, I'm not from the South, but Ron is, and from his reaction, I don't think that "redneck piece of trash" is an expression of love. So Kelly has a problem. She's not showing love. My first instinct after hearing "redneck piece of trash" come out of Kelly's mouth, was, "Oh no. What a horrible Christian example! She told everyone she was reading the Bible, and now she's saying this awful, awful thing!"

But listen: though she may not be a great Christian example, she is a perfect example *of* a Christian.

We're just like Kelly on *The Amazing Race*. We can't hold to our good plans. Our lives spin out of control. In a matter of minutes, we go from "I will be patient with my loved ones" to calling them whatever name our sinful hearts have assigned them. When everything seems to be falling apart, when we feel the worst at loving each other, it is Jesus Christ who intervenes with His own great love. He gives His love to us even when we are unloving and unlovable. And it is because of Jesus, not our own efforts to love or quality of loveliness, that God loves us forever.

A few years back I was driving my oldest son home from his basketball game and he was crying. He's a great basketball player but had a less-than-stellar performance. After doing my best to comfort him through encouragement, I asked him why he was so upset. He told me plainly, "Dad, I was terrible." I said, "I know you think that, but why does not playing well make you so sad?" He said, "Because I'm a basketball player. That's who I am."

Somewhere along the way he had concluded that his value as a person was tied to his achievements as an athlete. If he was a good basketball player, then he mattered. If he wasn't, he didn't. So a bad game was more than a bad game. It was a direct assault on his identity. I realized helping him meant understanding that basketball wasn't the issue—identity was. This was not a basketball crisis, it was an identity crisis.

I reminded him of the gospel. I showed him how the gospel frees us from this obsessive pressure to perform, this slavish demand to "become." I showed him how the gospel declares that in Christ "we already are." While we are tempted to constantly locate our identity in something or someone smaller than Jesus, the gospel liberates us by revealing that our true identity is locked in Christ. Our connection in and with Christ is the truest definition of who we are.

I told him that since he was a Christian, who he really was had nothing to do with his works. I reminded him that his identity is firmly anchored in Christ's accomplishment. So much of parenting, I've discovered, involves reminding. Simply reminding our children of who they are in Christ, what they already possess in Christ, and how nothing—nothing—that Christ has secured for them can ever be taken away.

After listening to this, he stopped crying and from the backseat said, "Dad, why can't you preach this way all the time?" Feeling like a failure as a preacher in that moment, I realized that none of us ever outgrow our need for robust reminders of the gospel.

When Daniel worships his own God, Darius doesn't change the rules for him. This seems ridiculous. The king loves Daniel. He doesn't want Daniel to die. And he's the king! Why doesn't he just change the rules? Well, it doesn't work that way. The law is inflexible. "Not the smallest letter, not the least stroke of a pen" (Matt. 5:18) will be changed. There is no wiggle room. This is terrible news for us sinners.

One of the great misconceptions about Christianity is that grace involves setting aside, circumventing, or ignoring the rules (the law). At the very least, we think of Jesus's good work as lowering the bar of the law. He takes all of God's laws and turns them into, *Do your best to love God and love one another.*

But this is a profoundly flawed view of Christ's work. He spends the whole Sermon on the Mount, for instance, *raising* the bar of the law or, more accurately, showing *how high the bar of the law has always been.*

When we sin, God does not set the law aside. If He did, we could never have any assurance, or peace. What is He going to do next time? What if we do something worse? What if we *keep* doing the thing that we did? Is He going to *keep* setting aside the law? This is not grace, and it doesn't lead to peace. It leads, rather, to fear. When we count on the rules being relaxed for us, we're hoping on something in which we have no confidence.

The good news is that God does better than setting aside the law. He closes lions' mouths.

Jesus did not come to relax the law; He came to fulfill the law! When we find ourselves called onto the carpet of life, we don't have to hope that the law gets ignored. We don't have to hope that the law gets changed. We don't have to hope that we can bend the rules. We can know that the law has been placed on the shoulders of another and that He has been cast to the lions in our place. Daniel awoke the next morning without a scratch, saved by God. Jesus does one better. He was raised, victorious over sin and death—and not just for Himself, but for us.

What does it mean when Jesus gets angry? In this story from Mark 3, we have an example of what I call God-centered anger.

Jesus, the God man, was angry. The Pharisees were looking to accuse Him of healing on the Sabbath. And then we read immediately that He was also grieved, seeing the hardness of the Pharisees' hearts.

Here is a superimportant characteristic of God's anger that we need to understand: God's anger is a *grieving* anger. It grieves because it sees the devastation that sin has on human life.

Jesus was angry because God's ways were being maligned, and God was being dishonored by these legalistic Pharisees. But His anger was fueled by grief—He saw sin's deadening effects in the lives of these hardened Pharisees. It was as if He asked them, "Why do you continue like this? Don't you see that you were created and designed for so much more than this?" It grieved Him to see that these Pharisees, because of their sin, were only shadows of what God originally intended for them to be. They had been made to live for so much more.

God is grievingly angry when our sin causes us to become less and less of what He created us to be, because we were fearfully and wonderfully made to live for so much more.

So often Christians are merely angry—angry at the sins we see in others, angry at the state of the world. We fail to grieve. Our self-centered anger leads to bitterness, while Jesus's God-centered anger led—and still leads—to healing.

There's nothing wrong with acknowledging that things are not the way they're supposed to be. Jesus did that, emphatically. Anger that does not grieve, however, is ultimately ineffectual. A grieving anger can contain compassion and hope for a world that so desperately needs a Savior. In Christ, that Savior has come. Christ came into a world that was not the way it was supposed to be—locked into self-centeredness and sin—and was angry. But His was a God-centered anger, and He took God's anger at sin onto Himself, for us.

At one point, the Carroll Academy Lady Jags had lost 213 straight high school basketball games. They'd won six games in fourteen years. Let that sink in for a second.

Carroll Academy is no ordinary school. The school is for troubled teen girls, girls with incidents of violence or drug use in their past who are no longer allowed to attend traditional schools. There are regular security checks, and the girls who want to play on the basketball team have to show significant behavioral improvement. It's a story that would make for a great Disney-style family film, except that the team wouldn't win the big game at the end. But listen to some of the wonderfully profound things that the coaches and administrators say:

> This is nothing compared to what you're going to face in your life. Twenty, twenty-five, thirty years from now, when I'm gone, and you come home, and you find out your husband has lost his job, that's adversity.... This is nothing. This will prepare you for that.
> —Randy Hatch, head coach, speaking to the team

> The losses give us the tools we need to teach, to build self-esteem.
> —Patrick Steele, director of security

This is counterintuitive in the extreme. Normally, you'd expect coaches to say that learning to overcome adversity on the court will help you to overcome adversity in life or that learning to make the transition from losing to winning builds self-esteem. These coaches are saying something quite different: that adversity on the court will prepare you for the adversity that life is sure to bring you; that it is losing, not winning, that builds self-esteem.

God works *sub contrario*; that is, "under the opposite" of where we might expect him to. We think that He makes His home with winners and with those who have overcome adversity. We think that He must help those who help themselves. This is not true. God is to be found in the dark places, with the lepers, hanging on a cross. And at Carroll Academy. These are the places in which He makes His home. Which means He can be at home with us.

In a *Vanity Fair* interview in 2010, a megachurch pastor was asked if he had ever sinned. Here's a direct quote:

> "Oh, sure," he answered surprisingly. "I'm sure I have. I mean, I think we've all sinned, so I can't say that I've never …" He looked suddenly bashful. "I've never done anything you'd call 'terrible.' I haven't done drugs. Victoria's the only girl I've ever dated." Victoria, his glamorous wife of 22 years, is also a pastor. "I'm probably squeaky clean—I don't have to say it."

Now listen to Isaiah's description of the Messiah, our Savior: "He was despised and rejected by others; a man of suffering and acquainted with infirmity; and as one from whom others hide their faces he was despised, and we held him of no account" (v. 3 NRSV). They couldn't be more different.

Today, take time out to remind yourself of the thing you spend most of your time trying to forget. We are transgressors. We have iniquities. But we say to ourselves, "Well, I've never done drugs. I've never *killed* anyone. I've never robbed a bank." We may not be naïve enough to think of ourselves as squeaky clean, but we're able to convince ourselves that we're doing pretty well. After all, aren't we nice people? Don't we give to charity? Didn't we volunteer at the soup kitchen? Don't we go to church?

The more we protest that we are already healthy, the harder it is to accept true health. The louder we shout that we are already doing pretty well, the harder it is to accept true righteousness. The quicksand of self-sufficiency gets a stronger and better grip on us.

On the cross, Jesus took all of that upon Himself. He became the one who falls short. He became the one with infirmities, with disease. He became the transgressor. And God forsakes Him. God comes to us. We become the righteous. We become the healthy.

Peter said that for God, a day is like a thousand years, and a thousand years is like a day. In a sense, this doesn't surprise us, the idea that time might not work the same way for God as it does for us. But for people who feel stuck in a broken world? The news that, for God, a day is like a thousand years is not so encouraging. And so, we might say, where in God's name is our relief? Where's the good news? But Peter didn't get there. He just said that since we don't know when it'll be, we ought to be good so that when Jesus comes, we'll be found "without spot or blemish" and "at peace." Well, good luck with that.

We get so caught up in waiting for things to get better, for God's promises to come true, that we're almost able to forget the fact that Jesus has come! Here's why that's important: we don't wait not knowing what will happen. I always get in trouble with my wife because I can't keep myself from checking my Amazon.com wish list all throughout the Christmas season to see what people have gotten for me. I'm too excited to wait for Christmas morning! It drives her absolutely crazy. But it works for me, because when I come down those stairs Christmas morning hoping for some really great gifts, I know I'm not hoping in vain!

We have the same hope in Jesus Christ. We don't go through winter each year hoping spring will come. We know it's coming! We plan for it. We don't celebrate Advent or Good Friday merely hoping that Christmas and Easter will come—we eagerly anticipate them.

So as we spend our lives waiting for what seems like a thousand years, let us always remember that we know just what our Christmas present is going to be: the saving work of Jesus Christ, assured because it already happened, and has been given to us, for free.

The hymn below is by English poet and cleric John Donne (1572–1631). My friend Shane Rosenthal sent me a note explaining that there is a double meaning in the repeated phrase, "Thou hast done." It obviously refers to that which God has done for Donne. But the other meaning, especially clear in the last stanza, is a play on the poet's own name: "Thou hast Donne." Despite Donne's weak grip on God, God's grip on him is perfect and forever.

A Hymn to God the Father

Wilt Thou forgive that sin where I begun,
Which was my sin, though it were done before?
Wilt Thou forgive that sin, through which I run,
And do run still, though still I do deplore?
When Thou hast done, Thou hast not done,
For I have more.

Wilt Thou forgive that sin which I have won
Others to sin, and made my sin their door?
Wilt Thou forgive that sin which I did shun
A year or two, but wallowed in a score?
When Thou hast done, Thou hast not done,
For I have more.

I have a sin of fear, that when I have spun
My last thread, I shall perish on the shore;
But swear by Thyself, that at my death Thy Son
Shall shine as he shines now, and heretofore;
And having done that, Thou hast [Donne];
I fear no more.

When Christ receives you in His grace, He takes you and your sin together. You're a package deal. But when He died, your sin died too. And when He rose, your sin stayed dead, banished. It never ceases to amaze me that, if you are in Christ, you can never, ever, ever out-sin the coverage of God's forgiveness. Amazing love, how can it be?

In the movie *Rocky*, do you remember the scene on the night just before his big fight with Apollo Creed? Rocky knows he can't beat Creed and tells his girlfriend, Adrian, "All I wanna do is go the distance," something no other fighter has done with Creed. If Rocky can somehow stay standing the full fifteen rounds, then he'll know for the first time in his life that he isn't "just another bum from the neighborhood."

In my moments of gospel-disbelieving self-centeredness, there are certain things I look to so I'll know I'm not just another bum. That's when I have to be reminded of the truth: if you embrace what Christ has done on the cross for sinners, you're "in."

In fact, all of our desires for acceptance are really just pointers to what we really long for. They point to the one place, the one person, where we find real acceptance that can be experienced forever.

If you're a Christian, you're forever, unchangeably accepted by God, the only One who matters. When we grasp this, we realize that all those other things where we've searched for acceptance ultimately don't matter. They were never intended to be our saviors, our source of significance. They're too limited. All gods but God are way too small.

Daily rescue happens as we continually reorient ourselves to what Jesus has done for us. When we remind ourselves that Jesus came to reconcile sinners to God, and that as a result we now possess all the acceptance we need, it frees us from our slavery. It frees us from our idols. We no longer have to depend on those small things that will never be able to rescue us the way we long to be rescued. We become free of self-reliance and self-dependence.

That's good news.

"You only go around once, so you'd better make it worth it." Even people who give millions of dollars to charity usually do it to receive something in return: notoriety, reputation, a building with their name on it. We all want to leave a mark. We've heard it said that "you can't take it with you," but deep down, we're not 100 percent sure that the statement's true. At least, our lives of accumulation and aspiration would seem to reveal we don't think so.

One of the students in a high school youth group I was involved with asked me about the Golden Rule: "Do unto others as you would have them do unto you." This young man had completely misunderstood Jesus's words; he had turned them into a kind of karmic good advice: "Do good unto others and they will do good unto you." This understanding of doing good is probably most exemplified today with the "pay it forward" movement.

It seems so simple: if you want other people to do good to you, you should do good to them. But as Christians, we must read deeper into the Golden Rule. We ought to understand Jesus's words this way: "Do unto others as you would have them do unto you—with no expectation of the good in return." It's not "Do unto others *so* they will do unto you."

If you have not love, you have gained nothing. If you do good expecting good in return, that's not love. That's a business transaction. Love is doing good regardless of reciprocation.

Love must be one-way to be worth anything. If we "give away all [our] possessions," but do it with an eye on the return on investment, we gain nothing. Jesus Christ is the only one-way lover in the history of the world. He loved His enemies—not only those from whom He would get nothing, but those who were actively killing Him—asking God to forgive them because they didn't know what they were doing. We don't get out of life what we put in. What we "get out" of life is exactly what Jesus Christ wins for us—the very righteousness of God.

In 2 Kings 5, Naaman wants to buy a miracle. He has leprosy, and he wants to be clean. He hears about a prophet who can heal him, and so he goes to see that prophet, Elisha. Naaman brings truckloads of fine clothing and money. His plan is to buy his healing. He wants something so good that no one else can afford it. As a rich man, he wants VIP treatment.

But there's a problem. Elisha won't accept his money. Instead, Elisha tells Naaman to go down and wash in the dirty Jordan River. That's it. Naaman is furious.

Here's the thing: God can't be bought. There is no price that is high enough, because His value is infinite. Naaman wanted a high price (to prove how rich he was) and is infuriated to hear that his money is no good, even though he's offered the healing for free. He wants to be able to say, "Look what I did."

When Naaman is told to just go to the local river to wash, he thinks that it's something he could have just as well done for himself. Naaman is angry, because the thing he's been given to do is *too simple*. He wants a complicated ritual or a set of steps to follow. If he can't earn this healing with his extravagant wealth, he wants to earn it with his faithful obedience.

Naaman's servants have it right, though. Having prepared ourselves to do something hard, shouldn't we be grateful that we've been asked to do something easy? Having convinced ourselves that a righteous life is the path to God's love, shouldn't we be overjoyed to learn that God's love has been given to us for free? Our resistance to our no-cost salvation shows an ignorance of the most crucial tenant of our faith. While "no pain, no gain" is quite true, the pain was suffered by another, a substitute, a Savior, and need not continue. This easy thing, this free gift, is worth more than anything else in the world.

Our pain, no gain. Jesus's pain, our gain. No charge.

Among other things, the gospel is the good news that if we, by faith, embrace all that Christ has done for sinners, then we can be assured that absolutely nothing "will be able to separate us from the love of God that is in Christ Jesus our Lord" (v. 39). Once we know that we're forever loved by Jesus, we're free to love others regardless of the risk, because our deep need to be loved will be satisfied.

A friend once told me, "My home is an unloving place." When he returned there every day from work, he said he wasn't loved the way he longed to be loved by his wife and kids. I listened to him, and we talked further. Eventually I responded, "Maybe, just maybe, you're looking at this from the wrong perspective." I suggested that for six months, he ask himself the following question each day when he came home from work: "Who here can I love? Who here needs my love right now?" I told him to pray about this before he walked in the door, asking God to show him the answer to that question. This man did that, and things at home changed.

Unfortunately, the fear that our love toward others will not be recip-rocated is something that paralyzes many of us. It prevents parents from properly loving their kids, and husbands and wives from properly loving each other. We come to this conclusion: I will love you only to the degree that you love me. It's an attitude that enslaves us. But the gospel frees us from that.

I, too, enjoy receiving love from my family. I'm ecstatic when my kids love me and express affection toward me. Something in me comes alive when they do that. But I've learned this freeing truth: I don't need that love, because in Jesus, I receive all the love I need. This in turn enables me to love my kids without fear or reservation. I get to revel in their enjoyment of my love without needing anything from them in return. I get love from Jesus so that I can give love to them.

Love today, not to earn God's love, but as a reflection of His incredible and "unlosable" love that you've been given.

During the University of Louisville's Elite Eight win over Duke, on their way to the 2013 National Championship, Kevin Ware experienced what is probably the most gruesome injury ever broadcast on live television. If you were watching, you know what I'm talking about, and if you weren't, well, there's really no way to describe it. Everyone—coaches, players, and referees—instinctively moved away from Ware, horrified by his injury. Only one person, Ware's Louisville teammate Luke Hancock, went the other way. Here's a description of what happened next, from Grantland.com's Shane Ryan:

> But after turning his head with everyone else at the sight of the snapped bone, Luke Hancock was the one who came to Ware's side and gripped his hand. He said a prayer, guided him through the initial trauma, and stayed with him on the floor while the medical staff worked. It was because of Hancock, at least in part, that Ware overcame his initial horror and encouraged his teammates to keep playing, to win the game.
>
> In the days leading up to Louisville's Final Four game against Wichita State, the question Hancock faced over and over was *why* he'd done it. Why did he have the presence of mind to react the way he did?
>
> When he answered the question Friday in the Georgia Dome's media center, he probably could have recited a response from memory. He'd been the centerpiece of hundreds of stories for that one act, and was destined to be featured in a hundred more. Which is why it surprised me that his answer, simple as it was, still moved me.
>
> "You know, I don't really know why I went out there," he said. "But, you know, I just didn't want him to be alone out there."

Hancock, by some miracle (note that he said, even after having days to think about it, that he doesn't know why he went to Ware's side), was moved to go toward the grisly injury, rather than away from it. I don't know if Hancock is a Christian, but his rush to the horrifically needy is indeed Christlike.

My friend Mike Adams provides an amazing testimony:

> I had made theology my pursuit, my goal, my aim, my identity. And I was pretty good at it too. I could go toe to toe with the best, and I was proud of that. Don't get me wrong. Good theology is necessary. But theology apart from a heart captured by the gospel is reduced to dangerous information. It's ammunition to win an argument. It's fodder for a blog. It's food for one's pride.
>
> Something else that became my identity was my ministry. In almost forty years in the faith, I had been on the pastoral team of several different churches and my identity was wrapped up in being a pastor. I became proud of the fact that I was a pastor. Proud to be a servant. Go figure!
>
> Then one day, the structure I had built my idols on began to collapse. The building fell with me still in it and everything crumbled in the ashes. Brought to nothing. All I could do was watch it tumble. I didn't know what was going on, but I could feel my heart changing.
>
> That collapse was almost five years ago. I see more clearly now what I couldn't see then. The Holy Spirit was being merciful to me as He began to show me what had slowly happened to me over the years; who I had become. It was an intervention. I had become hard, indifferent, proud, cold…. My identity was wrapped up in me and my theology and ministry, not Jesus. Grace and the gospel had become theological categories to be mastered, taught, and filed away.
>
> Sometimes God breaks our legs and once we're immobilized, He begins His gentle work of rebuilding, restoring, and restoration. He rebuilds and renews our hearts with His unending grace. He takes damaged goods and makes all things new. He takes us in directions we never saw coming and would never have imagined. But most of all, He keeps loving us! Even in our foolishness He is full of rich mercy and grace.

There is a once-popular worship song titled "Refiner's Fire" that has always rubbed me the wrong way. The song suggests that the "Refiner's Fire" is (or ought to be) our "heart's one desire." I don't know about you, but I never felt like being put in a fire would be that pleasant! Far from being our "heart's desire," it seems to me that anyone who is coming into a refiner's fire ought to be scared to death.

Indeed, Malachi seems to think the same, asking, "Who can endure the day of his coming?" (v. 2). Malachi understands what a refiner's fire is in a way that many people don't: it's a fire used to purify a metal, forcing all of the contaminants and impurities out. This means it is super hot.

The law of God is the refiner's fire, and no one can endure the day of its coming. Thankfully for us, though, the coming of Malachi's refiner's fire is not the only arrival Scripture talks about. Perhaps the simplest arrival is the arrival of Jesus into a manger outside Bethlehem. The Savior of the world, come to be the rescuer of sinners. A baby in a manger is quite a different image than a raging fire, isn't it?

The two arrivals are different because God speaks to us in two ways: judgment and love. The law is the refiner's fire. The gospel is our powerful savior.

For which arrival do we wait? Of course, we await the arrival of our Savior. Because we know the good news, that love always trumps judgment, that the comforting power of the gospel trumps the condemning power of the law, and that grace trumps criticism. As we live these difficult lives, feeling like God might only relate to us in the fiery form of the refiner, we do well to remember that dark Christmas morning, and be reassured that, as we wait, we have assurance that the God who was born in that manger came here to answer Malachi's questions: "Who can endure the day of his coming? Who can stand when he appears?" (v. 2). Jesus Christ can, and He stands there for us.

At the end of the 2012 sci-fi film *Looper*, a mother calms her raging son down with two short phrases: "It's okay. I love you."

Now, this son is bad news. We've seen him earlier in the film destroying a man with nothing more than his mind. Not only is he bad news, he's bad news with a ton of power. But there's one thing with more power than the evil resident in this boy—his mother's words, "It's okay. I love you."

Christians have always known the power of "I love you" to break down barriers and to intervene between us and judgment, whether it comes from other people or from God. But what about the "it's okay" part? Many Christians hold to the "God loves you just the way you are" adage and would interpret the mother's words in this light: "You're okay. Therefore, I love you." They assume that God thinks the same way: "You're okay just the way you are. Therefore, I love you."

But this is not the logic of the gospel.

God's word to us is the same as that of the boy's mother: "It's okay. I love you." But it is most decidedly not "you're okay; therefore, I love you." God's word to us is, "You're okay because I love you."

I'm not okay; you're not okay. And admitting this is okay. Because it is the first step to receiving the peace of God in Christ's finished work.

Only God's love can cut through the violence and anger of our lives. When we believe that we're fine just the way we are, the sin remains. Only the knife's edge of "you're okay, but only because I love you" can perform the necessary surgery on our hearts. Christ comes for the undeserving, for the sinner, for the far from okay. In His saving work, though, He becomes God's love for us, creating us anew, and making us so much more than okay.

Today "it's okay," not because you're okay, but because you are loved in Christ.

The Bible makes it clear that self-righteousness is the premier enemy of the gospel. And there is perhaps no group of people who better embody the sin of self-righteousness in the Bible than the Pharisees. In fact, Jesus reserved His harshest criticisms for them, calling them whitewashed tombs and hypocrites. This is surprising to some: the thing that gets in the way of our love for God and a deep appreciation of His grace is not so much our unrighteous badness but our self-righteous goodness.

There is, however, another side to self-righteousness that we gospel types are sometimes blind to. There's an equally dangerous form of self-righteousness that plagues the unconventional and nonreligious types. We "authentic" anti-legalists can become just as guilty of legalism in the opposite direction. This is what I mean: We become self-righteous against those who are self-righteous. We become Pharisaical about Pharisees!

Many younger Christians today are reacting to their parents' conservative, buttoned-down, rule-keeping flavor of "older-brother religion" with a type of liberal, untucked, rule-breaking flavor of "younger-brother irreligion" that screams, "I thank you, God, that I'm not like those legalistic hypocrites!"

See the irony?

Listen: Self-righteousness is no respecter of persons. It reaches to the religious and the irreligious, the "buttoned down" and the "untucked," the plastic and the pious, the rule keepers and the rule breakers, the "right" and the "wrong." The entire Bible reveals how shortsighted all of us are when it comes to our own sin.

For example, it was easy for Jonah to see the idolatry of the sailors. It was easy for him to see the perverse ways of the Ninevites. What he couldn't see was his own idolatry. So the question is not whether you are self-righteous, but rather, in which direction does your self-righteousness lean? Depending on who I'm with, mine goes in both directions!

Thankfully, while our self-righteousness reaches far, God's grace reaches farther.

Jacob has his eye on one of Laban's daughters. Rachel, Laban's younger daughter, is beautiful, while the elder daughter, Leah, is described by the Bible as having weak eyes. This is the Bible's version of the backhanded compliment: "She's got a great personality!"

Laban pulls a switch on Jacob, sending Leah into his tent. Jacob is so dissatisfied with Leah that he agrees to work another seven years to get Rachel, the girl he wanted in the first place. So we get the bald words of Genesis 29:30: "He loved Rachel more than Leah" (ESV).

Jacob loves beauty more than ugly: it shows everyone how successful he is. God loves ugly more than beauty: it shows everyone how gracious He is.

Jacob is able to make a choice—beauty or ugliness. Is it any wonder that he chooses Rachel? Most of us would make the same choice. It is the way of the world.

But then we also assume that God is like Jacob (choosing the beautiful over the ugly), so everything we do in our lives—even our religion—is orchestrated to make us seem younger and more vibrant, to make us appear more impressive, to achieve more popularity, to garner us more power.

Whereas Jacob thinks that choosing the trophy wife will increase his glory, and we work to become more acceptable in God's eyes, God acts differently. He chooses "the foolish things of the world to shame the wise" and "the weak things of the world to shame the strong" (1 Cor. 1:27). It's through Leah that God gives Jacob an heir. This is good news for us because it means that God can work through us! We are the weak; we are the ugly. Isn't that how we feel in our least guarded moments?

God doesn't wait for us to become beautiful like Rachel. He chooses us while we are ugly like Leah.

God aligns Himself with the ugly, with the powerless, with the outcast. Jesus's mission is to the Leahs of the world—to you and to me. And because of Him, we have all the righteousness, power, and holiness that result from almighty God choosing us, today and every day.

Have you ever noticed how often you use the words *luck* and *lucky*? We use them so often we don't really think about what they mean. Recently, though, I looked *luck* up in the dictionary. Here's what it said: "The chance happening of fortunate or adverse events." At first glance this concise definition may seem helpful and harmless, but in reality, it is neither. In fact, if someone had told my wife on February 4, 1999, that her father's untimely death was nothing more or less than a "chance happening of an adverse event," she would not have been comforted or consoled in the slightest. To really believe that her dad's passing was simply a stroke of "bad luck" would have been debilitating to her. In that moment, what she needed to know with complete certainty was that there was something—Someone—above and beyond "chance," guiding and directing this heartbreaking event toward some ultimately good end. She needed to know that, even though this painful episode was impossible to understand or explain, there was purpose and meaning behind it. Luck, by definition, can provide neither.

The Bible makes it very clear that there is no such thing as chance or luck. These are simply words that many attach to circumstances they cannot understand, circumstances that they know lie outside of their control. But the Bible reveals a personal God who has always been and will always be in full control of all He has made. He is the King of creation who exercises power over all things. He is both absolutely sovereign and absolutely good. He does not always explain His actions, but He does make it clear that He has a perfect plan and will work out every detail of that plan to completion.

We have to remember that because we are both finite and sinful, we cannot fully understand or rightly interpret all of God's ways. God's ways are higher than our ways and His thoughts higher than our thoughts (vv. 8–9). God has His secret purposes (Deut. 29:29) that we are never great enough to see, but the Judge of all the earth always does right (Gen. 18:25). This is our only source of hope and calm in times of crisis.

Today, remember that God is both sovereign and good.

My friend had been through a difficult divorce after a marriage of significant emotional neglect. For more than a year after the divorce, she took two of her children to a therapist, who was impressed—the children were adjusting quite well. My friend was so proud of her little ones, and proud of herself for being the stable adult helping them weather the storm.

Earlier, after the first few months of staring down her demons in the waiting room while her children used play therapy to explore their own, my friend was asked by the therapist to come into her office. Once they sat down, the therapist asked, "How are you doing?" My friend just looked at her. In the months since her marriage ended, not one person had asked her that question. She was the rock. She hadn't shared her true feelings with anyone. No one had even asked.

Even though my friend wanted to appear strong, she decided to be real. Fighting back tears, she explained to the therapist that the week had been rough. On one afternoon, she broke down in tears in front of the children after a long day of work—staring at a messy house, a pile of bills, and frustrating homework assignments. "I feel horrible that they saw me like that." The therapist faced my friend, gently held her shoulders, and said, "Look at me. It's okay to be human in front of your children. They need to see that you aren't perfect—that you're not a robot. Everyone needs to see the authentic you, the broken you. No one can love a stone."

You see, for her entire life my friend had been taught that it was not okay to show her frailties. From her strict parents to her insecure husband, she was bound and gagged. So she lived a life where she guarded her heart and never let anyone see the cracks. That was, until she was finally given permission—first by a caring therapist and then by Jesus.

She has since soaked in the beautiful freedom of the gospel. Today, she is the first to admit that she is a mess. For the first time in her life, she says she's free to let her cracks show because she knows that a perfect offering was made on her behalf, setting her free from the need to be perfect all the time. She has discovered what Aladdin's genie (voiced by Robin Williams) longed for: "To be free. Such a thing would be greater than all the magic and all the treasures in the world."

Jesus came to liberate us from the pressure of having to fix ourselves and fix others.

The essayist Jason Heller once wrote, "The funny thing is, the older I get, the less enamored I am of choice. It's no longer a novelty or a rite of passage to pick what I want to eat or watch or read or buy or vote for. Often it's a chore—or, at worst, a source of mild anxiety. What once seemed like agency is now just another thing to worry about."

Choice, as such, is often held to be the Holy Grail of human possibility. It's the be-all and end-all in a "give me liberty or give me death" sort of way. If we perceive ourselves to have choices, we feel free. If we perceive ourselves to be without choice, we feel trapped and dead.

What Heller's claim belies is a startling fact: we don't use our agency very well! Martin Luther is said to have responded to someone's claim that their will was free by quipping something along the lines of, "Sure, you're free to make any bad decision you like." That's the reason that agency turns into a headache as we age. As our agency is used for more important things (from deciding what kind of juice to drink to deciding what job to take), we realize all the more how bound we are to mess up.

This, ultimately, is why a reduced view of free will is good news. It posits a God that intervenes in our affairs, not waiting for us to make good decisions (e.g., choosing to follow and serve Him), but making good and saving decisions on our behalf. In the drama of real life, God is the actor, we are the audience. Christ is the Savior, we are the saved. Our agency works itself out in action that is bound in one way or another—the attempt to please someone, to achieve something, to get somewhere. More often than not, we don't make it. God's agency cuts through our bondage, carrying us over the wreckage of our bound decision making by His unbound, free love in Christ. Human agency leads inevitably to cataclysm, fear, and despair. It is only God's finished adventure in Christ that leads to relief, rest, and restoration.

Jewish people had been hearing Isaiah 61:1–2 read to them for their entire lives. They would have known it by heart and been desperate for its promises: The Messiah would come! He would make everything better! Good news to the poor! Freedom for prisoners! Sight for the blind! Freedom for the oppressed! Truly, He would usher in the year of the Lord's favor!

And then one Sabbath morning, there in the temple during a regular service, this man, a man who they'd all seen as a little boy, as a teenager, stood up, read that sacred prophecy, and then said that *He* is the fulfillment of it! "Today this scripture is fulfilled in your hearing" (Luke 4:21).

It's hard to wrap my mind around just how good this news must have been to those who believed it. It must be said, of course, that not everyone believed it. In fact, before Jesus was even done with His sermon, the congregation had run Him out of the temple and tried to throw Him off a cliff! But to those who heard His words and believed them? They wanted to exalt Him.

Just a few verses later in Isaiah's prophecy, we get an explicit description of the good news. Isaiah said, "I will greatly rejoice in the LORD, my whole being shall exult in my God; for he has clothed me with the garments of salvation, he has covered me with the robe of righteousness" (Isa. 61:10 NRSV).

In that great moment on the cross, Jesus Christ, who wore, by right—by virtue of His holy life—the garments of salvation and the robe of righteousness, took off those clothes and gave them to us. His goodness for our sin. His yes for our no.

Jesus came to earth to be grace in the face of the world's judgment, to be love in the face of the world's critique, to be the gospel in the face of the law, and to be God's yes to us. Jesus came to earth to "bring good news to the oppressed, to bind up the brokenhearted, to proclaim liberty to the captives, and release to the prisoners; to proclaim the year of the LORD's favor" (Isa. 61:1–2 NRSV).

Thanks be to God.

The 2013 film *Warm Bodies* tells the story of a postapocalyptic world in which zombies roam the earth. Nicholas Hoult plays the protagonist zombie. Here's *Warm Bodies'* unique twist on the genre: Hoult finds himself falling in love with a female human, and all of a sudden his heart literally warms and he begins coming back to life! Now since it's a movie, the human he falls for, of course, is the daughter of the world's foremost zombie hunter.

There's a bit of resurrection theology embedded in this story. Love, we might say, is the opposite of judgment. The zombie hunter is pure judge. He says things like, "This is a corpse, infected with the plague. It is uncaring, unfeeling, incapable of remorse." In Romans 8:3, Paul makes a profound statement about the relationship between love, judgment, and zombies: "For what the law [judgment] was powerless to do because it was weakened by the flesh [zombies], God did by sending his own Son [love]."

Historically speaking, zombie movies have often carried an implicit philosophical statement about groupthink or the consumer culture. In *Warm Bodies*, we get a statement about human nature itself. In his zombie state, Hoult is a lost cause. Nothing can save him. The best he can say for himself is that he's "conflicted about eating anything with a heartbeat." At the beginning of the film, he proclaims himself dead—not nearly dead, not deathly ill, not even undead. He's dead. He is beyond saving. This is the ultimate judgment.

Ah, but for love.

Love (God's Son) accomplishes what the law (judgment) could not: bring life out of death. Start a stilled heart. Warm a cold body. And after Christ's work is done, God cries out like the prodigal's father: My son "was dead and is alive again; he was lost and is found" (Luke 15:24).

God's work is no less profound than resurrection. He creates life out of death, something out of nothing, and righteousness out of sin. And He has done that for you today.

There's no doubt, the *why* questions of suffering are utterly perplexing. And as we search the Scriptures and consider stories such as Job's, we are tempted to see those as worst-case scenarios designed to help us get our heads straight in relation to our comparatively small "first world problems." We medicate; we minimize; we moralize. We develop theories to explain what is happening to us. While they may temporarily help us categorize and compartmentalize our thoughts and feelings, when true suffering comes, all our speculations fall flat.

Since no one alive can see the beginning from the end, from the divine vantage point, we're left stranded in a prison of inscrutability. And sadly, we often prefer our confinement to the disorienting possibility that our suffering is actually ordained, that God is involved in it.

Fortunately, we worship a God who is in the business of freeing captives and creating trust where there was none before. In fact, the cross tells us that He does so (and has done so) *through* suffering, not despite it.

Justin Holcomb puts it this way in his book *On the Grace of God*:

> Grace is available because Jesus went through the valley of the shadow of death and rose from death. The gospel engages our life with all its pain, shame, rejection, lostness, sin, and death. So now, to your pain, the gospel says, "You will be healed."

The good news of suffering is that it brings us to the end of ourselves. It brings us to the place of honesty, which is the place of desperation, the place of faith, the place of freedom. Suffering leaves our idols in pieces on the ground. It puts us in a position to see that God sent His Son not only to suffer in our place but also to suffer with us. Our merciful friend has been through it all. He is with us right now! And while He may not deliver us from pain and loss, He'll walk with us through it.

As we do with most heroes, we want to emulate Esther. She is so brave. When her immediate predecessor as queen showed any kind of backbone at all, she was shunned. Esther is always walking on eggshells around her king. Then she hears about an edict that has gone out that all Jews will be slaughtered on the thirteenth day of Adar. She decides to act to save her people. She's willing to die if she has to (Esther 4:16). Esther stands in the inner court and wins the king's favor, getting him to make a second edict.

On the very day that was supposed to spell doom for the Jews, the king's second declaration was put into practice. Where the first declaration was a command to "destroy, kill and annihilate all the Jews—young and old, women and children" (Esther 3:13), the second called the Jews to "assemble and protect themselves; to destroy, kill and annihilate the armed men of any nationality or province who might attack them" (Esther 8:11).

The day of judgment and destruction had become a day of salvation and redemption. This is the theology of the cross, that tragic tool of criminal execution that is used by God to achieve our eternal salvation. Life where we expected death.

The king's two declarations bring to mind God's two words: law and gospel. The first brings death, the second brings life. The transition from one to the other requires an intervention. Esther risks her protected place in an earthly palace to intervene on behalf of her people. Jesus is evicted from His heavenly palace ("My God, my God, why have you forsaken me?") to intervene on behalf of His. Esther must risk her life, Jesus sacrifices His.

Now we live in Esther's kingdom. Our enemies, sin and death, have been destroyed by our Intercessor. The thing that was supposed to end our hope—the cross of Christ—has given us new life. Like the Jews in the kingdom of Ahasuerus, we are free to be ourselves. The Jews need know no fear while Esther is on the throne. We need know no fear so long as Christ reigns. And He does, forever.

One of the ways to translate the word *epiphany* is "sudden revelation," like an aha moment. In the church, it's referring specifically to the revelation of Jesus to the wise men. They have become witnesses to the manifestation of God. They know that they can't go back to Herod and sell out this newborn, because they've come into contact with God on earth. They've experienced an epiphany.

But get this: it is not the first time God has been revealed! The most notable previous time was when He gave the Ten Commandments to Moses on Mount Sinai. God is described—revealed—by the commandments. He is holy, perfect, and good, and so His commandments to us reveal aspects of what He's like. But we don't call that an epiphany. That's not an aha moment. We save the word *epiphany*, the sudden revelation of God, for the recognition of Jesus Christ, just as Paul uses the Greek word *epiphaneia* in Titus 2:11 to refer to the "appearing" of grace.

The law works just the way we expect things to work. Bad people get what they deserve, good people get what they've earned. But the gospel? The news that grace exists? That a sinner might not get what's coming to him but instead be given *more* gifts? For the wise men, it changed everything.

It is an earth-shaking epiphany when God becomes incarnate on earth and reveals that He is a Savior, not a judge, when He is a healer, a minister, an offering, and a sacrifice for others. Life makes more sense if we each just get what we deserve. But that's terrible news. We've got it so much better. The good news, the announcement that shakes the earth and shatters the way we think the world works, is that God Himself came down to earth and turned the axis of the world from our way, in which everyone gets what they deserve, to Jesus's way, in which everyone gets *way* better than they deserve. In fact, we get the perfection He deserves while He gets the death we deserve.

Aha!

People are inherently selfish. This is why it's noteworthy when someone does something legitimately *un*selfish, when someone does something for someone else with no regard for themselves. They usually end up on magazine covers and talk shows. Such behavior runs counter to our nature, so it stands out.

That's why what happened at the end of a recent Miami Heat game was so remarkable. In a world of prove-your-worth-to-the-world machismo and selfishness, Heat head coach Erik Spoelstra did something almost unprecedented: he took his hands off the controls. In a critical moment with time running out and his team trailing, Spoelstra elected not to call a timeout to diagram a play. He decided to let his players run free and decide the game. Here's ESPN's Henry Abbott on the decision:

> This is big.
>
> To understand how big, you have to understand how impossibly tough it is for coaches to come around to the idea that the best thing for their team might be … less coaching.
>
> By the time you have put in the insane hours that it takes to become an NBA head coach, often generally at the expense of a quality family life or anything else that matters much, you have to really be attached to something.
>
> For many coaches, the thing they're attached to is the idea of calling the shots.

We want desperately to take credit, both as people, in general, and as Christians, in particular. Many Christians loudly proclaim that they are saved by the grace of Jesus Christ, but that they had to choose to accept it. This would be like Erik Spoelstra saying, "All the credit goes to the players, but they do have to run the sets that I design."

Spoelstra's ability to let go would be a great model for us all—if we could do it. Unfortunately, God has to take control away from us. Fortunately, He does just that. Our salvation is accomplished by God's action: He comes to us, opens our eyes to our needs, and then announces that our needs have been met in Christ. We are addicted to doing. In Christ, the work is done.

A lot of preaching these days is too theoretical and disconnected from reality when it comes to the human condition and how real change happens. We use language like "indicatives" and "imperatives." We love phrases like "faith alone saves, but the faith that saves is never alone," and "grace is opposed to earning, not effort." And all of those categories and phrases are good. I affirm them all theologically. But none of them answers this question: How does change actually happen?

When it comes to real heart change, we have two options: law or grace. That's it. Two. At the end of the day, we either believe law changes or love does. I can tell people all day long about what they need to be doing and the ways they're falling short (that's important to keep them seeing their need for Jesus). But simply telling people what they need to do doesn't have the power to make them want to do it. I can appeal to a thousand different biblical reasons why someone should start doing what God wants and stop doing what He doesn't want. And I do. But simply telling people they need to change can't change them. Giving people reasons to change doesn't do it either. Both are necessary, but neither actually *works*.

Paul makes it clear in Romans 7 that the law endorses the need for change but is powerless to enact change—that's not part of its job description. The law points to righteousness but can't produce it. It shows us what godliness is but cannot make us godly. The law can inform us of our sin but cannot transform the sinner. The law can instruct, but only grace can inspire. To put it another way, love inspires what the law demands.

Think about it. Beneath your happiest moments and closest relationships inevitably lies some instance of being loved in weakness or deserved judgment. Someone let you off the hook when you least deserved it. A friend suspended judgment at a key moment. Your father was lenient when you wrecked his car. Your teacher gave you an extension, even though she knew you'd been procrastinating. You said something insensitive to your spouse, but instead of retaliating, she kept quiet and didn't hold it against you the next day. One-way love is the essence of any lasting transformation that takes place in human experience—a person loved in weakness blossoms.

John the Baptist was a master of fire-and-brimstone preaching. He said that the time was coming! The ax is lying at the root of the trees! Trees that don't bear good fruit are cut down and thrown into the fire! And the crowds asked him, "What should we do then?" The tax collectors asked him, "What should we do?" The soldiers asked him, "What should we do?" And John gives them the law, the rules, the requirements.

For the crowds: "Anyone who has two shirts should share with the one who has none, and anyone who has food should do the same" (v. 11). For the tax collectors: "Don't collect any more than you are required to" (v. 13). And for the soldiers: "Don't extort money and don't accuse people falsely—be content with your pay" (v. 14).

In their question, "What should we do then?" you can almost hear the fear in their voices.

John is the last law preacher. (Well, that's not quite accurate, because Jesus certainly preached the law too.) But John is the last preacher who didn't have access to the gospel. He's the last preacher who preached the law and then stopped. He's the guy who tried to save people by giving them something to do.

John thought that when Jesus came, He would continue this threatening kind of preaching ministry. He talked about the one coming after who would separate the wheat from the chaff and throw the chaff into unquenchable fire (Matt. 3:11–12). But Jesus didn't come to perpetuate the law. He came to be the gospel. Here's what He actually said when He came: "The Spirit of the Lord is on me, because he has anointed me to proclaim good news to the poor. He has sent me to proclaim freedom for the prisoners and recovery of sight for the blind, to set the oppressed free, to proclaim the year of the Lord's favor" (Luke 4:18–19).

John knew that our actions deserved death. Jesus accepted our death and gave us His life.

The 2012 film *Wanderlust* tells the story of a "normal" couple, played by Paul Rudd and Jennifer Aniston, who lose their jobs and home and find themselves starting life over in a hippie commune in Georgia.

Most of the comedy comes in fish-out-of-water form, with Rudd and Aniston trying to get used to a community in which there is no personal property and no boundaries, down to the absence of a door on the communal bathroom. Everything is free—love, flesh, and food. It is supposed to be a community of freedom, one devoid of the constricting rules of the outside world. Then Paul Rudd kills a fly and gets in trouble for it.

"I'm sorry," he says. "I'm trying to learn all the rules." "There are no rules here," responds the commune leader, Seth. "Except 'no swatting flies,'" says Rudd. "That's not a rule, it's just, uh …" Seth hesitates, "… a way of thinking about stuff."

As it turns out, then, there are rules. Of course there are. Hippie or preppy, we surround ourselves with rules. Without them, life doesn't make sense; chaos reigns. And even hippies try to avoid true chaos. Of course, hippies and preppies have different rules (for instance, a different make of car might be acceptable or forbidden in each camp), but they are rule-bound nonetheless.

Wanderlust's hippies show us our compulsion. They've been in rebellion for so long, the things they're rebelling against (for instance, Walkmans and fax machines) are all hilariously out-of-date. We need to rebel, but the object of our rebellion is secondary. We set up rules to organize our rebellion and find ourselves to be no different from those legalists we hate so much.

Armed with the knowledge that we, like everyone else, are in open rebellion, we come—once again—face-to-face with our need for a Savior. Whether we flout the rules or love them, we need salvation. In Christ, we have just such a Savior. He silences our internal lawyers by satisfying His eternal law.

I increasingly hear people talking about the need to be biblically balanced. I think they mean that we need to spend the same amount of time talking about everything the Bible talks about.

So, for example, since the Bible talks about what God in Christ has done and also what we ought to do in light of what Christ has done, to be balanced we need to give both themes equal airtime. Since the Bible talks about Jesus and about us, to be balanced we need to spend the same amount of time talking about both. The list could go on: since the Bible talks about x and y, to be balanced we need to talk about x and y the same amount.

But this is *not* the balance of the Bible. While the Bible talks about a lot of things, it does not give all of its themes equal airtime.

The overwhelmingly dominant message of the Bible is that God loves and, in Jesus, justifies sinners. There are myriad ways the Bible says this—the whore is made a bride, the dead are raised, the unrighteous are declared righteous, slaves are made sons, the blind see, the sick are healed, the unclean are made pure, the guilty are forgiven, sinners are saved, and so on. No Christian denies that the Bible says more than this, but the work of Christ on behalf of sinners is clearly the emphasis of Scripture from beginning to end. What we do in light of what Jesus has done is important. But it's not more important than, or even equally important as, what Jesus has done for us.

Martin Luther said that the story of the Scriptures—from front to back—is about Jesus Christ. The emphasis of the Bible, in other words, is on the work of the Redeemer, not on the work of the redeemed. As important as how we live is, the spotlight of Scripture is on Christ, not the Christian.

To be truly biblically balanced, then, is to let theology be proportioned by the Bible's radically disproportionate focus on God's saving love for sinners seen and accomplished in the crucified and risen Christ.

Like Job's law-loving, advice-giving friends, we naturally conclude that good people get good stuff and bad people get bad stuff. The idea that bad people get good stuff is counterintuitive. It seems terribly unfair. It offends our sense of justice.

Even those of us who have tasted the radical saving grace of God find it naturally difficult not to put conditions on grace (e.g., "Don't take it too far; keep it balanced"). The truth is, however, that a "yes, grace, but" posture is the kind of posture that perpetuates slavery in our lives and in the church. Grace is radically unbalanced. It has no "but." It's unconditional, uncontrollable, unpredictable, and undomesticated. As Doug Wilson put it, "Grace is wild. Grace unsettles everything. Grace overflows the banks. Grace messes up your hair. Grace is not tame.... Unless we are making the devout nervous, we are not preaching grace as we ought." Grace scares us to death because in every way it wrestles control out of our hands. However much we hate law, we are more afraid of grace.

Gerhard Forde, in his wonderful book *Justification by Faith: A Matter of Death and Life*, says that "the gospel of justification by faith is such a shocker, such an explosion, because it is an absolutely unconditional promise. It is not an 'if-then' kind of statement, but a 'because-therefore' pronouncement: because Jesus died and rose, your sins are forgiven and you are righteous in the sight of God!"

Contrary to what we conclude naturally, the gospel is not too good to be true. It is true! No strings attached. No buts. No conditions. No need for balance. If you're a Christian, you are right now under the completely sufficient imputed righteousness of Christ.

How can we avoid falling prey to those preaching false christs that John warns about? Sometimes what they preach doesn't sound that much different than what we preach. False teachers today have become very good at preaching *almost* the real thing. And people are deceived. *We* can be deceived.

Now, as then, people preach Jesus, either leaving out a lot of things about Him, or adding things to make Him seem "better." They've invented their own Jesus, a Jesus of their own creation. They preach about a man called Jesus, but is the Jesus they preach the Son that John refers to? Is the Jesus we preach the true Jesus, the Son of the Father? Is the Jesus we hear preached about the Messiah, the One who atones for our sins? How can we know?

"Let what you heard from the beginning abide in you," says John. "If what you heard from the beginning abides in you, then you too will abide in the Son and in the Father" (v. 24 ESV). John wants us to remember our first encounter with Christ, the encounter that opened our eyes for the first time. Can we remember how we were at the beginning? We were lost, powerless, and totally consumed by we-didn't-even-know-what. Then it was Jesus the Christ, the *Redeemer*, who, while we were incapable of love, *loved us*, and showed us our need for a Savior. He opened our eyes to our brokenness, and then rescued us from it.

Brothers and sisters, we are living in the last hour, just like the original readers of John's letter. Antichrists are here, proclaiming false things about Jesus. Sometimes these false things can sound enough like the real thing to fool us. So we must keep returning to our gospel beginnings. In the storm of lies that is the world, we abide in Jesus who loved us when we were loveless. We abide in Christ whose law overwhelmed us with the truth about who we were and destroyed us. We abide in Jesus, the Son of God, the Messiah, who reconciled us to the Father. It is only the true Christ who can look down from His throne and say, "Behold, I make all things new."

In the spring of 2013, Nike's new ad campaign featuring Tiger Woods began making the rounds. The ad showed Woods staring down a putt, with the tagline "Winning Takes Care of Everything." There was much debate about the taste level of this ad, considering Tiger Woods was recently divorced, a discovered philanderer, and a father with less-than-full custody of his children. Has "everything" really been taken care of? Is this an appropriate message to be sending to children?

Tiger Woods was, to borrow a phrase from the philosopher Paul Ricoeur, nothing if not an "exiled soul." Reparation needed to be made, and the Nike ad claimed that winning was the route. Christianity all too often uses this same exiled-soul story and simply puts the cross in place of victories on the golf course. In other words, the cross is a tool to get us where we want to go—back to glory. Still, it is "success," in one form or another, that is required for us to regain our former stature.

Nike's ad posits a thing that you can do to regain your purity—win. Christianity, as often practiced, posits something too—work hard, pray hard, be righteous, and you can regain that close relationship with God that your sinful life cost you. On the golf course, a theology of glory can work in the short term—win, and the accolades will come back. The money will come back. The sponsors will come back. Even the beautiful women will come back. But where your exiled soul is concerned, it is only the victory of another—achieved through death—freely given to you, that can offer new life.

Tiger Woods's life isn't new; it's merely buffed clean until new cracks appear, until he starts losing. We require something more permanent, something that will give us peace. "Thanks be to God, who delivers me through Jesus Christ our Lord!" (Rom. 7:25).

In 2011, a Hasidic Jewish rapper named Matisyahu achieved a moderate level of popularity. Part of the appeal, I think, was the odd visual of such a person (bearded and yarmulke-wearing) "reggae rapping." But then, in January of 2012, Matisyahu, whose real name is Matthew Paul Miller, had something of a spiritual crisis. On his website, www.matisyahuworld.com, he wrote:

> Sorry folks, all you get is me ... no alias. When I started becoming religious 10 years ago it was a very natural and organic process. It was my choice. My journey to discover my roots and explore Jewish spirituality—not through books but through real life. At a certain point I felt the need to submit to a higher level of religiosity ... to move away from my intuition and to accept an ultimate truth. I felt that in order to become a good person I needed rules—lots of them—or else I would somehow fall apart. I am reclaiming myself. Trusting my goodness and my divine mission.

Perhaps the most illuminating line is that "in order to become a good person," Matisyahu felt he "needed rules—lots of them" or else he would "fall apart." He said he approached this as his own choice. In other words, he chose to submit himself to the law in order to try to become a good person.

Did it work? Well, suffice it to say that in public appearances after this announcement, Matisyahu sported a clean-shaven face and a renunciation of Hasidism. So the evidence suggests that it didn't. More explicit is his statement that he was "reclaiming" himself and trusting his own goodness. I can't say that he's gone from the law to the gospel, necessarily, as he seems to still be relying on a goodness from within, but he does seem to have rejected the law's ability to create goodness.

Matisyahu discovered that the law can demand goodness but cannot create it. We'll discover the same thing. The only thing that keeps us from falling apart is the saving strength of another, Jesus Christ, the friend of sinners.

The subjective question, "How am I doing?" has become a more dominant feature of Christianity than the objective question, "What did Jesus do?" Perhaps you're aware of this in your own life. As a result, generations of Christians have been taught that Christianity is primarily a lifestyle, that the essence of our faith centers on how to live and that real Christianity is demonstrated foremost in the moral change that takes place inside those who have a personal relationship with Jesus.

To be sure, the Bible has plenty to say about our becoming like Jesus. But our transformation is a secondary theme. The primary theme of the Bible is Christ's substitution—the fact that Jesus became like us. Today, most people have reversed the order. The focus of the Christian faith has become the life of the Christian.

This shift in focus from the external to the internal has terrible practical consequences.

When we're on the brink of despair, looking into the abyss of darkness and experiencing a dark night of the soul, turning to the internal quality of our faith brings no hope, no rescue, no relief. We assume that people possess the internal power to get things right, so we turn them in to themselves. But as too many people already know, every internal answer will collapse underneath them. Turning to the external object of faith, namely Christ and His finished work on our behalf, is the only place to find peace.

The surety we long for when everything seems to be falling apart won't come from discovering the dedicated "hero within" but only from the realization that no matter how we feel or what we're going through, we've already been discovered by the "Hero without." Peace with God rests securely on the work of Christ for us, outside us.

The truth is, the more I look into my own heart for peace, the less I find. On the other hand, the more I look to Christ and His promises for peace, the more I find.

Jesus is the eternal and magisterial King, sitting at the right hand of God the Father. But sometimes, we choose to forget about the King. We don't really like the idea of having a King. The very notion infringes upon our ideas of personal freedom. I mean, it's not as if we voted for this King. And if I were going to vote for any king, I'd check the box on the ballot that had my own name next to it. The last thing I need is someone sitting on a throne laying down the rules by which I have to live my life.

And what terrible rules they are. "Honor your father and mother." "Don't lie." "Love your enemies." "Give away everything you have." Whoever heard of such ridiculous rules?

We try to forget about Christ the King, pushing Him into the margins where we like Him. Sometimes we do this by trying to water down the rules. We think to ourselves:

The real Jesus is the servant guy who loved everybody. This King stuff isn't the real stuff. He just wants me to try my best to follow Him. I'll honor my father and mother, unless they start treating me poorly. I'll be honest, unless I can convince myself that this lie is a little "white lie" that won't hurt anyone. I'll give away some of what I have but certainly not everything. I'll tell everyone that I'm loving my enemies but cultivate a seething hatred just below the surface. Then I can say, "Hey, I've done my best, and Jesus will be satisfied with that."

As Sean Connery says in *The Rock*, "Losers always whine about 'their best.'"

When we forget about Christ the King, we forget that our best isn't good enough, that Christ the King meant it when He said that we must be perfect, as our Father in heaven is perfect.

When we forget the kingly nature of Christ and water down the rules He's laid down, we forget that we need Christ the Savior.

In Peter Weir's 1998 film, *The Truman Show,* Jim Carrey plays Truman, a man who unwittingly lives inside a giant television studio. His family, friends, and neighbors—everyone in his life—are all paid actors. As the film opens, Truman begins to suspect that there is something false about his surroundings, and sets out to escape. In the film's climax, Truman gets to speak to the show's creator, Cristof, before heroically leaving the show.

Cristof, a clear God figure, tries to tell Truman that the world "out there" is no different than the world to which he's grown accustomed. But the audience knows the difference. Inside the studio, Truman isn't free in any real sense. Job, wife, friends—they're all props, leaving Truman feeling manipulated.

We hate feeling manipulated, which is why we leave, or have disbelief in, a God who is controlling and constraining our free will, and we embrace a "god" who supposedly gives us our freedom. But look at what Truman is leaving:

> In my world, you have nothing to fear. I know you better than you know yourself. It's okay … I understand. I've been watching you your whole life. I was watching when you were born, I was watching when you took your first step. I watched you on your first day of school … when you lost your first tooth … you belong here. With me.

Throw away the specific details of the plot, and you begin to see, when we throw off the shackles of a "controlling" God, we are running away from a loving deity who has watched over and cared for us our entire lives and who creates a place in which we belong. He calls us "okay," understands us, and promises us a life without fear, and yet we still celebrate our striving for freedom. We are sure that we can do better, if only we are allowed to exercise our freedom!

But Cristof is right. The world "out there" is just as controlling, just as enslaving as our God, and yet it's not at all caring like Him. Worse, outside of our "controlling" God, we are expected to save ourselves, to live lives worthy of eternal glory.

Inside, we have been chosen—a world has been created just for us—to be a part of God's life and family, forever. Our God is a loving Creator. Today, as always, we remain with Him.

The deepest fear we have, *the fear beneath all fears*, is the fear of not measuring up, the fear of judgment. It's this fear that creates the stress and depression of everyday life, and it comes from the fact that, down deep, we all know we don't measure up and are therefore *deserving* of judgment.

God's law realizes our fears, though. Our fears have come true. We don't measure up! In Psalm 24, you can almost feel the internal dread in David's lyrics: "Who shall ascend the hill of the LORD? And who shall stand in his holy place? He who has clean hands and a pure heart, who does not lift up his soul to what is false and does not swear deceitfully" (vv. 3–4 ESV).

Whoa. "Who can measure up to God?" David's asking. "Who can enjoy the presence of God?" The answer is this: only someone who is completely pure. Only someone who has never trusted in something other than God. Only someone who has never lied.

Does this description fit you? It certainly doesn't fit me.

The fear, the stress, the depression, the anxiety all just lie there heavily on David's heart. How can we ever find peace, satisfaction, joy? We hang our heads in defeat.

But wait. There's a turn in the psalm. A sudden light dawns. David sings, "Lift up your heads, O gates! And be lifted up, O ancient doors" (v. 7 ESV).

The law makes you hang your head in shameful dejection. But David cries out to lift up your head. Why? "The King of glory is coming!" he says.

"Who is this King of glory?" he knows you will ask. He answers, "The LORD, strong and mighty" (v. 8 ESV).

The good news is that the God who makes the demands of us now meets the demands for us. Let fear vanish suddenly like the darkness when light enters the room. The King of glory has come.

There are two different ways of seeing: God's way and our way. Our way of seeing is simple: what you see is what you get. If I smile a lot, people would begin to think I am a happy person. If I frowned all the time, they'd think I was a grouchy person. This is just the way our minds work. We look at the outside and make judgments about the inside.

Samuel looked at the outside of Jesse's oldest son and made a judgment about his inside: he must be the Lord's anointed. But Samuel was wrong. Samuel looked at the outside, but the Lord looked at the heart. God doesn't see someone the same way that we do. There was a time when this was of great comfort to me. I thought, *God's different from all those people at school; He doesn't judge the outside. He sees the heart!* I spent a long time comforting myself with the thought that the people who had rejected me at various times in my life were only looking at the outside. I knew that God looked at my heart. He saw the real me.

Then I realized an awful truth: I have hatred in my heart. I realized then, as I realize now, that I'd be a lot happier if the Lord saw how humans see. Far from taking comfort in the idea that the Lord saw the inner beauty that no one else saw, I realized that God saw the inner anger and envy that was really there. This implicates all of us. We're good at tricking people, though, because people see the outside. Unfortunately for all of us, God sees the heart.

Though I might wish God saw as people see, I don't wish that God did as people do. People only give me what I deserve; God gives me much better than that. God sees the real me, the me I hide, the me that others would run from if they could see. But God sees, and He stays, and He loves. He gives me what I don't deserve (grace) and withholds the condemnations that I do deserve (mercy).

It's been about five hundred years since God used a Roman Catholic monk named Martin Luther to turn the oppressive religious establishment of his day upside down. Historians refer to this as simply the Reformation, and it's high time for another one.

For too long, Christianity has been identified with political ideology, social agendas, moralistic activism, and other earthly things. The core of Christianity—the gospel message—has been obscured and, in some places, lost.

The church is in trouble because it has embraced the same pressure cooker we find everywhere else. In recent years, a handful of popular books have been published urging a more robust and radical expression of the Christian faith. The unintended consequence of this push is that Christianity becomes more about the sacrifices we make than the sacrifice Jesus made for us. My fear is that too many people, both inside and outside the church, have heard our "do more, try harder" sermons and pleas and have therefore concluded that the focus of the Christian faith is people behaving better.

The fact is that the foundation of Christianity is not about good people getting better. It is good news for bad people coping with their failure to be good. The heart of the Christian faith is good news—not good behavior, good technique, or good advice. This message desperately needs to be recovered in the twenty-first century. The church should be the one place in all of society where the weary and heavy laden should be able to come and find rest. But all too often they get to-do lists. This needs to change. We need a new reformation.

The grace of God does not play it safe and cannot be contained by the walls we build and masks we wear. Grace moves beyond deserving, pushing the envelope of forgiveness and dispersing the shadows of shame and guilt. God does not flinch from reality—our hopes and dreams, our hurts and disappointments, our proudest moments or most embarrassing failures. This is the inexhaustible message that needs to be recovered in our exhausted age of "doing more and trying harder."

During the 2012–2013 season, the Miami Heat won twenty-seven consecutive basketball games.

The all-time NBA record for consecutive victories is thirty-three, by the Los Angeles Lakers during the 1971–1972 season. Naturally, there was great interest to see whether or not Miami could break this record, which they didn't, but the interest didn't stop there. No. We had to know, for instance, if that Miami team was "as great" as that Laker team. Where did that Miami team rank historically? Would the streak have become meaningless if the Heat hadn't capped the season with a championship? It was a rare thing during that time to hear someone say, "Gosh, this winning streak is really a wonderful achievement," without moving immediately to someone trying to categorize exactly how wonderful it was.

We do the same thing with our Christianity. It isn't enough to be a Christian, is it? We must immediately know just how good a Christian we are. Most of the time, we do it subconsciously, when we think that "so-and-so is such a faithful woman of God," or that "he is such a prayerful man." It seems a steep slope from the prodigal son coming home and "becoming a Christian" to the categorization of our proficiency as a new follower of Christ. Just how closely are we following Him, anyway? How well are we doing?

Remember that line from John Newton's classic "Amazing Grace"? "How precious did that grace appear the hour I first believed!" The implication is clear: it's easy for us to forget how precious grace felt and how much we needed it at the beginning of our Christian lives. The moment we feel safe or that we're getting better, grace starts to become less amazing to us. We conclude that we needed grace a lot at the beginning but that as we grow and improve, we need it less and less. Big mistake.

The fact is, we never outgrow our need for grace. Growth is always growth into grace, not away from it. And the good news is that God's grace is inexhaustible. It was there for us at the beginning, it will be there for us at the end, and it is there every moment of every day in between.

The Alan Parsons Project album *I, Robot* contains a great song called "I Wouldn't Want to Be Like You." It could serve as a rallying cry for disaffected youth everywhere, whether Wall Street occupiers, Alex P. Keaton neocon types, or anything in between. We won't make the mistakes of the 1 percent, or of the current or previous administrations, or of our parents, right? There's always someone out there that we won't be like.

I love the story arc in *Field of Dreams* in which Kevin Costner goes from paralyzing fear of turning into his father to joining his cornfield-ghost dad on the field to have a catch. In the beginning of the film, he'll do anything to avoid being like his dad, down to obeying a mysterious voice, plowing under his crops, and putting his livelihood and family at risk. Through the meeting of other ghostlike characters and an almost magical sage (James Earl Jones), Costner realizes that the problem lies, not with his father, but with him. He says he "never forgave [his dad] for getting old."

Alan Parsons, the braintrust behind the Project, wrote a catchy tune, but he missed the point entirely. He wrote, "If I was high class, I wouldn't need a buck to pass. And if I was a fall guy, I wouldn't need no alibi." In other words, If I were in your position, I wouldn't make the mistakes you're making. The basic problems of the world are attributable to others, but not to me.

We make the same mistake, and it leads to slavery. It's not until we can admit that "I am the problem and I am culpable too" that we will ever be able to see the true magic of a Savior who comes to us and sets us free, not because we are innocent, but because we are guilty.

Rod Rosenbladt told me a story once about a middle-aged woman who needed help from her pastor.

She went to her pastor and said, "Pastor, you know that I had an abortion a number of years ago?" "Yes," the pastor replied. "Well, I need to talk to you about the man I've since met." "All right," replied the pastor.

"Well, we met a while back, and started dating and I thought, I need to tell him about the abortion. But I just couldn't. Then things got more serious between us and I thought, I need to tell him about the abortion. But I just couldn't. A while later we got engaged and I thought, I need to tell him about the abortion. But I just couldn't. Then we got married and I thought, I really need to tell him about the abortion. But I just couldn't. So I needed to talk to someone, Pastor, and you're it."

The pastor replied, "You know, we have a service for this. Let's go through that together." So they did—a service of confession and absolution.

When they were finished, she said to him, "Now I think I have the courage to tell my new husband about my abortion. Thanks, Pastor."

And the pastor replied to her, "What abortion?"

The gospel is the good news that Jesus offers forgiveness full and free. This is the hardest thing for us to believe as Christians. We think it's a mark of spiritual maturity to hang on to our guilt and shame. We've sickly concluded that the worse we feel, the better we actually are. The declaration of Micah 7:19 (and Psalm 103:12) is the most difficult for us to grasp and embrace: the Lord practices a "forgetfulness" for the repentant person's sin. As Corrie ten Boom once said, "God takes our sins—the past, present, and future—and dumps them in the sea and puts up a sign that says 'No Fishing Allowed.'" This seems too good to be true.

But it is true! If you are a Christian, you are right now under the completely sufficient imputed righteousness of Christ. Your pardon is full and final. In Christ, you're forgiven. When you bring your sin up in conviction to Him, it's as if He says, "What sin?"

In a final-season episode of *Frasier*, Niles's ex-wife is accused of murder, and Niles is implicated as a possible accessory to the crime. His life swirling out of control, Niles makes a big deal about "choosing to be calm." Martin, the Crane boys' father, observes, "Wow! He's really holding up well!" "A little too well," Frasier retorts. "I'm starting to fear that he's not dealing with his emotions at all!" Martin says, "Right. That's the whole secret to holding up."

This exchange illustrates a very common disconnect. What is the difference between what is on our outsides and what is on our insides? What is real? Which is more powerful? As Martin suggests, we often think of obscuring what's really going on as a skill. Think of the grieving mother who gets right back to work or the mourning father who never cries. In some circles this is called strength. But is this kind of strength worth anything?

Niles's life becomes more and more unbearable, and he becomes more and more robotic in his insistence that everything is fine. Finally, at a café, he is told that the previous customer got the last straw. This ends up being the last straw for him figuratively, too: he ends up having a sort of psychotic break in the café.

Whatever's underneath will eventually come out. We tell ourselves that people like Niles are exhibiting great self-control. Martin certainly thinks so. But he's not actually controlling his discomfort and stress; he's simply hiding it. We find that he's only acting calm, cool, and collected. And no one can hide their true selves forever.

Christians often feel it necessary to hide their insides (their sinfulness) from one another, fearing that they'll be revealed to be lagging behind on the great path to righteousness. It's a good thing that Jesus came for sinners and not for the righteous. It's a good thing that He came for those of us who can't handle our lives rather than for those of us who can. The gospel is good news that we are loved and accepted no matter what, even when we find ourselves exposed, as Niles does, by situations beyond our illusions of control.

J. Gresham Machen noted the counterintuitive truth that a low view of law always produces legalism; a high view of law makes a person a seeker after grace. The reason this seems odd is because most people think that those who talk a lot about grace have a low view of God's law and that those with a high view of the law are the legalists. But Machen made the very compelling point that it's a low view of the law that produces legalism because a low view of the law causes us to conclude that we can do it—the bar is low enough for us to jump over. It's this low view of the law that caused Immanuel Kant to conclude that "ought implies can." That is, to say I ought to do something is to imply logically that I am able to do it.

A high view of the law, however, demolishes all notions that we can do it. We'll always maintain a posture of suspicion regarding the radicalness of unconditional grace as long as we think we have the capacity to pull it off. Only an inflexible picture of what God demands is able to penetrate the depth of our need and convince us that we never outgrow our need for grace—that grace never gets overplayed. Our helplessness before the totality of divine expectation is what creates the space for God's amazing grace and the freedom it produces. The way of God's grace becomes absolutely indispensable because the way of God's law is absolutely inflexible.

As Christians, we still need to hear both the law and the gospel. We need to hear the law because we are all, even after we're saved, prone to wander in an "I can do it" direction. The law, said Martin Luther, is a divinely sent Hercules to attack and kill the monster of self-righteousness.

And then once we are crushed again by the law, we need to be reminded that Jesus paid it all. Even in the life of the Christian, the law continues to drive us back to Christ—to *that* man's cross, to *that* man's blood, to *that* man's righteousness.

New beginnings. Fresh starts. Clean slates. Second chances. We love 'em all. They carry so much promise. They give us so much hope. If we blow it today, we can start again tomorrow. We conclude that the answer to yesterday's failure is today's success. If I preached a bad sermon this past Sunday, I can fix my sense of failure by preaching a great sermon next Sunday.

In many ways, all of our striving under this performance idol is a grown-up re-creation of the adolescent playground cry: "I want a do-over!" Have you ever heard that? Watch children at a park playing a game like football or basketball. Maybe somebody messed up the opening kick. Maybe they weren't sure the ball stayed in bounds or not. So somebody proclaims, "Do-over!" And they start over. They have to get it right. They want the bad play erased and replaced by a good play.

We're still doing this in our adult years, trying to manage our lives in some bizarre system of spiritual checks and balances, trying to outweigh our bad plays with our do-overs.

But when we worship at the altar of performance, we spend our lives frantically propping up our images or reputations, trying to do it all—and do it all well—often at a cost to ourselves and those we love. Life becomes a hamster wheel of endless earning and proving and maintenance and management and controlling, where all we can see is our own feet. We live in a constant state of anxiety, fear, and resentment until we end up heavily medicated, in the hospital, or just really, really unhappy.

So what's the answer to this enslaving addiction that plagues us all?

The gospel of grace.

The gospel is God's announcement to failing people like you and me that we are now free from the slavery of "if at first you don't succeed, try, try again." We don't have to put all our weight into the do-over. We can put it on Jesus. Because Jesus succeeded for us, we're free to follow with abandon and fail without fear.

I thought the *Choose Your Own Adventure* books were great when I was a kid. Now? They just seem exhausting. I remember sticking my finger in the page where I had to make the choice, reading through the story as it unfolded after my choice, and then going back, making the other choice, and following that different path all the way to the end too. It used to take me hours to read those books! Now I feel that I'd rather have someone just tell me how the story turns out.

The truth is, when we feel that the twists and turns of the story—specifically, *our* story—are up to us, an unbearable amount of pressure is placed on our every decision. In the books, if a decision turned out to be a bad one, it usually led to death. *Choose Your Own Adventure* books were surprisingly grim. But you could always go back and make a different choice. Unfortunately, we don't have that luxury in real life.

How much more comforting would it be to have a guide through the story, someone who knows the safest route and who is willing to ferry us through? We'd never have to leave a finger tucked in the pages. We'd know we'd make it to the end.

In the story of reality, God is both the author and the star, and we are really just supporting characters. Christ is the hero; we are His sidekicks. The choices we make usually place ourselves in the starring role; we are always the protagonists in our own imaginations. But this is a kind of bondage. Thank God that, in Christ, He delivers us from it. Choosing our own adventure seems like the way to life, but it inevitably leads (as anyone who has read those books knows) to catastrophe. Only trusting in Christ's finished work leads us to rest from our self-interested "analysis paralysis."

A God who knows us can be a scary thing. It's the kind of thing that we say we want, but when the reality comes into focus, we can get a little scared. A God who knows us turns out to be something that we don't want and something that we want to hide from. We are sure we can escape God in the same way that we escape our parents or any of the other oppressive forces in our lives. Feeling a little put upon at home? Move to Portland, Oregon. Mom and Dad don't understand you? Get a job on Wall Street and get lost in a Lower Manhattan high-rise. Realize that a relationship isn't fulfilling anymore? Change your phone number and start going to different bars and clubs. We're all familiar with this kind of escape plan.

So what are we to do with a God who claims to "fill heaven and earth," a God who explicitly says there's nowhere we can hide from Him? Well, we have to hope that there's a disconnect between what we *fear* will happen when He finds us and what will *actually* happen.

The good news is that there *is* such a disconnect, and its cause is Jesus Christ.

We fear a holy God because we know when a holy God finds an unholy us, the only possible reaction is rejection and exile. We read all over the Bible about "the outer darkness" and a God who says "I never knew you" to people who don't live up to His standard. We sinners need this to not be the last word. And thankfully, it isn't.

On account of Jesus Christ and His sacrifice for us, when God finds us hiding from Him in the deepest, darkest corners of our consciousness, He actually says to us, "I love you." He seeks us out, finds us, dies for us, and raises us to new life in Him.

Today remember that although your impulse is to hide, you have been found by God and loved by Him in Christ.

Good advice and inspirational pick-me-ups rarely comfort a grieving person. The pain is simply too big to be penetrated by flimsy platitudes, especially for those grieving the loss of a loved one. The givers of such encouragement mean well, but they often lack the right kind of word. More than that, though, they often lack the right *timing*.

A simple word of encouragement can mean a lot at the right time, or it can mean next to nothing at the wrong time.

In a way, Paul does offer an inspirational pick-me-up of his own: "Where, O death, is your sting?" (v. 55). Depending on the timing, the declaration could be a sting unto itself. Someone freshly grieving a loss can say, "The sting is right here. I feel it deep in my bones."

But notice the timing of that verse in the context of 1 Corinthians 15. Paul begins by declaring and explaining the gospel. He situates the work of Christ in the midst of history, reminding us first of all that Jesus came into this world, entering into this kind of pain. He reminds us that Jesus felt this kind of sting.

Then he begins to talk about the implications of Jesus's resurrection, what it means for us, what it means for the world, what it means for death itself.

It is clear he is not simply throwing out religious clichés. He is digging deep into the reality of the brokenness of our world and the reality of what will fix it. And it's not until he reaches the climax of this careful and carefully plotted exploration of our broken world that he brings up the rallying cry: "Where, O death, is your sting?" He's not trying to toss a pick-me-up to a grieving person. He's showing the reality of the gospel, which is more powerful than pick-me-ups and much bigger than suffering. It's bigger even than death.

And when all may seem hopeless, when we finally reach the end of the world, figuratively or even literally, God's rescue will be right on time.

Paul calls the gospel "the power of God for salvation" (Rom. 1:16 ESV) and contrary to what some have concluded, he didn't simply mean the "power of God for conversion." The gospel remains the power of God for salvation until we are glorified, because we're all "partly unbelievers until we die," as John Calvin put it. We need God's rescue every day and in every way.

In his book *The Gospel for Real Life*, Jerry Bridges picks up on this theme that Christians need the gospel just as much as non-Christians by explaining how the spiritual poverty in so much of our Christian experience is the result of an inadequate understanding of the gospel's depths. The answer isn't to try harder in the Christian life but to comprehend more fully and clearly Christ's incredible work on behalf of sinners and then to live in a more vital awareness of that grace day by day. Our main problem in the Christian life, in other words, is not that we don't try hard enough to be good, but that we haven't thought out the deep implications of the gospel and applied its powerful reality to all parts of our lives. Real spiritual growth happens as we continually rediscover the gospel.

The same dynamic explains the primary purpose of corporate worship: to rediscover the mighty acts of God in Christ coming to do for us what we could never do for ourselves. We gather in worship to celebrate God's grip on us, not our grip on God.

Gospel-fueled worship exposes our sin and exposes the Savior of sinners. The faithful exposition of our true Savior in every element of worship, while liberating, will painfully reveal the subtle ways in which we, as individuals and as a culture, depend on lesser things than Jesus to provide the security, acceptance, protection, affection, meaning, and satisfaction that only Christ can supply.

When God gathers His people for worship week after week, He does so to show just how relevant and necessary Jesus is by telling and retelling the story that, while we are all great sinners, Christ is a great Savior.

Some people are better at hiding their messes than others. Some are quite accomplished at pushing their messes so far down into the cracks of their hearts and minds that it never becomes apparent to the rest of us just how extensive the mess really is. These people generally run important organizations such as banks, governments, and megachurches. Occasionally, their messes come out and it's pretty shocking, even though it shouldn't be.

Other people are simply a mess.

The other day I drove past a house with a yard that was out of control—if there weren't people in the house, I would have assumed it was abandoned. But then I noticed a sign out front that read:

> Native plants bring life to this landscape. This "Florida Friendly" property is a model landscape that conserves and protects our precious water resources and provides valuable wildlife habitat. It has been certified by Broward County as an official NatureScape property.

Now, I'm sure all of that is true. What I'm about to say doesn't mean I deny the value of protecting precious water resources and providing valuable wildlife habitat. But do you know what my first thought was? *What a great scam! They probably printed that sign up themselves to stop the neighbors from judging them for their disgusting yard! How can I get one of those signs?* My very first thought was that these people had hit on a great scheme to justify letting their yard go to South Florida hell.

That this was my impulse sheds light on a truth: when we can't hide our messes, we justify them.

You're a mess. So am I. If we're not so good at hiding it, we often try to claim that we like it this way. We know, though, that the truth is quite different. The gospel offers us a different way: instead of trying to pretend that we like our messes, we can cast our hopes on the One who came into the world to save messy people, on the One who became a mess for us by putting Himself in our place so that, before God, we could be squeaky clean.

Here are four of the most misunderstood words in the Bible: "Therefore let us also ..." There are two ways we can read these words in the context of running a race under the supervision of the "great cloud of witnesses." One is moralistic, and the other is according to the gospel, and these four words make all the difference.

When I first read these words, I thought I'd caught the Bible preaching moralism. We get a list of Old Testament heroes, a list of the great things they were able to do, and then we get "therefore let us also," followed by a list of things *we're* supposed to do! And then, as I read the passage again and again, I realized there was a key to properly reading this passage. The key rests in the list of heroes: Gideon, Samson, Jephthah, David, and Samuel. They are painfully flawed, to man. It's the list of who's who in the great cloud of witnesses that enables us to see that the writer to the Hebrews is preaching something much more powerful than moralism: he is preaching the very gospel of the crucified and resurrected Christ.

It is in our nature, because we desperately want to have something to contribute, to read Hebrews 12:1 this way: "Therefore, since we are surrounded by such a great cloud of witnesses, let us throw off everything that hinders and the sin that so easily entangles. And let us run with perseverance the race marked out for us." Therefore, because of the great cloud of witnesses around us, let us run the race that has been set before us with endurance, *as they did*. This, clearly, is moralism. But the writer here has something much deeper in mind: because you *are like* the great cloud of witnesses, you *are able* to run the race with endurance. We don't run the race to become something; we can run the race because we *are* something.

Moralism says to run the race with endurance in order to become the thing I should be. The gospel says that what enables me to run the race with endurance is that I have already been made the thing I should be.

We are chosen, like David, Gideon, and the rest. Because of this, we can run with Christ's endurance, needing none of our own.

During Robert Griffin III's rookie year with the Washington Redskins, some fans started calling him Black Jesus. The appellation rubbed me the wrong way at first, as you might expect. Maybe it does the same to you. But let me suggest that, at least in this one case, there might be at least an allegorical reason to be okay with it.

Listen to how teammate Fred Davis (who coined the term) used it: "You really can't say much more. I mean, like I said, he's Black Jesus right now. He saved us today. He's a great player. He makes plays. And he did what he had to do on that third down. We've been talking to him about protecting himself a lot more, but he seen an opening and made a play."

Whatever hesitation I have about the name of the Christ being invoked so flippantly is mitigated by the fact that the people who are using it are at least thinking in terms of Jesus as a Savior. This is rare enough to be remarkable (and important). Normally, for people—both Christian and non-Christian—Jesus is nothing more than a wonderful exemplar of love, care, and charity. He is the classic great moral teacher. Fred Davis, though, is thinking of rescue. Robert Griffin III saved the Redskins, and Jesus saves us. The defense rests: Black Jesus.

It's helpful to look at this from the other side. As I've said, most people see Jesus primarily as an example to be followed. Consider the way in which all of the New England Patriots have adopted coach Bill Belichick's "mum's the word" press conference style. No smiles, no extra words, just focus on the next game. No one, however, has ever been, nor will ever be, moved to refer to Belichick as Podium Jesus.

This, all in all, is a really good sign for the ways people are thinking about Jesus. Sure, it's less than devout, and you wouldn't really want to encourage it, but I'm in favor of anything that reminds me that Jesus is a Savior to be adored, not a role model to be followed.

In the summer of 2011, Pastor Joe Nelms was invited to give the opening invocation at a NASCAR race. He became a brief Internet sensation for his *Talladega Nights*-style prayer, which included thanking God for "Sunoco racing fuel and Goodyear tires," and climaxed by thanking God for his "smoking hot wife, Lisa."

Before I was a "professional" Christian, I never wanted to pray out loud; I never thought my prayers would be good enough to be out there, side by side with the prayers of the truly (poetically) spiritual. You know the kind of people I mean. After I became a pastor and became more comfortable speaking in front of people and more confident in my ability to think on my feet, I became less worried about the ability to pray in public and more worried about the motivation behind my praying publicly.

I mean, aren't we supposed to be praying *to God*? Certainly Pastor Nelms got some notoriety for his church and probably boosted attendance a little bit, but could anyone argue that his prayer was truly intended primarily for God's ears? Or is it more likely that he wanted, in some way, to impress the gathered assembly? Only God knows.

But it raises an interesting question: Are we praying to impress others or are we praying to God? What are we to do with Matthew 6:6, wherein Jesus told His followers that when they pray, they should go into a room and close the door? Jesus seems to be regularly at odds with public displays of religiousness.

Today, talk to God as if no one is listening. God doesn't need your flowery language or extensive theological vocabulary. In fact, He doesn't need anything other than the sin you come to Him with. Sin is the raw material from which God makes righteousness—a righteousness that He gives to you no matter the quality of your prayers.

An impartial God is a scary thing. 1 Peter 1:17 is a hard thing to hear, as we're accustomed to thinking of a relationship with God as perfectly loving and as an escape from fear, rather than a source of it. What Peter is elucidating here is really the thing that makes a relationship with Jesus unique.

We think that we want impartiality. We imagine our lives on a sort of cosmic scale: all the bad stuff we do gets piled on one side and all the good stuff we do gets piled on the other. At the end, whichever side weighs the most, well, that'll determine how it goes for us, right? Peter is acknowledging that this is the natural human way to think. But he cautions us: "Since you call on a Father who judges each person's work impartially, live out your time as foreigners here in reverent fear" (v. 17). When the standard is godliness, fear must win the day. A fair God is a dangerous God, at least to those of us who fail to live up to His holy standard.

But there is good news, and it is shocking to our sensitivity: God is unfair. God does show a special partiality. He is partial to His Son. And this is good news for us! The Bible says that everyone who believes has been clothed with Christ. That metaphor is used specifically to help us understand this verse. When God looks at us, He sees His Son! He's not fooled. We're not pulling a fast one, because Jesus Christ is God Himself! But we get sovereignly covered with the righteousness of the One to whom God shows partiality. Wearing our normal clothes, we're in trouble. Clothed with Christ, though, we partake in all the glory that comes with being the favorite. Not because of who we are, but because of who ransomed us and who paid for our freedom from the tyranny of trying so hard to be acceptable, and always being worried that we haven't done enough.

In the movie *Flight*, Denzel Washington plays a troubled-but-talented airline pilot who manages to successfully land a crashing commercial jetliner despite being under the influence of more substances than you could count and whose alleged inebriation causes his heroism to be called into question.

Flight spends most of its time painting a graphic, realistic, and relentless picture of the life of an addict and, therefore, of the life of a human person. It echoes Paul's lines from Romans 7, "For I do not do the good I want to do, but the evil I do not want to do—this I keep on doing" (v. 19), but with one important difference: Washington's character thinks he knows what he's doing! It's always worked out before, and even when things seemed to be going tragically wrong, he was able to perform in ways that no other pilot (even a sober one) could.

In the film's most powerful scene, a fellow addict (played by Kelly Reilly) tells Washington's character that she's worried about him. "Worried about me?" he responds indignantly. "Worry about you! We're not the same … I choose to drink!" "It doesn't seem much like a choice to me," she replies. Reilly's character has added the "I do not understand what I do" of Romans 7:15 and tears the blinders from Washington's flight from himself.

For every scene in which Washington promises sobriety (when it is in his obvious legal interest to remain sober), there is a companion scene, showing us his continued spiral toward bottom. In the end, it is the bottoming out that leads to freedom. "I might be a chump," he says in a final scene, "but I couldn't tell any more lies."

The most common lie we tell is one to ourselves—that we have it all together, that we know what we're doing, and that we're in control. It takes a bottoming out to lead us to the Promised Land. "My grace is sufficient for you," the tagline might as well read, "for my power is made perfect in weakness" (2 Cor. 12:9).

We Christians have a remarkable tendency to focus almost exclusively on the fruit of the problem. We do this as parents with our children, pastors with our parishioners, husbands with wives, and wives with husbands. We do this with ourselves.

The gospel, on the other hand, always addresses the root of the problem. And the root of the problem is not bad behavior. Bad behavior is the fruit of something deeper. Our chief problem, as Jesus made clear, is "not what goes into a man," but the defiled heart—the root.

Christian growth consists not of behavior modification but of the daily realization that in Christ we have died and in Christ we have been raised. Daily reformation, therefore, is the fruit of daily resurrection (Rom. 6:1–11). To get it the other way around (which we always do by default) is to miss the power and point of the gospel. In his book *God in the Dock*, C. S. Lewis makes the obvious point that "you can't get second things by putting them first; you can get second things only by putting first things first." Behavior (good or bad) is a second thing.

"Life is a web of trials and temptations," said Robert Capon, Episcopal priest and author, "but only one of them can ever be fatal, and that is the temptation to think it is by further, better, and more aggressive living that we can have life." The truth is, you can't live your way to life—you can only "die [your] way there, lose [your] way there.... For Jesus came to raise the dead. He did not come to reward the rewardable, improve the improvable, or correct the correctable; he came simply to be the resurrection and the life of those who will take their stand on a death he can use instead of on a life he cannot."

Moral renovation, in other words, is to refocus our eyes away from ourselves to that man's obedience, to *that* man's cross, to *that* man's blood, to *that* man's death and resurrection!

Learning daily to love the glorious exchange (our sin for His righteousness), to lean on its finished-ness, and to live under its banner is what it means to be morally reformed!

Nathanael's question for Philip, "Nazareth! Can anything good come from there?" (v. 46) is the eternal human question. "Can anything good come out of losing my job?" "Can anything good come out of someone who loved me turning their back on me?" "Can anything good come out of this life?"

The question is asked from a place of hopelessness. If Nathanael thought that good things could come from Nazareth, there'd be no need for him to ask the question. If we thought that good things could come from the terrible, intractable situations we find ourselves in, we wouldn't be wondering all the time: "What good could possibly come of this?" To all of these questions, all of these hopeless questions, Philip offered words of hope. He said, "Come and see."

Jesus has none of the qualities we traditionally associate with goodness and success. He's not rich, not a socialite, not beautiful. He wasn't attractive in any traditional sense (Isa. 53:2). God chose to come to earth in Him and as Him. He chose to be a citizen of Nazareth and chose to *remain* a citizen of Nazareth. When Philip said, "Come and see," he wasn't thinking of Jesus's wealth or His power or His intelligence or His beauty. He was talking about the gospel.

Can we believe that good things can come out of Nazareth? Yes, God always chooses to work in places like Nazareth. This is good news, because it means that God chooses to work in people like you and me. People who aren't successful. People who aren't rich. People who aren't powerful. People who aren't necessarily intelligent. People who aren't beautiful. God works in you, and He works in me! That is good news indeed.

I know that my Redeemer lives!

Now, if we're being honest with ourselves, who woke up this morning ready to make a proclamation like Job's? Don't we more often think, *I sure hope* my Redeemer lives! We envy the people who have this kind of faith. But us? We're a little more ... wobbly. We're freshly recovering from a fight with our friend or our spouse. We're trying to forget about the situation at work that might end up getting us fired. We can't stop thinking about the trouble that our children have gotten themselves into. We consider the people in our lives, wondering what they would think of us if they knew what was really going on. We *hope* that our Redeemer lives. We know for sure that we need redeeming, otherwise we wouldn't have opened a book like this one. But we're not 100 percent sure that redemption is available for us. We hope it is. Job, though, seems pretty confident.

But this is Job! Job, the one guy who doesn't seem to have any reason to be confident. Job is the guy who was minding his own business, living a good life, when he became the subject of a bet between God and Satan. Job, whose wife deserts him and whose children all die, whose cattle are killed and who is covered, head to foot, with sores. And yet, in his suffering—through his suffering—Job is aware that he has a Redeemer.

When Jesus hung on the cross, His cry was not for a redeemer. When He was abandoned by those who loved Him, when He was assaulted, beaten, scorned, mocked, tortured, and killed, He didn't say, "I know that My Redeemer lives." He said, "It is finished." He might as well have said, "You cry out for a redeemer. I AM the Redeemer, and I have done My work."

Jesus's "it is finished"—His life, death, and resurrection—is our assurance. We have a Redeemer, and He lives.

Jim Valvano (most likely known to those who aren't sports fans as the name-sake of the Jimmy V Foundation, a cancer research supporter that has given away hundreds of millions of dollars to fight cancer) was the subject of an ESPN *30 for 30* documentary in 2013, *Survive and Advance*. The film is about the unlikely path-to-a-championship of the 1983 North Carolina State Wolfpack, coached by Valvano, which included nine consecutive must-win games, many of which came down to the final seconds. The team's run (the final basket in the championship game was recognized by *Sports Illustrated* and ESPN as the "greatest moment in the history of college basketball") was fascinating, but also typical, in a Disney film sort of way. It played out in exactly the way you might expect. What's interesting to me is how the documentary treats Valvano's illness and eventual death.

Jonathan Hock, the film's director, has said that one of the things that interested him most about this story was that it was a wonderful tale of triumph after triumph being told about the life of "a doomed man."

Interviewee after interviewee (Valvano's players, wife, and friends, which include such luminaries as Mike Krzyzewski, Dick Vitale, and Sonny Vaccaro) told of how, when Valvano was diagnosed with cancer, they thought he'd "beat it." This is the language we use with cancer: the language of victory. Valvano's friends all spoke of being shocked as he became sicker and, eventually, astonished at his death. They'd thought he would win.

Even Jim Valvano died. The consummate winner didn't win. No one has or ever will. Except Jesus. Jesus wins.

As humans, our most desperate wish is to win. We try to win everything, up to and including the ultimate contest: us against our own deaths. The profundity of the cross is that it looks death in the face and confronts it directly. The cross is the end of the human contest. We lose. Even Jim Valvano lost. No one survives and advances.

God in Christ brings victory out of defeat. God in Christ brings life out of death. We all die, but in Christ we have the hope—no, the promise—of new and eternal life.

Essayist Chuck Klosterman wrote an article in 2011 arguing that *Breaking Bad* is the best of twenty-first-century television because it is the only show in which the characters' morality is not "static or contradictory or colored by the time frame; instead, it suggests that morality is continually a personal choice."

It is only *Breaking Bad* that gives its characters "personal agency," or what we might call free will, according to Klosterman. *Breaking Bad* is the story of a chemistry teacher diagnosed with cancer who takes to dealing drugs to provide for his family as he faces his own death. Klosterman describes a scene in which Walter White's hoodrat lab assistant Jesse Pinkman tells Walter he can't just "break bad." He was arguing that Walter couldn't simply make different choices and change. But the show itself argued that Jesse was wrong: *Breaking Bad* shows Walter White doing just that. Klosterman praises this supposedly "realistic" view of human ability and control. We know better. We've tried to change.

From a contradictory perspective, TV critic Steven Hyden highlights *Breaking Bad* for its depiction of "the fragility of life and family, the potential for evil lurking inside good people, the possibility that humanity is a ruthless me-first game with no rules or order."

What Hyden calls "the potential for evil lurking inside good people," the Bible calls original sin—that internal cancer that we can't cure on our own no matter how hard we try.

The psalmist said, "I know my transgressions, and my sin is always before me. Against you, you only, have I sinned and done what is evil in your sight; so you are right in your verdict and justified when you judge. Surely I was sinful at birth, sinful from the time my mother conceived me" (vv. 3–5).

If Klosterman is right and goodness and badness are choices—even if complicated ones—then the number of people making good choices is zero. He's wrong. We were sinful at birth. But good news has come: there is One whose every right choice covers our every wrong choice and, as a result, has earned our place at the table of joy and peace forevermore. There is a cure for our internal cancer—but it's not found in the right choices we can make but in the right choices Jesus made for us because we could never choose rightly.

What we do in life is look for hired hands. This means that we look for people to tell us what we want to hear: "You're a good mother, a good son, a good lover." All the while, though, we know deep down that it's just not true. That's why we keep asking. We think that if we get enough people to tell us that we're great, we might be able to believe it. But we never do.

Jesus is the Good Shepherd. He's not like the hired hands who run away when they see how bad things really are, when the wolves start to come, when your life starts to really fall apart, and when the "I'm okay, you're okay" charade starts to break down. And what does Jesus say? Not, "I'm the good shepherd. I know what my sheep need to hear." Not "I'm the good shepherd, I know how to get my sheep to relax." Not "I'm the good shepherd, and I know how to get my sheep in line." He says, "I am the good shepherd. I lay down my life for the sheep."

The wolves are real. We feel guilty about all sorts of things in our lives. We have not loved God with our whole hearts; we have not loved our neighbors as ourselves. These are the wolves that are coming for us. We look for hired hands to tell us that these wolves aren't really all that bad. "Oh, you're not a bad person," they'll say. "You're sure better than so-and-so." And that'll make us feel better, until we look over our shoulder and see the pack of wolves just a little bit closer. So we look for another hired hand. But then, as things get worse and worse, hired hands start quitting. When we do something that makes it impossible for someone to say, "You're not a bad person," we find that there's no one around anyway.

No one, that is, except Jesus, who lays down His life for us.

In Paul Thomas Anderson's 2007 oil epic, *There Will Be Blood*, no character can stand in the way of Daniel Day-Lewis's character, Daniel Plainview. Several try, but they are mowed down by his titanic force of personality and will. Day-Lewis's performance is so assured and immersive, his Oscar was a foregone conclusion.

Because of Day-Lewis's dominance on the screen, almost none of the other performances register, including Paul Dano's dual role as both Paul and Eli Sunday. Paul shows up in an early scene, selling information that his father's ranch has oil on it, and is then never heard from again. Eli, however, is Plainview's main antagonist. He's a fire-and-brimstone-style preacher who wants to make sure that the church gets a piece of Plainview's oil profits.

Unfortunately for Eli, he is not the landowner, and Plainview is able to swindle the naïve elder Sunday out of his ranch. Eli rails at his "stupid" father: "You've let someone come in here and walk all over us.... You're lazy and you're stupid. Do you think God is going to save you for being stupid? He doesn't save stupid people."

In another scene, Plainview refuses to let Eli bless the new derrick, which leads (according to Eli) to the death of a worker and an accident involving Plainview's own son.

These two scenes go together to illustrate Eli Sunday's view of God: basically, Eli thinks that we can control God. First of all, he thinks that his blessing can compel God's protective action. No blessing, no protection. Either way, it's Eli who's in control. Secondly, he tells his father that God won't save stupid people. Again, it's people who control their salvation, not God. Smart, saved. Stupid, lost.

We think too often about God in the terms that Eli does. We imagine that He is beholden to us, either to our prayer life, to our faithfulness, or to our bidding. In fact, God operates outside of us, and despite us, saving us in our stupidity, and saving the world despite our attempts to destroy it.

When God's good news met me in a very dark place during the summer of 2009, I started to see the many-faceted dimensions of the gospel in a more dazzling way. It's almost as if, for me, the gospel changed from something hazy and monochromatic to something richly multicolored, vivid, and vibrant. I was realizing in a fresh way the now-power of the gospel—that the gospel doesn't simply rescue us from the past and rescue us for the future; it also rescues us in the present from being enslaved to things like fear, insecurity, anger, self-reliance, bitterness, entitlement, and insignificance. Through my pain, I was being convinced all over again that the power of the gospel is just as necessary and relevant after you become a Christian as it is before.

And because the gospel is essentially the presence of Jesus Christ Himself and our being united to Him by God's grace through faith, we can expect that the gospel will be amazingly versatile, that it will be enough—more than enough!—for whatever situation we're in.

Maybe you'd like to think of the gospel as a diamond. It is one brilliant treasure—there is not more than one gospel—but it contains many different facets, each gleaming in distinct ways, providing new angles and levels of brilliance, all glorifying the same Savior.

Or maybe you like C. S. Lewis's *The Chronicles of Narnia* and remember how inside the wardrobe was an entire universe of lands to explore. The gospel is like that.

In 1 Peter 1:12, Peter tells us that angels long to look into the gospel. What might attract their gaze? Why would these supernatural creatures want to stare into the good news of Jesus Christ? Maybe, on one level, because it is not for them but for sinful man, and this fascinates them. But perhaps on another level, they find the good news eternally fascinating because it brings to bear the manifest glory of the Alpha and the Omega. The gospel is eternally fascinating because Jesus is eternally glorious.

Mark had just finished introducing John the Baptist when he abruptly moved on to introducing Jesus, and he made the most of his opportunity to show a profound difference in the message of the two men.

John's sermon basically went like this: The time is at hand! Repent! Change your ways or else! Repent! In a nutshell, John's sermon was "Time's up! Be good!"

And then Jesus came onto the scene: "After John was put in prison, Jesus went into Galilee, proclaiming the good news of God. 'The time has come,' he said. 'The kingdom of God has come near. Repent and believe the good news!'" (vv. 14–15). Very similar right? Well, it starts out very similarly, but it ends on a different note entirely. While John essentially said, "The time is now, repent, and change your ways," Jesus said, "The time is now, repent, and believe in the gospel."

John asked us to acknowledge the places in our lives that fall short of God's calling. Admit that you are not the person that you ought to be. And then: Do better! Try harder! That is not good news, which was John's point. Jesus, on the other hand, says, "You don't have to do better. I've done it. I've been righteous when you couldn't be. I've been loving when you couldn't be. I've been loyal when you couldn't be. I've been everything that you couldn't be, and then I gave it all to you. I didn't come for the people who could do it, I came for the people who couldn't. I came for the fool, for the failure, for the fraud. I am the Savior."

Praise God that He is. That's the best news of all.

Seemingly every day, we ask a question just like this one: How could that have happened? How can it be that our mother has cancer? How can there be a God who allows children to be molested by their fathers? When you read books and articles by people who don't believe in God—once you get through all the pseudo-intellectual jibber jabber—their arguments come down to: "I can't believe in a God who presides over a world that has come out like this."

We tend to think that God is present in comfort but not present in pain. We tend to think that if God exists, He wouldn't have let this place go off the rails so badly. If you're looking at the world from that vantage point, and you see it as it is—all the suffering that is apparently allowed to happen—you would naturally think either that God doesn't exist, that He's not a very nice guy, or that someone in the situation sinned, right? In response to questions like that, though, Martin Luther said a very interesting thing. He said that a "theologian of glory" ends up calling the good bad, and the bad good. What did he mean by that?

It's quite simple, really. The things that we think are bad—suffering, pain, and the like—are actually the things that strip away our ability to rely on ourselves. They show us that we are incompetent saviors, and they remind us that we need salvation from outside ourselves. On the other hand, the things that we think are good—prosperity, health, comfort—are actually the things that build up our defenses against recognizing our true needs.

This is why Luther promoted the "theology of the cross." This theology looks at the world as it is and proclaims a God active in suffering and who suffered Himself. It proclaims a God who comes to those in pain, a God who offers new life to the dying.

Sin has made the world the way it is, but Christ, on the cross, has redeemed it.

Baseball player Mike Piazza's autobiography, *Long Shot*, was called "a case study in narcissism" by reviewer Rob Neyer. Here's some of what Neyer had to say:

> He really wants you to think he was a great hitter. Piazza hit 427 home runs in his career, and he mentions something like a hundred of them. He's got the record for the most home runs by a catcher. And right after the section where he talks about breaking the old record, he launches into an extended discourse about what a great player he was. Like he's trying to convince us, yes ... but also as if maybe he's trying to convince himself.
>
> He really wants us to think ... that beautiful women—Playboy models mostly, and Baywatch actresses—find him incredibly appealing. I wish the otherwise-estimable index listed mentions of "Playmate", "Baywatch", and "actress". But there are a lot of them in there. And when relating how he met his future wife Alicia, he simply describes her as "a Baywatch actress, and a former Playmate, to boot."

We find the narcissism of others uncomfortable because we fear that it might shine a light on our own. Underneath it all (but not too far underneath!), we have a caustic narcissist who chomps at the bit of social convention. We know it's not okay to appear narcissistic, so we keep the little guy chained up.

Better, though, to call a thing what it is. We desperately search for the affirmation of others (whether for our athletic prowess, physical attractiveness, or devastating wit) due to our fear that our weakness, ugliness, and banality are obvious to all. In other words, we are sinners looking for someone—anyone—to tell us that we're not. We're looking for someone to save us without our having to die. But it doesn't work that way. For resurrection to occur, there must first be a death. We must admit our faults, allow Jesus to put the narcissist inside us beside Him on the cross, and be raised to a new life of blessed self-forgetfulness.

One of the most audacious con men in American history, Frank Abagnale Jr., flew for free on more than 250 Pan Am flights, impersonating a deadheading pilot. He forged a Columbia University degree and taught sociology at BYU for a semester. He pretended to be a pediatrician at a Georgia hospital for almost a year, and for another year, after forging a Harvard degree, he passed the Louisiana bar exam and worked in the Louisiana State Attorney General's office. All before he turned twenty-one.

You're probably familiar with the film adaptation of his autobiography, *Catch Me If You Can.* In the film, the event that is alleged to have started Abagnale on his life of crime is the divorce of his parents, brought about by his father's financial ruin in the face of an IRS investigation. Abagnale believed that his mother left his father because of the family's financial woes and that if their lifestyle could be restored (through his thievery), everything would be returned to normal.

The twisted lengths to which we will go to prove our love are astounding. And there's a bit of Frank Abagnale Jr. in all of us. We're all in some way working for love. Abagnale thought of it in literal financial terms: if he could "earn," in his own highly illegal way, enough money to set the family's lifestyle right, love would return. The IRS, in his view, was holding love hostage. Often Christians think of God as holding His love back until we earn it and acting according to that old extra-biblical proverb "God helps those who help themselves." Nothing could be further from the truth.

This is the truth, and it's a truth that Frank Abagnale Jr. probably could have stood to hear as a sixteen-year-old: the kind of love we actually need, the kind of love that satisfies, and the kind that really helps and changes people is not the kind that is deserved. In fact, real love is not handed out on merit at all. This is why the greatest love, the love that satisfies most deeply and changes us most thoroughly, is the love of God revealed in the free gift of grace in His Son, Jesus Christ.

Normally, the outdoorsy image of choice for spiritual growth is mountain climbing. You can picture it—new Christian at the bottom of the mountain, mature Christian near the top. But I want to take you a different way. Let's go spelunking!

Spelunking is cave exploration, and it's my suggestion for another way to think about spiritual growth. Instead of thinking of growth in Christ as a climb up a mountain, let's think of it as a trip into a cave. Where a mountain climbing expedition gets higher and higher (and as Christians, we might be tempted to think, better and better, however we define *better*), a caving exploration goes deeper and deeper, exploring the undiscovered depths. Spiritual growth is not about climbing a mountain, getting better, and therefore needing Christ less and less. Spiritual growth is about discovering more and bigger caverns of need into which more and more of Christ's grace can flow. We think spiritual growth is about height, when spiritual growth is about width. We think it's about the heights we've attained when, in truth, it's about the depth of our need.

True growth as a Christian involves recognizing that there is always another cavern to explore. There's always another crevasse of self-centeredness or stalactite of jealousy. The light of Jesus shines into deeper and darker corners and proclaims, "Yes, I can redeem this, too." True growth as a Christian means realizing that all the climbing we need to do is down into the depths.

We hear, "For God so loved the world that He gave his one and only son that whoever believes in Him may not perish but have eternal life," and we think, "Got it! Simple! What's next?" The Bible answers, "Like newborn infants, long for the pure spiritual milk, that by it you may grow up into salvation" (1 Pet. 2:2 ESV). It is this milk, the simplicity of the gospel message, that grows us into a deeper awareness of our desperation and therefore a deeper awareness of our deliverance.

In the 2011 film *Terri*, John C. Reilly plays a high school assistant principal. In one central scene, he's caught by a student in a lie. When confronted, Reilly's character responds in an interesting way. He shifts the focus away from the lie and tells the kid a story about a temp who's working in the school because his secretary is very sick and in the hospital. He says, just that morning, the temp had, through a series of sideways questions, tried to figure out just how sick the regular secretary was, because she would really like the job for herself. In a deep, dark secret place that she likely won't even admit to herself, Reilly says, a part of this temp wants the regular secretary to die. It'll get her the job.

When the secretary does die, and the temp finds out that she will be hired permanently, the temp makes a big show of being sad, even though she's happy about the job. Reilly finishes his story with these words: "Life's a mess, dude … Maybe I will do better, or maybe I'll do even worse. I don't know. I screw up all the time, 'cause that's what people do."

We think, as Reilly's temp does, that the important thing is how we appear. We know when it's appropriate to be sad, and so we make our display. We know we're supposed to love our neighbor, so we act the part. But Reilly (and, usually, the people in our lives too) see right through us. We are significantly more transparent than we believe we are, and everyone knows, inherently, that what's most important is what's inside us.

And then Reilly admits that, ultimately, he's just like his temp. He messes up. He does his best, but he's likely to keep messing up. This is true of enlightened guidance-counselor types and this is true of Christians. We screw up all the time, 'cause that's what people do. I have a good friend who once said, "People are bad, and Christians are people." Simple, yet profound.

As usual, the best news for us is the good news, and the good news is only good if it's true for Christians, too. Jesus said that the healthy don't need a doctor.

How do we use our freedom? Usually, it seems we use it pretty selfishly. A couple of years ago, then-Laker Andrew Bynum (an all-star center who plays close to the basket) took a ridiculous three-pointer in a game. It barely touched the rim, missing by a mile. Incensed, coach Mike Brown immediately called Bynum to the bench and put in a substitute.

"I'm good," Bynum said postgame. "I guess 'Don't take threes' is the message, but I'm going to take another one and I'm going to take some more, so I just hope it's not the same result. Hopefully, I make it."

So there you have it—message received, freedom asserted, and message ignored. People think that punishment will correct behavior. Andrew Bynum's postgame comments illustrate a competing (though more accurate) truth—punishment incites rebellion. The law (e.g., don't shoot three-pointers if you don't have a reasonable expectation of making them) asks for a certain behavior. Bynum got it right: don't take threes. When it doesn't get what it's looking for, the law inflicts punishment, hoping that a program of reeducation will produce better results the next time. Unfortunately, as Christian theologians have always noted, the law is much better at asking for a result than it is at achieving it.

Martin Luther likened the relationship of the law to the results of a lion held down by steel bands. As the lion fights against the bands, the tighter the bands become and the more viciously the lion fights. We fear freeing the lion because of the ferocity with which it strains, forgetting that, all the while, the lion is fighting the bands, not us. Released, the lion has nothing to struggle against and will likely cease its struggling.

The true freedom of grace overwhelms the asserted freedom that we shout in the face of the law. Here's real independence: the freedom that comes from the Savior who has kept the law in our place, allowing us to live and delivering us from bondage.

Normally when we think of people in need of God's rescuing grace, we think of the unrighteous and the immoral. But what's fascinating to me is that throughout the Bible, it's the immoral person who understands the gospel before the moral person. It's the prostitute who understands grace; it's the Pharisee who doesn't. What we see in Luke 7:36–50 is that God's grace wrecks, and then rescues, not only the promiscuous but the pious. The Pharisee in this story can't understand what Jesus is doing by allowing this woman to touch him, because he assumes that God is for the clean and competent. But Jesus here shows him that God is for the unclean and incompetent and when measured against God's perfect holiness, we're all unclean and incompetent. Jesus shows him that the gospel isn't for the well behaved, but the dead.

Jesus came not to effect a moral reformation but a mortal resurrection. As Gerhard Forde put it, "Christianity is not the move from vice to virtue, but rather the move from virtue to grace."

Wrecking every religious category the Pharisee had, Jesus tells him that he has a lot to learn from the prostitute, not the other way around.

The prostitute walks into a party of religious people and falls at the feet of Jesus without any care as to what others are thinking and saying. She's at the end of herself. More than wanting to avoid an uncomfortable situation, she wanted to be clean—she needed to be forgiven. She was acutely aware of her guilt and shame. She knew she needed help. She understood at a profound level that God's grace didn't demand that she get clean before she came to Jesus. Rather, her only hope for getting clean was to come to Jesus.

Everywhere else in the world, loveliness precedes love. Only in the gospel does love precede loveliness.

When Simon Peter met Jesus for the first time, Jesus told the fisherman where to fish. When Simon let down his nets, he caught so many fish that he struggled to get the boat to shore. So what were Simon's first words to Jesus after this unique encounter? Did he say, "Wow! How'd you know there'd be so many fish there? Is there a hidden camera around here somewhere? Are you the Fish Whisperer?" Simon said none of those things. He dropped to the floor of the boat in front of Jesus and said, "Go away from me, Lord, for I am a sinful man!" (v. 8 NRSV).

Now I'm going to suggest that this is not an overreaction. It certainly seems extreme to us, but we are unaccustomed to coming face-to-face with God. We've also become unaccustomed to thinking of ourselves as sinners. Neither is a very tasteful proposition, and we'd just prefer not to think about them. And yet, here's Simon, falling at the feet of Jesus and making this exclamation: "Go away from me, Lord, for I am a sinful man!"

Once again we hear the two words of God. The first, an implicit word of judgment; it doesn't even need to be spoken. Christ's mere presence caused Simon Peter to acknowledge his sin. He exclaimed, "I am a sinful man!" But as always, the first word is never the last word. Jesus said to Simon, "Do not be afraid." The final word completely obliterated the first word. Peter came to the shore, dropped everything he had, and followed Jesus.

When we come face-to face-with God, it's bad news. God's holiness, His perfection, His *very being*, causes us to say, "I'm not the person I want to be." Bad news. German theologian Rudolf Otto called this experience the *mysterium tremendum*, the moment of personal unraveling when overwhelmed by the glorious perfection of the divine. We cry out, "Depart from me, for I am a sinful man," and the good news is that God, knowing our hearts, knowing the depth of our selfishness, anger, frustration, and envy, hears our command to depart and simply says, "No."

He doesn't depart from us. Instead He draws near with words of comfort: "Do not be afraid."

I don't know about you, but I don't particularly like what God said to Noah after the flood. I mean, I like part of it, I like the part with the rainbow and the whole not destroying the earth part, but if you look carefully at the reading, I think you'll notice two pretty nasty things. First of all, God only promised not to destroy the earth again *with a flood*. That's sort of like someone promising not to punch you in the nose again … with their *left* hand. It leaves some flexibility. It's not the most comforting thing in the world: "Never again will there be a flood to destroy the earth" (v. 11).

This is the part of God's covenant with Noah that we remember: the promise not to destroy the world with a flood. But less easily remembered is the fact that God told Noah that He will "demand an accounting" from both mankind and animals for how they conduct themselves on this newly clean earth. God demanding an accounting is a scary thing.

But let's look at another covenant that God makes, this time with Abram. In Genesis 15, God told Abram to set up the butchered halves of several animals in the normal arrangement for covenant making. Ordinarily, both parties entering into a covenant would pass between the animals, implicitly saying that if they broke the covenant, they would end up like the animals.

But then God did something amazing: He put Abram to sleep and passed between the animals alone. He guaranteed both sides of this new covenant! This is the kind of deal God makes with us: instead of condemning His people for not living up to His standard, He comes Himself in the person of Jesus to suffer the consequences of our covenant breaking for us.

God says to us, "Our relationship doesn't depend on you. It depends on Me." And He shows His faithfulness in both calling for the accounting and then sending His Son, Jesus, to give the account. Through His atoning work, the account is settled.

A couple of NBA seasons ago, Andrea Bargnani, the number-one overall pick in the 2006 NBA Draft, was having a terrible season. So terrible, in fact, that he was being loudly booed by his home fans. Bargnani's case is certainly not unique. Underperforming players are often booed at home. But we have to ask: Does this strategy work?

In theory, home fans boo their own players to shame them into working harder. Some, of course, might be expressing simple hatred, but I think that most fans would prefer that their players actually play well. So let's take a quick look at Bargnani's stats: he's shooting 47 percent from the field on the road and an absolutely horrific 30 percent at home.

The apostle Paul said that "the law was brought in so that the trespass might increase" (Rom. 5:20). This is evidenced by Andrea Bargnani's stats at home. When subjected to the law (the chorus of boos that tells him he's not good enough), Bargnani's performance is significantly worse. The law comes in, the trespass increases. The more Bargnani is reminded of how terrible he is, the more terrible he becomes. The same is true of every one of us.

Christians have an outlet that Bargnani lacks: when we hit bottom, we have a Savior there to pick up the pieces, a Christ who substitutes His perfection for our failure. The more shots Bargnani misses, the more likely he is to be out of a job. The more we fail, the more likely we are to call out for that Savior.

So what are we left with? Does the strategy work? Well, yes and no. The application of the law only works to weaken. Those who are oppressed perform significantly worse than they do otherwise. The law, remember, was brought in so that the trespass might increase. But for the Christian? The law works, absolutely. Paul again: "Therefore no one will be declared righteous in God's sight by the works of the law; rather, through the law we become conscious of our sin" (Rom. 3:20).

Thank God Christ has come for failures.

The modern folk-pop group the Belle Brigade has a very catchy song called "Losers." The first lines really caught me:

> *There will always be someone better than you.*
> *Even if you're the best.*
> *So let's stop the competition now.*
> *Or we will both be losers.*
>
> *And I'm ashamed I ever tried to be higher than the rest.*
> *But brother I am not alone.*
> *We've all tried to be on top of the world somehow,*
> *'Cause we have all been losers.*

The song seems to be about the futility of attempting to live up to the inevitable comparisons and competitions of human life. It's also a sad-but-true diagnosis of the universality of human pain and struggle. But sadly, and perhaps predictably, the Belle Brigade's solution left me a little cold:

> *So I wanna make it clear now.*
> *I wanna make it known.*
> *That I don't care about any of that [expletive] no more.*
>
> *Don't care about being a winner.*
> *Or being smooth with women.*
> *Or going out on Fridays.*
> *Being the life of parties.*
> *No, no more, no.*

So the answer to the pressures of life is to … declare myself immune from the law's demand? I will *not* feel that I have to be a better father than I am. I will *not* worry that I am about to be discovered as the fraud I am. Sadly, the law's demands on us weigh heavily whether we acknowledge them or not.

The law is the terrible windstorm that threatens to blow our house down. Throwing open the door and shouting, "You will *not* destroy my house!" is not a winning strategy. It's best to get a new house; ideally, one with many rooms in which Jesus declares us a winner, despite all our losing.

Have you ever done something that won *almost* unanimous praise? Did the experience teach you what it taught me? That *almost* unanimous isn't worth much? As a pastor, I get a lot of feedback on things our church does, whether it's my sermons or the music or some other choices I've made, like my clothing or my haircut. I've been blessed to have had many people compliment me on the way things are done at our church. Occasionally, though, someone will have a criticism. And you know what? The criticisms are far more memorable than the compliments.

I think this is true for everyone. It seems like ninety-nine compliments can be swallowed up by one bit of criticism. It just goes to show you: for love to be love, it must be perfect. To feel loved, I can brook no criticism at all. In other words, it is only perfect love that can cast out fear.

So why are we still afraid of God?

To borrow the language of John's first letter, we fear because we "have not been perfected in love." Our loving is still addicted to the reactions we get. I love the positive comments, but that love dies under the poison of criticism. In other words, our love is reactive. We love the things that appear to be loving us, and hate the things that we think hate us. We assume that because this is the way we relate to the rest of the world—and the way the world relates to us—this must be the way of God, too.

But God loves differently than we do: we love, in fact, "because he first loved us." That God loved us *first* means He loved us before our performance. When someone walks up to me, I reserve my love until I hear what they have to say. God lavishes His love on us whether we're good or bad, to Him or to one another. We are only capable of love because of this radical, one-way love of God, a love that doesn't depend on anything I might give or withhold.

The greatest single question of the religious life is, "If I call out to God, will anyone answer?" In the gangster-slash-vampire movie *From Dusk Till Dawn*, Harvey Keitel plays a pastor who has lost his faith. At one point, his daughter says to him, "Daddy, don't you believe in God anymore?" and part of his answer is, "Every person who chooses the service of God as his life's work has something in common. I don't care if you're a preacher, a priest, a nun, a rabbi, or a Buddhist monk. Many, many times during your life you will look at your reflection in a mirror and ask yourself: Am I a fool?"

I submit to you that this is shared by the people in those congregations as well as those in front of them. Am I a fool? Am I calling out into the void? If I call out for help, will anyone answer me?

When Paul wrote that "everyone who calls on the name of the Lord will be saved," he did it in the context of law and gospel: he' was breaking down distinctions. When he said that there's no difference between Jews and Greeks (in Romans 10), he was saying something incredible: there's no difference between law keepers and law breakers!

The prophets of the Old Testament railed at Israel because they weren't living up to the law the Lord had laid out for them: "You're living just like the Gentiles," they'd say. "There's no distinction between you! You're not separating yourselves." So even when there was *supposed* to be a distinction between them, there was no distinction between the Jews and the Greeks. The Jews were just as sinful as the Greeks! Now, because of Christ, there is again no distinction. All are made righteous. Their shared sin becomes shared righteousness, the precious gift of the crucified Jesus. It is because of this gift, this gift of a holy and righteous law-keeping life, that when we cry out into the void, "Lord, Lord, help me!" the Lord is generous to all who call on Him and that "everyone who calls on the name of the Lord will be saved."

The ironic thing about legalism is that it not only doesn't make people work harder, it makes them give up. So we make a big mistake when we conclude that the law is *the* answer to licentiousness. In fact, the law tends to *stir up* lawlessness. People get worse, not better, when you lay down the law.

To be sure, the Spirit does use the whole Word in our sanctification—the law as well as the gospel. But the law and the gospel do very different things. The law reveals sin but is powerless to remove sin. It shows us what godliness is, but it cannot make us godly. As Martin Luther said, "Sin is not canceled by lawful living, for no person is able to live up to the Law. Nothing can take away sin except the grace of God."

The law apart from the gospel can only crush; it can't cure. Scottish churchman Ralph Erskine wrote:

> *The law could promise life to me,*
> *If my obedience perfect be;*
> *But grace does promise life upon*
> *My Lord's obedience alone.*
>
> *The law says, Do, and life you'll win;*
> *But grace says, Live, for all is done;*
> *The former cannot ease my grief,*
> *The latter yields me full relief.*

So the law serves us by showing us how to love God and others. But we fail to do this every day. And when we fail, it is the gospel that brings comfort by reminding us that God's infinite approval of us doesn't depend on our keeping of the law but on Christ's keeping of the law for us. And guess what? This makes me want to obey Him more, not less!

Indeed, it is the kindness of the Lord that leads to repentance.

Moses and Elijah, representing the law and the prophets, are shown in the story of the transfiguration to be less than equal to Jesus. The law and the prophets are overshadowed by the gospel. All three of them are standing there and the cloud comes, and the voice says, "This is my Son, whom I love. Listen to him!" (v. 7). And in case the disciples were confused about which man they were supposed to be listening to, when they looked around the other two were gone! Only Jesus remained! Peter's mistake (v. 6) is that he fails to distinguish the law from the gospel. He thinks that Moses and Jesus will make good equal teammates.

If we fail to understand how the law and the gospel work together, our struggle to obey the law will make us forget about the gospel completely. If you start to worry about how well you're doing in God's eyes, you will forget that He saved you as a sinner. Remember what Paul said: "Once I was alive apart from the law; but when the commandment came, sin sprang to life and I died. I found that the very commandment that was intended to bring life actually brought death" (Rom. 7:9–10). The commandment that we think will bring us life, like "be a good Christian," will actually bring us death. The way in which it brings us death is by making us forget the truth, blinding us to the good news that we once knew, that while we were yet sinners, Christ died for us.

Peter, by suggesting that Moses and Elijah be on equal footing with Jesus, is actually eclipsing the radical goodness of the good news that Jesus embodies. Both God's law and God's gospel are good. But only one of them is eternal. There will not be any sin to restrain in heaven, giving the law an expiration date. But the gospel's life is eternal, which is why Paul says in 2 Corinthians that the gospel's glory is far greater than the law's.

The cloud comes and the voice from heaven singles out Jesus. The gospel always has the last word. For the pardoned children of God, forgiveness always trumps condemnation.

Are you doing well as a Christian? It seems that often Christians are less concerned with the fact that they're a Christian than their proficiency at being one. Because of this, we envision our Christian lives as being like a ladder we have to climb. Sure, we think, Christ's great sacrifice for us was enough to get us on the ladder, but now it's up to us to move higher. We imagine the pope and Mother Teresa as being very high on the ladder and those people who don't read their Bibles every day as being very low. This concept makes sense to us, and it allows us to do one of our favorite things in the world—compare ourselves and our progress to that of others.

So what, then, are we to make of the Great Christian Tumble? You know what I mean: when someone considered "a great Christian" is revealed to have been engaging in reprehensible behavior. It's confusing. We don't know how to classify the event. Was this person not as high on the ladder as we had imagined? Perhaps they'd never really gotten on the ladder at all (i.e., they weren't really a Christian). The truth, though, is more profound: there is no ladder.

Each of us are, as Martin Luther said, at the same time justified and sinner, or in other words, we are both right before God and wrong in ourselves. We live our lives in the glory of the Holy Spirit even while we are getting in accidents, getting called names, and getting abandoned by our loved ones. Even while we are still dealing with sin. Our desperate need never goes away.

In ourselves, we are left in a crumpled heap at the bottom of the Christian ladder. In Christ, we are carried directly to heaven, no work necessary on our part.

Remember Tim Tebow? His career as a football player has been one of the most talked about in recent years and, as of this writing, is most likely over. This, in itself, is a strange phenomenon since he has a winning record as a starting quarterback in the NFL—a relatively rare achievement for a young player who came into the league with questionable talent onto a mediocre (at best) team. Heck, it's rare for any young quarterback to come out of the gate with a winning record. In any event, people have begun to speculate about what Tebow might do next, now that it appears his NFL career is over.

Tebow is a very serious Christian, and one of the career options that is open to him is mainstay on the inspirational and motivational public speaker circuit. Tebow could likely earn his weight in gold each year speaking to one packed stadium of Christians after another. But it might not be that easy.

In 2013, Tebow accepted an invitation to speak at a controversial church. Outcry was quickly and loudly heard. How could Tebow endorse this church's message by agreeing to speak there? After some thought, Tebow cancelled the engagement, saying that he "needed to avoid controversy at this time." Outcry was quickly and loudly heard. How could Tebow bend his faith to the will of the politically correct establishment?

Tim Tebow simply can't win. He's criticized for agreeing to speak and then criticized for what he doesn't say. One thing is clear: life itself is unwinnable.

In Matthew 5:21–48, Jesus makes life unwinnable. We think we can defeat adultery but must admit defeat to lust. We think we can defeat murder but must admit defeat to anger. We think we can defeat the inability to love our neighbor but must admit defeat to the requirement to love our enemies. No matter which way we go, left or right, we can never truly do what Jesus would do. He was perfect, after all. WWJD is too tall an order. We must rely on God's enlivening word in the gospel. It is God's word of grace alone that brings life out of death and victory out of defeat.

When Peter Pan tells the Darling children they can go with him to Neverland, they ask how to get there. He tells them that they'll fly. When they try and fail, Peter is puzzled. "This won't do," Peter murmurs. "What's the matter with you? All it takes is faith and trust." I could almost hear the frustrated preacher behind those words. "What's the matter with you, congregation of mine? Why aren't you doing Good Christian Thing A or Good Christian Thing B? All it takes is faith and trust!"

Most pastors, and for that matter, Christians in general, have too high a view of human ability. We are left wondering what's wrong when we try to do something and fail. We wonder why our minds drift to the same selfish or impure places day after day, despite our efforts to control them. We wonder why our relationships seem to falter when we've tried so hard to make them work.

But Peter Pan is forgetting something: "Oh! And something I forgot … dust! A little bit of pixie dust." And so, with the magic ingredient introduced into the situation, flight is possible. Sure it helps to set your mind on "the happiest things," but the pixie dust is the key. It's the fuel that makes the flight go.

In the same way, it is the Holy Spirit that makes our Christian lives possible. But unlike TinkerBell's dust, we can't grab the Holy Spirit and shake a little out. No, it's better than that. The Holy Spirit is promised as power to us, but He is not fairy dust or a magic potion. He is God! He is the third person of the all-powerful triune Godhead indwelling us, instructing us, and empowering us.

It's the Spirit that allows for flight, not the quality of our "faith and trust." Someone once said that as our opinion of human ability goes up, our reliance on Jesus goes down. Let's always remember that. A high view of ourselves gives us a low view of Jesus. But it's a low view of ourselves and what we can actually do that promotes a high view of Jesus and what He has done for us. Only the eye-opening power of the Holy Spirit can grant us this kind of gospel sanity and cause us to fly into the freedom that Jesus paid so dearly to secure for wingless people like us.

In 1 John 5:3–4 John makes what seems, on the face of it, to be a ridiculous claim: the commands of God are not burdensome. What? Has John not read the Old Testament with its 613 commandments? Was he not there for the Sermon on the Mount, complete with Jesus's proclamation that His followers are required to be perfect, just as their Father in heaven is perfect?

And as if those laws weren't burdensome enough, we could add all of the self-imposed Christian commandments, like the kinds of movies we allow ourselves to watch (maybe a swear word or two is okay, but nudity isn't), the cars we drive (we like nice things as much as the next person, but we don't want to be showy, do we?), or even the expressions on our faces (we want to be cheerful, to show people what a good life Christ has given us). We *are* burdened, perhaps more than anyone.

The idea that God's commandments are not burdensome seems diametrically opposed to our experience: they certainly feel burdensome.

And yet we do have Jesus's offer of an easy yoke and a lightened burden. He does promise rest. But how does that work? How is it that Jesus's yoke is easy when He is the One asking us to be perfect?

The answer is as simple as it is profound. Though the commandments are indeed burdensome, that burden has been laid on the shoulders of another. Jesus Christ achieves perfection in our place. Jesus Christ, the culmination of the Old Testament expectation, fulfills the Old Testament laws. That same weight that threatens to break our backs actually did crush our Savior. The weights that we bear every day are simply aftershocks of our human attempts to save ourselves. The weights we feel are a phantom. They've already been taken to the cross, carried up the Via Dolorosa on Christ's back. We are free. We are, in Christ, unburdened.

In a second-season *Frasier* episode, Frasier tries to help Sam Malone, his old friend and bartender from *Cheers*, reconcile with his fiancée, Sheila, whom he left at the altar just days before. Frasier realizes they both have infidelities in their pasts and decides, in the interest of saving their relationship, that Sam and Sheila should be honest with each other, and ask for forgiveness. "Honesty," he says, "is the cornerstone of any healthy marriage."

Sam confesses an infidelity to Sheila, and she forgives him. Sheila confesses an infidelity to Sam, and he forgives her. Everything seems to be back on track until Sheila says, "I have another one." "It's okay, don't worry about it," Sam says. "This is what it's all about—honesty and forgiveness." But then she says that it's Cliff, the frumpy mailman from the Cheers bar. "Cliff?" Sam explodes. This is over the line for him. He can't take it and storms out of the room, calling off the marriage.

Sometimes assurance of salvation eludes us because of just such a dynamic.

Like Sam, God might say, "Oh, it's okay, don't worry about your transgressions," but we'd always be worried about that one day when one of our transgressions would be a Cliff. What then? What if it stopped being okay? But God doesn't say it's okay. Paul said that God set our transgressions aside, nailing them to the cross. He paid the ultimate price, laying our sins on the shoulders of His Son. He doesn't ignore them; He pays for them.

We need never worry that when we say "we have another" indiscretion—when we add a sin to the enormous stack that separates us from God—He'll storm out of the room and call off our relationship. He has dealt with our sins forever, and cast them into the sea of forgetfulness.

A friend of mine recently told a silly story about a man standing at the gates of heaven waiting to be admitted. To the man's utter shock, Peter said, "You have to have earned a thousand points to be admitted to heaven. What have you done to earn your points?"

"I've never heard that before," said the man, "but I think I'll do all right. I was raised in a Christian home and have always been a part of the church. I have Sunday school attendance pins that go down to the floor. I went to a Christian college and graduate school and have probably led hundreds of people to Christ. I'm now an elder in my church and am quite supportive of what the people of God do. I have three children, two boys and a girl. My older boy is a pastor and the younger is a staff person with a ministry to the poor. My daughter and her husband are missionaries. I have always tithed and am now giving well over 30 percent of my income to God's work. I'm a bank executive and work with the poor in our city trying to get low-income mortgages."

"How am I doing so far?" he asked Peter.

"That's one point," Peter said. "What else have you done?"

"Good Lord," the man said in frustration. "Have mercy!"

"That's it!" Peter said. "Welcome home."

My friend who used this silly illustration ended it by saying, "Teach the law. The psalmist called it perfect. Teach it until people recognize their inability to keep it and cry out for mercy."

If heaven came down to earning points, we'd all be excluded. In fact, the place where this illustration really breaks down is that Peter gives the man any points at all. If points can be earned, then grace has no value at all. But if points are impossible to earn—and anyone who has ever tried knows that they are—then grace is imbued with surpassing value.

The law shows our failure to earn points, and grace—in the gospel of Christ—gives us all the points in the world, for free.

The emblematic sufferer Job maintained his joy and perspective in a season of suffering because he held on to a robust theology of grace. Job knew that he was not entitled to anything he had—God held the title to everything. He knew that everything he had was on loan from God—his money, his relationships, his place in society, his family. While he loved his health and children and reputation and role and wealth, he didn't locate his identity in those things.

This clearly shows that if the foundation of your identity is your things, then suffering will pull you away from the misplaced foundation of your joy. And that will make you bitterly sad. But if your identity is anchored in Christ, so that you are able to say, "Everything I need I already possess in Him," then suffering drives you deeper into your source of joy. Suffering, in other words, shows us where we are locating our identity. Our response to suffering reveals what we're building our lives on and what we're depending on to make life worth living.

This means that suffering itself does not rob you of joy—idolatry does. If you're suffering and you're angry, bitter, and joyless, it means that at some level you've idolized whatever it is you're losing. The gospel, however, frees us to revel in our expendability! The gospel alone provides us with the foundation to maintain radical joy in remarkable loss. Joylessness and bitterness in the crucible of pain happen when we lose something that we've held onto more tightly than God.

When we depend on anything smaller than God to provide us with the security, significance, meaning, and value that we long for, God will love us enough to take it away. Much of our pain, therefore, is God prying open our hands and taking away something we've held onto more tightly than Him. And when that happens, it may seem like He's killing us, but He's actually setting us free.

Casuistry is a fancy theological word that means something like "the search for special cases." It exists by necessity: the law abounds, and so we humans—who are born lawyers—are compelled to search for ways to get around it. In fact, one might argue that casuistry makes up the bulk of a lawyer's job description. A client is accused of some manner of law breaking, and the lawyer attempts to find a reason that, in at least this one instance, the law breaking was justified. We humans do this all the time.

There are a million examples of casuistry in the world: Lying is wrong … unless the truth will hurt someone's feelings. Stealing is wrong … unless it is from a big, faceless corporation. You get the idea.

We engage in the casuistic exercise because we are desperate to justify ourselves. If we find an instance in which we are out of line (and therefore not "justified"), we scramble for a reason. "I didn't claim that income on my tax return because it would have required a lot of paperwork and it was only, like, five dollars over the limit anyway." Casuistry comes from the desire to never have to throw oneself on the mercy of the court and beg for a savior. Casuistry is a problem, then, for the same reason that anything that keeps us self-reliant is a problem: it clouds our ability to see ourselves as profoundly needy.

The more seemingly successful we are in our casuistic enterprise, the longer we will hold on to our apparent ability to save ourselves. But this is a ruse, a fake. Making up reasons that our situations are tenable is not a long-term solution. It is much better to shout out for help now knowing there is a God of grace on the other end waiting to rescue us and set us free. He will not justify our sin; in fact, He'll punish it. But He will justify us, punishing His Son for our sin. We probably can't figure out the casuistry of the gospel, and that's okay. Grace is its own radical logic. It doesn't make sense; but it does make us secure.

Royce White was a great college basketball player who struggled with a serious anxiety disorder. His anxiety is greatly exacerbated by flying, and so there were many people who wondered whether or not he could function as an NBA player, with the huge amounts of plane travel involved. He was drafted and immediately began having problems. As of 2014, he was out of the league. While he was still a member of the Houston Rockets, however, he gave an interview to Chuck Klosterman in which he had some very interesting things to say about the human condition. Here's a tiny piece of it:

> **RW:** The majority is mentally ill, and we should base all our policies around the idea of supporting the mentally ill because they're the majority of people. But if we keep thinking of them as a minority, we can say, "You stay over there and deal with your problems over there."
>
> **CK:** OK, just so I get this right: you're arguing that *most* Americans have a mental illness.
>
> **RW:** Exactly. That's definitely correct.
>
> **CK:** But—if that's true—wouldn't that mean "mental illness" is just a normative condition? That it's just how people are?
>
> **RW:** That doesn't make it normal. This is based on science. If there was a flu epidemic, and 60 percent of the country had the flu, it wouldn't make it normal.

White has hit on something here, something that Christians have always known. Despite Klosterman's seeming confusion, what White is talking about is an idea as old as humanity itself: original sin. Humans all have a problem, and even though it's spread evenly throughout the entire population, it's still a problem. In other words, it's normative and problematic.

We like to think that it's mostly those "other" people who have a problem. It comforts us to be able to shunt them over to a corner to deal with the problems that we claim we don't have. No one is free of sin. But praise God! We have a Savior who only rescues sick people because sick people are all that there are.

In an interview shortly following the release of *The Social Network*, Conan O'Brien asked Jesse Eisenberg (who played Facebook founder Mark Zuckerberg in the film) if his life had changed in any way since the movie had come out. Eisenberg's somewhat cryptic answer was, "I have a lot more cats."

Here's the story: Jesse Eisenberg has always liked cats, so he's on a list of cat adopters—people who make themselves available as caretakers for strays—and his apartment is basically a cat boardinghouse. He said that it's full of cat food, cat litter, and nothing else. What's really interesting, though, is why the movie star is still doing it, and why a successful film leads to more cats. The answer? Guilt! Eisenberg said that he feels guilty for having such success in movies, and so he cares for abandoned cats. The more success he had, the more cats he adopted. More popular movie? More cats. The result? Some potentially (and temporarily) expiated guilt and a house full of cats!

Expiation is a theological word that refers to the process of making amends. In the Old Testament, sacrifices served as expiation for sins. Many people handle their expiation—something we all have to do to help us sleep at night—like Eisenberg does. They try to do good things to outweigh the bad things.

Isn't it great, though, that we have a God who accepted one expiation for every sin, and who doesn't require that we keep punishing ourselves by filling our homes with animals who think they're smarter than us? Jesus Christ is the once-and-for-all expiation for the sins of the world.

Today, remember that you don't have to pay God back for His gracious gift to you. Jesus Christ is our expiation, and His cry from the cross—that "it is finished"—means that our guilt has been atoned for once and for all. Amen!

The apostle Peter would not have made a good pastor. I can just imagine him sitting in his office, feet up on a chair, when distraught parishioners keep coming in. "Peter! My husband is leaving me!" "My kid won't return my phone calls!" "My mother is in the hospital!" "I got laid off!" Peter probably wouldn't even take his feet off the chair: "Beloved, do not be surprised at the fiery ordeal that is taking place. Nothing strange is happening to you. Rejoice! You are sharing Christ's sufferings!" (author's paraphrase).

Now this seems to be the worst kind of response to someone in pain. "Suffering? Relax! It's no surprise … actually, you should be happy!" As insensitive as this sounds, don't let yourself think that Peter isn't following the example of God Himself.

Consider the crucifixion. When Jesus told the disciples that He was going to be arrested, tried, convicted, and executed, Peter said, "Never!" And Jesus's response was, "Get behind me, Satan." Remember, God works *sub contrario*—"under the opposite"—of where we think He will be. He worked in the crucifixion to save us. He worked in Peter's abandonment and denial to restore him, and He works in our struggles and in our hurt to give us joy.

Jesus told His followers that in this life they will have struggles. "But," He said "take heart! I have overcome the world" (John 16:33). He didn't say that things would get better, although we wish He would (and sometimes things do). He simply said that He has overcome the world.

We suffer, but we never suffer alone. Jesus said that He came for the sick. The healthy have no need of Him. We never suffer alone. And our suffering, stinging though it may be, not only has an end, its end has already been assured. "The God of all grace, who called you to his eternal glory in Christ … will himself restore you and make you strong, firm and steadfast" (1 Pet. 5:10).

Remember today that you never suffer alone.

Paul spoke of our "having been buried with him [with Christ] in baptism," in which we "were also raised with him through faith in the powerful working of God, who raised him from the dead" (v. 12 ESV). Our old identity—the things that previously "made us"—has been put to death. Our new identity is "in Christ." We've been raised with Christ to walk "in newness of life"—no longer needing to depend on the "old things" to make us who we are.

Out of some very real incidents in mid-twentieth-century history comes the story that is now modern lore. Many years after the end of World War II, it was discovered that a lone Japanese soldier still occupied a Pacific island, harassing and attacking anyone who ever approached. He was considered a wild man, a crazy hermit of sorts but very dangerous. This fellow had never heard that the war was over, that his side had surrendered. Thus, he lived according to the old reality. He wasn't enjoying the peace coming from his side's defeat. He kept soldiering on, still warring according to his old identity.

Similarly, too many Christians continue living as if the death of sin is ultimately up to them. Or just as sadly, they continue on in sinful patterns of living, not realizing that they are living according to their old nature, not their new. This is why when Paul confronted Peter about his hypocrisy, he said that Peter was "not in step with the truth of the gospel" (Gal. 2:14 ESV). Peter was living as if the "old things" were still in effect and the new things had not come.

If you're a Christian, here's the good news: you're free! Now you can spend your life giving up your place for others instead of guarding it from others, because your identity is in Christ, not your place.

Now you can spend your life going to the back instead of getting to the front, because your identity is in Christ, not your position.

Now you can spend your life giving, not taking, because your identity is in Christ, not your possessions.

All this is our new identity—all because of Christ's finished work declared to us in the gospel.

David Gelb's 2011 documentary, *Jiro Dreams of Sushi*, is an interesting illustration of law and grace. Jiro Ono, the film's subject, is a master sushi chef whose restaurant is, according to a food critic interviewed in the film, the most expensive restaurant in the world.

Jiro relentlessly pursues the perfect piece of sushi. He has a routine and follows it religiously every day, even so far as to board the commuter train from the same point on the platform. However, this pursuit is offset by his knowledge that actual perfection will remain out of his reach. He acknowledges that just when you think you know everything, something happens to remind you how much more there is to know and how much more work needs to be done.

This is quite reminiscent of God's law and its demand for perfection, which is always beyond our reach. Ironically, and graciously, it is in our acknowledgment of our failure to live up to the law, whether it be the law of perfect sushi or perfect righteousness, that we can actually find true freedom.

Jiro's son Yoshikazu remains at Jiro's restaurant as a sous chef despite being fifty years old, because in Japan it is expected that the elder son will stay with the father and take over his position. Yoshikazu, of course, is in the unenviable position of following in a master's footsteps. One of Jiro's former apprentices notes that when Jiro does retire, even if Yoshikazu's sushi is the equal of his father's, it will be seen as inferior and that it will only be seen as equal if it is, in fact, twice as good. Again we come up against the face of the unyielding law. There is literally nothing Yoshikazu can do to fulfill the expectation that is placed on him.

In a happy postscript, it seems as though Yoshikazu may have gotten his miracle: it turns out that every time the Michelin inspectors ate at Jiro's restaurant in the first year, it was Yoshikazu who made their sushi. There is a gospel note in this "mistaken identity," if we have the eyes to see it, because when our heavenly Father makes His judgment on the quality of our righteousness, He judges us by the work of *His* Son. By grace, Christ's righteousness becomes my justification, and I'm now regarded not simply "just-as-if-I'd" never sinned, but "just-as-if-I'd" always obeyed!

Is preaching the gospel of grace really the means by which God will save licentious people? Or to put it another way, is preaching grace what our relativistic and morally lax culture really needs? I mean, surely God doesn't think that the saving solution for the immoral and rebellious is His free grace. That doesn't make sense. It seems backward. Given our restraint-free cultural context, what does make sense to me is that preachers in our day should be very wary of talking about grace at all. In fact, it seems logical to me that the only way to "save" licentious people is to more forcefully exhort them to behave.

The Bible, though, makes it clear that the power that saves even the worst rule-breaking sinner is the gospel (Rom. 1:16), and not the law (Rom. 7:13–24). As if that weren't enough, there's another reason why preaching the gospel of free grace is both necessary and effective even at a time when moral laxity reigns supreme: moralism is what most people outside the church think Christianity is all about. Unbelievers generally think the message of the church is "Behave!"

People believe that God is most interested in people becoming good instead of people coming to terms with how bad they really are so they'll fix their eyes on Christ, "the author and perfecter of faith" (Heb. 12:2 NASB). From a human standpoint, this is precisely why many people outside the church reject Christianity and why many people inside the church conk out: they're just not good enough to get it done over the long haul.

Paul was accused on more than one occasion of preaching lawlessness and in Romans 6, he answers the assumption that preaching grace produces licentiousness, not by backing off of the gospel, but by preaching the gospel even more. I imagine it would have been tempting for Paul to put the brakes on grace and give the law in this passage, but instead he gives more grace. Paul knows that licentious people aren't those who believe the gospel of God's free grace too much, but too little.

There is an all-important distinction Christians must make between horizontal consequences of sin and vertical condemnation for sin.

When a Christian friend falls into sin, lots of people confuse these two categories, which results in two basic responses. Some people question their friend's salvation: "How could anybody really be a Christian and do something like that?" Others say, "Just let it go. After all, nobody is perfect. Don't we believe in grace and forgiveness?"

The first group needs to be reminded that God's love for us and acceptance of us does not in any way depend on what we do or don't do but rather on what Jesus has done. Who we are before God is firmly anchored in Jesus's accomplishment, not ours.

The second group needs to be reminded that consequences on the ground of life are real. Real people make real mistakes that require real action to be taken. So for instance, we can talk bad about our boss without sacrificing one ounce of God's acceptance, because before God, our sin has been atoned for, our guilt has been removed (Isa. 6:7). But we might still lose our job. We can make the mistake of driving one hundred miles per hour without losing a bit of God's love for us, because nothing can separate us from the love of God in Christ Jesus. But we might still lose our license.

When we confuse consequences with condemnation and vice versa, we don't know how to make sense of things when our brother or sister makes a big mistake.

The truth is that when we are in the throes of consequences for foolish things we do, our only hope is to remember that "there is therefore now no condemnation for those who are in Christ Jesus" (Rom. 8:1 ESV). In fact, the kind of suffering that comes from the consequences of sin is like a brushfire that burns away every thread of hope we have in ourselves and leaves only the thread of divine grace—a thread that will never break no matter how foolish we may be.

In the Bible "law" does not always mean the same thing.

For example, in Psalm 40:8 we read: "I delight to do your will, O my God; your law is within my heart" (ESV). Here the law is synonymous with God's revealed will. A Christian seeking to express their love for God and neighbor delights in those passages that declare what God's will is. When, however, Paul told Christians that they are no longer under the law (Rom. 6:14), he obviously meant more by law than the revealed will of God. He was talking there about Christians being free from the curse of the law, not needing to depend on adherence to the law to establish our relationship to God: "Christ is the end of the law for righteousness to everyone who believes" (Rom. 10:4 ESV).

The reason Paul said that Christ is the end of the law in this sense is because, in the gospel, God unconditionally gives the righteousness that the law demands conditionally. So Christ kicks the law out of the conscience by overcoming the voice of condemnation produced by the condition of the law. In other words, the conditional voice that says, "Do this and live" gets outvolumed by the unconditional voice that says, "It is finished."

When this happens, we are freed from the condemnation of the law's conditionality (the law loses its "teeth") and are therefore free to hear the law's content as a description of what it looks like to love God and neighbor. But every day in various ways we disobey and stubbornly serve ourselves rather than others, thereby "submitting ourselves once again to a yoke of slavery." And when we do, it is the gospel that brings comfort by reminding us that God's love for us doesn't depend on what we do (or fail to do) but on what Christ has done for us. Jesus fulfilled all of God's holy conditions so that our relationship to God could be wholly unconditional. "There is therefore now no condemnation for those who are in Christ Jesus" (Rom. 8:1 ESV).

For a long time, I found Ray Lewis's persona, both on the field and off, to be oppressively distasteful. He seemed so boastful and hugely self-absorbed.

Also, in 2000 he lied to police in an attempt to impede a murder investigation, an investigation in which Lewis himself was implicated.

For many years, I used this information to justify my dislike of Lewis. Sure, some of that dislike came from his self-aggrandizement, but a lot of it came from my belief that he was a criminal who got away with a plea bargain. These feelings came to the surface again several years ago during the national discussion about whether or not Michael Vick, who was convicted of running a dog-fighting operation, should be allowed to play in the NFL again. It angered me that Lewis was never so much as suspended, while there was sentiment that Vick shouldn't ever be allowed to play again.

My ability to feel good about myself requires people to exist in the world who are worse than I am. Ray Lewis filled that role for a time. If I can't say that I'm better than Ray Lewis, who am I? What value do I have?

Then I met Ray Lewis. I was invited to do a chapel for the Baltimore Ravens and then have dinner with the team afterward. My two boys accompanied me, and I'll never forget the way Ray buddied up to Gabe and Nate. Soft-spoken. Kind. Funny. Didn't talk about himself and asked them questions about life and sports. As I watched the way he interacted with my boys, Ray won my heart.

Ray Lewis, by all accounts, has completely reformed his life since the incident in 2000. He is a devout Christian, a pillar of his community, and a mentor to many young men. His is a story of redemption, and such stories are what we, the redeemed, should be cheering. The fact is, I'm not better than Ray Lewis. We share an incapacitating compulsion to selfishness and sin, and we share in a regenerating love of a Savior infinitely better than both of us.

There are two kinds of stories that we hear in our lives, and one of them is much more prevalent than the other. We could call them the human story and the God story. John calls them "the testimony of men" and "the testimony of God." Perhaps most simply, they could be called the law story and the grace story.

The law story, unfortunately, is the prevalent one. You know this story well. It'll probably be the dominant story you deal with today. This-for-that, tit-for-tat, you-scratch-my-back, I'll-scratch-yours—all of these things typify the law story. The law story is the one you must familiarize yourself with and participate in if you want to get ahead in life.

If you want to be the one to get the promotion at work, you tailor your output to what will catch your supervisor's eye. You might do a favor for someone with the expectation that, should the need arise, they'll do a favor for you in the future. You might be willing to say something that you don't really believe in order to be seen in a certain light.

The God story, however—the grace story—isn't like this at all. Since God has already given us everything we need in Christ—all the affirmation, all the value, all the significance—we don't have to get any of those things from other people. That means we don't have to worry about scratching their backs in order to have ours scratched; our backs have been scratched in Christ, so we can find ourselves free to serve our neighbors without regard for what we might get in return.

Here's the good news: the God story always trumps the human story. The law is the way of the world—the people in your office will never let you forget it—but grace is not of this world. That's the truest testimony according to John: "God gave us eternal life, and this life is in his Son" (v. 11 ESV).

Anyone who went to high school knows about letter jackets. It was the thing all the jocks had and the thing they wore at every opportunity. I remember the practice of girls wearing their boyfriend's letter jackets. It was the easiest way to tell who was dating whom.

The most interesting thing about letter jackets, though, is what happens to them after graduation. In other words, where do letter jackets go to die? If there's one ironclad rule about letter jackets, it's that you can't wear them after you're out of high school. There's nothing lamer than holding on to past coolness.

In the brilliant sitcom *Community*, the jock character, Troy, is getting made fun of at community college for wearing his high school letter jacket. As he puts it to his friend Jeff: "People have been clowning me about this jacket since I got here, but if I take it off to make them happy, that just makes me weak, right?" Jeff's answer is wise: "Listen, it doesn't matter. You lose the jacket to please them; you keep it to piss them off. Either way, it's for them. *That's* what's weak."

This is a gorgeous illustration of the inescapability of the law. Whether we struggle to obey the law or we reject it, we are under its power. Think of your parents: whether you are just like them or are committed to being nothing like them, they are still the ones influencing you. Paul wrote, "Do not be deceived: God cannot be mocked" (Gal. 6:7). In other words, don't think you can avoid the reach of the law. You can run toward it or away from it, but it still controls you. There is no escape.

Well, there is one escape. When Paul wondered who would rescue him from "this body of death"—the inescapable reality of the law—he immediately turned to his Savior. "Thanks be to God," he said, "for Jesus Christ my Lord" (Rom. 7:24–25).

One of the marks of a truly maturing Christian is that he or she begins to love the things God loves and hate the things God hates. In this regard, the law (all of the imperatives we find in the Bible) guides us well and wisely. It tells us what God wants and who God is. Yes, the law is good.

But while the law guides, it does not give. To be sure, the Spirit does use the whole Word in our sanctification—the law as well as the gospel. But the law and the gospel do different things in sanctification. The law has the ability to reveal sin but not the ability to remove sin. It points to righteousness but can't produce it. Let me stress again that this is not a matter of whether obedience to God's law is important to us or to God. Of course it's important. The question is: Where does the power to obey God's commands come from? Does it come from the gospel—from what God has done for us? Or does it come from the law—from what we must do?

Paul lays out the intensity of his struggle in Romans 7 to make it clear that although the law can no longer condemn us (because Jesus has kept it perfectly on our behalf), it's still unable to produce in us the desire to keep it. It can only tell us what God requires, which it does. But the law is not the gospel.

We must understand the precise role the law plays for us today. The law now serves us by showing us how to love God and others, and when we fail to keep it, the gospel brings comfort by reminding us that God's infinite approval doesn't depend on our keeping of the law but on Christ's keeping of the law on our behalf. And guess what? This makes me want to obey Him more, not less.

Therefore, it's the gospel (what Jesus has done) that alone can give God-honoring animation to our obedience. The power to obey comes from being moved and motivated by the completed work of Jesus for us. The fuel to do good flows from what's already been done.

Are you concerned you're not giving enough money to your church? You should be! Consider Jesus's interaction with a rich young man in Mark 10:17. The man asks Jesus what he must do to be saved—a question that we all ask ourselves with regularity. But far from talking about faith in God or dependence on Himself, Jesus talks to the man about his money. The man who wants to know how to be saved says he's been keeping all the commandments since his youth. He's basically telling Jesus that those things are easy, child's play, even.

"'One thing you lack,' [Jesus] said. 'Go, sell everything you have and give to the poor, and you will have treasure in heaven. Then come, follow me'" (v. 21). Mark says that the man was shocked to hear this, "and went away grieving, for he had many possessions" (v. 22 NRSV).

When we think about how to be a good steward, we often use the tithe, or 10 percent of income, as the standard of good stewardship.

But Jesus doesn't ask the rich man for 10 percent. He doesn't ask him for 25 percent. He doesn't even ask him for 50 percent. He asks him for everything! Apparently for Jesus, the standard for good stewardship is nothing less than every stitch of clothing on your back and every stick of furniture in your house. You have to give everything away.

We might well echo the disciples, who, upon hearing this, whispered to one another, "Then who can be saved?" Jesus's response contains some of the most comforting words in all of Scripture: "With man this is impossible, but not with God; all things are possible with God" (v. 27).

The standard of good stewardship is too high. So with the pressure to be good removed, think about what you actually *want* to give. Just know, as you consider your giving of your time, talent, and your treasure, your relationship with God is secure in the gift of Jesus Christ, not in the size of your pledge. The righteousness God requires cannot be achieved. It can only be received. And thankfully it is given to the unrighteous for free.

While the gospel is very big and very multifaceted, I fear that some believers tend to make it a sort of catch-all word for anything that has to do with God. The most common way I've heard it misused is in the context of the phrase "living out the gospel." What people generally mean by this is "doing good things for other people." So the gospel must be translated, in this instance, to "good things for others." I submit to you that this is a gross misunderstanding of what the gospel is.

First of all, *gospel* is a word that comes from an old English translation of the Greek word *euangelion*, which means "good news." More specifically, the gospel is an announcement. But it has to be a good announcement. The announcement that you must "love the Lord your God with all your heart, soul, mind, and strength" is news, but it's not particularly good if you're a human being like me. Historically, Christians have defined the gospel as the announcement that Jesus has died to save sinners. So the phrase "living out the gospel" makes no sense when the gospel is understood in this way: an announcement of good news.

If you watch newscasts, you know you can't "live out" the news. You can react to it, certainly, and knowledge of it may well influence the things you do. The gospel is the same way. It will, no doubt, impact your life. But that impact is not the gospel. It can't be. It's the impact of the gospel. And it should be noted that the gospel itself does not demand a certain response. It makes no demands at all. Remember, it is an announcement. Hearers of the gospel, from the apostle Paul to the atheist Richard Dawkins, have recommended responses, but again, these responses are not the gospel.

The gospel is that Jesus has died to save sinners like me, and like you.

The *Wall Street Journal* ran a piece in the wake of Lance Armstrong's confession to using performance-enhancing drugs called "Behind Lance Armstrong's Decision to Talk," which describes a meeting between Armstrong and Travis Tygart, the head of the United States Anti-Doping Agency, the man who finally caught up with Armstrong's deception. In that meeting, Armstrong pointed to himself and said, "You don't hold the keys to my redemption. There's one person who holds the keys to my redemption, and that's me." The fascinating thing about this quote isn't the brazenness; it's the common nature of the refrain.

Everyone thinks that their redemption is up to them. Except, maybe, for Travis Tygart. Upon hearing Armstrong's claim, Tygart allegedly responded, "That's [expletive]." Tygart is right: the idea that we hold the keys to our own redemption is total [expletive].

That Armstrong might believe that baring his soul (or, at least, the contents of his medicine cabinet) to Oprah would lead to his redemption is, at worst, cynical in the extreme and, at best, evidence of a woefully weak definition of redemption.

When Christians talk about redemption, we don't refer to a return to a prior state of good standing. Some do, actually, but such thinking, as Gerhard Forde points out in his book *On Being a Theologian of the Cross*, hinges on the unbiblical notion of a "fall." We imagine that we were once at a certain place in our relationship with God, we messed that up, and Jesus gave us the ability to get back. That is, according to Forde, a theology that "uses" Jesus and the cross to "get" us something, rather than one that sees Jesus and the cross as the end of us, and our resurrection. The truth is so much better. In our redemption—in real redemption—we are saved to a state higher than we ever had before: we are regarded as one with Christ, as God's own Son.

How do we please God? According to the prophet Micah, the answer is actually very simple: act justly, love mercy, and walk humbly with Him.

Micah cut through all of the God-pleasing practices that were going on at the time and gets right down to the heart of the matter: You want to know how to please God? Don't give Him the usual sacrifices: rams, oil, firstborn children, or even your own body. You really want to please God? Merely act justly, love mercy, and walk humbly with your God.

Years later, it'll be said in a different way: "Love the Lord your God with all your heart and with all your soul and with all your strength and with all your mind; and love your neighbor as yourself" (Luke 10:27). Different words, same message: pleasing God is about these simple things: act justly, love mercy, walk humbly with God (v. 8). Simple, right? Of course, God has spent the years between Adam and Eve and John the Baptist being displeased with His chosen people. They rarely do what He wants. They always complain. They have not acted justly. They have not loved mercy. They have not walked humbly with their God.

Apparently, being told *how* to please God doesn't make us any more able to do it. And guess what? We proudly continue our ancestors' tradition. Act justly? Love mercy? Walk humbly with our God? This life we're living, if we're honest, is far from the perfection that God requires to be fully pleased.

Many Christians believe that the good news is that Jesus enables them to please God. And He does. But the real good news is so much better than that! If that's the good news, then I've got great news: Jesus perfectly pleased God for us. God did not tell Jesus, "You are My Son, the Beloved; You will give these others the ability to please Me." No. He said, "*You* are My Son. With *You* I am pleased." For those who are united to Christ and clothed in His perfect robe of righteousness, God is pleased with you.

In one episode of *The Simpsons*, Lady Gaga comes to Springfield. She's not planning to, but her joyful train only stops in town after Gaga notices what a sad and depressing place Springfield is (a billboard reads, "Springfield: The Little Town That Can't—and Won't"). All Springfield needs, she figures, is a dose of the Gaga magic.

"Never forget, you're all my little monsters," coos Gaga. "You should love yourself as much as I love you. Because …" and then she breaks into song:

> *When they're young, all little monsters learn that they are scary*
> *Ugly, stupid, shunned by cupid, overweight and hairy*
> *But every monster needs to find the secret deep inside*
> *That transforms Dr. Jekyll into sexy Mr. Hyde.*
> *All my monsters are so beautiful …*
> *Monsters don't need implants or [an awesome] monster car*
> *Monsters only need to love the monsters that they are.*

When she's finished singing her ode to self-love to the gathered residents of Springfield, she breathlessly asks, "Does everybody love themselves?" Someone in the crowd says, "That kind of thing sounds hollow coming from anyone but you!"

With that one sarcastic sentence, *The Simpsons* writers put the lie to Gaga's rhetoric. Of course her song is hollow: if loving oneself were so easy, we'd all do it. Immediately. Later in the episode, Lisa Simpson loudly denounces Gaga on the school playground: "I denounce thee! I denounce thee for giving people ambitions they cannot fulfill, [and] for positing a world where social acceptance and walking on heels are easy! I denounce thee, I denounce thee, I denounce thee!"

The world has no answer for the people who try and fail. Gaga suggests that we fall in love with our Mr. Hyde, but even a child like Lisa Simpson knows that that's worthless. Jesus does have an answer. Jesus *is* the answer. His saving deliverance is what we need.

What should a farmer do with a fig tree that doesn't bear figs? Well, he should cut it down, right? That ground can be used for some better use, some plant that will actually bear fruit. When Jesus tells the parable of the barren fig tree, though, the tree has an advocate. A vinedresser speaks up for the tree and offers to personally care for it for a year. He tells the owner of the vineyard that if there are still no figs next year, he will cut down the tree.

Don't you get the feeling that the vinedresser knows better? He knows that with some love and attention, that tree is going to bear fruit. Some people see only the law in this little parable: if you don't bear fruit, you risk being thrown out of the garden. Have you ever felt this way? That God is the owner of the vineyard and He comes around every day to inspect the fruit that you are—or aren't—producing? Are you terrified that, one day, you'll be found lacking and cast out of the garden? These are very common sentiments. It's important to note, though, that this isn't what happens in the story.

In the story, the vinedresser intercedes for the barren fig tree. On its own, the tree isn't going to bear fruit, and really will be thrown out of the garden. But with the careful attention of this gardener, the tree will do fine.

Under the law, we are all barren fig trees. Our fears that our fruit will be insufficient are well founded. But we can cast our hope on the vinedresser, Jesus Christ. He steps in and takes personal responsibility for us. Whatever fruit we bear is, according to Paul in Galatians 5:22–23, the "fruit of the Spirit," which he contrasts with the barrenness we bring to the table.

Today, remember that presence of fruit in your life is not your doing and that you, therefore, cannot take credit for it. But it's also true that the absence of fruit in your life is not something that can separate you from God's love.

In his *Commentary on Galatians*, Martin Luther makes a beautiful observation in response to Paul's letter-opening prayer, "Grace and peace to you from God our Father and the Lord Jesus Christ" (v. 3). Luther says that Paul chose those words carefully, and that those "two words [grace and peace] contain all that belong to Christianity." He says that "grace forgives sin, and peace makes the conscience quiet."

Despite our efforts to achieve peace through a host of other methods—sound financial planning, righteous behavior, whatever—Luther contends that Paul's claim is that true peace can only come through grace. He says elsewhere that our "quest for glory can never be satisfied. It must be extinguished." In other words, there is no plane to which you could ascend at which you couldn't imagine being more peaceful. The grass is always greener, and all that.

The fact is that, because of Christ's saving work, we actually have been given peace through grace. Luther goes on to say that although the words are simple, "during temptation, to be convinced in our hearts that we have forgiveness of sins and peace with God by grace alone is the hardest thing." And this is true to human Christian experience, right? When faced with a situation, to accept that our standing with God is secure even if we make the wrong choice is next to impossible. This is why our consciences are so often troubled. We just flat out can't really believe that God will be graceful to us, and we therefore cannot have peace.

This is why it is important for Paul to begin his letter by wishing the Galatians grace and peace through God and Jesus Christ. This is why it's important for all of us to hear it every week, every day, every minute.

Today, let us begin with grace and peace. Peace is the thing that, left to our own devices, we would spend all of today seeking. Instead, let us remember that, in Christ, true peace is already ours, through grace.

Psalm 40 was made popular by King David long before it was made popular by U2. "I waited patiently for the LORD; he inclined to me and heard my cry" (v. 1 ESV). This is the first step in a beautiful, poetic, and short description of the story of God's action in human life. This is the trademark of human life—waiting and crying. That might sound dark to some, but to those who have lived through it, who are familiar with grief, struggle, and tribulation, the poet has connected to our very core with his first lines.

"I waited patiently for the LORD; he inclined to me and heard my cry." The poet suggests a God who hears our cries and then springs into action. It's much more than a sympathetic ear: He stoops to us.

As is so often the case, however, God goes above and beyond. He doesn't merely stoop to hear our cries; He rescues us from our despair.

"He drew me up from the pit of destruction, out of the miry bog, and set my feet upon a rock, making my steps secure. He put a new song in my mouth, a song of praise to our God" (vv. 2–3 ESV). Here, the poet is describing the profound *result* of the human interaction with God. As always, just as it is God who stoops to those of us who cry, God is again the actor here. *He* drew me up ... *He* set my feet ... *He* made my steps ... *He* put a new song in my mouth. Our action is to wait and to cry. God's action is to stoop down and rescue. We go from existing in the pit of destruction and the mud of the swamp, to having our feet set on a rock, our footsteps firm, and with a new song on our lips.

On an episode of the TV show *The Big Bang Theory*, Sheldon discovers that Penny has gotten him a Christmas present. Angered, he reminds Penny that the "foundation of gift giving is reciprocity" and that she hasn't given him a gift, she's given him "an obligation." He says that he now has to go out and purchase for her "a gift of commensurate value and representing the same perceived level of friendship" as that represented by the gift she's given him.

His solution is to purchase three gift baskets (of various sizes) of bath products. His plan is to see what her gift to him is, excuse himself from the room, give her the appropriate gift basket, and return the other two baskets to the store. What happens, though, is that Penny has gotten Sheldon a napkin that Leonard Nimoy has used and autographed. Sheldon notes that he now not only has Nimoy's signature, he has his DNA.

After excusing himself, Sheldon returns with all three gift baskets, barely able to carry the weight. "I know, I know," he wails. "It's not enough!"

And that's the problem, isn't it? We don't know how to react when we get really good gifts. When the gift is *that* good, no response is good enough. Certainly a plain "thank you" won't cut it. There is no bath product cornucopia that can balance the scales when Leonard Nimoy's DNA is on the other side, and there doesn't seem to be an adequate response when Jesus's death for our sins holds that place, either.

Many of us Christians spend our lives trying to reciprocate for Jesus's gift to adequately say thank you. But if we turn a big enough gift into an obligation, we are crushed by it.

Let's acknowledge from the beginning, then, that this is a gift that tips the scales forever. Let's treat the gift like a child would, with excitement and joy, and go play, remembering that even our most heartfelt gratitude is not commensurate with His life-giving gift—liberating us from the impossible burden of repayment.

The Israelites are in the middle of their years wandering in the desert, looking for the Promised Land, and they're getting impatient. They complain about the lack of good food and water, and they wish they'd never left Egypt in the first place. God, hearing their complaints, sends poisonous serpents among them, and many of the Israelites get bitten and die.

Ah, the joys of the Old Testament. Am I right? Complain about how God's treating you? Here are some poisonous snakes! So the people come back to Moses and they say:

> "We have sinned by speaking against the LORD and against you; pray to the LORD to take away the serpents from us." So Moses prayed for the people. And the LORD said to Moses, "Make a poisonous serpent, and set it on a pole; and everyone who is bitten shall look at it and live." So Moses made a serpent of bronze, and put it upon a pole; and whenever a serpent bit someone, that person would look at the serpent of bronze and live. (vv. 7–9, NRSV)

There are a lot of foreshadowing elements in this story. Jesus references it in John 3 when He says that He, too, must be lifted up. In the same way that the elevation of the snake on a pole is the avenue for the Israelites' salvation, Jesus's hanging on a cross is the way in which eternal salvation comes to the world.

A particularly fascinating thing about this story is that God chooses the serpent to be the image lifted up on the pole—the very thing that is killing the people. Again, He is foreshadowing the final act of His plan of salvation. Jesus, who knew no sin, became sin on the cross so that we might become the righteousness of God. The very thing that is killing us—sin—is laid on Jesus and lifted up on the cross. The bringer of death—the serpents and the cross—becomes the way of life.

Today, know that Jesus took your sin onto Himself and gave you His righteousness, so that you might live, and live forever.

What people *want* to hear from a religion and what they *need* to hear are two very different things. I want to hear that I am fundamentally good, fundamentally in control, and fundamentally on the right track. I also want to hear that the problems I experience in my life are the result of outside forces and can be overcome by following a short number of simple steps. In essence, I want to hear that it's all good, and that if I start feeling life becoming less good, I can easily right the ship.

I don't think it's any coincidence that many large churches in America proclaim this kind of message. Tell people what they want to hear, then the people and the money roll in.

The problem with this "what I want" refrain is that it can't actually help me. When my life starts sliding off the rails, it's all well and good to go to the handy self-help manual (Ten Steps to Financial Security, Eight Steps to Recovered Relationships, or the like), but it becomes decidedly less "well and good" if the manual lets me down. What happens when I follow the ten steps and still find myself financially insecure? Or when I follow the eight steps and they only serve to further alienate my family?

As it turns out, I need something different than what I want. I need the truth.

What people need to hear from religion is an accurate diagnosis of their condition. Wanted Religion can't offer a profound solution because it refuses to diagnose a profound disease. Needed Religion recognizes our plight and can offer a weighty cure: a Savior who substitutes Himself for us.

It will probably always be true that Wanted Religion will rake in the money; it's offering a much more desirable front end. Needed Religion, however, will be there when the bankrupt devotees of Wanted Religion need somewhere to turn and have no money left to buy their way in.

Today, revel in a God who gives us what we need: a Savior.

On April 12, 2012, Philip Humber (who had never even pitched eight innings of a major league outing) pitched a perfect game. That is, he retired twenty-seven batters in a row, three up and three down, every inning for nine innings. No walks, no hits. Only eighteen other men in the 108-year history of Major League Baseball have accomplished the feat. In November of that same year, his team cut him, making him available to any team in the league. What happened?

In an interview with *Sports Illustrated*, Humber tried to explain it. The article is subtitled: "For one magical April afternoon, Philip Humber was flawless. But that random smile from the pitching gods came with a heavy burden: the pressure to live up to a standard no one can meet."

The ladder of perfection has no top rung. There is no platform upon which we can finally rest. Whether our goal is to be a good father, a good Christian, or a good pitcher, each exemplary act carries with it the expectation (the requirement) of another. And another. "Being like Christ" is not like throwing a perfect game. It is like throwing perfect games every day of your life, while never being proud of the fact that you're throwing perfect games.

The quest for glory, the chasing of perfection, killed Humber's season. He never regained the form that mowed down all those hitters, and his team eventually gave up on him. In order to move on, Humber had to give up, admitting that "he's done chasing perfection. He's done trying to be the pitcher with the magical fastball and the unhittable slider. He knows he's a 30-year-old pitcher with a fading heater and a curveball that doesn't bite like it once did, and he accepts that."

Humber came to grips with his limitations, the truth about himself. He knows that, in order to be a good pitcher, he has to let perfection go. Let's remind ourselves daily, hourly, and by the minute that we can let perfection go, because it is a mantle that Christ has taken up for us.

In a 2010 interview with Stephen Colbert, reggae legend Jimmy Cliff was asked if he was currently a member of a religion. He answered, "No, I've graduated from them." Colbert asked, incredulously, "You've graduated from religion?" and Cliff said, "Yes." Colbert then said that God is sitting up in heaven when we graduate from this life with a scorecard, and asked Cliff which scorecard (Christian, Muslim, Jew, etc.) he wanted to be graded on. Cliff said he would like to be graded on the scorecard of "truth and facts." Colbert's inspired response? "I'll take faith and grace."

Jimmy Cliff has decided to "graduate" from religion and wants to be assessed on truth and facts. Well, what are the facts? What is the truth? When the requirements are things like all of God's holy commandments, beginning just with the great Ten Commandments, the real truth would reveal that we're not doing so well. We can't graduate if we can't pass the class.

To be judged on the scorecard of truth and facts is a hard yoke and a heavy burden. Truth and facts lead to a heavy burden because it involves a righteousness required. Jesus, though, said that His yoke is easy and His burden is light. He was talking about a righteousness *given*, not earned. He was talking about faith and grace. Truth and facts mean we're judged on our own merits, or lack thereof. Faith and grace mean that we're judged on Jesus's merits, and judged righteous.

May we always rely on a righteousness that is given and never fear a righteousness that is required. And may we never, ever "graduate" from a yoke that is easy and a burden that is light.

Imagine that you are an arrow in God's quiver. If you were to try to do God's work for Him, it wouldn't go well. An arrow can't do any good if it tries to wriggle away from the archer and do the work on its own. Even if an arrow could jump out of the quiver, somehow hop up to a target and hit it, it would just bounce harmlessly off.

Now imagine an arrow in the hands of a skilled archer. The arrow needs to do nothing but remain in just the form that the archer made it. It is the archer who sharpens the arrow and the archer who hides it away in the quiver. It is the archer who takes the arrow out of the quiver and the archer who puts it on the string. It is the archer who uses *his* strength to pull the arrow back, and the archer who aims. Finally, it is the archer who decides when to release the arrow. Only then will the arrow hit the target and stick. The arrow needs the strength of the archer to accomplish its purpose. If I were to ask you who did the work, the archer or the arrow, what would you say? If I tried to tell you that it was the arrow that did the work, you'd call me crazy. The archer is in control at every point, from sharpening the arrow to sticking it into the target.

How is it that we are to be servants of God? How can the arrow best be the servant of the archer? The way for us to be the best servants of God is to realize that He doesn't need us to do His work at all. He chooses to use us. A true servant is used by the master, the same way an arrow is used by the archer, to accomplish his purposes. Thankfully for the arrow, it is the archer who does all the work. And thankfully for us, it is *God* who is in control.

John Brzenk (icon of the documentary *Pulling John*) became the world arm wrestling champion in 1983 and didn't lose an arm wrestling match (a "pull") for the next twenty-five years. *Pulling John* follows his decision about whether or not to retire as he approaches age forty. The main story line of the film, though, is the collision course of Alexey Voyevoda (a demure Russian giant) and Travis Bagent (a bombastic American braggart), two young challengers to Brzenk's throne. Both men revere Brzenk and understand that they must each go through the other to get to Brzenk's level.

At the world championships in 2003, Voyevoda and Bagent met in the super heavyweight final. In a huge upset, Bagent soundly defeated the heavily favored Voyevoda. If you're familiar with stories like this, you know what happened next. Bagent got even cockier, while Voyevoda went back to Russia to work out. It's during these Russian post-loss scenes that Voyevoda discusses losing, what it means to him, and how acceptance of the loss can bring greater strength. At a critical point, one of his coaches says, "If you're strong, losing can make you stronger."

It is only from deaths that new lives are born. Voyevoda begins to know himself as someone who can lose, and, through that knowledge, gains strength. When he meets Bagent again, with the winner to face Brzenk, it's not close.

Martin Luther said that the cross was the end of us. Losing to Bagent was the end of the invincible Alexey Voyevoda. A new life was created. It was this new creation that dominated Bagent and moved on to face Brzenk.

It is when we are shown our need, which happens exclusively against our will, that we reach out for a Savior. Let us recognize that need today.

There is no question that Christians are to "work out [our] salvation with fear and trembling" (v. 12) and that the sanctification process will be both bloody and sweaty. Daily Christian living is daily Christian dying. Jesus likened the pain of Christian growth to "gouging out an eye" and "cutting off a hand"—indicating that growth in godliness requires parting with things we initially think we can't do without.

There does seem to be some question, though, about the nature and direction of our efforts. And at the heart of this question is the relationship between justification and sanctification.

Some think that justification is just the first rung on the sanctification ladder, and that as you climb up and up, you never need to think about that "first step" again. Sanctification, in other words, is commonly understood as progress beyond the initial step of justification. But while justification and sanctification are to be clearly separated theologically, the Bible won't allow us to separate them functionally.

In her book *Because He Loves Me*, Elyse Fitzpatrick rightly says:

> One reason we don't grow in ordinary, grateful obedience as we should is that we've got amnesia; we've forgotten that we were cleansed from our sins. In other words … ongoing failure in sanctification … is the direct result of failing to remember God's love for us in the gospel.… *If we fail to remember our justification, redemption, and reconciliation, we'll struggle in our sanctification.*

In other words, remembering, revisiting, and rediscovering the reality of our justification every day is the hard work we're called to do if we're going to grow. When Paul says to "work out your salvation with fear and trembling," he's making it clear that we've got work to do—but what exactly is the work? He goes on to explain: "For it is God who works in you, both to will and to work for his good purpose" (v. 13).

Sanctification, as someone once put it, is not something added to justification. It is, rather, the justified life.

Jesus got word that a good friend was dying. Though He was a good ways away, Jesus told His disciples that the illness "is not to death" and that it was actually for God's glory. He waited with His disciples for two days before he even began the journey to see His friend. When He got there, not only was Lazarus dead, but he'd been dead for four days. In Jesus's time, people who weren't dead were declared dead all the time. After a while, they learned to wait a little bit before burying someone. Even as recently as the Victorian Age in England, being buried alive was so common that people were often buried with shovels, so it's not for nothing that John noted that Lazarus had been dead for four days.

Lazarus's resurrection was not just another healing. John's gospel systematically escalates Jesus's interaction with humankind. First, He baptized and preached, then He healed the sick, then He raised the dead. But we don't understand. We're like Martha, who could be paraphrased as having said, "Lord, if you'd gotten here sooner, my brother wouldn't have died." We want a Jesus who heals the sick because we don't trust Him to raise the dead. Mary and Martha thought that as long as they could get Jesus involved before things got too out of hand, everything would be okay.

Jesus is out to prove one thing: even death is "not to death." Not to Jesus. Jesus has something serious in mind. When Martha came to Jesus, He said, "I am the resurrection and the life. The one who believes in me will live, even though they die; and whoever lives by believing in me will never die" (v. 25). If we're honest with ourselves, Paul's description of us in Romans 3 is dead on: ruin and misery mark our ways. We're more than sick—we're falling apart. Actually, it's even more that. We're dead. Jesus Christ is a God who does something so much better than heal the sick. He raises the dead to new life.

This is how we imagine the relationship between our hearts, our wills, and our minds works: Your mind makes a decision—for instance, "I want to be in better shape." Then your will has to get involved: "I will wake up early every morning, go to the gym, and work out." It's not pleasant, so you've got to invoke the old willpower, right? And then if everything goes as planned, your heart comes around eventually: "I love working out!" So in a nutshell, we act as if the way things work is: what the mind chooses, the will works for, and the heart ... well, the heart will catch up. Sound about right? That's how we live. The only problem is, about 95 percent of the time, our hearts never come around.

The things we hate to do to improve ourselves usually remain intolerable burdens. This is why so many people have bought and cancelled dozens of gym memberships over the years: they don't actually fall in love with the gym the way they thought they would. The reason is the above order of things isn't at all accurate. Here's how it really works: what the heart desires, the will chooses, and the mind justifies. We all follow our hearts and then make excuses later. Paul gave this truth words when he said he did things he didn't want to do and didn't do things he wanted to do. It was his mind losing to his sinful heart.

English theologian Thomas Cranmer wrote a prayer that is perfect for today:

Almighty God, you alone can bring into order the unruly wills and affections of sinners: Grant your people grace to love what you command and desire what you promise; that, among the swift and varied changes of the world, our hearts may surely there be fixed where true joys are to be found; through Jesus Christ our Lord, who lives and reigns with you and the Holy Spirit, one God, now and forever. AMEN.

Today, remember that God has given you a new heart, permanently aligned with His.

In 2013, you couldn't search the name "Chris Tang" anywhere on the Internet without finding an attendant mention of Jeremy Lin. At the time, Tang was a Chinese American player at Virginia's Oak Hill Academy, a school famous for producing NBA talent such as Kevin Durant, Carmelo Anthony, and Rajon Rondo. He toiled in total obscurity until those magical nights in the winter of 2011–2012 when "Linsanity" struck New York. Tang was then labeled, for better or worse, "the next Jeremy Lin."

For the rest of his basketball life, Tang will likely be required to labor under the "next" banner. He can never just be Chris Tang, as long as there's a Jeremy Lin.

This reminds me of Peter's description of the Devil: "like a roaring lion, looking for someone to devour" (v. 8). The law of "be the next Jeremy Lin" has devoured Chris Tang, and it will continue to devour Chris Tang until he eventually surpasses Lin. But the law will not then be satisfied. It never is. It will merely morph into "be the next Chris Tang." The law is a roaring lion, looking for someone to devour.

But whence this lion? This can't be an infinite regression. It must have begun somewhere. Long ago, someone was the first "one you've got to be like." In basketball, it was perhaps George Mikan, the first "unstoppable force." In the world? It was God.

The reason that we all experience an irresistible desire for perfection is that God is actually perfect. His law is a reflection of that. Then the Devil comes like a lion to accuse us and to proclaim—rightly—that we in deserve condemnation.

There is, unfortunately, no cure for the law. As Martin Luther famously said, the quest for glory can never be satisfied; it can only be exterminated. And this is precisely what Jesus does with that roaring lion, Satan. He shuts his mouth, crushes him to death, and throws him into his own fire.

One of the greatest documentaries of the last several years is *Murderball*, the story of the United States quad rugby team, a Paralympic team of quadriplegics. A fascinating thing to watch in the film is the interplay between physical disability and mental attitude. As you might imagine, the quadriplegics who play murderball (quad rugby's nickname) are some of the most competitive and independent spirits in the world. They would kill themselves before letting anyone take pity on them. One of the players, Mark Zupan, tries to start physical altercations so that he can taunt people for not wanting to hit a wheelchair-bound man. He is trying to call attention to his self-sufficiency and strength in the face of his obvious weakness.

Of course, it's overcompensation. Feelings of weakness (the film begins with a painfully long scene of Zupan simply getting dressed) lead to professions of strength. The truth is, though, that these quadriplegics are suffering—you can see it on their faces. They live their lives in denial of it, in much the same way that we deny much of our suffering. Do we, knowing that Christ came to and for sufferers, wear the thorns in our flesh as badges of honor? It doesn't seem like it. We are more like quad rugby players, keeping our needs deep beneath our surface, in the hope that Jesus won't have to come for us at all.

In a profound sense, I am just like Mark Zupan. I'm spoiling for a fight. I want to be able to stand before Jesus and say, "Lord, You know I'm not perfect! Look, I've suffered. My family is broken, my self-esteem is low, I'm confined to a wheelchair. It was a long, tough road, and I'm a little woozy. But the important thing is, here I am." I want to think I made it myself. The truth is, I can't. I need Jesus.

Perhaps your life has made you aware that you're not making it. Today, remember that, though you may not be okay, Jesus gave His all for you and you are deeply loved.

I'll bet you twenty dollars that as you think about the gifts of the Holy Spirit, you go through a mental checklist, hoping to find one of the gifts that you might actually have. I've done this a hundred times. Wisdom, knowledge, faith, healing, miracles, prophecy, discernment of spirits, tongues, the interpretation of tongues. My bet is you get through the list and come out the other side (like me) worrying that you might not have any spiritual gifts at all. You're not alone.

The problem is simple: we are human. It is our nature to take control. We do it every day. We do it every hour. We do it in the morning. We look at ourselves as the main actors in our little dramas, and so when we think about the spiritual gifts, we think only of ourselves, and what gifts we might possess. We don't think about the Holy Spirit for a second, even though they are His gifts! Because of that moment on the cross a couple thousand years ago, when Jesus took our works of the flesh upon Himself and gave us His fruit of the Spirit, we are still regarded, whatever our fleshly works look like, as bearing the fruit of the Spirit and as possessors of all kinds of spiritual gifts.

When Jesus went to be with His Father, He sent the Holy Spirit to be with us, and to give us all the good gifts we could never earn on our own. When God looks at us, His gaze finds what His voice has declared! We have been given gifts by the Holy Spirit. And the real miracle is, it actually happens! We have faith where none existed before. We are given wisdom in a difficult situation. We understand God's will in a situation without even knowing how we do so. Each one of these things is a miracle, because they come directly from God. They are *His* gifts, freely given to us.

In the 1997 Luc Besson film, *The Fifth Element*, there is a confrontation between the villain, Mr. Zorg, and a priest that perfectly illustrates the contrasting and complementary roles that the law and the gospel play in relation to one another.

Mr. Zorg claims that he and the priest are really in the same business: that of life. The priest accuses Zorg of only wanting to destroy life by being an agent of destruction and chaos, while Zorg insists that life cannot exist *without* destruction and chaos. They both have a point.

Zorg embodies the law. He causes death. As Paul so eloquently says in Romans 7, when the law came, "sin sprang to life and I died" (v. 9). Elsewhere, he famously said that the wages of sin is death (Rom. 6:23). So the priest's argument is true: Zorg, by his very existence, destroys life. But Zorg is right too.

At the beginning of Romans 7, Paul discusses his covetousness. He says, in essence, that he had no idea how much he was coveting, until the law came and told him, "Thou shalt not covet." All of a sudden, he realized the extent to which he wanted things that weren't his! That's when he says that he dies. There's a point for the priest. But then, most profoundly, Paul recognizes his need for a Savior: "Who will rescue me from this body that is subject to death?" (Rom. 7:24) and finds his need met: "Thanks be to God, who delivers me through Jesus Christ our Lord!" (Rom. 7:25). It was the law, and the resultant death (by "destruction, disorder, and chaos"), that led Paul to real life, that is, in Jesus Christ. There's a point for Zorg.

These two forces belong in the same room. Zorg and the priest. Law and gospel. The disorder and chaos of our lives drives us to an epiphany: We're dying! We need a Savior. Thankfully, the gospel always trumps the law, bringing us from death to life.

Can you believe the goodness of the good news? Can you believe that we're promised an inheritance that is imperishable, undefiled, and unfading? Never were three more beautiful words spoken. And the fact that Peter was the one who wrote them amazes me. Peter, who denied any relationship to Christ whatsoever while his innocent friend was being tortured. Peter may have been in the best position ever to believe that his inheritance had perished, been defiled, or faded. He must have been *sure* of it! It is only those who are convinced of their own badness who can perceive the incredible goodness of the good news.

Peter follows up these words with: "In all this you greatly rejoice, though now for a little while you may have had to suffer grief in all kinds of trials" (v. 6). He knows what that week between Jesus's resurrection and Jesus's appearing was like. It was full of suffering. He spent the whole time, I guarantee you, going over and over those three denials in his mind. "I do not know the man! How could I have said that! I don't believe that ... what was I thinking?" He must have been *sure* that Jesus would show up holding that cassette tape, like Charlie Sheen's character at the end of *Wall Street*: "I heard what you said, Peter. We recorded the whole thing." Peter is imagining an eternity spent separated from this man he denied. And yet, wonder of wonders, miracle of miracles, when Jesus walks into the room that night after He's resurrected, He doesn't even mention it! It's as if Peter's inheritance is ... could it be? Imperishable? Undefiled? Unfading? Peter might have started putting these words together in his head that very night.

We are like Peter. We are sure that our relationship with Christ has perished. That it has become defiled. That it has faded. And if our relationship was based on our performance, we'd be right. Thankfully for us, our relationship with Christ is based on His performance, His fidelity, and His love. Because His love for us is imperishable, undefiled, and unfading, so is our connection to Him.

A king throws a wedding banquet for his son. He sends out the wedding invitations, probably to the best and brightest. When he sends his servants out to pick up the people he's invited, they say they don't want to come! He tells the invited guests how great the party is going to be, but they make fun of it. Some of the guests even mistreat and kill the messengers! Talk about not wanting to go to a party! The king decides that he wants a full house at the wedding party, so he sends his servants into the streets to bring in whoever they can find.

This is a great story for us. More than just being about a people who had the opportunity to accept the message of Jesus and didn't, it's about the *next* group of people ... the ones who get the *next* opportunity. The original wedding guests were the sort of people who get to go to the real Hollywood power weddings. It's as if when Brad Pitt and Angelina Jolie got married, no one on their guest list had accepted their invitation. Imagine if Brangelina announced their wedding, and then ended up inviting hundreds of people just off the street. I don't know what street it would have been, maybe in California or in France or in Rwanda. Anyway, that would be quite the situation, wouldn't it? Hundreds of Joe Schmoes going to the wedding of celebrities?

And we like stories like this, right? This is good news for you and me. If the A-listers don't get to go, maybe our name will eventually come up. This is the gospel: Jesus didn't come for the good, fancy people who are self-sufficient, successful, and glamorous in their own eyes. He came for the needy, the weak, the unpolished. The gospel, in other words, is for *the rest of us*—the street people who live our lives in perpetual fear that we'll never make it, that we'll never be invited. The gospel is for us, and Jesus is saying that we're the ones who end up inside the wedding feast.

For various reasons, a recent year was the most painful year of my life by far. The following year, God graciously gave me a mild reprieve, but I still spent a lot of time thinking about all that had happened during that hard year and the way God used trials and tribulations to remold and reshape me.

As crazy as this might sound, I have finally come to the place where I am genuinely thankful for all of the pain, difficulty, and loss I experienced during that year. As much as my family and I suffered, I look back on the way God used our desperation to make us more dependent on Him, and I am deeply grateful. In fact, I told a friend the other day that I wouldn't trade one desperate, difficult day for all the dollars in the world. Seriously!

I've discovered that being thankful for pain is such a hard concept to grasp because we live in a world that has convinced us that the pursuit of happiness and comfort is our inalienable right. Therefore, when our comforts, conveniences, and cushions are threatened, we cry "foul." This has deeply affected our understanding of what it means to give thanks and the types of things we are to be thankful for.

Charles Spurgeon once said, "Health is a gift from God, but sickness is a gift greater still." Throughout his time in this world, Spurgeon suffered with various physical ailments that eventually took his life prematurely. He longed to be well but he recognized the supreme value of being sick and he thanked God for it because it was his pain that caused him to desperately draw near to God.

The paradox of Christianity is that if you want to find your life, you must lose it (Matt. 10:39). In the world's economy, life precedes death. In God's economy, death precedes life—the cross always precedes the crown. The good news—the thing that should cause us to be supremely thankful—is that when we lose our worldly comforts, we gain heavenly ones.

When the disciples have an argument about which among them was to be regarded as the greatest, Jesus gives a little illustration about a dinner, and asks them, "Who is greater, one who reclines at table or one who serves?" He answers His own question: "Is it not the one who reclines at table? But I am among you as one who serves" (v 27 ESV). It is easy to think that, here, Jesus is redefining greatness; that to be really great, we need to "become as one who serves." So we Christians start trying to be great, but through obvious acts of service, rather than by trying to get to the front. It's like when you were at camp, and everyone raced for the back of the line, knowing that the counselors would say that "the last shall be first and the first shall be last." Though the route is different, it's still a race to the front.

So how can we be great if our only way there is cut off? It seems like a cruel trick: servanthood is the way to greatness, but servanthood, true, honest, and pure servanthood, turns out to be impossible. Jesus said that the one who reclines at table is greater, and He's right! And here's the kicker: I want to recline at table! I know the right answer is to serve, but sitting at the table is so much better. Left to my own devices, I don't really want to serve—I want to *be* served.

Thankfully, Jesus isn't just giving us a new route to greatness. He's showing us that we're not great. The great have no need for a Savior, and we are in desperate need. It was on the cross, because of our inability to be great, that the Great One, Christ Jesus, was stripped of His greatness. It is in our recognition of our lack of greatness that we can clearly see the greatness of Christ, manifest in that least great of events, a public execution. The less great we find ourselves, the greater we find His gift.

In the 2010 film *127 Hours*, James Franco plays Aron Ralston, a hiker who got his arm stuck under a rock while canyoneering in Utah in 2003. Even if you haven't seen the film, you're probably aware of the story. After being trapped for 127 hours, Ralston amputated his arm with a dull pocket knife and walked to safety, having long since run out of food and water.

As he's running out of water and energy, but before he decides to cut off his arm, Ralston gets out his camcorder and records a good-bye to his parents and family. Then, as his delirium increases, he starts talking about other things in his life. One of the things he reminisces about is his tendency to tell no one his canyoneering plans, as the solitude adds to the adventure: he's more of a heroic character if there's no possibility of rescue. The director's mistake is introducing this potentially powerful idea more than halfway through the film.

As he faces his more and more imminent demise, Ralston chastises himself about this sort of faux heroism and terminal self-reliance. After the self-amputation, he walks out of the canyon and spots some other trekkers. Everything is shown out of focus, Ralston unable to muster the strength to speak. Finally, he shouts, "Help me!" Then the picture cuts into a crystal-clear close-up in which Ralston exclaims, enunciating clearly, "I need help!"

This character arc is a distinctly Christian one. The law, says Paul in Galatians 3, served as a taskmaster until Christ came. In other words, the law functions to drive us to Christ, to our need for a Savior. That rock in the Utah canyon was Ralston's taskmaster, driving him to his sober admission that he needs help.

Of course, now that Christ has come, Paul says that we are no longer under a taskmaster. We are now under the tutelage of a gracious Father who, even when He disciplines us, is loving us unconditionally all the way home.

Barry Zito was once known as one of the most dominating pitchers in Major League Baseball, winning the 2002 Cy Young Award. Then in 2006, he signed a huge free agent deal with the San Francisco Giants and became known as the worst signing in recent memory, a choke artist who never lived up to a tenth of his contract, much less the entire $126 million.

Finally, during the 2012 playoffs (and eventual World Series victory), Zito began pitching well, in the face of all expectations. In an interview, he tried to explain why. He said he had been raised by a grandmother who had founded her own religion, called Teachings of the Inner Christ. It was finally in 2012, he said, that he realized how exhausted he was from "relying on his own strength for so long." He realized that he needed to find "a strength outside" of himself.

He also talked about a "very odd" injury that he had in 2011—a Lisfranc ligament tear—that taught him about his lack of control. He illustrates it with a story: "A shepherd will be leading his sheep, and one of the sheep will be walking astray from the pack. The shepherd will take his rod and break the sheep's leg, and the sheep will have to rely on the shepherd to get better. But once that leg is completely healed, that sheep never leaves the side of the shepherd ever again."

Doesn't the name of Zito's grandmother's religion say it all? "Teachings of the Inner Christ"? That "religion" failed him. Zito finally realized he needed to find an outside strength, since the strength from within wasn't doing him any good.

Barry Zito needed the freedom that came from a reliance on the Outer Christ. It took a "very odd" injury for him to have his eyes opened. In the same way, having our leg broken by the shepherd is never something that we would choose for ourselves, but it is often the only way for God to open our eyes to our paralyzing need, and to the truth that there is a Shepherd there to nurse us.

What's your job description as a Christian? That's a little bit of a dicey question, isn't it? Most of us have job descriptions that we agreed to when we accepted our current role. Certain tasks we need to perform and certain levels of accomplishment we have to meet or else we get shown the door, right? We Christians often feel as if we have a job to do, and it's pretty common for people to take this section of Luke 4 as their Christian job description. After all, it's what Jesus said He had come to do, so shouldn't we do the same?

The people who think this way end up exhausted, burned out, and resentful. Thinking of this passage as your job description misses a crucial point: Jesus has fulfilled His job description. In other words, He did His job and did it so well that it no longer needs doing, and it certainly doesn't need doing by the likes of us!

So as we go about this life, let's be honest about who is poor, who is held captive, who is blind, who is oppressed. Sure, it's the people on street corners, the people in Third World countries, but it's also the people to the right and left of you. The people in your house. The preacher at your church. Everyone you see as you walk down the sidewalk. You. But know, always know, that on that day, all those years ago, Jesus unrolled the scroll and found the place where it was written:

> "The Spirit of the Lord is on me, because he has anointed
> me to proclaim good news to the poor. He has sent me
> to proclaim freedom for the prisoners and recovery of
> sight for the blind, to set the oppressed free, to proclaim
> the year of the Lord's favor." And He rolled up the scroll,
> gave it back to the attendant, and sat down. The eyes of
> all in the temple were fixed on Him. Then He began to
> say to them, "Today this scripture has been fulfilled in
> your hearing." (vv. 18–20)

Jesus's job is finished. Forever.

Filmmaker John Hughes was the poet laureate of the 1980s teenager. In 1987, he gave us the movie *Some Kind of Wonderful*, telling the story of a guy (played by Eric Stoltz) who falls in love with a girl (Lea Thompson) who is completely out of his league. He recruits his best friend (Mary Stuart Masterson) to help him win Thompson's heart, never knowing the obvious truth: Masterson is desperately in love with him.

In true romantic-comedy form, Thompson proves to be not as perfect as she seemed from afar, and Stoltz realizes that the girl he really wanted, Masterson, was right there all along.

Many people I talk to recognize that life on their own is heavy and unsatisfying, so they set out to "find God." Many seek earnestly. They set their minds on getting clean, believing that if there is a God, He will only take notice of them if they're worthy and lovable. Eric Stoltz's character thinks that he can turn himself into someone that Lea Thompson's character will love. This is the normal, though misguided, approach of many spiritual seekers. But it doesn't work. Lea Thompson is inscrutable. Hard to understand. Counterintuitive. Like God, she can't be "gotten to." It just doesn't work.

It is Mary Stuart Masterson, in the Christ role, who has been there all along. It is Jesus who is there to pick us up when our quest for God ends as it must—in bitter defeat and failure.

John Hughes puts in our common language what John the Evangelist said in theological terms: we cannot get to God. But God has come to us in Jesus Christ. As Os Guinness points out, "We cannot find God without God. We cannot reach God without God.... The secret of the quest lies not in our brilliance but in his grace."

The bad news is that we cannot ascend to God. The good news is that God descended to us in the person of Jesus—the One who promised to never leave us or forsake us.

As beautiful and lifesaving as grace can be, we often resist it. By nature, we are suspicious of promises that seem too good to be true. We wonder about the ulterior motives of the excessively generous. Grace offends our sense of justice by being both implausible and unfair.

We are uncomfortable because grace turns the tables on us, relieving us of our precious sense of control. It forces us to rely on the goodness of Another.

Robert Capon articulated the prayer of the grace-averse heart this way:

> *Lord, please restore to us the comfort of merit and demerit. Show us that there is at least something we can do. Tell us that at the end of the day there will at least be one redeeming card of our very own. Lord, if it is not too much to ask, send us to bed with a few shreds of self-respect upon which we can congratulate ourselves. But whatever you do, do not preach grace. Give us something to do, anything; but spare us the indignity of this indiscriminate acceptance.*

The idea that there is an unconditional love that relieves the pressure, forgives our failures, and replaces our fears with faith seems too good to be true. As we long for hope in a world of hype, the gospel of Jesus Christ is the news we have been waiting for all our lives. God loves real people like you and me, which He demonstrated by sending His Son to set us free.

Jesus came to liberate us from the weight of having to make it on our own, from the demand to measure up. Jesus came to release us from the slavish need to be right, rewarded, regarded, and respected.

Once this good news grips your heart, it changes everything. It frees you from having to be perfect. It frees you from having to hold it all together. In the place of exhaustion, you might even find energy.

A king has just invited people off the street into his wedding feast because the original invitees turned down his invitation. But when he comes into the room and notices a guest without a wedding robe, he has the guy thrown into "the outer darkness." What gives? It would be easy to interpret this story wrongly: the invitation is open to all, but to *stay* in, you have to look the part.

But Jesus isn't talking about keeping up appearances. When Jesus's listeners heard the word "robe," it would have brought up instant images for them of status symbols. The robes in biblical cultures weren't like our common bathrobes today. For instance, when Joseph's father wants to give him a really nice present, he gives him a robe of many colors. One of the important garments for a priest to wear was a robe. In fact, many pastors still wear robes in church. When the prophet Samuel's parents make the annual sacrifice, they make Samuel a special robe to wear for the occasion.

As you can see, robes carry a lot more meaning in the Bible than they do today. Today, robes go with slippers. Then, robes went with sacrifice. Samuel wore a robe when an animal was slaughtered in the annual sacrifice to God. Priests wore robes when they made the sacrifices on behalf of the people. Even Joseph's robe of many colors ends up drenched in blood as his brothers pretend that he's been murdered. In Revelation 19, Jesus is described as wearing a robe dipped in blood.

To be at this party, you need to be wearing a wedding robe. Jesus is, Himself, this wedding robe. To be in the kingdom of heaven, you must be covered by the blood of Christ. In Galatians 3, the apostle Paul said that all of you who were reborn into Christ have clothed yourselves with Christ (v. 27). So it is the blood of Christ alone that affords us entrance into the wedding feast of the kingdom of heaven.

Are you growing as a Christian? For a while when I was younger, this seemed like the most important question in the world. My friends would ask me how "my walk" with Jesus was going. What they meant, of course, was, "Are you improving?"

I feel like many of us still operate like this. Imagine coming into church and having someone ask you, "So how was your week?" We're not inclined to be honest in our answer anywhere, but how much *less* likely are we to be honest in church? In church, maybe more than anyplace else, we're expected to be growing. But of course, it's not just church. Think of the years your mother spent asking you when you were going to make her a grandmother. Or when you were going to settle down with someone. Or when you were going to stop playing video games. Or when you were going to get it through your head that you weren't going to be the next Mick Jagger. Think of the look on people's faces when they realize that you *still* have the same job you've had … you know, the one that's beneath you.

We all know that we're expected to grow up. We've heard it our whole lives, even from the Bible. Colossians 1, Ephesians 4, and 1 Corinthians 3 all ask us to grow up. The pressing question is *how*.

Listen to Jesus: "The kingdom of God is as if someone would scatter seed on the ground, and would sleep and rise night and day, and the seed would sprout and grow, *he does not know how*" (Mark 4:26–27 NRSV).

God gives growth. We work the soil but it is God alone who gives the growth. We think Christian growth is all about willpower. But the good and relieving news is that Christian growth is not about our willpower in the same way that planted seeds do not grow themselves. Christian growth is all about grace—the grace of a Father who works in us to will and to work for His good pleasure (Phil. 2:13).

In Galatians 5, Paul describes the fruit of the Spirit: "love, joy, peace, patience, kindness, generosity, faithfulness, gentleness, and self-control" (vv. 22–33 NRSV). Most Christians, when they read this list, immediately begin a kind of self-evaluation: How is my fruit? Is it the good stuff that Paul lists here, or is it the bad stuff that he lists a few verses earlier? Fornication, impurity, licentiousness, idolatry, jealousy, anger, and so on?

This kind of thinking, which we can fall into so easily, is one of the most common mistakes of Christianity, comparing the fruit of the Spirit with what Paul calls "the works of the flesh." People forget that you can't compare the fruit of the Spirit to the fruit of the flesh, because it's the *works* of the flesh, not the fruit. People confuse *fruit* with *works* and think they're the same thing, but they're not.

Paul is making an important distinction between work and fruit. He's saying that when we work, when we're active, these bad things come out. But when we allow the Spirit to bear fruit, when we're in a certain sense *passive*, these good things come out. This doesn't mean Christians are to be lazy. This isn't a "let go and let God" kind of thing. But it falls in line with what Paul says elsewhere in Galatians about being crucified with Christ. He says, "It is no longer I who live, but it is Christ who lives in me" (Gal. 2:20 NRSV).

Now he gives us this distinction between the fruit of the Spirit and the works of the flesh. Notice that the works of the flesh are things we *do*. The fruit of the Spirit look more like things we *are*—they are less behaviors and more qualities, characteristics. Paul is contrasting *doing* with *being* here.

When Paul relies on his flesh, it looks like fornication, impurity, jealousy, anger, and envy. But when Paul dies, and Christ lives, it looks like love, joy, peace, patience, kindness, and generosity. Works come from us, but fruit comes from the Spirit.

One of the most powerful scenes in the musical adaptation of Victor Hugo's *Les Misérables* is a song Inspector Javert sings. Javert embodies our natural addiction to law and our natural aversion to grace. Committed to the rigorous inflexibility of the law, Javert is haunted and radically disoriented by the grace and mercy of his prey, Jean Valjean. He sings:

> *Who is this man?*
> *What sort of devil is he,*
> *To have me caught in a trap*
> *And choose to let me go free?*
> *It was his hour at last*
> *To put the seal on my fate,*
> *Wipe out the past*
> *And wash me clean off the slate!*
> *All it would take*
> *Was a flick of his knife.*
> *Vengeance was his*
> *And he gave me back my life!*
>
> *Damned if I'll live in the debt of a thief!*
> *Damned if I'll yield at the end of the chase!*
> *I am the Law and the Law is not mocked.*
> *I'll spit his pity right back in his face!*
> *There is nothing on Earth that we share!*
> *It is either Valjean or Javert!*

Javert concludes that he would rather die than deal with the disorienting reality of grace, and so he jumps into the Seine. He chooses death over grace. For Javert (as with all of us), the logic of law makes sense. We love the if/then proposition: if you do this, then I will do that. It's easy to comprehend, formulaic, and best of all, it keeps us in control. Grace, on the other hand, feels risky and unfair. It wrestles control out of our hands. The grace of God is scandalous and scary, unnatural and undomesticated, but it's the only thing that can set us free.

The annual Burning Man event in Black Rock Desert in northern Nevada is often thought of as a judgment-free environment. Can this be true? Is Black Rock City heaven on earth? If so, no wonder people go every year and weep when they have to rejoin the rest of us out here in the "default world," as they call it.

In truth, though, Burning Man is a lot more like the outside world than Burners would ever admit. There are plenty of rules; they're just unofficial. For instance, once you park your car, you're expected to leave it parked. The rule doesn't exist, but, you know, don't break it. People have to be at Burning Man for "the right reasons" to be trusted. The only economy is a gift economy … except when the goods in question are actually valuable, like ice, which is the only product that you must buy with cash. Earning respect from old-timers matters. Sound familiar? It's just the "alterna-vision" of your subdivision, your school yard, your office, and your in-laws' house.

Even at the Burning Man free-for-all, we discover that God has put His law into our minds and written it on our hearts (v. 10). We carry it wherever we go. And if God's law is there, its pale human shadow is there too: be how you're expected to be; go along; fit in; earn respect.

The reality is that rebels are just as bound to the law as the conformists they so loathe, and they're just as in need of a Savior. They do the opposite of what the law requires, but are still living their lives in reaction to it, and forming their own laws to organize their reaction. Burning Man, apparently, isn't savior enough, despite the protestations of its citizens. The rain falls on the Burners and the Squares alike, we find that the law finds us all bent in upon ourselves, and we are grateful that Jesus died for the sins of the whole world.

The word *imputation* is the best attempt to translate into English a Greek word that means things like "regard," "attribute," or "credit." In a nutshell, it boils down to something like "the treatment of something as having attributes that it does not intrinsically have." Here's an example: in the 2003 Wayne Kramer film, *The Cooler*, William H. Macy plays the unluckiest guy in the world, working for a Las Vegas casino, "cooling" tables. He is so unlucky that his unluckiness exudes out of his pores and infects those around him. Winning streaks become losing streaks, hot streaks become cold streaks, and good rolls become bad ones. One day, though, he does a favor for cocktail waitress Maria Bello, and things begin to change. She starts to have feelings for him, and consequently, he begins to be less unlucky. In a sense, she treats him as though he is desirable, when he is clearly not. Then, because of this attribution—this imputation—he becomes desirable.

Bello begins to treat Macy as desirable for only one reason: she loves him. There is no ulterior motive. Of course, she's a character in a movie, so she's immune to the vagaries of human nature to which the rest of us real people are beholden. The classic human example, the incontrovertible fact that we are inevitably attracted to the person who loves us when we feel unlovable, still feels (and is) like a lightning bolt out of heaven, a pure miracle. True imputation can only come from God, because only God's words create that which they speak.

So if the bad news is that only God imputes, the good news is that God *does* impute! In the same way that William H. Macy becomes the person Maria Bello regards him to be, we become the kind of people that God regards us to be. We are regarded as righteous when we are not, and are therefore made righteous. We are "counted righteous" in Christ.

For a long time now, I've been convinced that the way most Christians think about redemption is influenced more by ancient Greek philosophy than by the Bible. We think of ultimate redemption as being redemption *from* the body, not *of* the body, and redemption *from* the world, not *of* the world. This, however, goes against what the Bible clearly teaches about redemption.

In the Lord's Prayer we see that God's ultimate goal for earth is that it become like heaven. God's mission is to bring heaven to earth!

There are many people who believe that God will destroy this present world—all of it—and start over, creating a new world from scratch. The truth, though, is that God plans a radical renovation project for the world we live in today. The Bible never says that everything will be burned up and replaced. Rather, it says that everything will be purged with fire and restored. God won't destroy everything that now exists, but He will destroy all the corruption, brokenness, and chaos we see in our world, purging from it everything that is impure and sinful.

Understanding God's mission fuels our hope and summons our engagement in a world that desperately needs to hear that one day the fraying fabric of our world will be perfectly rewoven. For those who have found forgiveness of sins in Christ, there will one day be no more sickness, no more death, no more tears, no more division, no more tension. For the pardoned children of God, there'll be complete harmony. We'll work and worship in a perfectly renewed earth without the interference of sin. We who believe the gospel will enjoy sinless hearts and minds along with disease-free bodies. All that causes us pain and discomfort will be destroyed, and we will live forever. We'll finally be able, as John Piper said, "to enjoy what is most enjoyable with unbounded energy and passion forever."

Jesus tells a story about wise and foolish bridesmaids who either remember to bring enough oil for their lamps (the wise) or have to run out and get more when they hear that the bridegroom is coming (the foolish). When the foolish bridesmaids get back, the door to the wedding feast is closed, and they're not allowed in.

At first this seems to be the biblical equivalent of the Boy Scouts motto "Be Prepared." In Christian terms, we would usually translate that as something like "be good."

"When Jesus comes back," I can imagine someone saying, "are you going to be prepared?" In other words, is your house going to be in order when He shows up? But this is not at all what this story is about!

This story is about what we do when we get caught unprepared. Think about it: How would you act if it came on the news right now that Jesus was returning? Would you feel elated and eager to welcome your returning Lord? I know I wouldn't. I'd be terrified! I'd immediately try to run out and reconcile any broken relationships that I might have. I'd probably dash out a quick check to charity, just in case. In other words, I'd be just like the foolish bridesmaids, and I bet you would be too.

Here's the foolish bridesmaids' mistake: they try to save themselves. They're caught without oil, and they try to fix the situation. They want the bridegroom to come, see that they have lamps full of oil, and congratulate them. Their fatal error is, in their urgency to save themselves, they're not even there when the bridegroom arrives!

We have a forgiving Bridegroom, Jesus Christ, who said clearly that He came for the people who didn't have it all together. He came for the bridesmaids, like you and me, who are forever running out of oil. He is primed to forgive. When we're caught unprepared, we need only to admit it and throw ourselves onto His never-ending mercy.

We have an allergy to weakness. So even when we are compelled to fess up to a weakness, like in a job interview, we think of a *strong* weakness, like perfectionism or "sometimes I work too hard." We pick a weakness that we hope will actually be perceived as a strength. This is not the kind of weakness that Paul seems to be talking about in his second letter to the Corinthians. He talks about being given a thorn in his flesh, a thorn that he apparently begged God to take away from him, but a thorn that he still carries nonetheless. When he appealed to the Lord to take away this thorn, the Lord's answer was this: "My grace is sufficient for you, for power is made perfect in weakness" (v. 9 NRSV).

Jesus's power isn't made perfect in our strength; in fact, we tend to ignore Jesus when we feel strong. But when we have those moments of bracing honesty in our lives, when we come to grips with how weak we really are, our realization of our need comes through, and Jesus's power is realized in us.

But that's not all we're promised. We're also promised that God's grace is sufficient for us. Now I think we have a pretty insufficient idea of what the word *sufficient* means. When we think about sufficient, we think "barely enough to meet our needs," right? But God's making a much bolder promise. When He says His grace is sufficient, it means that *you don't have to add anything to it*! And this is great news for those of us who have come face-to-face with our weaknesses. God's grace, that free gift to the undeserving, is sufficient. It's all you need! The price, in other words, is paid.

In Romans 9 Paul pushes the radical one-way-ness of God's rescuing love to an uncomfortable extreme. He shows just how single-handedly we are saved by God, who saves us from beginning to end.

When it comes to the mysterious (and controversial) doctrine of election, we tend to be scandalized in the wrong direction: we're scandalized by who it leaves out rather than being scandalized by who it lets in—the weak, the rebellious, the immoral, the adulterer, the liar, the thief, you, and me.

Romans 9 changed my life. It turned me inside out and upside down.

God's rescue of me was dramatic and, for a while, I couldn't talk about God's amazing grace in saving me without crying. But after a while the novelty of grace wore off. I remained grateful for God's blood, sweat, and tears in getting me in, but my focus shifted to the amount of blood, sweat, and tears of mine it would take to keep me in. I was appreciative for God's work, but I was especially focused on my own. I had come to view grace as divine assistance for the process of moral transformation rather than as a one-sided divine rescue—I had lost sight of the beauty and brilliance of Romans 9.

This chapter reoriented me back to the size and scope of God's grace in a way that changed me forever. After reading it, my estimation of God grew larger and my estimation of myself grew smaller. These verses made me feel silly that I would ever want to shift the spotlight from God's action for me to my action for Him.

Romans 9 anchors our identity in God's action for us. He does all of the acting and all of the choosing; we do all of the receiving.

Romans 9 is intended to make us aware of the fact that we are deeply loved by Jesus and have done nothing to earn it or deserve it. In the face of all our doing, striving, toiling, and laboring, Romans 9 sings about a God who has done everything for us from before the foundation of the world.

There is a great crossroads in life, a place described by two verses from the Bible. The first comes from Jesus during His Sermon on the Mount, where He describes what righteousness looks like: "Be perfect, therefore, as your heavenly Father is perfect" (Matt. 5:48). Crossing this road is another thoroughfare, this one described by Paul: "There is no one righteous, not even one" (Rom. 3:10). We all find ourselves at this crossroads, desiring to be righteous but prevented by our humanity from getting there.

Remember the scene in Wolfgang Peterson's classic film *The NeverEnding Story* in which Atreyu must pass through the Sphinx Gate? He has to be worthy to get through without getting blasted by the sphinxes' laser eyes. Atreyu and the tiny scientist look on as a worthy-*looking* knight fails to make it through.

Though the scientist phrases it differently ("aware of your own worth"), clearly it is righteousness that will allow a person to pass through the sphinx gate. There's even a little shot at the "whitewashed tombs" of pharisaism (Matt. 23:27) when the fancy-looking knight gets his.

It is a staple of fantasy books and movies for there to be a chosen one who is pure, even though those around him don't know it. King Arthur is able to pull Excalibur out of the stone, Aladdin is a "diamond in the rough," and so on. Atreyu, at first, seems to follow that mold. But then the sphinxes' eyes start to open! Even Atreyu is revealed to be impure, and it's only his cat-like reflexes (and some pretty severe limitations on the eye-shooting abilities of the sphinxes) that allow him to escape with his life.

For the sphinxes, nothing less than perfection will do. This is true of God. The sphinxes can see right through a shiny exterior and see into your heart, and so can God. No one is worthy, not one. Finding ourselves at this crossroads, where requirement meets ability, we must rely on a Savior from outside ourselves who, as Paul said, "at just the right time, while we were still powerless ... died for the ungodly" (Rom. 5:6).

On a Saturday morning in December of 2012, there was an unspeakable tragedy. Kansas City Chiefs linebacker Jovan Belcher shot and killed his girlfriend, then drove to the Chiefs' facility and thanked his coach and general manager before shooting himself.

The next day Bob Costas blasted people who spouted an old cliché: "This really puts things in perspective." "That sort of perspective," he said, "has a very short shelf life, because we will inevitably hear about the perspective we have supposedly regained the next time ugly reality intrudes upon our games."

Costas's diagnosis is on target. But he has no solution. He is precisely correct that everyone will be saying the same thing after the next tragedy. I'm reminded of *The Onion* article "Nation Somehow Shocked by Human Nature Again." There are, however, two truths that Costas is missing.

First, no one has any perspective. We are all absolutely convinced we are the center of the universe, good deeds reap good rewards, and a host of other "truths" define our lives when they do not.

Second, everyone needs profound events for recalibration. Indeed, it is our lack of perspective that requires them. This is the genius of the church. Each week, we must be brought again into contact with a truth that we forget, week by week: our righteousness is secured by the perfection of another, and this righteousness has been gifted to us with no expectation of recompense. The way in which we commonly view the world (that we are the center of things, in control, and will get what we deserve) is so profoundly backward that it takes a profound event (a humble deity dying a criminal's death) to recalibrate us.

As the days pass and we forget, as we inevitably will, the ugly truth about the world and about ourselves, let us rest on the truth that the "profound event" of the gospel of Jesus Christ's life, death, and resurrection has happened, and that it alone can recalibrate us, give us hope, and offer true perspective.

It was in the context of my begging my kids, probably for the fifteenth time in ten minutes, to say thank you, that I thought of Jesus's warning that "whoever does not receive the kingdom of God like a child shall not enter it" (v. 17 ESV). Jesus is telling us to be like children? Really? Doesn't He know what children are like? Especially *my* children?

I think, however, it just may be (in a certain sense) our kids' obliviousness to say thank you that Jesus is suggesting we emulate.

Saying thank you is a particularly adult practice. And interestingly, the quality of our thank-you varies depending on the quality of the thing we've been given. It's as if we want our thank-you to repay the original kindness. Big kindnesses get big thank-yous. This is why we get uncomfortable when we get really good gifts. We know that simple thank-yous won't cover the debt we owe. If someone gives us a truly wonderful gift or helps us in a really selfless way, we'll do anything we can to balance the scales again. Being in someone's debt rankles.

Kids have no such problem. When someone gives them a gift, they unwrap it and begin to play immediately. It's we parents who chase after them pleading, "Say thank you!" We might as well be saying what our subconscious is screaming: *You're going to anger the gift giver!*

Jesus wants us to receive the wonderful gift of the kingdom of God as a child would: running off immediately to play with this wonderful gift. After all, doesn't the gift giver want to see his gift played with? Wasn't that the whole point of giving it? The most glorious irony is this: Our unfettered and without-thought play turns out to be more law abiding than our starched-shirt and pleated-pant thank-yous ever could be. Our joy in a wonderful present engenders the kind of thanks (that which is from the heart) that the gift giver was interested in.

Let's receive God's gift of Jesus as if we were children. Your enjoyment of the gift of God is a precious kind of thank-you to Him.

In a first-season episode of *Frasier*, the radio psychiatrist is offered the opportunity to make some extra money by personally endorsing products. As is his custom, he goes to his brother for advice.

"Let's face it, Frasier," his brother Niles says. "You talk about wanting to safeguard your professional dignity, but the first time you went on the air, you got out of medicine and into show biz." Crestfallen, Frasier asks, "So what you're saying is that I shouldn't do it?" "No, no, no," concludes Niles. "I'm saying it doesn't matter."

Niles points out the truth of Frasier's situation, and the truth of the human situation. We let our ethics go long ago. We excuse all manner of sin. We say things like, "No one will ever find out," or, "No one is getting hurt." Niles urges us to stop being so defensive. It doesn't matter! You're already too far gone! This illustrates what happens when this realization hits home. We believe that we are simultaneously justified and sinful. In fact, we urge sinners to take note of the depth of their sin, to be able to see the corresponding grace. But what about the next step? Doesn't such unmerited grace encourage licentiousness? Won't people just do whatever they want, knowing that, as Niles puts it, it doesn't matter?

No! Paul asked, "Shall we go on sinning so that grace may increase? By no means! We are those who have died to sin; how can we live in it any longer?" (vv. 1–2). Robert Capon puts it this way: "To sin so that grace may abound is like a lover desiring to return to a state of unloving in order to experience falling in love again. It's impossible." Frasier *can't* lose his medical ethics. They're gone! So what does he do? Knowing he has the freedom, being already a "sinner" and forgiven by Niles, does he endorse the snack-nut commercial? No, Dr. Joyce Brothers does. Freedom in the gospel does not create license. It creates the thing that the law wanted in the first place: righteousness.

I used to think that when Paul told us to "work out [our] salvation" (Phil. 2:12), it meant go out and get what you don't have—get more patience, get more strength, get more joy, get more love, and so on. But after reading the Bible more carefully, I now understand that Christian growth does not happen by working hard to get something you don't have. Rather, Christian growth happens by working hard to daily swim in the reality of what you do have. Believing again and again the gospel of God's free justifying grace every day is the hard work we're called to.

I'm realizing that the sin I need removed daily is precisely my narcissistic understanding of spiritual progress. I think too much about how I'm doing, if I'm growing, whether I'm doing it right or not. And what I've discovered, ironically, is that the more I focus on my need to get better, the worse I actually get. I become neurotic and self-absorbed. Preoccupation with my performance over Christ's performance for me makes me increasingly self-centered and morbidly introspective. After all, Peter only began to sink when he took his eyes off Jesus and focused on "how he was doing." As my friend Rod Rosenbladt wrote to me recently, "Anytime our natural *incurvitas* [fixture on self] is rattled, shaken, turned from itself to that Man's blood, to that Man's cross, then the devil take the hindmost!"

So by all means, work! But the hard work is not what you think it is—your personal improvement and moral progress. The hard work is washing your hands of you and resting in Christ's finished work for you, which will inevitably produce personal improvement and moral progress. Martin Luther's got a point: "It is not imitation that makes sons; it is sonship that makes imitators."

Jesus caused such a stir in the crowds that, at one point, officers were sent to arrest Him. When they came back empty-handed, the chief priests and Pharisees asked why. Their answer: "No one ever spoke like this man!" (v. 46 ESV). So what was it that Jesus said that made these officers, sent specifically to arrest Him, turn and walk away? I think the answer is found in John 7:37–38, when Jesus said, "If anyone thirsts, let him come to me and drink. Whoever believes in me, as the Scripture has said, 'Out of his heart will flow rivers of living water'" (ESV).

It might not seem like it at first, but Jesus was turning conventional wisdom on its head. Religious people are wired this way: When we thirst for a relationship with God, we participate in the things that are meant to get God interested in us. We pray, we read the Bible, we serve those less fortunate. We work. We think that the good we do will cause God to take notice of us. Jesus basically tells us, "If you thirst, just come. Come as you are. Come thirsty. Come in need. *After* you get close to Me, *then* out of your heart will flow the good works." He's reversing the order! We think it's our good works that bring us close to God, when in fact it's our closeness to God that produces good works.

Of course, the same words that got Jesus out of an arrest here eventually got Him crucified. The temple authorities, who were mediating the relationship between God and humankind, could only let Him go for so long. He was giving it away for free! What had once required hard work, this working our way toward God, was now being offered to anyone.

Jesus met all of God's qualifications so that your relationship to God could be unqualified. If you're thirsty, drink. If you're hungry, eat. If you are a sinner, be saved. It is Christ's, and through Christ, it is yours.

Doesn't it sometimes seem as though all our problems started after we became Christians? Before we were Christians, we had an excuse for all the bad things we did, right? But now, all of a sudden, there are these expectations on our lives, some put there by other people, some put there by the Bible, some put there by ourselves. We hear phrases like, "God loves you just the way you are, but He loves you too much to leave you there." We hear people tell us what "the Christian life" is supposed to look like. For many of us, when we first started with this Christianity thing, it was very much "Your word is a lamp to my feet and a light for my path. I have taken an oath and confirmed it, that I will follow your righteous laws."

But then "the Christian life" actually started happening, and we realized that we couldn't *keep* all of those righteous judgments.

Anyone who makes an honest assessment of the state of their Christian life might well come away saying, "I have suffered much; preserve my life, LORD, according to your word," the Psalm's *very next verse*! We Christians are troubled because we worry that Jesus knows how we sometimes feel about our parents, how we often feel about the poor and needy, and all the other deep, dark secrets we keep locked away, the stuff that seems left over from a time before we were Christians but that we just can't seem to get rid of. We are troubled because we're worried about what Jesus will do. We don't feel more righteous. In fact, we often feel *far* from the Christians we want to be; *far* from the Christians we're expected to be.

Here's some good news: the gospel is for Christians, too. Jesus has paid for your Christian sins just as completely as He paid for your non-Christian sins. There is no condemnation—none—for those in Christ Jesus. Before God, the righteousness of Christ is all we have. Before God, the righteousness of Christ is all we need.

Imagine you're in bed, comfortable and at peace. A knock comes on your door in the middle of the night. Wouldn't you tell the person to go away? We don't want to help when it's inconvenient. Consider the friend who calls and needs to talk *just* when you're on your way out the door to a nice dinner. The child who wants to go to the bathroom during the bottom of the ninth inning.

Sidetracked by a million petty annoyances, we become unable to simply give somebody something they need. We're always calculating the impact it's going to have on us. We say things like, "Ordinarily I would, but ..." or "Any other time ..." People often have to hound us to get what they need. Even our friends. This is what Jesus is telling us about in Luke 11:5–13. He's not saying this is what God is like. He's saying this is what *we* are like. And by contrast, He's saying that God is *not* like this!

If we, who are evil and who need to be hounded into doing even basic good things for those around us, don't give our children snakes instead of fish or scorpions instead of eggs, how much better a gift giver is God? If we, who often can't even do a favor for a friend, know how to give good gifts to our kids, imagine the surpassing splendor of the gifts that God gives! Jesus told the story of the two friends and the locked door to draw attention to the kind of gift giver God is—an awesome one. God is an awesome gift giver in two ways: first, He's always there, and second, His gift is amazing.

We give reluctantly; God gives overflowingly. We give after being hounded; God gives without even being asked. We give to people we think deserve it; God gives to the undeserving. We give only when there's something in it for us; God gives the life of His most beloved Son.

Is it ever appropriate to use the word *sinner* to describe Christian identity? Once God saves us, aren't we new creatures?

My good friend Jono Linebaugh (New Testament professor at Knox Theological Seminary) wrote a clarifying explanation of Luther's famous phrase explaining what is and what is *not* meant that the Christian is *simul justus et peccator*—"at the same time righteous and sinner":

> "Sinner" is an identity word and is misapplied if it's used to name the Christian's identity—their person. Before God, identity is not a both/and (sinner *and* righteous); it is an either/or (sinner *or* righteous). The basis of this difference is not anthropological (what I do or don't do). It is strictly and solely Christological: to be in Christ is to be righteous before God.
>
> Paul does something unprecedented in that he designates all people outside Christ with the identity "sinner" (e.g., Rom. 5:8). But even more novel and scandalous is his corresponding claim that it is precisely "sinners" who are identified as "righteous" *in Christ* (Rom. 3:23–24). So, to borrow an expression from a Reformation confession, while the old Adam is a "stubborn, recalcitrant donkey," this does not define Christian identity before God.... What it is, however, is a description of the both/and that characterizes the Christian life *as lived*.
>
> [This] enables us to affirm (without crossing our fingers) that in Christ—at the level of identity—the Christian is 100 percent righteous before God while at the same time recognizing the persistence of sin. If we don't speak in terms of two total states (100 percent righteous in Christ and 100 percent sinful in ourselves) corresponding to the coexistence of two times (the old age and the new creation) then the undeniable reality of ongoing sin leads to the qualification of our identity in Christ: the existence of some sin must mean that one is not totally righteous. This is acid at the very foundation of the peace we have with God on the other side of justification.

Does being a Christian take practice? This question, though it might seem absurd on the surface, seems to inform a lot of what we spend our time as Christians doing. We think that, like friendships, familial relationships, and intimate relationships, our bond with Christ must be managed, tended, and cultivated, or else we will forever lose it.

The ways in which we Christians endeavor to remain (or become) close to Jesus are often referred to as spiritual "disciplines" (or "practices"). Meditation, prayer, fasting, and solitude are just some of the "practices" that Christians engage in to cultivate "A Closer Walk with Thee." Yours and mine might be different, but we all have things that we do to get the thing that we want most—intimacy with Jesus. In other words, practice makes perfect. The better you practice, the more perfect your relationship with Christ becomes.

Let me suggest to you that, while spiritual practice can help you feel closer to Christ (which is a wonderful thing), it is not our disciplines that establish God's closeness to us.

More so than we would like to admit, our practices can oftentimes be subtle ways we try to climb our way to God. But there is good news! It is not up to us to climb our way to God. In Christ, God has come down to us. Remember: Christianity is founded on, and grounded in, a cross—not a ladder.

So let us pray, have quiet times, fast, worship, and do myriad things to cultivate our relationship with our Savior. But let us never worry that He is absent or estranged, for He has assured us that He will be with us "always, even to the end of the age" (Matt 28:20 NASB). For Christians, then, it is not "practice makes perfect." It's something closer to "Christ's perfection frees you to practice." In Him, our relationship is always secure, and in Him, our practice, whatever it is, is made perfect.

Have you ever watched the high jump event in the Olympics? One of the interesting things about a high jump competition is that competitors can "pass" attempts at lower levels, waiting to jump until the higher, more impressive rounds. Sometimes they do this to save their strength. Sometimes they do it for other reasons. Of course, you only get credit for heights that you actually clear, so passing can be a risky strategy. Here's an example of what I'm talking about. During one Olympic competition a number of years ago, a competitor—who was expected to compete for a medal—passed on all the lower and intermediate heights. So confident was he in his ability, and so desirous of instilling fear in his opponents, he waited until the bar was set only a few inches below his personal best before taking off his sweats and joining the other jumpers.

This is what many Christians do when we think about the law. We imagine that the lower levels are easy: honor your father and mother, don't murder, don't steal. We don't pay a moment's attention to these things, focusing on the things that we think are harder—lust, jealousy, and the like. But it turns out that we've made a terrible mistake.

The high jumper in that Olympic competition knocked the bar off the standards in all three attempts at his first height. He was out of the competition, but more important, he had not cleared a single height. All the other competitors went out on the same height as he did, so if he had cleared even one previous height, he would have been assured a medal. As it was, he went home empty-handed.

What we need to understand as Christians is that the "easy" laws are actually not easy: they condemn us just as readily as the "difficult" laws. We go away sorrowful, realizing that we didn't even clear a single height, unless we reach out our hands for our Savior, who leaps the high bar of the law for us, and gives us His medal.

In the 2006 indie-comedy *Little Miss Sunshine*, there's a family dinner table scene. One member of the family, Uncle Frank, has just come home from a treatment facility after attempting to commit suicide. The daughter of the family, Olive, is obviously itching to ask Uncle Frank about the suicide attempt, but her father, Richard, doesn't want her to spend any time opening herself up to a "loser" like Frank. Finally, though, Frank says that it's okay if they discuss his recent stint in treatment, and so he begins to tell his story.

Frank describes a heartrending descent into depression. Every time Olive says, "And that's when you decided to kill yourself?" he goes a step deeper. Doesn't this often seem to be the way of things? Our disappointments, struggles, and painful experiences often seem to pile on one another until they threaten to overwhelm us.

This truth of life seems to be incontrovertible. Everyone deals with stuff. The bigger question is: What do our failures mean? Do we, as Richard does, think that the onus is on us to fix ourselves? Have we just "made a series of poor choices" that we "right" if we just get our act together? Many people do think this way.

Wouldn't you rather hear the life-giving truth that our relationship with God is not dependent on our making better choices? That though we may give up on ourselves, God never gives up on us? And that, not only does God refuse to give up on us, He comes down to us in Jesus when we fail, again and again?

Thank God we have a better answer than Richard does. Who will rescue us from this body of death? Praise be to God, He delivers us through Jesus Christ our Lord (Rom. 7:24–25).

How can God ask Abraham to sacrifice his son? It's terrible. And then, in the final analysis, it was all just a test. That almost makes it worse, doesn't it? For some people, this is the kind of thing about God that they just can't get past. Sure, God created humankind in His image, gave us dominion over the earth, and blessed us with the ingenuity to create things like art, fine wine, and HDTV. But how could He ask a man to sacrifice his son?

God asks Abraham for something that no father ought to have to do. It seems so out of bounds, so out of the ordinary. But here's the thing: it's actually not at all out of the ordinary. Not for God. God asks us for impossible things *all the time*. He asks us to turn the other cheek, to give away all of our possessions, to have a pure heart, and to have no love for money. Not to mention commanding us to be perfect.

The story of Abraham and Isaac isn't just a thing that happened to a guy one time, an example of a man asked to do an extraordinary and awful thing to prove his faith in God. This story is the ultimate example of what is ultimately true of God. He asks for the impossible. But then He provides.

When the moment comes for Abraham and Isaac, God provides another way. A ram caught in the thicket. This is our story. We are asked to prove our faith, and we fall short. And in that final moment, at that ultimate time, God provides another way. He sacrifices His Son, and we are set free. "'The LORD will provide', as it is said to this day, 'On the mount of the LORD it shall be provided'" (v. 14 ESV).

Today, remember that the Lord has provided the impossible. The God who makes the impossible demands, meets the impossible demands in the giving of a substitute—Jesus.

I remember reading an article about Netflix (the wildly successful video-rental and streaming company) a few years ago that points to how grace actually works. Netflix, it turns out, has no official vacation policy. They let their employees take as much time off as they want, whenever they want, as long as the job is getting done. The article, after noting that "ever more companies are realizing that autonomy isn't the opposite of accountability—it's the pathway to it," quoted Netflix's vice president for corporate communications, Steve Swasey, as saying:

> Rules and policies and regulations and stipulations are innovation killers. People do their best work when they're unencumbered. If you're spending a lot of time accounting for the time you're spending, that's time you're not innovating.

Their policy, or lack thereof, has not resulted in the company going out of business, which many of us, if we were stockholders, would fear it would. In fact, just the opposite. Freed from micromanaging bosses, their employees work even harder. Obviously this is not the same thing as the assurance we have in Christ, but perhaps it is not so different either.

The gospel breaks the chains of reciprocity and the circular exchange. Since there is nothing we ultimately need from one another, we are free to do everything for one another. We can spend our lives giving instead of taking, going to the back instead of getting to the front, sacrificing ourselves for others instead of sacrificing others for ourselves. The gospel alone liberates us to live a life of scandalous generosity, unrestrained sacrifice, uncommon valor, and unbounded courage.

This is the difference between approaching all of life from salvation and approaching all of life for salvation; it's the difference between approaching life from our acceptance, and not for our acceptance; from love not for love. The acceptance letter has arrived, and it cannot be rescinded, thank God.

You've probably heard the story of Peter walking on the water. He gets out of the boat to walk to Jesus, and is miraculously doing just fine. Until, that is, he notices what it is that he's doing. Then he begins to sink. The usual interpretation of this event is that, to be successful, we've got to keep our eyes on Jesus, not on ourselves. This is perfectly true. But there's another thing to notice in this parable, something that's better news than just "Don't make the same mistake that Peter did."

The first thing to note is our current position. Are we in the boat? Are we on the water? I don't think we're in either of those places, so the message to "keep your eyes on Jesus" isn't really appropriate. Or at least, it's not timely. Here's why: *we're already sinking!*

We never do as well as we'd like. We're not the kind of people we'd like to be; we're not the Christians we wish we were. Like Peter, we get out of the boat intending to do well, brimming with faith. But our desire doesn't stop us from starting to feel overwhelmed after just a few steps.

If the bad news is that we're already sinking, the good news is that Jesus is right there. When we start to falter, Jesus is there to reach out His hand. As Peter begins to sink, and calls out, "Lord, save me!" Jesus doesn't step back. He doesn't say, "Let us see how Peter handles this situation. He got himself into it; let's see if he can get himself out." Too many Christians treat sinking with swimming instructions—"Paddle harder, swim faster."

Thankfully for Peter (and for us), when Peter calls out for a Savior, Jesus springs into action. Matthew says that, "Jesus *immediately* reached out his hand and caught him" (v. 31 NRSV). There is no hesitation. No requirement. Just salvation. As we live our lives in Christ, trying to be the faithful people we're called to be, let us never forget that, in this world, we are always sinking. But more than that, let us never forget that, in Christ, we have an intervening Savior.

In Deuteronomy 8, we find a little story that shows clearly that the themes of law and gospel, the two words of God, are carried throughout every page of the Bible, and have always typified God's relationship with His people. In this chapter, we find Moses telling the Israelites that God has *let* them hunger and then given them a food they were unfamiliar with, to humble them so that they would learn a lesson about where real satisfaction comes from. Now this is a kind of God that we feel a little funny about, right? We're on board with a God who *loves us*. Who sacrifices for us. Who puts our sins as far away from us as the east is from the west. *That* we like. We're not quite sure what to make of a God who makes His people go hungry to teach them a lesson.

Moses has given the people the law, the first word of God, to prepare them for the gospel, the second and final word of God. He's talking about giving the people bread they're not acquainted with so that He can introduce them to the bread from heaven. He's talking about acquainting them with trials so that He can acquaint them with a Savior. He's talking about bringing them down low so that He can raise them up. This is why we say, "Swing low, sweet chariot, comin' for to carry me home." Where we are living now is low: we're hungry, we're thirsty, we're lonely. We feel oppressed and like prisoners. We need that chariot to swing low!

The gospel gets low enough. "I am the living bread that came down from heaven. Whoever eats this bread will live forever" (John 6:51). God comes *down*. He never waits for us to go up. He goes to the suffering places, the lonely places—the places in which we live—to bring us home. Out of hunger He brings true fulfillment and out of a crucifixion He brings salvation—for you, for me, forever.

In the Christian soft-rock group 4Him's anthem "Measure of a Man," they sing this:

> *Oh I say the measure of a man*
> *Is not how tall you stand*
> *How wealthy or intelligent you are*
> *'Cause I found out the measure of a man*
> *God knows and understands*
> *For He looks inside to the bottom of your heart*
> *And what's in the heart defines*
> *The measure of a man*

4Him is on the right track. It's not all the stuff on the outside that can be measured that determines who you are. That's how the world thinks. 4Him reminds us that it's "what's in the heart" that defines the measure of a man. But the problem is, they say it like it's good news!

Jesus knows better. He agrees with 4Him that who you are isn't made up of what goes into you. He says none of those things can defile you. According to Jesus, it's not the things that you *do* that get you into trouble, it's the content of your heart. It's the person that you *are*!

Listen to Jesus's description of your heart: "For out of the heart come evil intentions, murder, adultery, fornication, theft, false witness, slander. These are what defile a person" (Matt. 15:19–20 NRSV). We react and say, "I don't do any of those things!" Well, there are those among us who have. But that reaction is just us going back to the worldly way of measuring: forgetting that God looks deeper. "For *out of the heart* come evil intentions, murder, adultery," and so on. It is the seed of these things that is the problem for us.

Today, remember the fact that *God measuring you by your heart* is the worst news of all. But also remember that we are judged on the pure contents of *Jesus's heart*, a heart He has given to us.

Are your friends "keeping you accountable"? If so, do you find yourself lying to them in order to make your Christian life look better than it is? If not, wonderful. If so, you might be in the wrong kind of accountability group.

For those who have been spared, an accountability group is a single-sex, small-group Bible study on steroids. A group of friends arrange for a time each week to get together, ostensibly to encourage one another by upholding standards of personal righteousness in a confidential context. What actually happens is that everyone, in an earnest desire to progress spiritually, begins to concoct an appropriate narrative of improvement.

Listen carefully: Christianity is not first and foremost about our behavior, our obedience, our response, and our daily victory over sin—as important as all these are. It is not first and foremost about us at all. It is first and foremost about Jesus! It is about His person; His substitutionary work; His incarnation, life, death, resurrection, ascension, and promised return. We are justified—and sanctified—by grace alone through faith alone in the finished work of Christ alone. Even now, the banner under which Christians live reads, "It is finished." Everything we need, and everything we look for in things smaller than Jesus, is already ours in Christ.

So I'm all for accountability—but a certain kind. The accountability we really need is the kind that corrects our natural tendency to dwell on ourselves. It sometimes seems that we can't help ourselves from turning the good news of God's grace into a narcissistic program of self-improvement.

The gravitational pull of conditionality is so strong, our hardwiring for law so ingrained, that we need real friends to remind us of the good news every day. In fact, our lives depend on it! So instead of trying to fix one another, perhaps we might try stirring one another up to love and good deeds by daily reminding one another, in humble love, of the riches we already possess in Christ.

Remember the Ben Stiller/Vince Vaughn movie *DodgeBall: A True Underdog Story*? Vaughn and Stiller run competing gyms, and they each have TV ads that play in the film. Here's Stiller's: "I'm here to tell you, you don't have to be stuck with what you've got. Here at Globo-Gym, we understand that 'ugliness' and 'fatness' are genetic disorders ... and it's only your fault if you don't hate yourself enough to do something about it. That's where we come in." He then goes on to describe the "staff of personal alteration specialists" and the on-site plastic surgery center. "Of course," he concludes, when Globo-Gym is finished with you, "you'll still be you in a legal sense, but think of it as a thinner, more attractive, better you than you could ever become without us."

Vaughn's ad takes a totally different tone: "I'm Peter LeFleur, owner and operator of Average Joe's Gym, and I'm here to tell you that you're perfect just the way you are. But if you feel like losing a few pounds, getting healthier, and making some good friends in the process, then Joe's is the place for you."

Theologians might call these two gyms Law Gym (Globo-Gym) and Grace Gym (Average Joe's). The law says "Be fit!" but doesn't have anything other than the commandment itself to get you there. So it keeps yelling, telling you that you're not good enough, that you're not skinny enough, that you should hate this you and move on to a better one. Grace, on the other hand, says that you are beloved, despite yourself. In Christianity, we understand that this belovedness is on account of Jesus Christ (in other words, it's not "you're perfect just the way you are").

Surprisingly, belovedness despite perceived fault is the only true motivator. Vince Vaughn is right: when you feel loved and accepted in advance, you can begin to consider what you really want to do. People who live under the weight of the law will, over time, self-destruct. It is only grace that leads to a "healthy life."

Bill Simmons has popularized an idea that he calls the Ewing Theory. From Simmons's Wikipedia page: "The Ewing Theory claims that when a longtime superstar who has never won a championship leaves the team via injury, trade, or free agency, and the media writes the team off, the team will play better."

The theory takes its name from Patrick Ewing, the all-star center for the New York Knicks, due to the fact that the Knicks always seemed to play better when Ewing was either injured or had to be benched due to foul trouble. In the theory's most classic example, during the 1998–1999 playoffs, Ewing sustained an Achilles tendon injury, and it was widely assumed that the Knicks' season was over. However, they promptly defeated the Pacers, even without an answer for Indiana's giant center, Rik Smits. They did ultimately lose in the finals, to the San Antonio Spurs.

So did the Knicks get better by losing a great player? Did addition by subtraction occur?

Of course, the addition-by-subtraction model is as familiar to Christians as a Thomas Kinkade print. A common prayer is to ask that "we might decrease so that [Christ] might increase." What is less familiar to Christians is the underlying truth of the addition-by-subtraction formulation: no one subtracts on purpose.

The Knicks discovered by accident that playing without Ewing made them better. They would never have intentionally played without him. And in the same way, we never consciously decrease so that Christ might increase. This is something that God does to us, for our benefit, not something that we do for ourselves. We think too highly of our own abilities to ever think to add by subtraction. So, much like a torn Achilles tendon, God must break us down against our will in order to resurrect us. I've heard it said that one of God's jobs is to destroy the idols in our lives. Unfortunately for us, our main idol is ourselves. We must be destroyed in order to be remade. Fortunately, God promises to do just that.

Are you worried that your kids are rebelling against you? The thing is this: no matter what we do, whether we reject the kind of childhood we had or try to re-create it, law will engender rebellion.

Neither rejection nor assumption can relieve the weight of law on our shoulders. We either terrorize ourselves trying to find the right blazer for the occasion, or terrorize ourselves when our kids do. The only way out from under is to answer our fearful question—*Am I screwing it up?*—in the affirmative.

"Yes," we must say, "certainly you are. I am too." We need to confess to ourselves and our kids that we are messing up and ask for forgiveness.

Law is merciless. It crushes both our attempts to appease it and our attempts to escape it. Thankfully, the gospel describes a way to freedom: the law crushes Another. "Surely he has borne our griefs and carried our sorrows; yet we esteemed him stricken, smitten by God, and afflicted. But he was pierced for our transgressions; he was crushed for our iniquities; upon him was the chastisement that brought us peace, and with his wounds we are healed" (vv. 4–5 ESV).

As parents, words like *grief* and *sorrow* are familiar. Words like *peace* and *healing* are so gloriously foreign that we barely comprehend their meaning. Perhaps there is no person more in need of substitutionary atonement than a parent with a severely difficult child.

But there is substitution! The weight of the law has been put on Another. Our failures as parents have been carried and nailed to the cross. The laws we place on ourselves and create for our kids are taken up by Christ and defeated forever. The only thing that can save us—the intervention of a substitute—has actually taken place. Our efforts to live up to the laws in our lives, and our efforts to subvert them, have only led to grief and sorrow. Christ alone is the Source of peace and healing.

"Unconditionality" is incomprehensible to us. We are deeply conditioned against unconditionality because we've been told in a thousand different ways that accomplishment always precedes acceptance, that achievement always precedes approval. When we hear, "Of course you don't deserve it, but I'm giving it to you anyway," we wonder, "What is this really about? What's the catch?" Internal bells and alarms start to go off, and we begin saying, "Wait a minute … this sounds too good to be true."

You see, everything in our world demands two-way love. Everything is conditional. If I achieve, we reason, only then will I receive everything I long for. That's how our world works. But grace isn't from our world. It's otherworldly. It's unconditional.

Even those of us who have tasted the radical saving grace of God find it intuitively difficult not to put conditions on grace. Don't take it too far! Keep it balanced! But grace is, by its own definition, unbalanced. Grace is a gift, not a wage. It's a gift of love, and lavish love gifts never sit quite right with the bookkeeping, wage-earning, responsible citizen that resides in our own hearts.

Need proof? We need look no further than Mary's profligate anointing of the Savior in preparation for His death for a snapshot of our own hearts. She was both misunderstood and censured by those ever-so-responsible disciples in attendance. The giving of something costly to another simply because one loves, without expecting anything in return, is inequity in action. We recoil at it. What could ever be balanced about something as lopsided as one-way love? One-way love has no qualifiers, no conditions, no buts. It's unconditional, unpredictable, and undomesticated. You can't put brakes on it because it's not yours to measure out or control.

Contrary to what we conclude naturally, the gospel is not too good to be true. It is true! It's the truest truth in the entire universe. No strings attached! No fine print to read. No buts. No conditions. No qualifications. No footnotes. And especially, no need for balance.

Some of the best, mind-blowing paragraphs I've ever read on grace come from Robert Capon. The following sentences on preaching made me sing:

> I think good preachers should be like bad kids. They ought to be naughty enough to tiptoe up on dozing congregations, steal their bottles of religion pills ... and flush them all down the drain. The church, by and large, has drugged itself into thinking that proper human behavior is the key to its relationship with God. What preachers need to do is force it to go cold turkey with nothing but the word of the cross—and then be brave enough to stick around while [the congregation] goes through the inevitable withdrawal symptoms.
>
> But preachers can't be that naughty or brave unless they're free from their own need for the dope of acceptance. And they won't be free of their need until they can trust the God who has already accepted them, in advance and dead as doornails, in Jesus. *Ergo*, the absolute indispensability of trust in Jesus' passion. Unless the faith of preachers is in that alone—and not in any other person, ecclesiastical institution, theological system, moral prescription, or master recipe for human loveliness—they will be of very little use in the pulpit.

Amen and amen!

There are way too many "good, religious kids" in the pulpit these days pushing the idea that is most naturally comfortable to all of us: proper human behavior is key to our relationship with God.

May God raise up a generation of preachers who fearlessly storm the gates of "just do it" religion with the jaw-dropping, chain-breaking, cage-rattling, freedom-inducing words of our Savior from the cross: "It is finished." I pray every day for God to unleash desperate preachers who are bold enough to push the irrational logic of His grace in the face of enslaved people.

So go on, preachers, I dare you. In fact, I double-dog dare you. There's no better time to abandon your preaching to those three game-changing, paradigm-shattering words than today.

There's a scene in *Fight Club* in which Brad Pitt's character explains to Edward Norton's that if he wants to be free, he has to give up the things he holds most dear. "First you have to give up," he says. "You have to know—not fear, *know*—that someday, you're gonna die." To drive his point home, he burns Norton's hand with lye, to show him the weakness of his body. Pitt might be crazy, but he's also right. This is the first step to freedom—to know that the road of the cross leads to Calvary. He goes on: "It's only after we've lost everything that we're free to do anything."

We resist. "Lose everything? Deny myself?" we protest. "But that'll mean weakness … and death. That'll be the end of me!" The somethings we hold on to, the things we imagine are keeping us alive, are the very things that are killing us. The things we own end up owning us. Ed Norton puts our greatest fear into words: "You don't know how this feels!" We cry so to God, "You rip my desires, my hopes, my dreams—my life!—away from me. You don't know how this feels!" Brad Pitt holds up his hand, with an identical lye burn scar, proving to the faithless that he's been here before.

Like Thomas, converted by the wounds of the risen Christ, Norton is converted by Brad Pitt's wounds. He has passed this test. He has carried this cross. Jesus Christ has borne His cross so that death can be not just an end for the old us, but a beginning for the new us. Christ died so that we might live. He died, and we died with Him (Gal. 2:20), so that now we can be free. We have to know, not suspect, the reality of the cross. It is only then that we can really be free.

The good news is, in those moments when you feel as if God is killing you, He is. But He's killing you to make you alive. Behold, says Jesus, the old has passed away. The new has come.

All good theology is an exposition of the gospel.

In his letter to the Christians of Colossae, the apostle Paul portrays the gospel as the instrument of all continued growth and spiritual progress, even after a believer's conversion. In Colossians 1:6, he speaks of the gospel as some kind of holy spiritual force—a power—hijacking all creation.

A friend once told me that all our problems in life stem from our failure to apply the gospel. This means I can't really move forward unless I learn more thoroughly the gospel's content and how to apply it to all of life. Real change does not and cannot come independently of the gospel. God intends His good news in Christ to mold and shape us at every point and in every way. It increasingly defines the way we think, feel, and live.

And since the gospel is the "power of God for salvation," we know that even for the most saintly of saints, the gospel is wholly relevant and vitally necessary. This means heralded preachers need the gospel just as much as hardened pagans.

The gospel doesn't just ignite the Christian life; it's also the fuel that keeps Christians going and growing every day. It impacts my longing for approval, my tendency to be controlling, and my fear of the unknown. When I experience agitation, impatience, unease, and anxiety, I try to identify where my restlessness is rooted, because that's where a confrontation with the gospel is needed. Whatever deficiency lies at the deepest root of our restlessness—no matter how big or small, whether it's life gripping or comparatively trivial— the missing component is something very specific that Christ has already secured for restless sinners like you and me.

The good news of the gospel is that we have been captured and are daily recaptured by the "God of great expenditure" who gave everything that we might possess all.

Musician Rich Mullins once wrote:

> I have attended church regularly since I was less than a week old. I've listened to sermons about virtue, sermons against vice. I have heard about money, time management, tithing, abstinence, and generosity. I've listened to thousands of sermons. But I could count on one hand the number of sermons that were a simple proclamation of the gospel of Christ.

It's not just Rich. I received the following letter recently from someone I've never met. He wrote:

> Over the last couple of years, we have really been struggling with the preaching in our church, as it has been very law laden and moralistic. After listening, I feel condemned with no power to overcome my lack of ability to obey. Over the last several months, I have found myself very spiritually depressed, to the point where I had no desire to even attend church. Pastors are so concerned about somehow preaching "too much grace" (as if that is possible) because they wrongly believe that type of preaching leads to licentiousness. But I can testify that the opposite is actually true. I believe preaching only the law actually leads to lawless living. When mainly law is preached, it leads to the realization that I can't follow it, so I might as well quit trying.

So sad. You see, the ironic thing about legalism is that it not only doesn't make people work harder, it makes them give up. It is no coincidence, for example, that the straitlaced *Leave It to Beaver* generation preceded the "free love" movement of the 1960s.

We make a big mistake when we conclude that the law is the answer to bad behavior. In fact, the law alone stirs up more of such behavior. This isn't to say the Spirit doesn't use both God's law and God's gospel in our lives and for our good. But the law and the gospel do very different things. Thankfully, it is the gospel, not the law, that has the last word over you today.

Do you have a piece of art in your house that says, "As for me and my house, we will serve the Lord"? Many people do. I think this verse makes up part of one of the funniest parts of the Bible. It's not intended to be funny, but to me it is. After Joshua makes this great proclamation of faithfulness, he tells the people to choose whom they will serve. That's the freedom that William Wallace—"They may take our lives, but they will never take our freedom!"— and Patrick Henry—"Give me liberty or give me death"—wanted, right? Joshua is allowing the people to choose. "Choose this day." And it seems as though they've made a good decision, right? They say, "We too will serve the Lord, because he is our God" (v. 18).

What's funny to me is what comes in the very next verse. Usually, when we think of these verses, we stop right after the choosing part, don't we? But listen to Joshua's response to the people: "You are not able to serve the Lord. He is a holy God."

So Joshua seems to think the people are a lot less free than they think they are, doesn't he? Sure, they're free to *say* that they'll serve the Lord, but according to Joshua's view of their human nature, they're not free to *actually do it*. They're bound to sin, just as we are.

To the extent that we have freedom, we use it in our humanity and therefore we use it to sin; we use it to serve other gods, gods of our own creation. Praise God, we're nowhere near as free as we imagine that we are! That's good news. Jesus said that we did not choose Him, but that He chose us, and gave Himself for us, as an offering and sacrifice to God.

This is the gospel, that even when we use our freedom—such as it is—to run from God, Jesus chooses us, dies for us, and rises to earn us new life.

In a critical scene in the film *Batman Begins*, Rachel Dawes accuses Bruce Wayne of being too busy being a billionaire playboy to care about the welfare of Gotham City. She even goes so far as to say that, "It's not who you are underneath; it's what you do that defines you." Little does she know, of course, that he's Batman, fighting to save Gotham by night. She's doing what we all do: judging the man by his actions (or at least, what she knows of them). This way of judging was put forward by Aristotle in his *Nichomachean Ethics*. A man, according to Aristotle, acts in good ways and bad. If his good deeds outweigh his evil deeds, then he is good. Pretty standard stuff.

But the Bible says something quite different: "The LORD does not look at the things people look at. People look at the outward appearance, but the LORD looks at the heart" (1 Sam. 16:7). Jesus also called the Pharisees whitewashed tombs, claiming that though they were beautiful on the outside, inside they contained only death (Matt. 23:27). It seems, then, that the Bible would dispute Rachel's claim that it doesn't matter who you are on the inside. Jesus said quite clearly that it doesn't matter what you do on the outside; it's the content of your heart that counts.

Sometimes, we can actually convince ourselves that this is a good thing: *Good*, we think, *God doesn't care about my embarrassing actions; He sees my good intentions.* It never takes too long, however, for us to realize that, most of the time, our intentions are even more embarrassing than our actions. We survive other people seeing the things that we do. But can you imagine surviving other people seeing what you *think*?

Today, remember that we have a Savior whose work is more profound than just covering our sinful exteriors. He sees, knows, and forgives (on account of His death and resurrection for us) our wicked insides along with our wicked outsides.

Have you heard the old worship song "Lord, I Lift Your Name on High"? I spent years singing that song. I really never thought twice about it until an older pastor that I knew started grumbling about how he didn't like it. At first, I just assumed he was being an old curmudgeon who didn't like guitars in church. Finally, I asked him what the problem was, and I was surprised at his answer: he said that he didn't agree theologically with one of the lines in the song, which went, "He came from heaven to earth to show the way." According to this old pastor, Jesus didn't come to earth to show the way, He came to *be* the way. You know what? That old pastor was absolutely right.

When we think primarily of Jesus as a trailblazer, someone who came to show us the right things to do, we operate in the realm of the law. Of course, Jesus *did* come to show us the right things to do. The law is good, right, and true. We should live the lives that Jesus exemplified. But of course, we run into a problem: the law is *too* good, right, and true. The bar that Jesus set by His life is too high for us to clear. We strive and we strive, but we still cannot accomplish what God requires—perfection. There is good news even in our failure though: trailblazer is not Jesus's final, or most important, job.

My old pastor friend was right: Jesus came for a much better and more profound reason than to show us the way. He came to be the way. At the end of His life, Jesus traded in His trailblazer job description for that of a Savior. He did not hang on the cross and shout, "Now live as I have lived!" He shouted, "It is finished!" This is the realm of the gospel.

Josh Hamilton was a great baseball player. Then he lost it all in a wave of drugs and alcohol. Years later, amazingly, he became a great baseball player again. He gave his faith all of the credit for his renaissance. But then, after another several years of sobriety, he was photographed drinking in a bar in 2012. What happened?

Here's a bit of a 2012 article on Hamilton by Bryan Curtis:

> The problem with The Story [of Hamilton's recovery from drug and alcohol addiction and development into one of baseball's best players] wasn't that Hamilton was telling it too much. The problem was that The Story was too perfect. Its happy ending left no room for a fourth act. Which is to say, the improbable, occasionally strange life that Hamilton was continuing to live and the odd turns of fate that would occur over the course of a baseball season. Here, we come to the 2012 Texas Rangers.
>
> In February, Hamilton went out in Dallas and started drinking. At some point during the night, he called Ian Kinsler. Hamilton committed no crime, and a relapse is about the most predictable thing that can happen to an addict. But drinking didn't jibe with The Story. For if faith had helped Josh ward off Satan's stench, why was Satan back?

In other words, how can Christians be such bad people sometimes?

Remember once again Martin Luther's famous formulation *simul justus et peccator* ("at the same time justified and sinner"). Paul felt this simultaneity an incredible struggle, calling out for rescue from his "body of death" (Rom. 7:24 ESV).

Of course, Josh Hamilton has led a life that seems to belie all the good he's done: he's human (*peccator*). How sweet, then, is the news that our Savior came to save (*justus*) those who consistently slip back into sin, who know what they ought to do but cannot carry it out, and who consistently fail. Christianity is not a religion to help bad people get better, but a faith in a God who came to die for bad people.

When I was younger, we were told that the person we were to imitate was Michael Jordan. We all wanted to "be like Mike." It's what we do: we're imitators. We sort of hate that about ourselves. We'd really *like* to be unique, singular people, but we're terrified that it's not true. That's why we act out.

There's a scene in the movie *Garden State* where Natalie Portman stands up, walks to a certain place in the room, and does a really random thing, saying that at least *that one thing* has never been done before, in that particular place. If nothing else, she can lay claim to *one* unique action. But despite our attempts to be unique, I think we find it much safer to imitate. We want to be like Mike. We want to be like Rosa Parks, or Mother Teresa, or Jasper Johns, or John Irving, or Steve Jobs, or, as Homer Simpson says, "sort of like Jesus, but not in a blasphemous way."

Interestingly, when Paul writes about imitation, he suggests that we imitate *him*! This is the height of self-absorption, isn't it? But look closer: Paul never mentions anything good about himself! In fact, he is constantly referring to himself in a state of need. "Our citizenship is in heaven," he says. "It is from there that we are expecting a Savior, the Lord Jesus Christ. He will transform the body of our humiliation that it may be conformed to the body of his glory" (vv. 20–21 ESV). How is it that Paul wants us to imitate him? He might as well be saying, "Stop trying to imitate everyone you look up to. It's just making your life hurt. Instead, imitate me by waiting for a Savior. He will take the humiliation you feel, having failed to live up to expectations, and turn it into His glory."

Today, don't worry about imitating Michael Jordan, Rosa Parks, or Mother Teresa. Imitate Paul. Know that Jesus has come for you even when your imitation of Him is sorely lacking. He won't wait for you to be like Him. He loves you now.

Jeremiah described God's speech in two kinds: destructive (pluck up, pull down, destroy, overthrow) and constructive (build, plant). Both are essential.

God's first word is one of judgment and destruction. He's sending His prophet to announce plucking up and pulling down. God will get rid of everything in our lives that is not of Him. He's going through the rooms of our hearts, and it's spring-cleaning time. He's clearing out the cobwebs, taking out the garbage, and mopping the floor. And our hearts are in need of renovation. Later in his book, Jeremiah wrote about us humans: "The heart is deceitful above all things, and desperately sick; who can understand it?" (Jer. 17:9 ESV). Our deceitful hearts are the reason that God's first word is a word of destruction.

But remember, God's first word is never God's last word.

After plucking up and pulling down, after destroying and overthrowing, there is always building and planting. In fact, you *can't* build and plant until you've destroyed and overthrown. Land must be cleared for new growth. We plant in the winter for growth in the spring. You can't have resurrection until you've had crucifixion. Jesus said, "Unless a grain of wheat falls into the earth and dies, it remains alone; but if it dies, it bears much fruit" (John 12:24 ESV).

And so today we see again that weakness is the key to the whole thing. Our weakness reminds us, ultimately, of our death, which is the avenue of Christ's power. And honestly, who doesn't feel weak? Jesus's message is a message for the weak. We've already been plucked up and pulled down … we've already been destroyed and overthrown. We're ready for building and planting.

We are weak, but Christ is strong. And in the same way that God puts words in His prophet's mouth, He puts Christ in our place, giving Him up to death so that we might live.

In *The Mission*, Robert De Niro plays the New World slave trader Rodrigo Mendoza. Mendoza returns from a slave-gathering trip to find that the woman he loves has fallen in love with his brother. In a fit of rage, and being a violent man, Mendoza duels with and kills his brother.

He is immediately wracked with overwhelming guilt, and imprisons himself. It is there that he is visited by a priest who broaches the subject of forgiveness. Being Catholic, expiation takes the form of penance, and the priest asks Mendoza to choose his penance. "There is no penance hard enough for me!" growls Mendoza. But as those of you who've seen the movie know, Mendoza comes up with something.

Mendoza carries all of his armor (his identity as a slave trader and mercenary) on his back up a mountainous waterfall toward the local indigenous Guarani community. His statement that there is "no penance hard enough" for him is a common, though oft-suppressed, human sentiment. We feel that we are beyond the reach of grace. We are too far gone. With all our heart, we work for righteousness, all the while cultivating a certainty that we can never be good enough. Mendoza attempts to cleanse his soul through work.

When he finally gets to the summit, hours later and covered in mud, one of the Guarani runs up to him and holds a knife to his vulnerable throat. Mendoza, however, is now without the strength necessary to protect himself. In an act of amazing forgiveness, the Indian, rather than cutting Mendoza's throat, cuts the armor from his body, freeing him.

The Guarani has no reason to forgive Mendoza, but does. Mendoza's tears after the armor is cut away betray his feeling that the forgiveness is still unmerited. Indeed, how has his "work," the penance for his brother's murder, benefited the Guarani? It hasn't. Yet Mendoza is forgiven anyway. So are we.

Today, remember that you are forgiven by the quality of God's grace, not by the quantity of your work.

When Paul is at the Areopagus, he sees evidence of what we might call "universal law" or simply, "universal demand." The Athenians are worshipping a lot of gods, but just in case they've missed one, they've set up an idol to a sort of miscellaneous god. On the off chance there is some deity out there who must be appeased, they hope that this generic altar will get the job done.

We spend our whole lives in unconscious pursuit of something that can never be achieved—perfection. The ongoing and vague dissatisfaction we have with our lives can only be explained by the fact that we are only satisfied by perfection. As long as we aren't quite perfect, we aren't quite happy. So we do what the Athenians did, and erect an altar to an unknown god.

We try to give this god of perfection appropriate sacrifices. Our lives are full of unknown gods, and we spend our lives building altars to them.

Paul doesn't tell us to stop trying. Paul gives perfection a name: God the Father. And in that name, he gives us a way out: the sacrifice of God the Son.

We know that telling ourselves we don't need to be perfect doesn't work. We also know that continuing to strive toward perfection doesn't work either. The answer can only be repentance. We throw up our hands at our failure to be acceptable and rest on the One who was and is acceptable: Jesus Christ.

You've probably heard that the Bible has 613 laws in it. That sounds like a tough number to follow, doesn't it? But what if I told you that there were really only two? Then, perhaps, you'd think you have a chance.

Jesus took all the rules and translated them into, "Just love God with everything you have, and love your neighbor as yourself." That's a load off, right? Or is it? Is loving my neighbor as myself really a lightened load? To really think of others before I think of myself? A while ago, I was an angry and self-centered person for two days because I had a piece of meat stuck in my teeth. I'm serious! I was ornery, annoyed. Because of a piece of meat. I know I'm supposed to love my neighbor, but I was completely helpless. A piece of meat defeated me. I was an utter failure at loving my neighbor, let alone loving God.

It turns out, as I actually live my life, that loving my neighbor as myself is impossible for me, even when I have clean teeth. I'm always thinking of myself. I want to watch the movies that I want to watch, I want to eat the food that I want to eat, I want to sleep as late as I want to sleep, and so on. Wherever I turn, people are getting in the way of my doing what I want to do. And don't even get me started about all the ways my kids infringe on what I want to do.

I wish it were true that I could read the great commandment, "Love the Lord your God with all your heart and with all your soul and with all your mind…. Love your neighbor as yourself" (vv. 37, 39) and feel good about it. The truth is, it makes me feel like a failure. Jesus didn't come to make the laws easier; He came to show how hard they really are.

But today, remember that He also came to follow them in your place and to give you His perfect obedience as a free gift.

Doesn't it often seem like the harder we work to make something happen, the further and further that thing gets away from us? Like there are cosmic forces at work preventing us from getting the thing we want, the thing we deserve?

Drop Dead Gorgeous is a mockumentary about a small-town beauty pageant and the lengths to which the girls will go to win the title American Teen Princess. It's also a funny reflection on human inability to achieve the ends we want. There's one girl in town, Becky Leeman, who wins everything. As much as the Leeman family tries to make sure that Becky wins the pageant (which she does), the victory is a Pyrrhic one, lasting only for an evening before everything is taken from all of them. Kirsten Dunst plays the runner-up who benefits from the Leemans' downfall. It's noteworthy that Dunst doesn't move on to the state or national pageants because of her talents; she moves on, as one might say, by the grace of God. At one point, when she bemoans the circumstances by which she won the local pageant, her aunt says, "You are a good person. Good things happen to good people." This is what we all think, or at least wish was the case.

A world in which God rewarded good people and punished bad people sounds good to us; it sounds fair. Of course, it only sounds good to us to the extent that we are able to convince ourselves that we are good.

When Dunst questions her aunt's assumption that good things happen to good people and says, "Really?" the aunt cracks, "No, it's pure [expletive], sweetie. You're lucky as hell." What one woman calls luck another might call divine intervention.

It is good news that God doesn't reward the good and punish the bad. If He did, that would be bad news for all of us. Our God comes to the bad people, giving them His Son's righteousness in exchange for their sins.

Jesus tells a fascinating parable about a dishonest manager. About to be fired, the manager reduces the debts of his master's clients, so that they'll think well of him when he's thrown out on his ear. Despite everything the story may teach us, this is a simple parable about a guy who finds himself in a tight spot, a position where he's caught between the boss and the people who owe money to the boss. He's going to have to pick between them. Does he side with the boss, his superior, perhaps by collecting more than is owed, or does he side with the debtors, those below him, by cutting debts?

On the one hand, he can ingratiate himself to the higher-ups. This is probably the first thought most of us have. This is our natural instinct.

The same is true of our relationship with God. If we think of God as our angry employer, we begin to feel the pressure to be the best employee, the best Christian, of all time. "I'll help the most homeless people," you might say. "I'll give more to the church than I've ever given before." "I'll be so nice to that person I hate, God will surely notice!" This is how many of us live our lives, treating God as if He were our boss and we were on probation.

But the manager goes the other way. He aligns himself with the people who owe the boss. He goes with the people below him, rather than with the person above him. And he's right. Both the boss in the story and Jesus telling the story commend him. This is the choice to make.

We are debtors, just like the dishonest manager. Thankfully, we have an Intercessor, Someone who comes and pays our debts, Jesus Christ. We don't need to impress the boss; Jesus does that for us and makes us impressive *in Him* in the process.

In the 2012 playoffs, the Yankees went down in flames, and they did it in a way that no one expected: the Bronx Bombers couldn't hit! Long known for using their high-priced "murderer's row" offense to make up for shaky starting pitching, the 2012 Yankees lost close, low-scoring games because they couldn't score any runs. Alex Rodriguez took most of the blame because of his overwhelming contract.

Yankees fans, used to cheering the long ball, got frustrated. For one game, a fan took the time to paint a giant sign saying "A-Rod: Redeem Thyself" and bring it to Yankee Stadium. How do you think Rodriguez felt, looking up into the stands and seeing that sign? I know how I would feel. I'd want to jump over the wall, clamber up to that fan's row, and scream in his face, "Look, I'm *trying* to get hits! Don't you think I'd be playing better if it were up to me? Don't you think I'd redeem myself if I could?"

Self-redemption is every human being's fondest hope, but it's also our impossible dream. In sports, people always talk about the disaster that can come from trying to make up for failures on the next play. The assertion is simple: we can't redeem ourselves.

Humans refuse to believe that we are beyond helping ourselves. In fact, we often protest that God only helps those who do help themselves. We dearly wish that we could atone for the mistakes of the past, and say, "Thanks but no thanks" to the offered atoning death of Another. We're uncomfortable owing someone so much.

We only acknowledge our need for a savior when the idol of self-salvation is unceremoniously ripped from our grasp. A few days after the "Redeem Thyself" sign appeared at Yankee Stadium, the Detroit Tigers' Justin Verlander annihilated the Yankees with a three-hit shutout. This loss served as the hammer of God, finally convincing the Yankees and their fans that a savior from within is not enough.

Today, let us celebrate the good news that we have a Redeemer, and He is not us.

Do you know the story of the *Little Red Hen*? It's the children's story in which a little red hen finds some grains of wheat and asks the duck, the pig, and the cat for help in all the different stages of making bread. None of them want to help her plant the wheat, harvest wheat, take the wheat to the miller, and so on. When she finally takes a hot and fresh loaf of bread out of the oven, though, and needs help eating it, the other animals finally do want to help! "No you won't," said the Little Red Hen. "You wouldn't help me plant the seed, cut the wheat, go to the miller, make the dough, or bake the bread. Now my three chicks and I will eat this bread ourselves!"

This is how the world works: if you don't put in, you don't get to take out. You don't get to reap where you did not sow. Ronald Reagan even told a version of this story in which the Little Red Hen was *forced* to share her bread with those who hadn't worked for it and lost her motivation to keep working hard, which resulted in the entire barnyard ending up in poverty! If the moral of the story is that you can't reap the benefits of something you didn't work for, Reagan took it one step further and said that if you were to get the benefits of something you didn't work for, it would ruin everything.

Though the world works this way, Christianity doesn't. We have a God who doesn't require that we be involved in the recipe for salvation. We have a God who does the planting, the cutting, the carrying, the kneading, and the baking all by Himself, and who then offers us delicious bread to eat. We take out, though we don't put in; we reap where we do not sow. God's generosity doesn't ruin everything; it pours out every good gift on us, His undeserving children.

I once had a youth pastor point out the incongruity of Christians wearing cross jewelry. It's like someone walking around wearing an electric chair necklace. You'd start to wonder about that person, right? But Christians have seriously adopted as our central symbol the device that was used to execute the worst criminals the first century had. It would be gruesome, if it weren't so important. The importance and centrality of the cross is what led Paul to tell the Corinthians that when he came to them he "decided to know nothing among you except Christ and him crucified" (v. 2 ESV). He's putting everything else aside.

This means that for Paul, Jesus was not primarily a teacher, or a healer, or a social activist. This means that Jesus was, first and foremost, a Savior.

This, of course, is not revolutionary, but it is easily forgotten. There's a reason we talk a lot about the cross. It changed everything. There's a reason the earliest Christians chose a method of execution as the symbol with which they would identify themselves. It was through a death that the world was saved. In the same way Paul said he came to the Corinthians humbly, we read about Jesus humbling Himself, even so far as to die on the cross.

This is the most powerful thing in history. Sally Lloyd-Jones's *The Jesus Storybook Bible* puts it like this:

> The full force of the storm of God's fierce anger at sin was coming down. On his own Son. Instead of his people. It was the only way God could destroy sin, and not destroy his children whose hearts were filled with sin. Then Jesus shouted out in a loud voice, "It is finished!" And it was. He had done it. Jesus had rescued the whole world.

Jesus was humbled, taking the sin of the world onto Himself and offering His righteousness to us, His sinful people.

This quote from Robert Capon is one of my all-time favorites:

> The Reformation was a time when men went blind, staggering drunk because they had discovered, in the dusty basement of late medievalism, a whole cellar full of fifteen-hundred-year-old, two-hundred proof grace—bottle after bottle of pure distillate of Scripture, one sip of which would convince anyone that God saves us single-handedly. The word of the Gospel—after all those centuries of trying to lift yourself into heaven by worrying about the perfection of your bootstraps—suddenly turned out to be a flat announcement that the saved were home before they started.… Grace has to be drunk straight: no water, no ice, and certainly no ginger ale; neither goodness, nor badness, not the flowers that bloom in the spring of super spirituality could be allowed to enter into the case.

Are you busy mixing or do you drink grace straight? Are you always in a spiritual hurry or is your soul free to rest and raise a glass? Is it possible that free grace in Christ causes people to love like Christ?

Reflecting on the Capon quote, John Dink wrote:

> We want so desperately to mix in some of our rule-keeping or our performance … we'd give anything to add something of our own label! But it never turns out as we had hoped. We start to feel like we can't keep up our end of the bargain—we feel as though we've failed. But … what if we don't need our own label? What if Jesus kept up our end of the bargain for us? Those who are broken and bold enough to ask the questions, find themselves seated at a table with smiling sinners—too drunk on grace to remember the rules, and yet, they all seem to know them by heart. We're served glass upon glass and something happens … the Gospel becomes the power of God and the wisdom of God. The power of God, because we taste something strong enough to save us. The wisdom of God, because we taste something good enough to change us. The bar is always open and the drinks are all paid for—just thank the Bar Tender, raise your glass and drink it straight. It's all Grace.

Days of Thunder is such a fun movie. But it contains at least one moment of true profundity. After Cole Trickle has had a terrible accident, he's badgering his doctor, Claire, to let him race again. She says, "You shouldn't be driving a car anywhere. You're selfish, you're crazy, and you're scared. You want to control something that's out of control; that's what you said to me, wasn't it? Well I'm going to let you in on a little secret that almost everybody else in this world automatically knows: control is an illusion, you infantile egomaniac."

Though I don't think that most people "automatically know" that they are basically unable to control anything about their lives, I do think that Claire is right in her main assertion. Control is often an illusion. Cole's assertion that he desires to "control something that's out of control" (his race car) is an obvious contradiction in terms. Even if he is able to control the car he's in, he can't control the other "infantile egomaniacs" on the track.

As Claire points out, we can't even control the goings-on within our own bodies! We can exercise, eat right, take vitamins, use medicine, and even buy plastic surgery, but we can't really forestall that thing we're hoping to avoid. Everybody dies.

This urge to control goes all the way back to Eden when Adam and Eve desired to "be like God," in other words, to be in control. The result of their decision is that we all desire control and, more nefariously, have convinced ourselves that we have it. The upshot of this delusion is that, as our sense of control rises, our feeling of need (especially for a Savior) wanes. Better to acknowledge the truth of the situation, that we are perilously out of control, both internally and externally, and are just moments away from a debilitating crash.

Eyes open to the realities of life and our lack of control, we are much more likely to cry out for help. The good news of Christianity is that, in Jesus Christ, that help has come.

The parable of the eleventh-hour workers is well known. The master of the house hires laborers in the morning to work his vineyard at an agreed-upon wage. At different points throughout the day, he hires more workers, including some that are hired at the eleventh hour, that is, an hour before the end of the workday.

At the end of the day, he paid the workers who had worked the least first and decided to pay them the same amount that he had promised the laborers who worked all day.

When the workers who had worked all day were paid the wage they'd agreed to, they were angry. After they saw what the eleventh hour workers had made, they'd expected more. When we read this story, it's easy enough to understand why they felt cheated. Wouldn't you?

But we forget that in the economy of the gospel, *we are the eleventh-hour workers*. Some people are pretty good at keeping it together, so it's easy to convince ourselves that we deserve some greater reward. But the truth is, we're far worse off than we think. Are you ever not "all you can be"? Do you have regrets from a damaged relationship? Do you have a dark secret that you can't share with anyone? Jesus says, "You. You there that no one else thinks deserves much of anything. I'm here for you. Not because you worked hard, but because I am generous. I give you the same free gift, bought and paid for with My own life, that I give to those who you think are better than you." This is a free gift of love and a free gift of grace. It's a love that is *given*—a love for which you never have to work.

Psalm 26 is a gorgeous poem, but it rings a little hollow for me. Lines such as "Vindicate me, LORD, for I have led a blameless life" (v. 1) and "I do not sit with the deceitful, nor do I associate with hypocrites" (v. 4) and "I wash my hands in innocence" (v. 6) just seem like lines no human being could ever have written. Is there really someone so righteous that these lines wouldn't seem like the height of self-delusion? Was this poem written by Jesus Christ Himself?

Well, that's an interesting question.

Psalm 26 was written by David—the same David who murdered Uriah in order to take Bathsheba as his wife. So what happened? How can this man write these things about himself?

The answer can be found in a single sentence spoken to David when his crime and sin became public. The prophet Nathan reveals David's sin to him, causing David to say, simply, "I have sinned against the LORD." It's the sentence that Nathan then speaks over David that allows him to proclaim his innocence in Psalm 26 despite being anything but: "The LORD has taken away your sin. You are not going to die" (2 Sam. 12:13).

For us, it is at the cross of Christ, in the blood of the Savior spilled for us, that we are washed clean and declared innocent. David was told that God would not hold his sins against him. We are told, through Christ and the cross, that we are made innocent, through the innocence of Him who died for us. And so we remember the One who came to die, the One who came to trade His righteousness, His innocence, for our sin, for our guilt. Looking to the cross, we can say with David and Psalm 26, "Do not take away my soul along with sinners" (v. 9), and know that, in Christ, it is finished, and we, therefore, are innocent before God.

Perhaps my favorite illustration of our relationship to the law in Christ comes from Paul Zahl's *Who Will Deliver Us?*:

> [We are] a little like the duck hunter who was hunting with his friend in a wide-open barren of land in southeastern Georgia. Far away on the horizon he noticed a cloud of smoke. Soon, he could hear the sound of crackling. A wind came up and he realized the terrible truth: a brush fire was advancing his way. It was moving so fast that he and his friend could not outrun it. The hunter began to rifle through his pockets. Then he emptied all the contents of his knapsack. He soon found what he was looking for—a book of matches. To his friend's amazement, he pulled out a match and struck it. He lit a small fire around the two of them. Soon they were standing in a circle of blackened earth, waiting for the brush fire to come. They did not have to wait long. They covered their mouths with their handkerchiefs and braced themselves. The fire came near—-and swept over them. But they were completely unhurt. They weren't even touched. Fire would not burn the place where fire had already burned.

The point here is that the law is like a brush fire that takes no prisoners. It cannot be escaped or extinguished or circumvented. But if we stand in the burned-over place, where law has already done its worst, we will not get hurt. Its power has not been nullified nor has its necessity and authority been denied. Yet because of where we are standing, not a hair on our heads will be singed. The death of Christ is the burned-over place. There we huddle, hardly believing, yet relieved. Christ's death has disarmed the law, and where there was once guilt, now all that remains is gratitude.

The gospel declares that Jesus came, not to abolish the law, but to fulfill it—Jesus met all of God's holy conditions so that our relationship with God could be wholly unconditional. The demand maker became a demand keeper and died for me—a demand breaker.

We read, "If your eye causes you to stumble, pluck it out" (v. 47) and turn it into, "If a certain person in church causes you to become angry, avoid that person." We do this because we want to soften what Jesus is saying. We can say to ourselves, "Well, it's not my eye that's causing me to stumble, it's the presence of this catalogue!" or, "It's not my brain that's causing me to get angry, it's this incredibly trying person!" In other words: "It's not me that's causing me to sin, it's this or that."

We get, intuitively, that when we steal, it's not really our hands that are causing it. When we look at someone with NC-17 thoughts in our heads it's not really our eyes that are at fault. We're willing to admit that Jesus can't be saying that. We can see that He's asking us to consider the question, though: "What is it that causes you to sin?"

Jesus locates the cause of sin in our hearts. So He is leading us in a different direction with His discussion of hands, feet, and eyes. But He's not leading us outside ourselves. He's leading us inside. It's not a metaphor; it's just not the right body part! He's saying, "It's not your hand that causes you to sin. And it's not your eye either, but you'll wish it were. Because you can lose a hand, a foot, and an eye and live. The problem is your heart. And if you tear out your heart, the thing that really causes you to sin, you'll die."

The good news is that, while our hearts are the real problem, Jesus's heart is the only solution. He came to rescue internally corrupt people like you and me because internally corrupt people are all that there are.

On an October Sunday in 2012, the crowd at Kansas City's Arrowhead Stadium was getting tired of quarterback Matt Cassel's poor play, so they began to chant backup quarterback Brady Quinn's name. In the fourth quarter, Cassel had to leave the game with a head injury. As Cassel lay on the turf after the hit that injured him, his home crowd seemed to cheer in relief. "Finally! No more Cassel!" The stadium certainly cheered as Quinn entered the game. After the game, Chiefs lineman Eric Winston called the fans' behavior "sickening" and "embarrassing."

The next day, television personality Tony Kornheiser suggested that if this happened, it was illustrative of the "darkest part of human nature." Interestingly, both Kornheiser and his cohost, Michael Wilbon, expressed surprise that this kind of thing could happen in Kansas City, traditionally believed to be home to one of the nicest and most loyal fan bases in the NFL.

As they expressed their surprise, I couldn't help but think of the similar surprise that Christians express when their heroes falter. Ted Haggard comes immediately to mind. "Really?" we exclaim. "Him? How could someone who seemed so faithful fall so far?"

The impulse that led Kornheiser and Wilbon to assume that the citizens of Kansas City were above cheering a quarterback's injury is the same impulse that allows us to convince ourselves that we would be above that kind of thing too, that we're "not like other people" (Luke 18:11). It only takes the right situation, however, to show us that our grip on righteousness was nonexistent and that our falls can be as spectacular as anyone else's.

Today, let us remember that we are like other people, and have no righteousness of our own. But our salvation is a gift that covers the darkest part of human nature, and redeems us forever.

Why do people desire that which is bad for them? I'm reminded of an old Halloween episode of *The Simpsons* in which the whole town (except for Bart) is turned into zombies by infected hamburgers. After days without one, Bart decides he *needs* a burger and risks life and limb to navigate a sea of zombies to get his hands on what appears to be the last remaining burger in town. He bites.

What could compel Bart to do this, to act against his best interests? This convention is well known in horror films: "No group of nubile teens has ever returned from that campground alive!" "*Oh, I'm sure we'll be fine.*" Or, "This house, built on an ancient Indian burial ground, has phantasmagorical blood pouring down the walls, and the Realtor, a crusty old woman with one eye and a goiter, told us not to stay here." "*I'm sure it's nothing to worry about.*" Bart's been given information that can save his life: "Don't eat that burger." He does anyway.

And Christians? What's with them? Why the resistance to the good news? In the end, Bart's hunger gets the best of him. His need for a burger overrides the logic of avoiding zombies. For Christians, our need to contribute, to self-justify, and to be active overrides the logic of accepting what appears to be the best option: a free gift for which we must do nothing and which requires no response.

In *As Good As It Gets*, Jack Nicholson pays for Helen Hunt's son's medical care that she can't afford. When he tells her that no thanks are required, that it's a free gift and he doesn't want to read her thank-you letter, she becomes angry. People want to contribute. People need to self-justify. People desire to be active.

Today, remember that God has overcome your need to contribute and to self-justify. He has already justified you.

Halloween has become more Christian than Christmas. Now before you freak out, let me explain. Of course, Christmas for Christians is the celebration of the birth of our Savior. And Halloween has its roots in some bad stuff. But in the ways that they are *currently* seen and celebrated by the world, Halloween is more Christian than Christmas.

Consider the theological implications of Halloween (again, the way it is *currently* celebrated). Halloween is the ultimate equal opportunity holiday. *Everyone* gets candy. On the surface, it's a picture of the gospel. There is no checking of qualifications at the door. You come, you receive.

Christmas, on the other hand … well, you know the song: "He's making a list, checking it twice, gonna find out who's naughty or nice. Santa Claus is coming to town." Yikes! You'd better hope that you're on the good list, or you're not getting any presents! David Sedaris wrote in one of his essays that in Holland, if a child is bad, Saint Nicholas and his helpers beat the offending child with a switch. If a child is *really* bad, they throw him into a sack and take him to Spain. Our punishment isn't as harsh as the Dutch one, but it's still based on judgment. If you're good: presents. If you're bad: lump of coal.

In his letter's opening lines to the Ephesians (a sinful people: see 4:1, 4:17, 5:3, etc.), Paul made clear what the foundation of the Christian faith actually is: the free gift of God in Jesus Christ. Paul didn't say, "Shape up!" Instead, he said, "I have heard of your faith in the Lord Jesus and your love toward all the saints [and for this reason], I do not cease to give thanks for you!" (ESV). He didn't go all Christmas on them. He didn't check his naughty-and-nice list! He treated them like it was Halloween.

This life—the years we live, the loves we have, the losses we suffer, offset by the celebrations we cherish—is an ordeal. In the movie *Magnolia*, Jason Robards plays a man dying of cancer. He is a tragic figure, divorced from his first wife, estranged from his son, married to someone who loves only his money, and cared for by a nurse from a service, the only person who seems to care about him at all. As he lies there dying, struggling for each breath, and slipping in and out of consciousness, he says, "Life ain't short. It's *long*."

We often hear, and say, that "life is short." What we mean is, "Enjoy it while you can." Or, "The good times don't come around all that often or last all that long, so take advantage." We might as well say, "Life is short on joy and long on tragedy." Now don't get me wrong. There is joy in life, and I praise God for it. But there's no arguing that we are broken people living in a broken world with other broken people. And that means that life is, and will always be, hard.

Jesus speaks specifically to this most human of conditions in the beginning of His Sermon on the Mount, commonly called the Beatitudes. He names the human sufferings, and then pronounces His blessing. For instance, "Blessed are the poor in spirit, for theirs is the kingdom of heaven. Blessed are those who mourn, for they will be comforted" (vv. 3–4).

Jesus is calling out the painful things of human life. Poor in spirit, mourning, meekness, hunger and thirst for things that are beyond our grasp, persecution, slander. He names them, *and then He blesses them.*

Today, know that Jesus knows your ordeal and your pain. And know that He promises to never leave you nor forsake you. Jesus came for, and rescues, broken people, because broken people are all that there are.

On another episode of *Frasier*, Frasier and Niles gain access to a fabulously exclusive day spa. After an amazing afternoon of coddling, they say, respectively, "I feel like I've been rubbed by angels," and "I've never felt better in my life." All of a sudden, they see a golden door through which they are forbidden to go. It's for gold-level members only. Immediately, the wonder of the day turns to hatred. "Just how are we supposed to enjoy this?" wonders Frasier angrily. Back at home when asked what kind of place it was, he says, "It was a hellhole!"

Later, Frasier and Niles are having coffee with their friend Roz, who chides them: "You only want to go in there because you can't. And what if you do get in the gold door? What's next, the diamond door? And after that a titanium door?" Roz knows there is no end to the human struggle, the human quest for achievement. For Christians, the analogy is our quest to get to God. There will forever be another door through which we must pass.

Eventually, Frasier and Niles do get through the gold door, and it's great ... but there's a platinum door. When Niles wants to go through the unguarded door, Frasier cries, "This is heaven! Right here and now! Why do we have to think about someplace else!" Niles retorts, "This is only heaven for people who can't get in to the real heaven, the *platinum* heaven!"

Finally, Frasier and Niles go through the platinum door, and the truth is revealed to them. There is no platinum-level spa. They are outside, with the Dumpsters and garbage, locked out of the spa altogether. For us, we can say that there is no such thing as a "close enough" relationship to God. We would all affirm this, and yet we all chase this mythic state. As Frasier and Niles realized too late, the profundity of the gospel is that we are in the best place already! Let's stop trying so hard to move up and enjoy the beauty of a God who has given us all that we need right here, right now.

Jesus tells the story of a man who had two sons. The man asked each son to go work in the field. The first one told his father that he would not go but then later changed his mind and went. The second son told his father that he would go but ultimately didn't. When Jesus asks the gathered chief priests and elders which son did the will of his father—the one who obeyed social convention by not saying no to the patriarch or the one who actually did what the father asked—they say that the first son did. Jesus then chastises them for not changing their minds about the coming of the kingdom of God even after they had seen it.

This little story—this parable of two brothers—is fascinating. Neither kid wanted to do the work. The chief priests and elders thought the first son was righteous because he was obedient. But they miss the point. The first son had a change of heart. That's the key.

Grudging obedience is not what Jesus wants. Imagine a third brother, who said he would work in the vineyard, even though he didn't want to, and then went and did it, grumbling the whole time. If that had been a choice in the story, the chief priests and scribes would have picked that kid every time! Isn't that how we think about life? Your heart doesn't matter in the least; it's whether or not you're obedient!

The law has the power to show us what to do, but only grace has the power to make us want to do it. Paul told us in 2 Corinthians 9:7 that "God loves a cheerful giver." And it is only the amazing grace of God given over and over again to self-absorbed sinners that can change our hearts and make us want to do the things we ought to do.

We can all think of the big moments of our lives. The moments when it seems like everything depends on what happens next. For many people, these moments start when you're asking someone out on a date. You barely get the question out, and then you wait. That's the moment—when you're waiting to see what the next word will be, the moment when there are two possible words, one of which means "you're not good enough" and the other, which means "you're perfect." Everything in the world comes down to those two words.

The writer of the letter to the Hebrews talks about these same two words. He terms them somewhat differently. The word indicating "you're not good enough" is what he says "makes you subject to weakness." He calls this word "the law." The other word indicating "you're perfect" is what he considers "the word of the oath."

The law, in other words, makes you subject to weakness. That's why your stomach knots up so much when you ask the question. The other person's answer determines your value. Are you good enough or not? It's up to them. That makes you weak. The law always makes us weak.

"The word of the oath," on the other hand, doesn't have anything to do with weakness, because *it doesn't have anything to do with you*. Hebrews applies it to Jesus, our new High Priest who has offered Himself as a sacrifice once and for all, promising that no more sacrifices will ever need to be made.

Before God rescued us, whenever we heard that tiny voice whispering, "You're not good enough," we had to just sit there and take it, or get to work trying to silence it. Now, when that accusatory voice comes, we have a place to run. Jesus says, "In Me, you're perfect."

The Astronaut Farmer is a cute movie in which Billy Bob Thornton plays Farmer, an ex-NASA astronaut who builds a rocket in his barn. He intends to use it to go into space, fulfilling a never-realized dream. His plan is going swimmingly (in that no one except his family and small-town neighbors knows what he's doing) until he tries to buy fifty thousand gallons of high-test rocket fuel over the Internet. In comes the FBI, suspicious that he might be building a weapon, and the FAA, concerned he will show their multibillion-dollar budget to be unnecessary at best and might set a dangerous precedent for other amateur space enthusiasts at worst.

At the FAA hearing to discuss his submitted flight plan, Farmer stands up and makes a stirring speech, saying, "When I was a kid, they used to tell me that I could be anything I wanted to be. No matter what. And maybe I am insane—I don't know—but I still believe that. I believe with all my heart. Somewhere along the line, we stopped believing that we could do anything. And if we don't have our dreams, we have nothing."

The problem with claims like Farmer's is that they overestimate human ability. In any kind of honest assessment, we would have to admit we can't do anything we set our minds to, and sometimes, desire is not enough.

If it were true, for instance, that God helped those who help themselves, then hard work would be a necessary ingredient for salvation. But thank God that phrase is not in the Bible. Instead, we get good news—God helps the helpless, those of us who can't win the big game, make the big shot, land the big role, or even competently live our own average lives. God doesn't help those who help themselves; He only helps those who can't help themselves. That's all of us.

Think of a story you've read in which the plotline goes something like this: A flawed hero (we'll make this character a man) is presented with a task at home that he cannot complete, is rejected in some way, and must begin a journey. He leaves home and has many adventures. Finally he returns, having been changed by his adventures into a man who can do the things he was supposed to do in the beginning. This is the epic story of life. Except it is not the spiritual life of a Christian.

In Christianity, you come up against a task you cannot complete. You're not enough. The army, before it asked you to be "army strong," asked you to "be all you can be." You're not. You've tried hard; you've tried everything you can think of. Yet there's still that feeling of insufficiency, that feeling of not quite measuring up to the life you've been asked to lead. You might feel like a failure.

Christianity's story doesn't end there: a God who, seeing His broken, suffering, and sinful children, does not demand that they clean up their act and come to Him, but sends His Son to live in this broken, suffering, and sinful world, and to die for us—the ones who know they can't do it. Jesus came to live our lives for us and to die our deaths for us, so that we, like Him and because of Him, could be crowned with glory and honor, forever.

Remember the Fail Mary pass during the 2012 NFL season, the one presided over by the league's replacement referees? During a Monday Night Football game between the Seahawks and the Packers, calls were missed or made incorrectly all game long, and the coup de grâce was a time-expired Hail Mary pass that seemed, in replay, to be awarded to the wrong team, completely altering the outcome of the game. For the first time, it seemed inarguable that the replacement refs had cost a team a game.

The problem, of course, was simple: these replacement refs were totally in over their heads. They were incapable of doing the job they'd been given. Didn't you feel badly for them? I did.

Paul says that "sin, seizing the opportunity afforded by the commandment, deceived me, and through the commandment put me to death" (v. 11). When Moses came down the mountain with those commandments, and then Jesus clarified and sharpened them in the Sermon on the Mount, we were given a job that we're not qualified to do, a task that is beyond us. We look as hopeless in our trying as the replacement refs looked on that Monday night. But, as Paul also says, "I would not have known what sin was had it not been for the law" (v. 7). We wouldn't know how hard it is to referee an NFL game if the replacement refs hadn't failed so spectacularly. We wouldn't know how far from the righteousness of God we are if the commandments hadn't been brought down from the mountaintop to show us.

Failure is the only thing that leads to an openness to salvation. Jesus promises to be that Savior for His creation. Paul rejoices, "Thanks be to God, who delivers me through Jesus Christ our Lord!" (v. 25).

Cartoonist and author Lynda Barry produced a short comic strip called *Two Questions*. This strip is Lynda's autobiography, in terms of her work. It tells how she started drawing as a kid and how it made her feel. She says: "When I was little, I noticed that making lines on paper gave me a floating feeling. It made me feel like I was both there and not there. The lines made a picture and the picture made a story."

Lynda is describing the way in which we discover things we love to do. We try them out, and they give us a special feeling. They don't seem like work at all; we do them because we love them, and the results come, flowing freely. We don't really know how to describe the process at all; all we know is that we are free. "Before the two questions," Lynda continued, "pictures and stories happened in a way that didn't involve much thinking. One line led to another until they somehow finished. I never felt like I was trying."

But then, Lynda says something very profound: "But the two questions find everybody."

And what are the two questions?

They are questions we are all too familiar with: "Is this good?" "Does this suck?" Lynda said that the two questions found her in the form of the two most popular girls in her first-grade class. She says, "They liked me more after I made that picture. My teacher liked me more too. It lasted a few days."

Aren't these the two questions we ask about ourselves? Am I good? Do I suck?

These are questions that the law asks, and Lynda notes that the law oppresses everyone. It is inescapable. Outside of the two questions, though, we never feel as if we're trying. We have a certain floating feeling. We're working, but it doesn't seem like work. In fact, eliminate the two questions, and we actually work harder because the pressure of evaluation is off. This is the gospel. It is freedom.

Early in Isaiah 40, we are compared to grasshoppers in light of the awesome majesty of our God (v. 22). Not a very flattering description, right? But then, Isaiah does something amazing. He describes the same almighty, all-powerful, awesome God: "He will not grow tired or weary, and his understanding no one can fathom" (v. 28), and in the most profound thing you'll ever hear, he describes *God giving these attributes to His chosen people, His children.* "He gives strength to the weary and increases the power of the weak" (v. 29). He is described as not growing tired or weary, and then that *exact same description* is given to us! "The LORD will renew their strength. They will soar on wings like eagles; they will run and not grow weary, they will walk and not be faint" (v. 31).

This is Christianity: an awesome God, majestic and holy (He makes us feel like grasshoppers), who nevertheless gives wholeness to us. The classic ratification of this is the thief on the cross. He had no time to change his life, no time to get better. He comes into contact with Jesus, and his first thought is of his own imperfection in comparison to Jesus's righteousness. He reaches out for a Savior, saying simply, "Jesus, remember me when you come into your kingdom" (Luke 23:42). Jesus looks at him, and with words that make the hair on the back of my neck stand on end every time I hear them, says, "Truly I tell you, today you will be with me in paradise" (Luke 23:43).

The disciple John wrote, "If anybody does sin, we have an advocate with the Father—Jesus Christ, the Righteous One. He is the atoning sacrifice for our sins, and not only for ours but also for the sins of the whole world" (1 John 2:1–2). We worship a God who is so glorious, so magnificent, and so holy that we feel miniscule and unworthy—like a grasshopper—by comparison. But we worship a God who sent His Son to give us what we lack, so that He can look at us and say, "Truly I tell you, one day you will be with Me in paradise."

Do you remember the scene in which we are introduced to Annette Bening's character in Sam Mendes's 1999 film, *American Beauty*? She's a real estate agent arriving at a house—a house she's determined to sell. Before she even gets started, though, she notices a house across the street that also has a For Sale sign, this one sporting the smiling mug of Buddy Kane, the "king" of real estate. Bening frowns and gets to work.

Throughout her work cleaning and staging the house, Bening intones, "I will sell this house today," almost as a meditative mantra. She hangs all of her value on her ability to sell the house, and—underneath that—to beat the king of real estate. Buddy Kane is the embodiment of the law to her. Bening thinks that the law says, "Sell this house," or, "Be a successful real estate agent." These laws are arguably fulfillable. The underlying law, though, is the one with real teeth: "Be Buddy Kane," or as Christians hear, "Be perfect."

Despite all of Bening's hard work (we might say, her "good works"), she is unable to sell the house. She has failed. And now the law begins operating on her in a new way: she hates herself for being weak.

In the classic hymn "Rock of Ages," Augustus Toplady asks that Christ "Be of sin the double cure / Cleanse me from its guilt and power."

The only way out from under this vicious cycle of sin's guilt and power is the Toplady way: admit the guilt and power, and ask for the cure. Today, remember that the law is not something you can fulfill by the sweat of your brow or the strength of your character. The law doesn't say, "Be good." It says, "Be perfect." Praise God that Jesus Christ was perfect on our behalf, the double cure for sin.

When I was twenty-five, I believed I could change the world. At forty-two, I have come to the realization that I cannot change my wife, my church, or my kids, to say nothing of the world. Try as I might, I have not been able to manufacture outcomes the way I thought I could, either in my own life or in other people's. Unfulfilled dreams, ongoing relational tension, the loss of friendships, a hard marriage, rebellious teenagers, the death of loved ones, remaining sinful patterns—whatever it is for you—live long enough, lose enough, suffer enough, and the idealism of youth fades, leaving behind the reality that we live in a broken world as broken people. Life has had a way of proving to me that I'm not on the constantly forward-moving escalator of progress I thought I was on when I was twenty-five.

Instead, my life has looked more like this: Try and fail. Fail, then try. Try and succeed. Succeed, then fail. Two steps forward. One step back. One step forward. Three steps back. Every year, I get better at some things, worse at others. Some areas remain stubbornly static. To complicate matters even more, when I honestly acknowledge the ways I've gotten worse, it's actually a sign that I may be getting better. And when I become proud of the ways I've gotten better, it's actually a sign that I've gotten worse. And round and round we go.

If this sounds like a depressing sentiment, it isn't meant to be one. Quite the opposite. If I am grateful for anything about these past fifteen years, it's for the way God has wrecked my idealism about myself and the world and replaced it with a realism about the extent of His grace and love, which is much bigger than I had ever imagined. Indeed, the smaller you get—the smaller life makes you—the easier it is to see the grandeur of grace. While I am far more incapable than I may have initially thought, God is infinitely more capable than I ever hoped.

The other day, I saw a truck that made me laugh out loud. It was a truck from Premier Booting Services, one of those companies that puts a bulky metal "boot" lock on your front tire when you've parked illegally. Not that funny, right? What was funny was their slogan: "Your Source for Parking Compliance." Something about that line struck me as appropriate for the Ministry of Truth in George Orwell's *1984*. So I laughed. But while I was laughing, I realized that their slogan had profound—and unintended—theological implications as well.

Premier Booting Services doesn't actually want to ensure parking compliance. It would put them out of business. Their business model, in fact, depends on people getting booted, and then getting booted again. It's not in Premier's best interest for people to learn their lesson and start parking legally. They're not actually in the compliance business; they're in the punishment business. They say that they provide "compliance" services because it doesn't sound as nasty.

Preachers who think that simply telling bad people to be good—applying a boot to the tires of their spiritual lives—will actually produce compliance misunderstand the law's purpose. The law tells us that compliance is required, but the law is incapable of producing a compliant heart. We would all agree that compliance is a laudable goal. We want people parking legally, and we want people loving their neighbors as themselves. But how might compliance actually happen?

Counterintuitively, it is grace that produces compliance. Grace—that love that comes to the undeserving—is the only thing capable of causing the kind of heart change that generates true obedience. Punishment and judgment don't create a reformed heart; they create—at best—a heart full of fear, and—at worst—a heart full of rebellion. Love and grace replace a fearful heart with a grateful one—a heart that desires whatever the lover asks.

Writer Jonathan Merritt once asked me, "What are the ways in which you—yes, you, as a clergy person—have been complicit in perpetuating this system of works righteousness?"

I responded this way:

> I'm so embarrassed by many of the sermons I preached early on. I wish I could go back and apologize to all the people who heard them. My primary concern at that time was to get people to do more, try harder, and change. The end result was stunted spiritual growth for our people because I was causing them to fix their eyes on themselves rather than on Christ.

Ironically, I've discovered that the more I focus on my need to get better, the worse I actually get—I become neurotic and self-absorbed. Preoccupation with our performance over Christ's performance for us actually hinders spiritual growth because it makes us increasingly self-centered and morbidly introspective—the exact opposite of how the Bible describes what it means to be sanctified. Sanctification is forgetting about yourself. As J. C. Kromsigt said, "The good seed cannot flourish when it is repeatedly dug up for the purpose of examining its growth."

In those early days, I was treating the Bible as if it were a heaven-sent self-help manual. The fact is, unless we go to the Bible to see Jesus and His work for us, even our devout Bible reading can become fuel for our own self-improvement plans, the place we go for the help we need to conquer today's challenges and take control of our lives.

What I've learned since those days is that the Bible is not a record of the blessed good, but rather the blessed bad. The Bible is not a witness to the best people making it up to God; it's a witness to God making it down to the worst people. The Bible is one long story of God meeting our rebellion with His rescue; our sin with His salvation; our failure with His favor; our guilt with His grace; our badness with His goodness.

No doubt you're familiar with Jesus's telling the disciples that if they had faith the size of a mustard seed, they could tell a mulberry tree to be uprooted and planted in the sea and it would obey them. But did you know that this scathing criticism came in response to what seems, at least on the face of it, an innocuous request, maybe even an honorable one?

Jesus told the disciples that they have no faith after they come to Him and ask Him to increase their faith. Isn't that strange? Doesn't it seem like requesting greater faith is what the disciples ought to be doing? It does seem that way to us, but that's only because we suffer under the same delusion the disciples did. We think we just need a helping hand.

You see, the error the disciples made in asking for increased faith was that they were assuming they had faith in the first place! Jesus disabused them of this notion pretty quickly, telling them if they even had the tiniest bit of faith, they could do truly miraculous things. Jesus was showing them what the law shows us: that we're worse off than we think we are.

Like the disciples, we can often assume we're doing fairly well. None of us would admit that we're perfect—we're too smart for that—but we like to think we're not the worst, either. We say, "I'm not perfect, but ..." Jesus's response shows He didn't come to earth to improve the pretty good. He didn't even come to build up the not-that-good. Jesus came to create goodness where there was no goodness before. He came to give faith to the faithless and life to the dead.

Before Oscar Pistorius was known for—allegedly, as of this writing—murdering his girlfriend, he was known simply as an inspirational story. Pistorius is a double-amputee sprinter who runs on carbon-fiber blades that replace the lower half of both of his legs. In 2012, he was the first such competitor to be allowed to compete at the Olympic Games. This didn't occur without fuss. There was at least some question about whether or not the blades gave Pistorius a competitive advantage over runners forced to use their own, God-given legs. Pistorius sued for the right to be allowed to compete and won.

Pistorius seemed to say all the right things during each of his interviews, always remarking that he was "happy just to be" there and honored and humbled by the attention he was getting. For Pistorius, it seemed that it wasn't about winning.

But then, Pistorius was beaten by Brazil's Alan Oliveira in the Paralympic 200-meter dash, ending an almost unparalleled dominance (he'd won the 100-, 200-, and 400-meter dashes at the previous Paralympic Games). In interviews following the race, Pistorius suggested that Oliveira ran with longer prosthetics than should be allowed, saying, "We aren't racing a fair race. I gave it my best. He's never run a twenty-one-second race, and I don't think he's a twenty-one-second athlete."

I was glad that Oscar Pistorius revealed himself to be a human being rather than a selfless superhero. He did what we all do—apply a scaled law to ourselves and the full law to others. This is the theological version of "running from the bear": you only have to be faster than one of the other people trying to get away.

Until we can start seeing the law as applying fully in all cases—and that we're no exception—we'll always find ways to exempt ourselves and, thereby, put a bandage on the gaping wound of our human needs.

Today, let us recognize the depth of our desperation, so we can see the depth of our deliverance by the One who came to do for us what we could never do for ourselves.

Remember when Simon Cowell was a judge on *American Idol*? I've become less aware of the show as the judges have changed, but there was a time when Simon Cowell was famous for his vicious takedowns of singers who came up short. One of the things that always amazed me most about *American Idol* was the fascination—at least in the first few weeks of each season—with the terrible singers who would try out. It was Cowell who would level the truth laser at these people. Many of them were undone by it. A lot of them seem to have truly believed they were wonderful singers, and when they hear they're awful, they completely crumble. Some cry, some beg, some ask for another chance or offer to sing another song, and some get really angry. And something Cowell often said was, "Who has heard you sing? Have you ever sung in public? How do people react when they hear you sing? Who *told you* that you could sing?"

The story in Genesis 3 about Adam and Eve's first interaction with God ("Who told you that you were naked?") after eating the fruit is a story about people having their eyes opened. Everything's fine until they eat the fruit of the tree and see themselves with shame. They hear God walking around in the garden, and their shame turns to fear. The *American Idol* contestants have their eyes opened by Simon. Some of them are there for a joke, but some of them actually believe they can sing well. Walking into that room with Simon Cowell is like eating the fruit from the Tree of the Knowledge of Good and Evil. Your eyes are opened when you leave.

So much of our lives are marked by this shame. Today, remember that our Savior died the most shameful of deaths so we can come face-to-face with our holy God shame-free on account of what Jesus accomplished for us and has given to us free of charge: His righteousness.

My wife and I have three children: Gabe, Nate, and Genna. In order to function as a community of five in our home, rules need to be established, laws need to be put in place. Our kids know they can't steal from one another. They have to share the computer. Since harmonious relationships depend on trust, they can't lie, and so on and so forth. Rules are necessary. But telling them what they can and cannot do over and over can't change their hearts or make them want to comply.

When one of our kids breaks a rule, we can take away some of his or her privileges. And we do. But while this may rightly produce sorrow at the revelation of sin, it does not have the power to remove sin. In other words, the law can crush but it cannot cure. If Kim and I don't follow up the law with the gospel, our rule-breaking child would be left without hope—defeated but not delivered.

But the law does defeat us, and so it becomes all the more necessary to be reminded that, in the words of William Cowper, "There is a fountain fill'd with blood drawn from Emmanuel's veins; and sinners, plunged beneath that flood, lose all their guilty stains." We need to be told that the sins we cannot forget, God cannot remember. We need to be told over and over that there is no condemnation for those who are in Christ Jesus, that nothing can separate us from God's love, and that Christians live their lives under a banner that reads, "It is finished."

With Christ's first coming, God began the process of reversing the curse of sin and redeeming all things. In Christ, God was moving in a new way. All of Jesus's ministry—the words He spoke, the miracles He performed—showed that there was a new order in town: God's order. When Jesus healed the diseased, raised the dead, and forgave the desperate, He did so to show that with the arrival of God in the flesh came the restoration of the way God intended things to be.

In his book *This Beautiful Mess*, Rick McKinley describes a pastor's response to the death of a friend:

> A pastor friend of mine told me that as he was preparing for a funeral once, he decided to go through the Gospels to see how Jesus dealt with funerals. What he discovered was that Jesus did not much care for them. Every one He went to, He raised the person from the dead. Jesus doesn't do funerals, not even His own.

The resurrection of Jesus is the greatest proof of God's intention to revitalize this broken cosmos. His rising from the dead was "just the beginning of the saving, renewing, resurrecting work of God that will have its climax in the restoration of the entire cosmos," as K. Scott Oliphint and Sinclair Ferguson remind us. Christ's resurrection is both the model of and the means for our resurrection—and the guarantee that what He started, He will finish.

The day will come when Christ returns and *completes* this process of transformation (read Revelation 21, for instance). Psalm 96:11–13 gives us a poetic glimpse of what will happen when Jesus returns to rule the earth:

> Let the heavens be glad, and let the earth rejoice;
> let the sea roar, and all that fills it;
> let the field exult, and everything in it!
> Then shall all the trees of the forest sing for joy
> before the LORD, for he comes,
> for he comes to judge the earth.
> He will judge the world in righteousness,
> and the peoples in his faithfulness. (ESV)

So take heart, weary soldiers. The best is yet to come.

In Paul Zahl's wonderful little book *Who Will Deliver Us?*, he writes:

> Law with a small "l" is any voice that makes us feel that we must
> be something or do something in order to merit the approval of
> another. In the Bible, the Law comes from God. In daily living, law
> is an internalized principle of self-accusation. We might even say
> that the innumerable laws that we carry inside us are the bastard
> children of the capital "L" Law.

You're familiar with this kind of law, even if you've never used that word
to describe it. The "musts" of life are numerous. You feel them every day:
infomercials promising a better life if you work at getting a better body, a
neighbor's new car that you can't afford, a beautiful person you can't hope to
compare to, the success of your more talented coworker. We almost always
feel as if life is telling us that we're not enough.

The force of "little-L" law is felt when we become aware of an expectation that our spouses have of us that we can never seem to meet. It resides in
a deadline at work, or in the pressure we feel to fix our kids. It roosts in the
desire to make a name for ourselves, to leave a mark. Because of our nature,
we conclude that if we're going to experience these things, we're the ones who
must make it happen. We think we must find salvation from these myriad
laws within ourselves.

Into the prison of ruthless musts and demands comes God's second
word: His gospel. The gospel declares, because of Christ's finished work for
you, you already have all the approval, all the security, all the love, all the
worth, and all the rescue you long for and that you desperately look for in a
thousand places, all of which are infinitely smaller than Jesus. We're working
so hard to appease those little-L judges, we forget that the big-L Judge—
almighty God—has already been appeased in Christ!

In Craig Brewer's 2006 film, *Black Snake Moan*, Christina Ricci plays Rae, a sex-addicted girl, and Samuel L. Jackson plays Lazarus, the man who finds her beaten at the side of the road and nurses her back to health. In a twist, though, Lazarus chains her to a radiator when he discovers her compulsions in order to "cure [her] of [her] wicked ways."

Do you think that Rae's chain tames her? Of course not. It does nothing but drive her wild, even pushing her so far as to attack a prepubescent boy. Eventually, though, over the course of the film, Rae and Lazarus develop a relationship. What is antagonistic at first becomes friendly and finally truly loving. Lazarus eventually frees Rae from her bondage, saying, "You're an adult. You should live however you want to." Do you think Rae immediately runs out to fulfill her rampant sexual desires? Does she use her freedom to sin all the more? Of course not. In fact, Rae is domesticated to the point of cooking dinner for Lazarus, the young boy she attacked, and the local pastor!

When the condemning weight of the law is removed, people don't react with wild sin, as we might expect; they relax in their new freedom.

Given the freedom to run, Rae stays by the side of the man who loved her when no one else would.

Many fear that the grace-delivered, blood-bought deliverance of radical freedom will result in loveless license. But as the story above illustrates, redeeming unconditional love alone (not law, not fear, not punishment, not guilt, not shame) carries the power to compel heartfelt loyalty to the One who gave us (and continues to give us) what we don't deserve (2 Cor. 5:14).

There's a classic *New Yorker* cartoon of a man sitting down with a woman, having dinner, saying to her, "Look, I can't promise I'll change, but I can promise I'll pretend to change." Sadly, that idea characterizes more churches than you think. Instead of a hospital for sufferers, church becomes a glorified costume party, where lonely men and women tirelessly police one another's facade of holiness.

Contrary to popular belief, Christianity is not about good people getting better. If anything, it is about bad people coping with their failure to be good. That is to say, Christianity concerns the gospel, which is nothing more or less than the good news that "Christ Jesus came into the world to save sinners" (v. 15).

The prevailing view in much of contemporary Christianity is more subjective. It tends to be far more focused on the happiness and moral performance of the Christian than the object of faith, Christ Himself.

But in the gospel, we learn that we don't have to pretend to be or do anything. We don't even have to change anything to be loved by God! His grace comes to us unilaterally, and it does indeed change us, but as a consequence of His saving work, not a prerequisite for it. When we sit down to the table of salvation with God, we don't have to make promises to get His love. We receive Him by faith. It's His promises we hear, and He makes them not to who we pretend to be, but to who we actually are. He loves the real us.

The you that you are right now, the one that's tired, hurt, upset, afraid, or whatever—that's the you He loves.

In a parable, Jesus tells the story of a landowner who plants a vineyard, leases it to tenants, and then goes to another country. After a time, he sends servants to the vineyard to collect the fruit. Rather than give the master his profit, the tenants beat one servant, stone another, and kill a third. In response, the landowner sends more servants, only to see the same thing happen to them. Finally, thinking surely they will respect his son, the landowner sends his heir to the vineyard. Believing they will be able to keep the vineyard for themselves, the tenants kill the son. At that point, Jesus asks the Pharisees what the landowner will do in this situation.

The Pharisees say what we would all say; they suggest doing what we would all want to do: "He will put those wretches to a miserable death" (v. 41 ESV). In other words, he's going to turn that place into an Arnold Schwarzenegger movie: no survivors. You see, the Pharisees, like us, are tuned in to the law. They're thinking in terms of an eye for an eye and a tooth for a tooth. They can't see Jesus's underlying point: they're the tenants.

Jesus quotes them Psalm 118, saying that the stone the builders rejected has become the chief cornerstone. The son sent to the vineyard was rejected by the tenants … but that's not the end of our story. Jesus says that anyone who comes into contact with this stone will be broken. All of our efforts, whether aimed at rebellion or at righteousness, will cease. The chief cornerstone will break us.

There's one important difference between the heir in the parable and Jesus. Jesus didn't stay dead! And because Jesus was raised to new life and has given that new life to us, we can leave all our striving behind.

The world tells us in a thousand different ways that the bigger we become, the freer we will be. The richer, the more beautiful, and the more powerful we grow, the more security, liberty, and happiness we will experience. And yet, the gospel tells us just the opposite. The smaller we become, the freer we will be. This may sound at first like bad news, but it could not be better news!

In the Bible, slavery is equated with self-reliance and self-dependence, the burden of depending on yourself and controlling your circumstances to ensure meaning and security, safety and significance. But as we know, the burden of self-determination is enormous. When your meaning, your significance, your security, your protection, your safety are all riding on you, it actually feels like slavery. This is a burden we were never meant to bear, and yet after the fall, self-reliance became our default mode of operation. Mine as well as yours. You might even call it our inheritance. In our exile from Eden, we naturally tend toward self-reliance.

Thankfully, God does not leave us there. God wants to free us from ourselves, and there's nothing like suffering to show us we need something bigger than our abilities, our strength, and our explanations. There's nothing like suffering to remind us how not in control we actually are, how little power we ultimately have, and how much we ultimately need God. In other words, suffering reveals to us the things that ultimately matter, which also happen to be the warp and weft of Christianity—who we are and who God is.

The gospel is for those who have realized they can't carry the weight of the world on their own shoulders. Only when God drives us to the end of ourselves do we begin to see life in the gospel, which is another way of saying that only those who stand in need of a Savior will look for or recognize a Savior. Fortunately, Christianity in its original, most authentic expression understands God chiefly as Savior and human beings chiefly as those in need of being saved.

Having small children made me a connoisseur of Disney movies. When you watch these movies over and over again, things start to jump out at you. And sometimes, believe it or not, they can be useful, theological things.

One of these things has ruined *Aladdin* for me forever. The thing I noticed is this: the genie mis-grants one of Aladdin's wishes! Aladdin wishes to be a prince so he can impress and marry Jasmine, but the genie only makes Aladdin *appear* to be a prince! He gets the trappings but not the juice. Obviously, this is important, as it provides the story's main conflict, but it's a huge plot hole. When Jafar controls the genie and wishes to be sultan, he is made the actual sultan. When he wishes to be an all-powerful genie, he is made an actual genie (complete with the itty-bitty living space). In neither case does Jafar's wish only grant him the appearance of his wished-for state.

Aladdin got robbed.

If we can liken our omnipotent God to Aladdin's all-powerful genie, we need to make sure we don't get robbed too. When we're promised righteousness and salvation as a free gift (a granted wish), we need to make sure it's real and not a shadow or a trick. It can't be something we're called to account for later, as Aladdin is.

And, in fact, our righteousness is precisely the opposite of Aladdin's princehood. Aladdin appears to be a prince, but isn't. All the genie's power went into the robes, menagerie, coterie, and theme song. And it's a catchy song. But there's no magic left to make Aladdin *an actual prince*, which is all that really matters. We, on the other hand, can sometimes appear to be unchanged in the slightest. We are beset by the same selfishness, the same mercurial nature, the same everything. What has happened, though, is a total renovation of our nature. We have become the righteous people God calls us to be, no matter what we think we look like on the outside.

Contrary to what some Christians would have you believe, the biggest problem facing the church today is not "cheap grace" but "cheap law"—the idea that God accepts anything less than the perfect righteousness of Jesus. As essayist John Dink wrote:

> Cheap law weakens God's demand for perfection, and in doing so, breathes life into the old creature and his quest for a righteousness of his own making.... Cheap law tells us that we've fallen, but there's good news, you can get back up again.... Therein lies the great heresy of cheap law: it is a false gospel. And it cheapens—no—it nullifies grace.

Only when we see that the way of God's law is absolutely inflexible will we see that God's grace is absolutely indispensable. A high view of the law reminds us that God accepts us on the basis of Christ's perfection, not our progress. Grace, properly understood, is the movement of a holy God toward an unholy people. He doesn't cheapen the law or ease its requirements. He fulfills them in His Son, who then gives His righteousness to us. That's the gospel. Pure and simple.

Sanctification, simply defined, is love for God and love for others. But what actually produces love for God and love for others? Not the law. Nowhere does the Bible say the law produces love. Nowhere. What the Bible does say is love for God and others is produced only by God's love for us. We love because He first loved us. And this radical one way–ness of God's love is alone the impetus to realizing the very things the law required in the first place, and the things for which every Christian longs.

A "religious" approach to marriage is the idea that if we work hard enough at something, we can earn the acceptance, approval, and life we think we deserve because of our obedient performance. My friend Justin Buzzard rightly points out in his book *Date Your Wife* that "religion" governs how most of us approach God and our wives:

> If we live as a basically good person, we can earn God's favor and get the decent life we deserve. If we stay committed to our wives and don't go anywhere, God will give us a decent marriage with decent sex in a decent American town with a decent church down the street.

Justin argues against a guilt-driven, performance-oriented, approval-seeking, "do more, try harder" approach to marriage. Instead, he argues for a gospel-empowered approach to marriage. Justin wrote, "A man comes alive when he finally feels in his guts that religion can't fuel his life or his marriage, when he makes the painfully sweet discovery that there is only one fuel source that can get the engine running again: Grace."

Sadly, fearing our love will not be reciprocated is something that paralyzes many marriages and prevents husbands from loving their wives "as Christ loved the church," deciding instead to "love you to the degree that you love me."

I enjoy receiving love from my wife and love her expressing affection toward me. But I've learned I don't need that love, because in Jesus I receive all the love I need. This liberates me to love her without apprehension or condition, and she can enjoy my love without my needing anything from her in return. I get love from Jesus so I can freely give love to her. The gospel sets us free to become the romantic leaders of our marriages without fright or hesitation.

I was once asked what I felt when I read this section of Matthew 6 about not worrying, and my answer was: "I feel like I have no faith!" Jesus even said it! "Consider the lilies of the field, how they grow: they neither toil nor spin, yet I tell you, even Solomon in all his glory was not arrayed like one of these. But if God so clothes the grass of the field, which today is alive and tomorrow is thrown into the oven, will he not much more clothe you, O you of little faith?" (vv. 28–30 ESV). Jesus is calling us out! *You of little faith.* "Why are you so worried?" He's saying. "You don't have to be!"

And this is what's so messed up about the human condition. We hear this message from Jesus—Don't worry, God's going to take care of you—and we don't believe Him for a minute. We think, *Why would God get involved in what I've got going on? Doesn't He have better things to do? I'm not worth His time.* And just like that, Jesus's comforting words—Don't worry, God's going to take care of you—become almost judgmental: you faithless one. So we're either worried that God's not actually going to take care of us, or we're worried that we don't have enough faith to believe God's actually going to take care of us!

We have little faith. We're worried about what we'll eat. We're worried about what we'll drink. We're worried about what we'll wear. We're worried about *everything.* We wish we *were* the lilies of the field or the birds of the air! We do not trust that God will take care of us.

There is good news for those with little faith: God is faithful. Abraham's disbelief didn't stop Isaac from being born. Peter's unfaithfulness didn't stop Jesus from keeping His promise. Thomas's doubt didn't stop the resurrected Christ from showing up. Our God comes incessantly to His enemies; He relentlessly pursues rebels. He has taken the worries of today to the cross with Him.

It wasn't until LeBron James decided to return to his hometown team, the Cleveland Cavaliers, that I finally realized what it was about LeBron that has entranced me for the last four years as he played his guts out for my beloved Miami Heat.

In 2010, Cleveland had disowned and betrayed LeBron—from his once-beloved fans to his former teammates to the owner to the city itself—and he lived with this in his heart for four years. But, despite the fact that he wasn't welcome there (he was, in fact, booed every time he went back there to play with the Heat) nor had he ever achieved championship status there, LeBron forgave them all before they had even asked. LeBron's love for "his people" compelled him to leave a city that loved him for a city that disowned him. He wrote:

> The letter from Dan Gilbert, the booing of the Cleveland fans, the jerseys being burned—seeing all that was hard for [my family]. My emotions were more mixed. It was easy to say, "OK, I don't want to deal with these people ever again." But then you think about the other side. What if I were a kid who looked up to an athlete, and that athlete made me want to do better in my own life, and then he left? How would I react? I've met with Dan, face-to-face, man-to-man. We've talked it out. Everybody makes mistakes. I've made mistakes as well. Who am I to hold a grudge?

LeBron's decision to return to a city he loves with a desire to bless the same people who cursed and ridiculed him four years ago is a remarkable picture of grace.

It reminds me of the humility and courage that a grace-captured heart can have, to endure the harsh opinions of the world and not be controlled by them. To not return anger for anger. Only a heart set free in some way can do that. And only the gospel can truly set a heart free.

For a while, my parents were getting *Reader's Digest* every month while I was growing up. Because they were stored in the bathrooms, they were widely read. In each and every issue there was an interview with some celebrity, usually an actor or an athlete.

Reader's Digest's favorite kind of celebrity was the self-made variety— someone who had come from nothing, preferably a broken home in which the single mother had to work multiple jobs to afford the windows that protected the family from the ceaseless gunfire outside. The interviewers inevitably ended their pieces by asking the celebrity something like, "If you could offer one piece of advice to our readers, what would it be?" (In fact, this makes up the bulk of *Reader's Digest* … the part that isn't ads. It's full of pithy little pieces of advice for an improved life: "For a fun afternoon with the kids, try making caramel apples!" "To sleep better, try eating more blueberries!" "For a more fulfilling marriage, try going camping together!") The celebrity would always say something like, "I would like to tell your readers that you can't let anyone tell you you can't accomplish your dreams. I'm walking evidence of that. If you want something badly enough and work at it hard enough, you can accomplish anything at all."

The Kingston Trio has a great song called "Desert Pete" about a man crawling through the desert, dying of thirst, who comes upon a decrepit old water pump. Next to the pump he finds a bottle of water. There's a note, too, that says he has to use the water to prime the pump before he can drink any. Here's part of the chorus:

> *You've got to prime the pump. You must have faith and believe.*
> *You've got to give of yourself 'fore you're worthy to receive …*
> *You've got to give until you get.*

That sounds like a lot of preaching these days. "Do for God and then He'll do for you." "Do your best and then God will do the rest." It's *Reader's Digest* Christianity.

Remember: the gospel is good news, not advice.

At first glance, the story of the widow's interaction with the unjust judge seems like bad news. But we're reading it wrong! Our habit when reading parables is to find the character who is playing the role of God and the character who is playing the role of us. In this case, our first instinct is to say that, okay, the judge is God, and the widow is us. The widow came to the judge to get justice from her opponent. The judge, who didn't "fear God or care what people think," refused to give her the justice she sought. But apparently, she came back and asked again … and again … and again. Finally, the judge gave in just to get the widow off his back. Jesus made sure to put those words in the judge's mouth: "… I don't fear God or care what people think." Jesus made sure the people knew that the judge didn't feel any sort of moral obligation—religious or humanistic—to give justice to the woman.

Jesus made it crystal clear that the only reason the judge granted the woman's wishes was sheer annoyance. If God is like this, it's bad news. The normal interpretation of this story—persistence in prayer—is bad news. If God will only give us what we ask for if we ask persistently enough, it puts the onus of answering prayers on us. Did we keep asking for long enough? Were we patient enough?

But read on to the next sentence: we've gotten it all wrong! Jesus went on to say, "Listen to what the unjust judge says. And will not God bring about justice for His chosen ones, who cry out to Him day and night? Will He keep putting them off? I tell you, He will see that they get justice" (vv. 6–8). So here is the good news. Our God is not like the unjust judge! The unjust judge made the people cry day and night before he'd help them. Our God, on the other hand, will not delay in helping us.

Today, remember that we have a God who rushes to our side in our hour of need, not requiring anything of us before intervening on our behalf.

I can boil down the human problem really quickly: we trust the thieves and robbers! Jesus said that thieves will try to break in and steal His sheep but that He's the Good Shepherd. Our problem is that we get enticed by the robbers, the people offering us something that seems good but isn't. The promise of something that is never quite delivered. We feel that, well, maybe we're not working hard enough or doing enough yoga or going to enough of our kids' softball games or being clear enough about our needs with our spouses or any number of other things that are supposed to bring us the peace of a secure pasture. We give our lives over to these things and then we're very surprised when we feel robbed by life. We thought they were the shepherd.

Oprah, Dr. Phil, Tony Robbins, whoever, even the good pastors—even me!—we give something of ourselves to these people and they steal it. The Good Shepherd, though, lays down His life for the sheep. That's how you know the Good Shepherd. When's the last time Oprah died for someone? They don't even do that on *Extreme Makeover: Home Edition*! I don't do it. But Jesus actually did. The Good Shepherd laid down His life for the sheep. And you know what? If nothing else, just hearing that enables us to find a little bit of pasture.

Can you imagine? A person, a good person, thinking to die for you? And I don't mean in some abstract sense, like "Jesus died for the whole world." I mean specifically. Jesus died for *you*! Paul Tripp has said that, "Jesus took names to the cross."

You want some peace? You want to find some pasture? A place where you can just relax and be yourself? Well, that's what Christianity is selling. In fact, we give it away. We can give it away because it's not ours. It belongs to the man who called Himself a Good Shepherd, and who, at the right time, when we needed it most, laid down His life for His sheep.

In Alexander Payne's 2002 film, *About Schmidt*, Jack Nicholson plays Warren Schmidt, an aging recent retiree. An insurance actuary from Nebraska, Schmidt is a normal guy. That is, he's basically selfish. He interacts with his life in the standard human way: himself at the center. The only seeming exception to this—he financially supports an African child—actually isn't. His letters to the child, Ndugu, are full of complaints about Schmidt's situation in life, his wife, and his future son-in-law.

At the end of the film, Schmidt breaks down. He wonders what difference he's made in the world and he can't think of any. He assumes that when he dies, and everyone who knew him dies, it will be as though he never existed. He sits at his desk and weeps.

Then he gets a drawing in the mail from Ndugu, the African child he supports, showing the two of them holding hands. He breaks down into tears again, but this time with a smile on his face.

So Schmidt has realized, maybe just for a moment, that it is not "about Schmidt." His depression changes, if only briefly, to joy. And the reason? A little boy, many thousands of miles away, has loved him. Sure, Schmidt sends the money that makes the boy's life a little bit better, but you sense that it is the letters that he loves. Schmidt, of course, has been using these letters as an opportunity to vent on his own issues and to dispense ridiculous advice (at one point, he suggests that Ndugu save some of this money for college), not to build a relationship with the child.

The relationship between Schmidt and Ndugu is one way. At first, it's from Schmidt to Ndugu, and Schmidt is unmoved. But when that changes—when Schmidt feels Ndugu's one-way love in a moment of need—he is reborn. It is when we are loved that everything changes. Like Schmidt, who appreciates one-way love that comes when he hits bottom, we find it is when we feel no one could possibly love us that we are most eager for a God who says, "I came to love the unlovable."

In 2011, the BYU men's basketball team was on a roll until Brandon Davies, a starter, was dismissed from the team for the remainder of the season for "a violation of the school's honor code," which turned out to be having sex with his girlfriend. The day after the announcement was made, ESPN conducted a poll asking readers if they felt they could live up to BYU's Honor Code for a year. Here is BYU's Honor Code in its entirety:

1. Be honest.
2. Live a chaste and virtuous life.
3. Obey the law and all campus policies.
4. Use clean language.
5. Respect others.
6. Abstain from alcoholic beverages, tobacco, tea, coffee and substance abuse.
7. Participate regularly in church services.
8. Observe the Dress and Grooming Standards.
9. Encourage others in their commitment to comply with the Honor Code.

My college had a similar code of conduct that I had to sign before being admitted. I signed it, knowing that I could fulfill it only by the broadest and most superficial definitions of the "commandments."

ESPN posed the question, though, and what do you think the answer was? Interestingly, almost 50 percent of people said that, yes, they could live up to the Honor Code for a year.

What are people thinking? That they can be completely honest for a year? How regular does regular church attendance have to be? How clean does clean language have to be? That a virtuous life only refers to their "naughty bits" and not to their minds? And that's not even bringing up the totally amorphous "respect others" dictum. Are 50 percent of people being dishonest about their human capability, or do 50 percent of people underestimate the power and depth of a commandment like "be honest"?

Today, let us worship a God who, when we failed to uphold His code of conduct, sent a Savior to uphold it in our place.

Do you watch *The Bachelor*? Millions do. Over several months, a man sifts through dozens of women vying for his attention, hopefully—for the television producers, at least—ending with a proposal to the last woman standing. Throughout the show, though, the man takes women on dates to see if he wants to keep them around.

Picture it: a man and a woman go on a date. Will it work? Is there chemistry? Questions abound on any date. On *The Bachelor*, the question is, "Will he give her a rose or won't he?" This is how the bachelor lets us know that he wants to go on another date with this woman. The wrinkle is that if he doesn't give her a rose, she has to go home immediately. She has to be packed and ready to go before the date.

The hilarious (and profound) addition on *The Bachelor* is that they turn the ethereal pressure of a standard date into a physical object: a rose. And then, they have the rose sitting there for the whole date! Both people comment about how the rose ruins the evening. They can't stop looking at it, wondering what the outcome will be.

Judgment kills love. This is a truism of human life. The presence of the rose is the embodiment of judgment. The knowledge of impending judgment kills any possibility of love. Rather than discovering whether or not she is in love with the bachelor, the woman toils under the weight of being the kind of person who gets a rose. And so love dies.

Love can thrive only without judgment, without roses. What if the bachelor gave the rose to the girl at the beginning of the date? Before she proves her worth? What might happen then? They could get to know one another without the pressure, without the judgment, and see if they might fall in love.

Today, remember that God in Christ has already given you your rose. There is no judgment.

Is it possible to believe the promise that we have a Rescuer? Sometimes, it just seems as if life applies too much weight, too much pressure. Like the trash compactor in the first *Star Wars*, the walls are closing in, and eventually there'll be nowhere for us to go. There doesn't seem to be any C-3PO shutting off the power to save us.

Here's a sobering—but true—thing about Christianity: it's not about us being rescued at the last minute. There's a funny scene in the film *Galaxy Quest* in which a giant explosive device aboard a spaceship is counting down to explosion. The heroes get there in time and disarm it with seven or eight seconds left on the timer. To their horror, the clock just keeps on ticking. They worry that they've done something wrong and they're all still going to die, until the timer gets down to one, and stops there. The joke is that, in these kinds of movies, the countdown clocks are *always* stopped at one. The only rescue is the one that happens at the last second.

We are inclined to think of Christianity in the same way. It seems to us that Jesus's job is to rescue us from our almost-certain-death predicament, and that the gospel—the good news—is that the power to the trash compactor *will* be shut off, the countdown timer *will* stop at one, and we won't have to die.

But we are not promised this kind of salvation. We are not saved from death as much as we are saved through death. The old us, the us that was trying to get out of our situation by our own efforts, must be put to death. Otherwise, we might be tempted to take a little bit of the credit for our rescue.

Today, acknowledge that you have troubles. The Lord has rescued you, not by avoiding death, but by embracing it, taking the old you to the cross with Him. Today, and every day, in Christ, you are made new.

In the 1998 Adam Sandler movie *The Wedding Singer*, Sandler's character, Robbie, is in love with a girl who is engaged to a jerk. When he feels that he's lost her for good, he goes out for a drink with his best friend, Sammy, an inveterate ladies' man. Assuming that Sammy is living the high life and is totally content, Robbie is shocked when Sammy admits, "I'm not happy." In the ensuing conversation, he explains that he's worried that, as he gets older, his life of chasing women is just going to seem more and more depressing. He compares his life to that of The Fonz and Vinnie Barbarino, whose shows got cancelled because no one wants to see an old guy chase after girls. Sammy ends the scene with a profound line: "What I'm saying is all I really want is someone to hold me and tell me that everything is going to be all right."

Sammy is expressing a basic human need, something that we all share: we want someone to love us when we feel unlovable.

I think it's important to note that Sammy doesn't want someone to tell him that everything *is* all right, because it isn't. He doesn't want to be lied to. The "power of positive thinking" movement is all about claiming that things are not the way they seem. "Don't dwell on it," they'll say. "It's not real." But it is real. *Happy Days* (The Fonz's show) *did* get cancelled. Everything is not all right. It's not helpful, but insulting, to say that it is. What we can hope for is that it will be all right one day.

This is God's promise to us. In Christ, the not-rightness of the world is already defeated. Jesus's cry of "it is finished" from the cross was true and real. When things aren't all right now, take comfort in the fact that they will be, forever.

I'm sure you've heard a number of sermons, talks, and messages about the parable of the talents. It's a favorite of Christian motivational speakers, a great story to get you to use the talents and skills that God has given you. God has even gone to the trouble to name this first-century unit of money with the same word that we use for our innate gifts. It's almost as though God has gift wrapped the interpretation for us—don't hoard your talent for yourself. God has given it to you, so go out into the world and use it. That way, it will multiply!

But let's hang on just a second.

It seems to me that this is a misreading of the parable, and it stems from our knee-jerk impulse to make whichever character in the parable is the most powerful into God. The third servant, entrusted with a single talent, said that he knew the master to be a hard man, reaping where he did not sow, and gathering where he had scattered no seed. So it can't be quite right that the master in the story is God. The master in the story is the law. The third servant is judged harshly, just as he feared he might be. In other words, this parable is a picture of the interplay between people and the law *without the presence of an intercessor*!

Our God is so much more than "a hard man," deciding who fulfills His requirements to His satisfaction. He is also a lover of souls, the God of love, who sends His Son to earth for all the fearful servants who hide the gifts they've been given.

We are poor stewards. We imagine God to be a hard man, ready to throw lightning bolts and cast us into the outer darkness if He is displeased. But because of Jesus, God's love for you does not depend on what you do or don't do. God's love for you is firmly established because of what Jesus has done for you.

In my life, I've played on two different kinds of softball teams: I've played primarily on church-league teams, which is a different experience than the town leagues in which I've played. The church league has prayers before and after the games, and we players keep our anger and competitiveness jailed beneath our surfaces. So, you know, "Christian."

One day in the church league, as we all gathered at home plate for the pregame prayer, something wonderfully oxymoronic happened. The pastor of the church we were playing against bowed his head to pray and began, "Dear God of grace …" before looking up and barking, "Hats off!" Everyone scrambled to take their hats off while I chuckled to myself. So is God a god of grace, or is he a god who doesn't listen to the prayers of those currently sporting a baseball cap?

I think this little episode shows the disconnect many Christians have when they think about God. We say that He is a God of grace. We know the word, and we know that it's important, but we don't actually believe it. Our actions betray how we really feel: we think that God isn't gracious at all, that He won't answer our prayers unless we do it right (hats off!), and that if we mess up, we're in trouble.

The trick is that both things are true. We mess up, and we're in trouble. "But God" (v. 4) is a God of grace. God is full of requirements, and Jesus said that He's not going to change one jot or tittle (Matt. 5:18). Jesus, however, is also the embodiment of God's grace to us.

You've heard that He who knew no sin became sin, but how's this for a translation: He who always prayed with His hat off became our hat-wearing prayers so that we could become the righteousness of God (2 Cor. 5:21)? God's first word is a word of law, of requirement: Shape up! Hats off! God's final word is a word of gospel, of grace: I love you.

The young Martin Luther was a monk, obsessed with living a pure and holy life. Long before he started the Protestant Reformation, Martin Luther was just about the best Catholic ever. No one worked harder at religion than he did. No one was more faithful. No one prayed longer or ate less or said more Hail Marys. But then one day he was reading his Bible and came across Paul quoting this verse from Habakkuk: "The righteous person will live by his faithfulness" (v. 4). This caused a huge existential crisis for Luther.

How do you know if you have faith? The only way to really know, he guessed, was to prove your faith by your faithfulness. This is why he worked so hard at his religion, and why Christians continue to work so hard today. We do it because we are so afraid that we don't have enough faith.

The realization that sparked the Reformation came from Luther's ongoing realization that there was never enough proof. He could never look at his life and say that it was "faithful enough." So he began to see this verse as an intolerable burden. The requirement that he have faith was killing him. Finally, he had an epiphany: *It's not our faith that we live by; it's God's.*

Jesus doesn't look at our worry-filled lives ("Do I have enough faith?") and say, "Hey, guys, get some faith! Stop worrying so much!" He does say, "O ye of little faith," and, "Oh, you faithless generation." He accurately diagnoses our faithlessness. But He's not finished with us. He says, "I came for the unfaithful, because the faithful have no need of Me. I came not for the healthy, but for the sick." In the gospel, God reveals His righteousness through faith for faith. It is not our own faith that saves us, but the faith that is given to us, on account of the faith of Christ.

Every year around this time we start hearing the word *Advent*. It literally means "coming" or "arrival." It's the four weeks of the year leading up to Christmas when Christians all over the world look back to the first coming of Jesus and look forward to His second coming. In one sense, Christians are always to be doing this. But these four weeks are meant to be an intensified celebration of Christ's first arrival that, in turn, is meant to fuel our anticipation of His second arrival. This means that Advent is a season marked by hopeful anticipation.

During one recent Advent, there were three things in particular I was looking forward to, things I was anticipating: a friend's wedding, a football game, and the arrival of out-of-town guests. Whether it's something as significant as the wedding of a friend or something as trivial as a football game, the capacity to anticipate is a gift from God—God designed us to anticipate. So it's fine to anticipate things such as the ones I mentioned. But as I thought a bit harder, I realized those anticipations are never meant to serve as ends in themselves. They are intended to nurture and expand our God-given anticipatory capacities so that we will anticipate something greater: secondary anticipations are designed by God to point to the primary anticipation.

The weakness of our anticipation for Christ's return is not because it is uneventful or unimportant. It's because we keep ourselves stuffed with smaller anticipations. As C. S. Lewis said, "We are far too easily pleased." Momentary expectations will never fulfill our deepest anticipations. These are shadowlike anticipations; Christ is the substance. These are streamlike anticipations; Christ is the ocean. These are beamlike anticipations; Christ is the sun.

So the next time you find yourself anticipating anything from a good meal to a good vacation, take a moment to trace that anticipation to its end: Jesus. This is what Advent is meant to do.

In Tony Gilroy's 2009 film, *Duplicity*, Clive Owen and Julia Roberts play corporate spies who may (or may not) be planning to double-cross each other. They also may (or may not) be in love. They spend the entire film lying to one another, falling in and out of bed with each other, and just generally degrading any hope they ever had of trusting each other.

These are two people in a relationship of sorts, but they haven't been able to trust each other since the day they met. They've just stolen a formula, worth billions, and are both pretty sure that the other is going to try to get all the money for themselves. In a situation like this, love cannot exist. But then, almost out of nowhere, Julia Roberts begins to play the God role. She says, "I know who you are. And I love you anyway." What a statement! These two sentences, when placed one after the other, have insurmountable power. Clive Owen is powerless before them. But more important, he is *transformed* by them. His distrust becomes trust. Not knowing what Roberts has, he offers the formula. And in this wonderful scene he tells us his reasoning. "I look at you … I can't stop looking at you … and I think, 'That woman. She knows who I am and loves me anyway.'" Walker Percy rightly put it this way: "We love those who know the worst of us and don't turn their faces away."

Now, it's important to note that God loves us despite our unlovable nature *on account of Christ*—not "just because." The fact remains, however, that God knows us in all our conniving, self-centered, and jealousy-laden splendor and loves us anyway. And this love is a creative love, creating trust where there was distrust, care for others where there was self-centeredness, and love where there was jealousy.

Today, remember that when God looks at you—when you fear that He sees only the unlovable you that you see in the mirror—He sees only His holy and righteous Son.

Do you remember Manti Te'o? He was the Notre Dame football player (now in the NFL) who had the imaginary girlfriend who "died"—making him a short-lived heroic figure—a couple of years ago. Te'o's mental suitability for the NFL was questioned when the full story came out. After all, how could someone fall for such a scam: hours on the phone with what turned out to be a man, Skype conversations where "the camera broke," plane trips from Indiana to Hawaii only to find that she was "too busy" to get together, and so on? How could someone be so obtuse?

Here's the answer: we would do anything for love. Full stop. Manti Te'o was ready to believe any ridiculous excuse or story because he thought his girlfriend loved him. And so would we.

Here's the kicker: our truest Friend, the Friend of sinners, *doesn't ask us to do anything for love.* We would do anything for love and spend our lives trying to win it, earn it, and possess it. Jesus is there when we exhaust ourselves. When it all turns out to be a hoax, He is there. When it is revealed that no one really remembered our birthday, He is there. When we desperately want love but are totally undeserving of it, He is there. He is there.

He is love for the unlovable, and though we'd do anything to get to Him, He has come to us first. While we would do anything for love, Jesus gave everything for love. This is that love: While we were at our worst, God gave us His best. He always meets our mess with His mercy, our guilt with His grace, and our failures with His forgiveness. That's true love—*one-way* love.

With Christ there are no exceptions—not even the ignominy of the crucifixion. Jesus did everything for love, for us.

Once when I was getting off a subway train in New York City, I saw two movie posters not a foot apart from each other that illustrated the difference between the law and the gospel.

The first poster was for the film *Extraordinary Measures*, which stars Brendan Fraser and Harrison Ford. The tagline for the film is "Don't Hope for a Miracle: Make One." This is the law in its most condensed form: You are on your own. Your salvation, however you define that word, is up to you. Don't hope, for there is nothing to hope in. Make your salvation, and if you fail—when you fail—you will have no one to turn to. The law makes a demand without offering any comfort. The law is devoid of hope.

Literally, right next to the *Extraordinary Measures* poster, was a different poster with a different message. This one was for the movie *The Book of Eli*, starring Denzel Washington. Its tagline could not have been a more stark contrast from the *Extraordinary Measures* tagline. It simply said: "Deliver Us."

The law (Make Your Own Miracle) is designed to elicit a plea for help (Deliver Us). The gospel is an answer to this plea. The gospel is God's answer: "I have delivered you." When we get too lost in the world of *Extraordinary Measures* and forget that miracles happen, when we believe that we must make our own, failure delivers a crushing blow. The gospel offers comfort without making any demands. The gospel abounds in hope. We can say, "Deliver us," and hope, and know, that God has done it.

We need hope. We have been crushed under the weight of the expectation that we create our own miracles. We have tried. We have failed. We have called out to Someone, "Deliver us." The good news of the gospel is that our cry has been heard. Our Savior has come. We need to be delivered … and Jesus has done it.

The tendency of preachers from my neck of the woods (theologically minded, seminary trained, book readers) is to preach in such a way as to impress our seminary professors or theological heroes or favorite authors—none of whom are actually sitting in front of us as we preach. And as a result, we end up failing to connect with the very people God has called us to bring His good news to.

I like to say that preachers are called to comprehend high and communicate low. Read, study, think, wrestle (comprehend high), then distill everything big that you learn in easy-to-understand words and sentences (communicate low). As John Reisinger has said, "God has called us to feed sheep, not giraffes." It was Luther's commitment to put God's Word into the everyday, average language of the ordinary person that launched the Reformation.

This speaks to how the power of the gospel goes out in mission. The effect of the gospel on sinners is not in the impressiveness of Christians or their eloquent arguments, but in the gospel itself. Paul writes in 1 Corinthians 2:1–5:

> And I, when I came to you, brothers, did not come proclaiming to you the testimony of God with lofty speech or wisdom. For I decided to know nothing among you except Jesus Christ and him crucified. And I was with you in weakness and in fear and much trembling, and my speech and my message were not in plausible words of wisdom, but in demonstration of the Spirit and of power, so that your faith might not rest in the wisdom of men but in the power of God. (ESV)

And this is certainly reflective of the gospel itself, which tells us that God the Most High has come to the lowliest of men—you and me—in order to redeem us.

When it comes to engaging and influencing culture, too many Christians think too highly of political activism. As Vern Poythress has pointed out, the political arena is not the most strategic arena for cultural influence:

> Bible-believing Christians have not achieved much in politics because they have not devoted themselves to the larger arena of cultural conflict. Politics mostly follows culture rather than leading it. A temporary victory in the voting booth does not reverse a downward moral trend driven by cultural gatekeepers in news media, entertainment, art, and education. Politics is not a cure-all.

Even political insiders recognize that years of political effort on behalf of evangelical Christians have generated little cultural gain. American culture continues its steep moral and cultural decline into hedonism and materialism. Why?

Virtually every social scientist I've ever talked to agrees that what happens in New York (finance), Hollywood (entertainment), Silicon Valley (technology), and Miami (fashion) has a far greater impact on how our culture thinks about reality than what happens in Washington, DC (politics). It's important for us to understand that politics are reflective, not directive. That is, the political arena, the place where policies are made, reflect the values of our culture and the habits of heart and mind that are being shaped by these other, more strategic arenas. As the Scottish politician Andrew Fletcher said, "Let me write the songs of a nation; I don't care who writes its laws."

So, as important as politics is, and as important as it is to be interested and involved as a citizen of this country, let's keep some perspective. Politics is not a cure-all. Only Christ can heal cultures.

We Christians may talk about God being loving and forgiving, but what we often mean is that God loves and forgives those who are good and clean—who meet His conditions, in other words.

Author Jerry Bridges put it perfectly when he wrote:

> My observation of Christendom is that most of us tend to base our relationship with God on our performance instead of on His grace. If we've performed well—whatever "well" is in our opinion—then we expect God to bless us. If we haven't done so well, our expectations are reduced accordingly. In this sense, we live by works, rather than by grace. We are saved by grace, but we are living by the "sweat" of our own performance. Moreover, we are always challenging ourselves and one another to "try harder." We seem to believe success in the Christian life (however we define success) is basically up to us: our commitment, our discipline, and our zeal, with some help from God along the way. We give lip service to the attitude of the Apostle Paul, "But by the grace of God I am what I am" (1 Cor. 15:10), but our unspoken motto is, "God helps those who help themselves."

The liberating truth of the Christian gospel is that God's love for us and approval of us has nothing to do with us. The Christian life commences with grace, continues with grace, and concludes with grace. Jesus met all of God's holy conditions so our relationship with God could be wholly unconditional.

Thanks to Jesus, I am clothed in an irremovable suit of love and forgiveness.

Martin Luther shows how probing the problem of presumption is and reveals that our so-called progress may not be as impressive as we think it is:

> Presumption follows when a man sets himself to fulfill the Law with works and diligently sees to it that he does what the letter of the Law asks him to do. He serves God, does not swear, honors father and mother, does not kill, does not commit adultery, and the like. Meanwhile, however, he does not observe his heart, does not note the reason why he is leading such a good life. He does not see that he is merely covering the old hypocrite in his heart with such a beautiful life. For, if he looked at himself aright—at his own heart—he would discover that he is doing all these things with dislike and out of compulsion; that he fears hell or seeks heaven, if not also for more insignificant matters: honor, goods, health; and that he is motivated by the fear of shame or harm or diseases.

Luther also said that one of our biggest problems was our own "good" works. They obscure our need for a Savior. "At the cross," said Gerhard Forde, "God has stormed the last bastion of the self, the last presumption that you were really going to do something for him." Genuine freedom awaits all who stop trusting in their own work and start trusting in Christ's work.

In the 2002 Joel Schumacher film *Phone Booth*, Kiefer Sutherland plays a deranged moralist bent on showing "bad" people the evil of their ways. He does this by calling them on a pay phone in New York City while aiming a high-powered rifle at them and telling them that if they don't admit their mistakes and right their wrongs, he'll kill them. In the course of the narrative, it is revealed that Colin Farrell, our flawed protagonist, is his third target. The first two were a prolific pornographer and a dishonest Wall Street fat cat. Here's where it gets interesting: Farrell protests that his sins are not in the league of these other targets. All he's done is talk on this pay phone every day to a girl who is not his wife. He admits that he's invited her to a hotel with the intention of sleeping with her, but she has refused, so nothing has happened. "These are my sins?" he protests.

Sutherland asks him, quietly, "How many times have you slept with her—in your head?" Here Sutherland is echoing (the morality, at least, of) Jesus: "You have heard that it was said, 'You shall not commit adultery.' But I tell you that anyone who looks at a woman lustfully has already committed adultery with her in his heart" (vv. 27–28 NRSV).

Sutherland, deranged as he is, has caught on to a central principle of Christianity. The deep, dark recesses of our hearts are more important to God than our shiny surfaces. It is easy—and very pleasant—for "good" people to think themselves better than "bad" people; it helps us good people sleep at night to place ourselves above at least *someone*. But the truth is more stark: All have sinned. All have fallen short of the glory of God.

In the film, Farrell confesses, and is set free. Admission is his path to release.

Today, let us remember that our sin is deeper than we're willing to admit, and then let us celebrate our Savior, whose righteousness is beyond our reach but given to us for free.

Because we are so naturally prone to look at ourselves and our performance more than we do to Christ and His performance, we need constant reminders of the gospel.

If we're supposed to preach the gospel to ourselves every day—what's the actual content of that message? What is it exactly that I need to keep reminding myself of?

If God has saved you—if He's given you the faith to believe, and you're now a Christian—then here's the good news: you've already been qualified, you've already been delivered, you've already been transferred, you've already been redeemed, you've already been forgiven.

It's been widely accepted that in the original language of Greek, Ephesians 1:3–14 is one long sentence. Paul becomes so overwhelmed by the sheer greatness and immensity and size and sweetness of God's amazing grace that he doesn't even take a breath. He writes in a state of controlled ecstasy. And at the heart of his elation is the idea of "union with Christ." We have been blessed, he writes, "in Christ with every spiritual blessing" (v. 3 ESV): we've been chosen (v. 4), graced (v. 6), redeemed (v. 7), reconciled (v. 10), destined (v. 11), and sealed forever (v. 13). The everything we need and long for, Paul says, we already possess if we are in Christ. He has already sweepingly secured all that our hearts deeply crave.

We no longer need to rely, therefore, on the position, the prosperity, the promotions, the preeminence, the power, the praise, the passing pleasures, or the popularity that we've so desperately pursued for so long.

Because of Christ's finished work, Christians already possess the approval, the love, the security, the freedom, the meaning, the purpose, the protection, the new beginning, the cleansing, the forgiveness, the righteousness, and the rescue that we intensely long for and look for in a thousand things smaller than Jesus every day—things transient, things incapable of delivering the goods.

The gospel is the only thing big enough to satisfy our deepest, eternal longings—both now and forever. Grace, redemption, reconciliation, every spiritual blessing—these things are yours in Christ today.

In his letter to the Galatians, Paul uses the strongest terms possible in exhorting believers to go back to the gospel as the one and only basis for their Christian lives.

In chapter 3 he launches a series of rhetorical questions to jolt their thinking on this. He takes them back to the beginning of their Christian experience—a beginning whose essence never changes. "Let me ask you only this," he says. "Did you receive the Spirit by works of the law or by hearing with faith?" (Gal. 3:2 ESV). It was, of course, always the second, never the first. He then asks, "Are you so foolish? Having begun by the Spirit, are you now being perfected by the flesh?" (Gal. 3:3 ESV). In other words, having trusted in Christ's work to get you in, are you now trusting in your work to keep you in? Paul is helping them return to the truth: the Christian life begins with the Spirit's work, it continues in the Spirit's work, and it culminates by the Spirit's work. Paul's making the point that our works have nothing to do with God's love and acceptance of us, either at conversion or after conversion. At no point in time, either before God saves you or after, does your behavior or work or performance determine God's love for you.

He drills ahead with more questioning: "Does he who supplies the Spirit to you and works miracles among you do so by works of the law, or by hearing with faith?" (Gal. 3:5 ESV). From first to last, it is faith alone (which is itself a gift from God)—in Christ's finished work alone (not our work)—that's the essence of our right response to God's grace. By faith alone we believe and are saved ... by faith alone we're sanctified ... by faith alone we shall be glorified. As Paul will state a bit later, it is "through the Spirit, by faith" that "we ourselves eagerly wait for the hope of righteousness" (Gal. 5:5 ESV). He urgently wants them to see: we're justified by grace alone; we're sanctified by grace alone; we're glorified by grace alone. There's no other way.

Mary's response to the announcement that she, a virgin, will conceive and bear a son who will be the Son of God is remarkable. After gently suggesting that such a thing is impossible—and being reassured that, with God, nothing is impossible—she agrees simply: "Here am I, the servant of the Lord; let it be with me according to your word" (v. 38 NRSV). Though this reaction seems logical—when an angel tells you something, you agree to it—it's actually wildly unique.

When God told Abraham that Sarah was going to have a child, Sarah, who overheard him, laughed! I don't know about you, but this is much closer to my own reaction when God tells me what He wants me to do. When a friend first told me that I should consider the ordained ministry, I pulled a Sarah. I laughed. I laughed for a while! Then, as you might imagine, I wasn't laughing anymore. You've probably heard the saying "We make plans, and God laughs." Well, I submit to you that the saying ought to be "*God* makes plans, and *we* laugh." And the reason we laugh is because we don't believe God would ever do what seems so far-fetched for us to imagine.

God's plans always seem impossible, right? Giving birth to His Son by a virgin. Bringing John the Baptist into the world by a woman who was barren. Making Abraham and Sarah, an old couple who could no longer have children, ancestors to many nations. Bringing the nation of Israel out of slavery in Egypt, not around the Red Sea, but through it. Making me a preacher. This is what God does. This is His preferred method! "For nothing will be impossible with God," said the angel.

God does the impossible to *show us that He is God*. Any fertile woman can have a baby. God chooses to bring a prophet and our Savior out of barrenness and virginity.

God accomplishes the impossible, including saving you and me.

When the angel told Joseph that he didn't have to be afraid, he said, "The child conceived in her is from the Holy Spirit. She will bear a son, and you are to name him Jesus, for he will save his people from their sins" (vv. 20–21 NRSV). Listen to the simplicity of Christ's mission statement: "For he will save his people from their sins." Matthew wanted to get Jesus's job description clear right from the very beginning. Jesus was coming as a Savior. That's it. It's funny—and depressing—that in the intervening years, we've come up with all sorts of other things that Jesus is—healer, lover, example, unifier, friend (even, as some trucker hats would have us believe, homeboy)—and Jesus is all of those things. But Jesus, above all else, is Savior. Period. Anything else Jesus is, is a by-product of His saving work.

It's interesting that the angel (and Matthew) inserted Jesus's ultimate job into what is basically His birth announcement. Traditionally, we don't start hearing about Jesus as Savior until the end of His life. At His birth, we're much more interested in magi, gifts, and no room in the inn. The Bible seems to have another agenda, though. The very first thing God—through His angelic messenger—told Joseph about his son is that He's coming to save people from their sins. Not to lead them, not to teach them, not even to love or comfort them, but to save them. This is what John was talking about when he says in his Revelation that Jesus is the Lamb slain from the foundation of the world. This was always the plan!

Jesus's death, resurrection, and ascension isn't a story about God making the best out of a bad situation. The end of Jesus's earthly life—and the beginning of His eternal heavenly life—is about a plan working to perfection and an ultimate triumph, and it's a plan instituted at His birth announcement. We can take comfort in the words of the angel to Joseph: into this sinful world a Savior has come, and His name is Jesus.

The three dimensions of Christ's finished work—His life, death, and resurrection—are individual and cosmic. They range from personal pardon for sin and individual forgiveness to the final resurrection of our bodies and the restoration of the whole world. Now that's good news—gospel—isn't it? If we place our trust in the finished work of Christ, sin's curse will lose its grip on us individually, and we will one day be given a renewed creation. The gospel isn't only about reestablishing a two-way relationship between God and us; it also restores a three-way relationship among God, His people, and the created order.

Of course none of this is available for those who remain disconnected from Jesus. Sin's acidic curse remains on everything that continues to be separated from Christ. We must be united to Christ by placing our trust in His finished work in order to receive and experience all the newness God has promised. For, as John Calvin said, "As long as Christ remains outside of us, and we are separated from him, all that he has suffered and done for the salvation of the human race remains useless and of no value for us." But for all that is united to Christ, everything false, bad, and corrupting will one day be consumed by what is true, good, and beautifying.

As the beloved Christmas hymn "Joy to the World" puts it: "He comes to make His blessings flow, / Far as the curse is found."

In this remarkable line, we broadcast in song a gospel as large as the universe itself. The good news of the gospel is that the blessings of redemption flow as far as the curse is found. This hymn reminds us that the gospel is good news to a world that has, in every imaginable way, been twisted away from the intention of the Creator's design by the powers of sin and death, but that God in Christ is putting back into shape.

In C. S. Lewis's masterful children's story *The Lion, the Witch, and the Wardrobe*, he tells of a country, Narnia, which is under the curse of the White Witch. This evil queen places a spell on the land so that it's "always winter and never Christmas." Under her control, the future of Narnia looks bleak until word gets out that "Aslan is on the move." In the story, Aslan is a noble lion who represents Christ. He's coming to set things straight. He's coming to destroy the White Witch and thus reverse the curse on Narnia. The first sign of Aslan's movement toward this cursed land is that the snow begins to melt—"spring is in the air." The cold begins to fade as the sun's rays peer through the dark clouds, promising the dawn of a new day. Everything in Narnia begins to change.

You'll have to read the book to see how the story ends, but when I'm asked to describe the true meaning of Christmas, I like to say that the birth of Christ is the sure and certain sign that "God is on the move." The arrival of Jesus two thousand years ago ensured that God had begun the process of reversing the curse of sin and re-creating all things. In Jesus, God was moving in a new way and, in the words of C. S. Lewis, "winter began stirring backwards."

All of Jesus's ministry—the words He spoke, the miracles He performed—showed that there was a new order in town: God's order. When Jesus healed the diseased, raised the dead, and forgave the desperate, He did so to show that with the arrival of God in the flesh came the restoration of the way God intended things to be. New life was given and health was restored. God was reversing the curse of death, disease, and discomfort. The incarnation of Christ began the "great reversal."

I hope and pray that today is a day of restful reorientation for those of you who are weary and heavy laden, for those who feel the weight of trying to make it on your own.

For those who feel the acute pressure of thinking you have to change your spouse if you're going to be happy, that you have to be on top of everything if you're going to make it, that you have to do everything right with your kids if they're going to turn out okay, that you have to control what others think about you if you're going to feel important, that you have to be the best if your life is going to count, that you have to be successful if you're ever going to satisfy the deep desire for parental approval, and so on and so forth, *Christmas is for you.*

The incarnation of Christ serves as a glorious reminder that God's willingness to clean things up is infinitely bigger than our willingness to mess things up. The arrival of God Himself in the flesh sets us free from the pressure we feel to save ourselves from loneliness and lostness, despair and dejection.

In short, Christmas is God's answer to the slavery of self-salvation.

Jesus came to liberate us from the pressure of having to fix ourselves, find ourselves, and free ourselves. He came to rescue us from the slavish need to be right, rewarded, regarded, and respected. He came to relieve us of the burden we inherently feel to trust in ourselves in order "to get it done." Because Jesus came to secure for us what we could never secure for ourselves, life ceases to be a tireless effort to establish ourselves, justify ourselves, validate ourselves.

The incarnation is God's shout: "You're free!"

As everything, He became nothing so that you—as nothing—could have everything.

Merry Christmas!

When Ebenezer Scrooge inquires about the nature of the chain that Jacob Marley's ghost is wearing in Charles Dickens's classic *A Christmas Carol*, Marley's ghost says, "Ah! You do not know the weight and length of the strong chain you bear yourself! It was as full and as long as this seven Christmas eves ago and you have labored on it since. Ah, it's a terrible, a ponderous chain!"

In light of Marley's message for Scrooge, listen to how Paul greets the Corinthians in his first letter to them: as "sanctified in Christ Jesus" (v. 2), "enriched in every way" (v. 5), and not lacking "any spiritual gift" (v. 7). He says that he thanks God for them "because of his grace given [them] in Christ Jesus" (v. 4). He also says that God will keep them "firm to the end, so that you will be blameless on the day of our Lord Jesus Christ" (v. 8). If only people thought I was worthy of such a greeting!

Paul's greeting stands in stark contrast to Marley's. Marley has come to Scrooge to warn him to change his ways, lest he bear a similar burden in the afterlife. Paul seems to be saying, "You're great, and you're going to *keep* being great." And the difference between Scrooge and the Corinthians seems obvious: the Corinthians are faithful Christians, while Scrooge is a terrible sinner.

But look closer.

In chapter 5 of his letter to these Corinthians, Paul exclaims that "it is actually reported that there is sexual immorality among you, and of a kind that even pagans do not tolerate: A man is sleeping with his father's wife. And you are proud!" (vv. 1–2). So the Corinthians are, at the very least, getting something of a mixed message. But it's a mixed message that contains the very truth of the gospel.

Marley's message for Scrooge is, "You are a sinner. Better become a saint."

Paul's message for the Corinthians, and the Bible's message for us is, "You are a sinner, and yet, you are a saint."

Like Scrooge, we have forged for ourselves a ponderous chain. And yet, every single link is worn by our Savior, Jesus Christ.

In a 2014 episode of the television show *Louie*, an overweight female character suggests that the meanest thing you can say to a fat girl is that she isn't fat. While this might sound counterintuitive, it actually makes a lot of sense. Essayist Libby Hill, commenting on the episode, said:

> To tell a fat woman—who's fully aware of her weight, her size, her body, who gets up every morning and looks in the mirror the same as anyone—that she's not fat confirms all of her worst fears about herself: Ultimately, being fat is something to feel intensely ashamed of. It's so shameful that loved ones will deny it to her face, lest her heart break at the realization.

We all have that mirror moment, every day. We have that feeling of disappointment at what we see, that longing to be more—or better—than we are. It's never comforting to be told that some terrible thing you know to be true about yourself isn't true. Instead, it's comforting to be told that you are known, cared for, loved, and redeemed from your regrettable state.

God never looks at a Christian and says, "Good enough." There's no such thing. Instead of waiting for us to become something we can never be, God gives that which He requires—perfection. In exchange, He takes our imperfection onto Himself. He speaks a loving word over His righteous Son and that word is applied to us. He calls us perfect, He calls us holy, and He calls us beloved. And since God's words call into being the thing which He speaks, we become what we are naturally not—perfect, holy, and beloved.

It is this exchange that forms the center of Christianity and allows Christians to be honest with themselves and with others. We can say, "I am fat." We can say, "I am a liar." We can say, "I am selfish." We can say, "I am a sinner." Into the darkness of those admissions comes the fire of new truth: though I am not good enough, Christ was good enough for me.

Near the end of *Saving Private Ryan*, Tom Hanks is dying. He's just sacrificed the lives of almost everyone in his squad to save the life of Private Ryan. He's lying in Ryan's arms, drawing his last breaths, and he looks up at Ryan and says, "Earn this." His implication is clear: "My men and I have given you an extraordinary gift. We've given our lives so that you can have a life. Make it worth it. Earn the sacrifice we've given you." Ryan goes home and lives his whole life, trying desperately to earn that gift. At the end of Ryan's life, he tearfully begs his wife to tell him that he's been a good man. He's terrified that he hasn't been good enough.

This movie knows what we're like! When someone gives us a great gift, we go about the business of trying to retroactively earn it. We think something like, *I'll become the kind of person for whom this extravagant gift makes sense!* This happens with great negative impact to Christians as they react to Jesus's gift of His life.

We often put Tom Hanks's dying words into the mouth of Jesus as He hung from the cross: "Earn this." When we become acquainted with what Jesus did, separating Himself from God, living life as a human, being betrayed by His best friends, sold out by His closest followers, and shamed and executed in front of everyone, all so that we could be reconciled to God and spend eternity with Him, we get that embarrassed feeling again. How are we supposed to respond to such a gift? So we get to work, trying to earn it.

But Jesus didn't say "earn this" from the cross. Far from it! He said, "It is finished."

"It is finished" means no repayment is necessary, and no retroactive earning is possible.

Today, because Jesus didn't say "earn this," let's rejoice in the fact that His saving gift to us is free, forever.

The more we reflect on the gospel, the more we let our hearts and minds soak in it, the more we see how the gospel is saturated with the dynamics of nothing and everything.

This Jesus who is so infinitely everything—this same Jesus "made himself nothing" (Phil. 2:7). In Jesus "God was pleased to have all his fullness dwell in him" (Col. 1:19); nevertheless, "being in very nature God," He "did not consider equality with God something to be used to his own advantage" (Phil. 2:6). He "emptied himself" (Phil. 2:7 NASB).

The everything became nothing.

And this is how far it went—here is what God, "for our sake," did through Christ: "God made him who had no sin to be sin for us, so that in him we might become the righteousness of God" (2 Cor. 5:21).

The everything became nothing. For our sake.

On the cross, Jesus took our sin—our corrupt, fatal nothingness—upon Himself and placed His righteousness—His "everythingness"—on us. It's what has been called the glorious exchange.

That's the gospel. It takes those who essentially are nothing and have nothing, and brings them to a glorious completeness of wholeness and perfection. Not a single one of us could ever have done anything close to that for ourselves, because "we were dead in transgressions" (Eph. 2:5). The next move had to be His.

"This is how God showed his love among us: He sent his one and only Son into the world that we might live through him" (1 John 4:9). A restored relationship with God never happens by us climbing up to Him. It happens only in Jesus who came down to us.

Grace is descending, one-way love!

Jesus is everything, and, therefore, for mankind the gospel is everything. That's why Paul told the Corinthians that he resolved "to know nothing while I was with you except Jesus Christ and him crucified" (1 Cor. 2:2). It's why He told the Colossians of His ministry commitment "to make the word of God fully known" (Col. 1:25 ESV).

This vast gospel in its fullness is now ours to fully know, to fully experience, to fully embrace.

Paul says that the law was our guardian, which also carries the connotation of disciplinarian. It's like being sent to the principal's office. The law told us what to do, and when we messed it up, as we were sure to do, we get pulled out of class. We all feel this separation between who we are and who we should be. The law (and the law giver) tells us how we've messed up and gives us our punishment. All laws—godly and worldly—do this.

Here's an example. The law of God says that your body is a temple of the Holy Spirit … treat it accordingly. The law of the world says to be attractive and physically fit. And so, faced with these laws, most of us feel a separation. We agree with the laws but don't find ourselves able to rest easy in the face of them. They make us nervous. They judge us. They are our disciplinarians. And so we have labored under these laws, both the laws of God and the laws of man.

Paul says that's why Jesus came! "When the fullness of time had come, God sent his Son, born of a woman, born under the law, in order to redeem those who were under the law, so that we might receive adoption as children" (Gal. 4:4–5 NRSV). So Jesus came to redeem us from the oppression these laws of life put upon us. The laws of sexuality. The law of preppy clothing. The law of having the right smartphone. The law of loving your neighbor as yourself. The law of loving God with all your heart, soul, mind, and strength. The law of having read classic literature. The law of knowing something about politics. These laws oppress us. And Paul says that Jesus has come to redeem us from that oppression.

Christ has fulfilled all laws—God's and the world's—on our behalf. They cannot condemn us any longer. The captives (that is, you and me) have been set free.

There's a coffee shop I like to go to in which the bathroom walls are completely made out of chalkboard. They provide chalk and encourage patrons to write things on the walls. There are the usual things you'd imagine to find there: expressions of love for people, ads for websites and other restaurants, taunts about sports teams, and the like. Once when I went in there, there was one phrase that was chalked thicker and larger than any of the other writing, as though someone really took the time to make it look good. Someone was serious about it. It simply says, "Inner Peace."

I wonder what the person who wrote it was thinking. Did they have inner peace? If they did, they certainly didn't clue any of us readers in on how to get it. Were they seeking inner peace? There's no question mark; it's simply a bald statement. I know what I feel like when I read the words: I want some inner peace.

You can tell from the other writing on that bathroom wall, the lengths some people will go to get some inner peace. Some of them are trying to drum up business for their bar or restaurant, hoping that some financial success will give them inner peace. Some are loudly proclaiming that the team they root for is the best, hoping that being aligned with victory will bring them some inner peace. Some are looking for a no-strings-attached anonymous sexual encounter. Maybe that kind of release will bring some inner peace. The people proclaiming love for another set of initials within a heart come the closest, probably, but I wonder how many people will want to erase those in a few weeks, days, or months.

True inner peace can never be achieved; it can only be received. The gospel of grace is the good-news announcement that Jesus delivers true—and lasting—inner peace by giving us His righteousness and taking from us our guilt and shame.

Today, and forever, remember that your peace is not dependent on anything but the one-way, never-ending love of Jesus.

THE
ELEPHANT
IN THE GYM

WINCHELSEA
MEDIA

Winchelsea Media
6479 Ptarmigan Way
Nanaimo, BC V9V 1V7
www.winchelseamedia.com

ISBN: (print) 978-1-99949089-0-9
ISBN: (ebook) 978-1-9994089-2-3

Ordering Information:
Special discounts are available on quantity purchases by corporations, associations, and others.
For details, contact Winchelsea Media at the address above.

THE
ELEPHANT
IN THE GYM

YOUR BODY-POSITIVE GUIDE TO
WRITING YOUR OWN HEALTH AND FITNESS STORY
GILLIAN GOERZEN

To the people who challenged me,
pushed me and told me I wasn't enough.
Thank you.

To the family, friends and mentors
who told me I was.
My deepest gratitude.

DISCLAIMER

This book provides general health-related information and is intended for healthy adults, age 18 and older. The information provided is for information and education purposes and does not constitute medical advice. Simply put, a book cannot replace a physician, dietitian, counsellor, psychologist, psychiatrist or other medical professional! I highly recommend you speak to your medical or health professional(s) of choice before you begin making any changes. There may be risks associated with participating in activities or making nutritional changes for people in poor health or with pre-existing physical or mental health conditions. I encourage you to work with your medical and health professionals to ensure you're ready and capable of the changes suggested in this book. Speak to them about your desire to make changes in your health and get them on board before you begin so they can provide you with on the ground support along the way.

This book contains anecdotes and stories from my work with clients. These case studies have been written to clarify points and while some may be based upon real client stories, all names and identifying features have been changed to protect privacy.

CONTENTS

INTRODUCTION

It's everywhere you look.

Billboards with perfect bodies inviting you to try a revolutionary new program. Magazine covers with meals perfected by cuisine artists who claim they are easy to make and healthy! Social media feeds of sweaty selfies meant to inspire us off the couch and into action…

But if you're like most people – they don't make you leap into action.

In fact, they can leave us feeling…Not. Quite. Enough.

Not fit enough, strong enough, young enough, determined enough, good enough….

ENOUGH!

We live in a world of never-enough-ness. Chasing perfection. Always seeking more and better. And never quite measuring up.

I don't blame the marketing gurus or your friends on social media. They're just out there doing their thing. My intention isn't to call out an industry or shame your friends – far from it. It's to bring your attention to what you don't realize is holding you back from truly being healthy and fit by naming The Elephant in the Gym.

Sure, the billboards, magazines and ads don't help; and there are plenty of reasons to advocate for that to change – but that's not what this book is about.

This book is about YOU.

I want to show you the light switch – so you can turn it on and *see* the Elephant. As for kicking the Elephant out of the gym, that may take some time – and a lot of work; and frankly I don't think that's the solution. True power doesn't come from removing the challenges we face, but from seeing them, owning them – and being empowered to work *with* them, not *against* them.

There is a First Nations story about two wolves that is often shared by elders, and it speaks to this eloquently. A Grandfather is telling his Grandson about a battle he has going on within himself – between two wolves, one good and one evil. The Grandson asks, "Which one will win?" To which the Grandfather replies, "The one I feed."

As the story goes, it's not about eliminating the evil wolf; it's about nourishing the wolf that you want to thrive.

Instead of seeing the Elephant as the evil wolf – something to fight against and using up your precious energy – let's shift our focus to the good wolf. The wonderful things I know you are likely *already* doing. Let's build from those and build your strength and your confidence in your capabilities.

Instead of fighting the Elephant, let's get to know him. Let's befriend him. Let's gain clarity and understanding around how we can make peace with him. So he can stay or go – and so can we. Instead of being tethered to the Elephant and allowing him to pull us along this path to health and wellness, let's unleash him so we can be empowered to determine our own path.

My Battle Becomes My Mission

My mission is not just driven by my professional experience as a personal trainer and coach, with nearly 20 years of experience in the fitness industry. It is deeply rooted in my personal experience... and this is my story…

My battle with my body began when I was *five years old*.

It was June of 1983, and as part of year-end celebrations, our school hosted an afternoon of activities, relays and outdoor games. The sun was beaming and it was remarkably warm for late June. I remember feeling hot and uncomfortable in my blue terry shorts and tank top – the top was too tight across my belly and I felt even more self-conscious than usual. I was already feeling tired, and the next event was a physical relay. I can still recall the feeling of the butterflies flipping and flitting in my stomach as I waited for my turn. When it was finally my turn, a Grade 7 student guided me through the obstacle course. I remember her pulling at my hand as I struggled to climb up and over the final ladder, and the disappointed faces of my teammates as we came in *dead last*. In that moment, I decided I was fat, slow, and not good enough.

Once you decide something about yourself, the evidence mounts. As humans, we make meaning out of everything, and I was not immune. From the way my ballet teacher looked down at me when I couldn't quite remember all the positions, to the 'harmless' teasing on the playground, my inner critic developed a strong case at an early age.

This lens came with me through a move to a new town, and it gained strength with every negative experience I had. Whether it was struggling to keep up in gym class, being excluded from games on the school ground, or always being picked last for sports teams, the evidence was clear to me – when it came to my body, it did not measure up.

But people, particularly children, are resilient. And I discovered ways to protect myself. I created a confident and carefree façade, and I excelled in other areas. I was very musical: I sang in choirs and festivals, and I performed in musical theatre. I was also strong academically, and I was generally well liked by my peers.

I can honestly say I had a happy and fulfilling childhood. But my body was always a thorn in my side.

My parents recognized my struggles and did their best to support me. But my mom struggled too; like many of her peers, she was typically on some form of a diet. Because that's what women do, right?

I learned early that my body was a problem that needed fixing – and that the solution was dieting.

I was nine when I put myself on my first diet, and my parents had no idea I was dieting. We lived next door to the school, and in Grade 3 I was allowed to go home for lunch and be there by myself. From what I could tell from watching my mom and the ads on TV, the *trick* to dieting was eating salads, so that is what I ate. But salads left me hungry, so all my midday resolve was wasted when I would come home after school and proceed to eat anything and everything I could find.

The bullying started early and escalated to a fever pitch in high school. I acted as if I didn't care, but I did – deeply. I was hungry and I was sad, and food was my solace. Food didn't call me names or make thunder noises as I walked down the hallway. So I continued to eat after school. I remember eating ice cream straight out of the bucket, but doing it in a way that 'no one would notice.' After evenly taking spoonfuls from around the edge, and then washing the spoon by hand and putting it away, I was sure no one knew – except me. And I was my own worst enemy. I berated myself for my lack of willpower and self-control. I compared myself to my classmates and friends, and to strangers in magazines, and I longed to be anyone other than me.

I'd always been told that I had "a pretty face," so I thought that if I could *fix* my body, everything would be perfect! That boy I liked would like me back. I would be the star of the musical (instead of always being in supporting roles). And I could finally wear the same styles as all my friends and not feel horribly uncomfortable.

Each morning would start with fierce resolve, and then each afternoon I'd find my solace in food.

By age 15, the guilt and shame of my after-school binges overtook me and I sought solace in purging. I knew better; I knew it wasn't okay – but I didn't know how to stop. And I was ashamed and scared to ask for help.

Thankfully, the move into university residence and a shared bathroom curtailed my purging, but only in the short term. I replaced my purging with bouts of intense exercise and extreme dieting. I started going to the gym and I developed a 'blood, sweat and tears' approach to fitness. I remember being so sore from a workout that getting up and down from the toilet seat was miserable – and being so proud of it. I developed weird food rules around fat, and I ate a strange concoction of cafeteria rice, veggies and cold tofu for dinner almost nightly. It was weird – but hey, for the first time in my life, I was thin!

But getting thinner didn't make me happy.

All my life I'd pinned my hope on being thin. But it turned out that thin wasn't the answer. I was deeply depressed and I suffered alone.

Thankfully, life intervened, and a transition from the University of Victoria to Simon Fraser University meant moving back in with my parents and having a fresh start. I spent the summer exploring my new life and myself. I knew that something needed to shift and I was drawn to the self-help section of our local bookstore. I read more books that summer than I could count, and I made my first steps toward peace with my childhood struggles. Slowly, I began to realize my personal potential…

When I wasn't working or reading, I was off hiking or cycling, and I also began running. Inspired by my work colleagues, I discovered running as a pastime rather than a sport – and I was hooked. When my first semester of Kinesiology began at Simon Fraser that fall, I was happier than I had been in months, and possibly in my whole life – and I was ready to embark on a new chapter.

I knew that in order to truly have a fresh start, I needed to finally release my struggle with food and my body. While I had stopped many of my bulimic behaviors, I knew in my heart that the hurt beneath it needed to be healed.

A family friend who had quite publicly shared her own struggles with bulimia as a teen was also attending Simon Fraser University, and one day I bumped into her. Gathering all my courage, I told her about my own struggle with bulimia. I remember feeling so nervous as I was telling her about it, and then feeling an immense relief as soon as I had spoken my truth.

She understood my struggles. She gave me a hug and empowered me to get the support I needed. She gave me hope and I did get support.

That was a pivotal day! Not just because I resolved to get help, but also because it was the first time I had acknowledged my struggle to a peer – and I realized I wasn't alone.

That day I began my journey to create a truly healthy relationship with my body… but it didn't happen overnight.

It's just not that simple, and at times it was downright hard. It took focus and time and work, but with dedication and perseverance I began to find peace – for the first time in my life.

I was enrolled in Kinesiology with the intention of pursuing Physiotherapy. But as I learned more about the human body, I became fascinated with its capacity and capability. I gained a deep understanding of how the body works, and with that I developed a profound sense of awe and respect. My studies, in combination with therapy, resulted in a transformational shift in my life.

I started to see that my purpose could be to help others develop this same awe and respect for their body; and I became a sponge for any and all information about the human body. I focused my Kinesiology studies around Fitness and Nutrition and earned my Bachelors of Science in Kinesiology. During my studies I also became a registered group fitness instructor and then a personal trainer. As I gained experience in the field through volunteer practicums and then work placements, I knew I had found my calling.

I've been working in the industry for nearly 20 years now, and the fire that was lit at age 19 burns even brighter today.

My mission is so much bigger than my clients reaching a certain goal or finally losing weight. I see a world where people aren't stuck in an endless battle with their body; where they have a tremendous amount of awe and respect for their body, and a profound sense of peace and joy around food and fitness. Where they feel empowered and unstoppable – capable of anything they set their mind to. Where they acknowledge and own their struggles – and honor their intrinsic value. Because without struggle we can't find our strengths. It is clear to me that the struggles I've faced, paired with my education and experience, have brought me to this place where I have a clear purpose to help others.

I have seen the freedom and joy my clients experience when they break through these barriers and release this struggle. I felt called to write this book because I wanted more people to experience this freedom and joy.

I want to help you experience it too. Are you ready?

Making Peace with the Elephant

In the gym, the 'Elephant' will represent different things to different people. It may represent:

- The myths and misconceptions that permeate health and fitness.
- Or the social norms perpetuated by the media regarding what health and fitness *should* look like.
- Or your personal struggle to have a healthy relationship with fitness and food.

This book isn't a call for activism or an effort to change society. My goal is to help *you* name the challenge or struggle you are facing, and to help *you* to end the battle – so you can make peace with the Elephant and shift your relationship with health and fitness to one that brings you joy, happiness and fulfillment.

Sound like a pipe dream? It's most certainly *not* a pipe dream!

It starts with curiosity and then dedication, and a certain amount of grit and determination. You won't change your relationship with the Elephant over-night; it will take time. But slowly and surely, as you unleash the Elephant, you will begin to notice that you can breathe; and that you're no longer living in the shadow of that giant animal. And you will finally find a path to health and fitness that feels right for you!

I don't have all the answers – far from it. But I do have 20 years of experience helping others as well as myself. Over the years, I've developed insights, strategies and solutions that have worked for me and for my clients, and that is what I would like to share with you…

You'll have the opportunity to get very familiar with the challenges you face. You'll acknowledge the Elephant hiding in plain view, and you'll stand in front of him.

In the following pages you will be able to:

- Explore 10 principles of sustainable and healthy lifestyle change.

- Discover the 5 variables that form the current paradigm of 'fitness' and how they work together to keep an $80 billion dollar industry continually growing without actually helping *you.*
- Understand the 4 challenges of change and strategies to overcome them.
- Learn the 1 crucial thing you truly need to set the foundation for success.
- Uncover the truth about failure, and why failure is actually essential to your success.

This book is filled with real stories from the front lines. Some are painful, some are heart-wrenching, and some are inspiring. I hope that by sharing these personal experiences, case studies and anecdotes, you will see how a new approach could work *for you.*

No other person on this planet has your unique genetics, history, values, priorities and commitments. You deserve an approach to health and fitness that is right for you. As you read this book, I encourage you to reflect on what I've written and consider how it fits for you as an *individual.*

My goal is to assist you with figuring out what is right for *you.* Some things will feel like a good fit; some will not. Please take the strategies, tools and tips that you think will work for you and leave the ones that *don't.* Some might fit now, and others might fit later.

My hope is that you will see your own health and fitness through a new and inspired lens. I want you to feel excited about creating a healthy lifestyle that you love, and about learning some new approaches to make it happen, ones that work for your unique life! This will include practical advice such as:

- What you really need to know about 'fitness' (no gym required).
- 10 simple tips for healthy eating (without depriving yourself!).
- Why setting goals might be your Achilles heel (and what to do instead).
- How to master a self-compassionate approach to health and fitness so you can create a healthier and happier life!

It took a lot of work for me to make peace with my inner five-year-old. What

I didn't expect was the incredible freedom I'd feel on the other side of the guilt and shame!

You too can achieve this freedom! You can be strong; you can be confident; you can be truly unstoppable. The journey that you are starting on today transcends your relationship with food and fitness – it will positively impact every choice you make and every interaction you have.

Are you ready to shift your relationship with health and fitness to one that is more peaceful and more joyful?

Naming the Elephant

Unrealistic and ridiculous expectations are everywhere. We are bombarded!

Fitness and diet industries play a big part, and social media isn't helping either.

Green Juice. Sweaty Selfies. Meal Prep. Flex Fridays. Smoothie Bowls. Mason Jar Salads. We live in a time where these are 'things.' Being healthy is in vogue.

Everywhere you look, there is a fitness fad to be followed or a new nutrition program to tackle. The global fitness and health club industry alone generates more than 80 billion U.S. dollars in revenue per year!

If you believe social media, it might seem like most people are nailing their nutrition, slaying their workouts and pretty much rocking life. Sometimes it feels like you're the *only* one that isn't quite 'getting it.' But you're not! Social media promotes a false sense of reality. People don't post their failures (unless they're funny); they post their good stuff – their 'highlight reels.' So it's easy to think they're rocking it. But really, they're not. And I've got proof.

Let's start by simply looking at the statistics. According to a 2016 review of the health status of Canadians, 80% of Canadian adults do not meet *basic* physical activity guidelines. These guidelines are not about peak physical fitness; they're designed to promote general health and well-being and prevent the development of lifestyle–related diseases such as heart disease, diabetes and osteoporosis.

Let that sink in... it means that only 20 percent of Canadians are moving enough to simply stay healthy and well!

The U.S. has a similar story. According to the Department of Health and

Human Services, "Less than 5% of adults participate in 30 minutes of physical activity each day, and only one in three adults do the recommended amount of physical activity each week."

So we certainly don't have the physical activity piece nailed. Just in case you thought I might be picking on North Americans, I'm not. According to the World Health Organization, "recent figures from member states of the European Union indicate that 6 in every 10 people above 15 years of age never or seldom exercise or play a sport, and more than half never or seldom engage in other kinds of physical activity, such as cycling, dancing or gardening."

Our European cousins might be doing better, but they're not getting it either.

I know what you're thinking: Who designs and *develops* these guidelines anyway? Who says how much I need to move my body? Valid question! In Canada, these guidelines were developed by leaders and experts in the field of exercise physiology and health – through a rigorous process that included a thorough evaluation of the available research and consultation from experts in the field from all over the world.

Research and comparisons aside, I think we can all agree that being physically active on a regular basis is widely accepted to be good for our health, and yet, the majority of us aren't doing it, or aren't doing it consistently.

What about those friends of ours who seem to have their nutrition figured out? According to the US Department of Health and Human Services, "typical American diets exceed the recommended intake levels or limits in four categories: calories from solid fats and added sugars; refined grains; sodium; and saturated fat." Additionally, "Americans eat less than the recommended amounts of vegetables, fruits, whole-grains, dairy products, and oils."

We categorically do *not* have nutrition 'figured out.'

Have you ever started an exercise program or diet, only to quit? Maybe you lasted a week, or a month, but one day that little voice inside said "not today," and you agreed?

You are not the only one struggling. Research suggests that 50 percent of people starting an exercise program will drop out within the first six months.

So those people snapping sweaty selfies when they've just started a program? Half of them won't be doing it in six months, and many of them will be dropping out long before that. People making changes to their nutrition aren't achieving long-lasting success either. According to research that examined long-term results from dieting, while participants typically lose 5 to 10 percent of their starting weight in the first six months, at least one-third to two-thirds of those individuals regain more weight than they lost within four to five years.

As a society, we are conclusively NOT rocking this. Not even close.

When you feel like you're all alone, failing miserably at this, you are not. That's not reason to conclude that creating a healthy lifestyle is a hopeless endeavor – because it's not! But in order to be truly successful, you need to know what you're up against – because if you understand what you're up against, and the challenges you're going to face, you can go in with your eyes wide open. With increased awareness and a few new tools in your toolkit, you'll be able to tackle the challenges along the way.

It's time to shine a light on the Elephant in the Gym...

The Fitness Paradigm is Broken

You've been set up to fail. Yup, you read it correctly.

But before you sound the alarm and start pointing fingers, this is not some grand cover-up. There is not one person or industry to blame, but a whole host of factors that have led us to this point. And the point is this: There is a major problem with how we are approaching lifestyle change – and it is this paradigm that is setting people up for failure.

The paradigm can be roughly translated into this formula:

$$\text{Desire to Change} + (\text{The Program} \times \text{Hard Work}) = \text{Desired Outcome}$$

You have a *desire* to make a change; you pair that with a *program* and some good old-fashioned *hard work* … and ta-da! You get the outcomes you desire.

Makes sense, right?! Except it doesn't. Not in real life. Why? Because the formula is corrupt at every level. And what that means is that instead of being set up for success, you've been set up to fail – again and again. The result is a never–ending negative feedback loop of starting, failing, and starting again. Like that movie *Groundhog Day* where Bill Murray's character has to re-live the day again and again until he gets it 'right' by examining his life and priorities. Except this isn't Hollywood, it's not funny, and the cost is your health. And it's got to stop!

Problem #1: "You can achieve any results if you follow the formula."

I've been blessed with two beautiful boys. With each pregnancy I was in awe of the miracle of life – I made two humans!

What wasn't I in awe of? The 70 pounds I gained.

I had the desire to change. I had the knowledge and tools I needed, and I've never been shy about working hard. But that desired outcome (a.k.a., my 'pre-baby body') eluded me.

I had hoped I'd be one of those women whose metabolism magically shifted after pregnancy so the weight would 'fall off' with breastfeeding – like the celebrities in the magazines! But 'fall off' it did not. Losing the weight was a struggle. I tracked my calories, I moved my body, and nothing happened. I knew it wouldn't happen overnight, I'd done this before – so why wasn't it working this time?

This was my first clue that the 'formula' that I was using – was missing something.

All I wanted was to be *me* again! But what if that goal wasn't actually possible?

And therein lies the first problem with this formula. The desired outcome sought after by so many people either doesn't exist or simply isn't a realistic goal for them or their life!

I was desperately seeking my 'pre-baby body,' but as any mom will attest to — having a child changes your body forever. And that needs to be okay!

There is a quote from actress Kerry Washington that beautifully sums this up:

> "You know what? I try really hard not to use that language (being 'back'), because it's not about going backward in life. I've been really focused on not being 'back' to anything, but being the best version of myself *right now*. My body is the site of a miracle now. I don't want to be pre-miracle."
>
> —Kerry Washington, *Self Magazine, September 2015*

Sadly, this is not how most women feel! Because we're bombarded by images that tell us this 'perfect' body we seek (post–baby or not) is not only *possible*; it's the *ideal* we should be seeking.

I'm not trying to be a buzz kill — far from it. I want you to feel empowered and inspired. But I also want you to be grounded in reality – so you can be successful. And as such, I need to say this: the image most people have in their head is not based on reality!

Our formula is busted right from the word 'go.' No matter how deep your desire to change, or how amazing the program is, or how hard you work – you simply cannot get *there*. Because 'there' isn't based in reality.

$$\text{Desire to Change} + (\text{The Program} \times \text{Hard Work}) = \text{Desired Outcome}$$

Let's dig into this desired outcome and bring the Elephant in the Gym into the spotlight.

For many, the desired outcome is to look better. That's not inherently bad; the problem is how we define 'better.' That definition is informed by cultural and societal norms, and it is driven by marketing and media that lacks diversity, or in some cases any sort of grounding in reality.

In a recent Australian study, researchers analyzed social media posts tagged with #fitspo (the search term for *fitness inspiration*). Of the 415 images from Instagram, Facebook, Twitter and Tumblr that the researchers analyzed, the posts of *women* (compared to men) were more likely to be sexualized, to show the full body, and to emphasize the buttocks. The women in these streams were characterized as "thin and toned."

Want to run your own little experiment? Head to your favorite social platform and use the hashtag #fitspo and see what shows up. Or Google "fit woman" and see what appears. When I did this as part of my research, the images that showed up were primarily professional images that showcased 20 to 30-year-old women wearing booty shorts and bra tops. They had very low body fat and strong muscle definition. The women were all made up to perfection, and very few of them were actually exercising. The one or two who were exercising were posed in postures that had more to do with a 'good shot' than exercise.

This imagery is meant to inspire and help us, but does it? The bottom line is *no*! A significant amount of research has been devoted to exploring whether exposure to media-portrayed images of body ideals impacts us. The answer is a resounding *yes*! But not in a positive way. Exposure to these 'body ideals' is associated with negative psychosocial outcomes, including low self-esteem, body dissatisfaction, disordered eating, and depressive symptoms.

And we haven't even gotten into the professional 'gloss' of lighting, filters, and Photoshop, and how *this* impacts us. It has come to be considered standard practice – something we expect. We know that, and we can spot it. Or can we? Research would suggest 'no.'

In one experiment, participants were asked to identify if an image was an original or if had been digitally altered. More than half could not identify if the image was manipulated. Even after media literacy training, "people's belief about the extent of image manipulation in general did not improve their ability to detect and locate the alterations."

And if you can spot the altered image? Even if you know the images are doctored, that doesn't prevent them from having an impact on your self-esteem and confidence. There is some interesting research on this. Dr. Renee Engeln is a psychology professor and body image researcher at Northwestern University. She conducted a study that looked at whether the increased awareness around Photoshop, lighting, etc. have impacted how images make us *feel*.

The bottom line was *no*. Even though we understand those images aren't realistic (or even real), we still feel crummy about ourselves after looking at them!

So even strategies, such as those employed by Israel and France, where doctored images are legally required to have *a disclaimer*, aren't really helping to solve anything. [13]

This could be the topic for an entire book, but here's the take away: you are impacted by the visuals you see. On a subconscious level, they are responsible for the desired aesthetic outcome you seek. Whether you like it or not, you are comparing *yourself* to these ideals, and this comparison is setting you up for failure because this ideal simply isn't possible for most people – because genetics, priorities, and interests are also at play in this formula. Health and fitness don't have a specific 'look', in fact, they will look different on every person, and they are a reflection of a multitude of factors. Which is why I will encourage you to explore what health looks like for *you* throughout this book.

For now, I invite you to begin to shift your desired outcome from a desired aesthetic to a desired *function*. Find a place where your health and fitness are focused around *what your body can do,* and *not* on how it looks doing it.

This shift will take time and work. Unraveling the years of programming and old ways of thinking doesn't just happen without commitment.

It all starts with *awareness,* and below are some simple tips to help you begin to make this shift:

- Become more aware of the *images* you see and how they impact you.
- If you see images that you find upsetting or not representative of health and fitness on your terms – unfollow, unlike, and don't support those companies.

- Be savvy to marketing that encourages a *singular* aesthetic or physique. Support companies that promote more diversity in their marketing, such as Fabletics or Nike.
- Focus on what your body *is capable of,* not what it looks like. As you begin to reframe your desired outcomes, consider this: What would you like to do with your body? Climb a mountain? Play soccer with your kids? Run a 5k?
- Be curious and consider what it would look and feel like if you moved away from a focus on losing a certain amount of weight or looking a certain way, and shifted that focus to how you would like your body to perform and feel.

Problem #2: One Size (or Program) Doesn't Fit All.

A good plan is fundamental to your success. But how do we qualify *good*? Where do we get the information we need? What will work? What won't? There are two major issues I see when it comes to 'The Program.'

Issue #1: Information overload is bogging you down.

Ketogenic, Drop Sets, HIIT, Low Carb, High Carb, Paleo, Circuit Training. There are more programs, fitness tools, and approaches to nutrition on the market than ever before. And thanks to the digital age, information is literally at our fingertips. Some is based on sound science, guided by common sense, and developed by qualified professionals – but others not so much. *Anybody* can post or provide information, workouts and tools, and share their thoughts on a topic. And while this is pretty cool, it also means there is an entire subset of 'experts' out there who are 'fitness famous' on social media and are gaining credibility. Not from their education, training and experience, but from their likes and follows... last I checked, having a notable rear doesn't give you a fitness qualification, nor does achieving the 'perfect body' after having a baby and shaming others for their failure to do so.

Clearly this is an issue that gets me hot under the collar – because all this noise is doing us a massive disservice.

For the majority of people, it is difficult to discern what programs are valid and based on credible methodology. The plethora of programs is overwhelming, and I find that clients often come to me with a serious case of analysis paralysis. Sometimes they're so caught up in researching the different methods and programs that they fail to do the one thing that would actually help them most – *just start*. For others, they've dabbled in this, dabbled in that, and nothing really 'takes' because they didn't do any of it for long enough.

Have you ever felt this way? Spinning from the pure volume of ideas, plans and programs, and not knowing which way to go?

ARE YOU READY TO "JUST START?"

Awesome! I have five simple actions you can take today that will help you move your health forward. For the FREE download head to www.elephantinthegym.com/resources and get started today!

We need to ask questions and to trust our own judgment and common sense. We also need to consider what will actually work for our body, our life, and our commitments. Many programs are so time-consuming to manage that they are just not realistic for most people. And most importantly – whatever we choose, we simply need to *do* it, and do it *consistently*.

But Gillian, *what* should I do? What program should I use?

This leads me to the next issue...

Issue #2: There isn't one best way to get healthy and fit.

Say what? Yes, there is no singular program that works for everybody. In fact, most programs will only work for a very small segment of the population, and often only for the short term. And this is a major flaw in the formula and a huge reason why so many people struggle.

This is why when your best friend gave up bread, she dropped 20 pounds, but when you tried it, all you lost was options for lunch. It's why Crossfit enabled your husband to be more fit than at any other time in his life, but all it did for you was give you back pain. It's why your 60-year-old neighbor is celebrating her tenth half marathon, but every time you try to run 5K it feels like a cruel punishment. Everyone is different!

Over the years, scientists have studied health and exercise science, and gained a significant amount of knowledge about the human body. But the truth is that while we know a lot about the human body, and about health and fitness, we don't know it all. There is much about how the human body responds to physical activity and nutrition that we simply do not understand.

Does that mean you can't try the program that worked beautifully for your sister? Not at all! If it speaks to you, and it feels like a good fit for your life and commitments, go for it! But go forward with an understanding that it will be a matter of trial and error – an experiment. Because *you* are the only person exactly like you.

We will dive deeper into the science and practice of your healthy lifestyle in later chapters. For now, consider these tips as you move forward with your health and fitness:

- Be critical when evaluating programs, but don't get stuck in analysis paralysis. If it seems too good to be true, it likely is. In Chapter 6, we'll get into more specifics about what exactly you should be looking for, but for now, just begin to be curious and to question.
- Remember that you are *unique*. Don't try to stuff a round peg in a square hole, and trust your instincts about what will work for *you*.
- Your 'program' may not follow one specific doctrine or methodology. You may need to modify, hybridize, or create your very own program.

- When you do start a program, do it and do it consistently. Give it *time* to work.

Problem #3: Punishing Yourself with Hard Work.

Ugh! That is pretty much how most people feel about the 'hard work' it takes to be healthy and fit. Somehow there is a negative association with doing the work of healthy living. We want the outcomes, but doing the work can feel cumbersome – even punitive. This is another major flaw in this formula – but likely not in the way you think.

Here's the thing about change, and about doing things that matter: *It takes hard work!*

Getting up before dawn to work out – is hard. Walking past the candy bowl at work – is hard. Juggling your schedule so you can make time for a daily burst of activity and still manage your work, family, and life commitments – is hard.

Change is inherently hard – but there are two key factors that make 'hard' work *for* you instead of against you.

Find Your *Why*

What if all this hard work was bearable? Enjoyable even? It comes down to the belief that what is on the other side of *hard* – is worth it! That *you* are worth it!

Shortly after I discovered my love of running, I was introduced to the sport of triathlon. My boyfriend at the time kept talking about this event he wanted to do – the Ironman, where people swim 2.4 miles, bike 112 miles, and then run a marathon of 26.2 miles. All in one day! I thought he was nuts – but I was also intrigued. I was still working through my 'not good enough' narrative, and this struck me as a pretty awesome way to prove to the world that I was good enough!

I also loved how accomplished I felt as I worked towards events and challenged my preconceived limits. The work to get to Ironman level was intense. It took me three years to work up to the full distance. At the peak of training, I was swimming, biking, and running 27 hours per week. And I did this while I maintained a full course load in Kinesiology and also worked. Did I have a busy social life? No, I definitely did not. If you didn't swim, bike, or run, my time with you was very limited. Instead of hitting the club on Saturday night, I hit the pillow so I could be up at dawn to train. Pursuing this goal was hard. I remember heading out on an early spring ride in the pouring rain and a stiff wind. It was miserable outside, but training my body to ride 112 miles wouldn't just happen. I had to make the choice…

Was it easy?

No.

Did it take some sacrifice? Discomfort?

Yes.

But I was willing to do it… I made the time, found the energy, and got it done because I knew the other side of that work was a huge victory for me.

And I was right. *Crossing that finish line* goes down as one of the proudest accomplishments of my life! It may have started as a venture to prove to others I was good enough, but what it showed *me* was far more profound.

This girl, who had struggled her whole life to keep up, to be fast enough to finish the obstacle course and make her teammates proud, competed in one of the most grueling physical events in the world – and made *herself* proud.

Ultimately, hard work is all about priorities – which means that each of us has to take a look at what is really *important* in our life. Because sometimes being successful involves shifting your priorities so you have the mental and physical real estate to make *the things that really matter* happen.

Like saying no to another social engagement so you can get in your daily walk. Or not pressing the snooze button because you know that if you just get up and get your sweats on, you'll be glad you did. As the meme says, "I really wish I hadn't done that workout – said no one, ever."

These days I'm not training for Ironman; I'm training for life (and the odd running race for fun). Every single morning when my alarm goes off, I think to myself, "Ugh, I don't wanna." But I also know that when I exercise first thing, the rest of my day changes shape. I feel energized, even before my coffee. I have more patience for my kids, and I'm clearer mentally (who doesn't need that?). So when that alarm goes off, I push past "I don't wanna," and I do it. And this doesn't mean I scrimp on sleep. Part of my commitment to early morning workouts means I also make sure I get to bed on time so I get my full 7 hours per night – because sleep is an unsung health hero (more on that in Chapter 8).

Whether I'm training for Ironman or training for life, keeping what is on the other side of the hard work is essential. As is reframing *how* I view the work.

Reframing *'Hard'*

Transforming your relationship with food and fitness can feel 'hard.' But the alternative is too. It's hard to feel uncomfortable in your own skin. It's hard to be breathless climbing a flight of stairs. It's hard to say 'no' to an activity with friends because you don't think you're fit enough. Or sitting on the sidelines as your child experiences their first ride at Disneyland *alone* because you don't fit in the seat – that's hard.

I invite you to choose which 'hard' you prefer.

Try this now:

- Make a list of all the things you can't currently do but would like to if you had better health and fitness.
- Make a list of the stuff in your life that you are willing to give up in order to make space in your life for your health and fitness (be honest with yourself about what you are actually willing and able to give up).

- We're going to really dig into this in Chapter 10, but for now keep your list handy and let it sink in.

Problem #4: Overnight Results and Instant Gratification.

Better abs in 21 days.
Toned legs in 2 weeks.
Release 7 pounds of fat in 7 days!

I got your attention, didn't I? That's part of the problem.

We want, and we *expect*, everything **now**.

In the digital age we're living in, life is moving quickly. As a culture we are impatient. If a website doesn't load in two seconds, we give up. We multitask at all times, and being 'busy' is a badge of honor.

Our hurried relationship with time impacts our health and fitness. We decide we want it, and we want it *now*. When clients come to me, they genuinely expect to see at least some results within a week, if not days. If it takes longer? They lose interest or worry that 'it's not working,' and they want to change strategies or jump ship.

This is why quick fixes and extreme programs spark a lot of interest. They state that they will give us fast results. But the methodology to make that happen simply isn't sustainable; it generally requires us to make significant changes to multiple areas of our life all at one time, and it is often intense and generally not personalized.

This is not to say they aren't effective.

That juice detox your friend did? I bet it worked.

The no-sugar, low-carb plan your colleague is doing? It will too.

And the 30-day fitness challenge advertised on Facebook? Follow it and you will likely see results.

Most things followed to the letter will work. Some of them may even have scientific validity. But the question is: will it work for *you*? And most importantly, will it work *for longer than a week or 30 days*?

I get it: extreme is enticing, results are motivating. But here's the problem: that magical motivation that seems so profound in the initial few days or weeks of a more extreme approach fades quickly. Life happens. Work gets hectic, schedules collide, and it all starts to feel impossible. All that food prep and getting up before dawn for workouts starts to feel like a daunting task. You feel overwhelmed and exhausted and then you quit. All that hope you felt in the initial phase fades, and you're left with another failed attempt added to the list. But it's not *you* that failed; it's the approach. And more specifically, it's because our brains aren't wired to respond to change this way. Let me explain...

Our brains are super cool. We have the capability to 'rewire' and learn new habits or change our behaviors, and that capability is called neuroplasticity.

It may not be as sexy as seven pounds in seven days, but neuroplasticity is key to creating sustainable habits – and *habits* are the key to lasting results!

The *challenge* with this super cool feature is that it is relatively *slow*. Rewiring your brain requires you to complete the new behavior repeatedly over time in order to lay down new neuronal pathways. But our brains can only focus on so many things at once. So in order to be successful in creating these new pathways, we need to be strategic and not overload the circuits.

Consider this analogy. Remember when you first learned to drive? Remember how overwhelming it felt to keep track of all the tasks at once? In order to support this learning environment, you likely took your first drive in a parking lot where there weren't as many distractions as there are on the road. With practice and patience, you reinforced the patterns in your brain, and you learned the skills and habits of a safe driver. So much so that years later, you've likely had the experience of safely getting somewhere without even thinking. Our brains are so malleable – so 'plastic' that they can practice learned habits pretty much without thought! That is neuroplasticity at work!

So how does this relate to my health and fitness and my love of quick results?

As a brand new driver, it was stressful for you to multitask and perform all those tasks at the same time, and it was important to minimize other distractions, like your siblings in the backseat or the car radio. Wiring and rewiring the brain to learn new skills or behaviors requires *energy and focus*.

So now think about trying to learn a whole series of new skills and behaviors as we do when we decide to tackle our health and fitness. Layer that on top of all your other life commitments and distractions and you can see why it can be overwhelming.

Here are some practical tips to help you move from 'new driver' to 'autopilot' with greater ease:

- Tackle one habit at a time. Focus on something simple that doesn't feel overwhelming. If you're just getting started, try swapping soda for water. Or wearing an activity tracker and setting a personal goal of moving for at least five minutes every hour. As you become proficient with your new habit, layer on another new habit, but make sure you give your brain time to rewire itself and reinforce your new habits!
- Think about the long game, but work with the short game. Start by looking at your long-term vision for your health and fitness. Where would you like to be in one year? Now take that vision and consider one thing that you can start with today. Be successful with that habit and build from there.
- Practice your new habits daily, and do so with patience.
- Celebrate the small wins. Celebrate the seemingly small singular choices you make that move you closer to your bigger vision, and this will help you to maintain your momentum.

Problem #5: Everyone Wants a Better Body... Right?!

We receive a lot of messages telling us we *should* want to change. But what if we don't really *want* to?

I once worked with a client who had great goals. Each week when we connected she would tell me her plans for the week – how she was going to set herself up for success, and how she was going to make it happen. The strategies she implemented were reasonable (a.k.a. 'The Program' made sense). I also knew she was capable of the 'Hard Work' required, and she had a lot of determination. She had a 'Desired Outcome' that was grounded in reality and connected to her personal values – for her, getting healthy was about being a great role model for her young girls, and being able to keep up with them as they grew.

But each week when we checked in, she'd tell me it didn't quite happen. When I'd inquire about *why*, she was honest, "I could give you a bunch of excuses, but I know that's what they are."

She was very self-aware, and she knew she was sabotaging herself. Finally, I asked her point blank, "Do you *want* to change?"

Her response was awesome (and somewhat unexpected), "No, I don't think I do."

Ultimately, she didn't put the Work in because her Desire to Change wasn't strong enough to override the energetic cost of the work to get there.

What drives Desire to Change is a complex aspect of this formula, but it's pivotal to your ability to achieve lasting success – so much so that we'll be exploring this in depth in the next few chapters. But *change*, no matter what is driving it, requires *work* – and changing your habits and routines also requires you *to step out of your comfort zone*. So what if you really aren't ready to do that work?

That's okay! You are awesome just the way you are. Give yourself space to just be *you*. Did you hear that? Let me repeat it, because it's essential that you hear it.

You are awesome just the way you are.

The size of your pants nor your level of fitness is a reflection of who you are and the difference you make on this planet. You are so much more than your physical body. So give yourself space to just *be* who you are with no change required. But what I think is not as powerful as what you believe. Give yourself five minutes right now to explore how you *really* feel about your Desire to Change or *not*. Consider the following:

- When you think about making changes, what is driving that desire?
- Who or what is telling you that you need to change?
- What is in it for you to make the changes?
- If nothing changes, what does the trajectory of your life look like?
- And are you happy with that trajectory?

I encourage you to write down your answers. As you begin to untangle your relationship with food, fitness, and your body, something beautiful can unfold: *you*.

A New Paradigm

"I want to be healthy!"

I hear this from clients pretty much daily. I bet you've said it too (I certainly have!). But what does that really mean? How do we define 'healthy'

The World Health Organization (WHO) defines health as "a state of complete physical, mental and social well-being and not merely the absence of disease or infirmity."

More importantly, perhaps, than the definition is how this translates into action in your actual life!

Recently I was speaking to a corporate group and I posed three questions to them.

"How do we define health?"

"What would being healthy mean for you and for your life?" and

"What are the habits and routines of healthy people?"

It was no different than any other time I've conducted this mini-experiment. When I asked the first question, the responses from the room were not unlike the WHO definition. "I'm not sick!" said one gentleman who was fighting a cold. A woman stated that health included body, mind, and spirit. Another participant spoke about feeling able-bodied.

When I followed up with the second question, the answers started to change.

One woman shared that she wanted "to be able to keep up with my active kids." Another said, "I love to hike, and I need the strength and stamina to do it." The same gentleman who shared the "I'm not sick" definition piped up, "I'd have the energy to fight off the bugs!" We all chuckled.

But when I followed that up with my third question, the answers varied dramatically – from more specific ideas like "practicing yoga every morning" to "walking three times per week" or "going to the gym five days a week" to notions such as "eating lots of veggies" and "getting eight hours of sleep every night!"

Any time I do this little experiment with a group, there are a plethora of answers that confirm my point:

How you define and implement health in your life is completely up to you. There is no one right way – just the right way for you!

Defining Health – Your Way

It is up to each individual to define *health* – from the perspective of a general sense of well-being to the particular habits and routines that support that sense of well-being.

Ask yourself: If you were healthy according to your terms...

- How would you feel?
- What could you do?
- What would it mean for your life?

When I explored these questions with Monica, she told me that health meant she had the energy and vitality to lead an active lifestyle with her family that included mountain biking, hikes in the summer, and skiing in the winter. When I had the same conversation with Sue, health was having the energy and vitality she needed to fight cancer. Those are different definitions that translate into very different habits and routines.

For Monica, the habits and routines associated with health included being well hydrated, participating in a fitness class three times per week to prepare for their weekly family adventures, and taking a balanced approach to nutrition that included lots of whole fresh foods from the farmers' market. For Sue, the routines and habits included a daily meditation practice, sleeping for at least eight hours each night, eating a specific diet recommended by her naturopath and her oncologist, and short daily walks in fresh air.

You will need to practice patience as you create a definition that helps you feel inspired but also feel grounded in the reality of where you are right now in your life. Take time gaining clarity around what it really means to *you* to be healthy because understanding what it means to *you* will set the groundwork for how you move forward from there.

I'll share my own definition of health and what being healthy means to me:

I choose to take care of my body, mind, and spirit in a way that enables my body to feel vital and alive, my mind to be inspired and curious, and my spirit to be vibrant and empowered.

In more practical terms it looks like this:

My health includes:

- *Physical: the health and vitality of my physical body.*
- *Mental: my emotional, social, and psychological well-being.*

- *Spiritual: my connection to a higher power, to my belief system, and to the values I consider important.*

As with the theme of this book, these are not concrete definitions; they are the definitions that connect for *me*.

To support your exploration and creation of a healthy lifestyle I've created a companion handbook, *Unleash the Elephant: Defining Your Practice.* You can download it for free from my website at www.elephantinthegym.com/resources. I will reference the handbook throughout the book and encourage you to make use of this resource.

Take a moment right now to download this resource and begin to explore your own unique definition of health.

In practice, my personal definition of my health changes, depending on my interests and priorities, but generally speaking it translates into the following habits and routines:

- Physical
  - I move daily, doing activities that bring me joy. Sometimes that means gentle yoga and other times a heart–pumping run.
  - I eat foods that nourish my body 80-90 percent of the time, and 10-20 percent of the time, I indulge in and enjoy foods that nourish my spirit (I like to have a little wiggle room).
  - I keep my body hydrated.
  - I sleep seven to eight hours most nights.

- Mental
  - I practice mindfulness and self-compassion in my daily moments.
  - I geek out to audiobooks and podcasts daily to explore new ideas.
  - I regularly take professional and personal development courses.
  - I actively take steps to manage my stress levels and anxiety.

- Spiritual
  - I connect with nature at least once a week.
  - I spend quality time with my immediate family daily (even if it's only five minutes).

- I invest energy in developing strong connections with my community through my extended family, friendships, and charity work.

I strongly believe that we cannot have optimal physical health without optimal mental health and spiritual health – and vice versa. Each area is contingent upon the other, and all three must be balanced, and given appropriate attention and care to ensure overall health.

I didn't develop this definition and working model overnight, and even as I wrote it this time, I considered whether what I wrote was accurate regarding my current practice. But overall, it is what I strive for.

How Do You Define Health?

We will take a deeper dive into these questions in Chapter 9, but for now, consider the following questions in a journal or with a friend:

- What does health mean to you? How would your body feel? What could it do? How would you feel mentally? Spiritually?
- What would being healthy mean for you and your life?
- What habits and routines do you associate with your definition of health?

Note: there are a few nuances included in my definitions above that I will share with you when we dig into creating your 'Vision' in Chapter 9. So don't worry if coming up with something right now feels daunting. Just start to be curious and explore.

Shifting the Paradigm: There Is No Wagon!

Oh, the wagon! You know that conceptual wagon that people 'fall off' as they try to adhere to various rules or improvements, or stick to a program that is truly only possible if you don't work, and you don't have kids, and you have no stress in your life…! If you're a human living on earth, you must know about the wagon. People typically get on it on Mondays or in January, and they typically fall off it when they hit stressful periods at work, or when the weekend arrives, or when they go on vacation.

But your health isn't a wagon. It's actually more of a continuum – or as I like to call it, your *Health Zone.*

On one end of Your Health Zone you have your basic health habits and routines that you maintain no matter what. These are the non-negotiables. We'll dig into more specifics about these in Chapter 9, but for now, consider them conceptually. Also, keep in mind that your lower limit will be unique (that should be no surprise by now).

On the other end of the continuum, you have your upper limit. This is not the 'ideal' of what you'd like to do; rather it's *the maximum you're willing to commit to* that works for your interests, priorities, and commitments.

Let's clarify this by circling back to Monica...

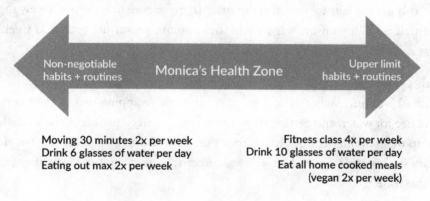

Each day and each week, Monica's habits and routines are somewhere between her lower and upper limits – her Health Zone. She knows that as long as she's living somewhere in this zone she's bringing her definition of health to life! Which, just in case you have forgotten, is to have the energy and vitality to lead an active lifestyle with her family that includes mountain biking, hikes in the summer, and skiing in the winter. Awesome. When life gets chaotic, instead of 'falling off the wagon,' Monica simply lives her lower limits – and she knows that, regardless of where she lands within the zone, she's still achieving *her* definition of health. Which means no wagon. No guilt. No pressure. *More* consistency and *more* life!

Why Is a Zone So Important?

I've seen it all too many times. Clients *start out* with a concrete plan. They're going to exercise three days per week for 30 minutes, drink eight glasses of water per day, and get seven hours of sleep per night. At first glance, these seem like completely reasonable goals. But what if I told you that the person starting on this plan was currently sedentary, drinking only coffee, and surviving on five hours of sleep per night? All of a sudden this seems like a much bigger deal.

Not only is this a huge change, it doesn't leave any wiggle room for real life. And when we don't have wiggle room, it leaves a lot of space for black-and-white thinking (insert wagon talk here). What happens when life gets busy and this person fails to meet these quotas? In my experience, they will view the shortfall as 'falling off the wagon' and then commit to starting back next week, next month, or at an undetermined date.

If this person had approached their health with a *zone*, they might have started with a 15-minute walk two to four days per week, swapping two to three cups of coffee for water, and getting six to seven hours of sleep per night. These goals bump them up higher from where they were, and *also* give them real-life wiggle room so they can still see themselves as successful – regardless of where they fall in this zone.

This mindset of success can go a long way when it comes to creating sustainable health habits!

Your Health Zone Is Evolving!

Now here's where things get really cool. Not only is where you land within your Health Zone responsive to your life, so is the Health Zone itself. Because how you define health *today* may not be how you define it in one year, or in five. You are constantly evolving, and so is your health. So your zones need to evolve as well. In addition to your values and priorities, your Health Zone needs to take into consideration where you are starting from.

Consider for a moment that 'Monica' and 'Sue' can actually be the same person at different stages of life. They have different interests, priorities, and commitments, a different definition of health, different habits and routines, and different upper and lower limits.

Often how we discover our lower and upper limits, or our evolving Health Zone, is by 'trying things on' to see if they fit with our goals and with our life! Monica tried on the concept of eating only plant-based foods. She found it overwhelming and struggled to get enough protein. She knew it was *possible*, but she found that it just didn't work for her life at that time. Then when Monica was diagnosed with stage III breast cancer, that changed. Her doctor advised her to follow a plant-based diet, and the reality of her situation shifted her priorities so this time she made it happen. In a short period of time, her definition of *health* shifted, and her Health Zone did too.

Our best Health Zone is what works for us *now* - with our *current* health level, fitness level, priorities, and commitments.

Part of defining health for yourself is about recognizing that, much like the seasons, it will *change*.

Cool news: you get to choose what *all* of this looks like. We will explore this in more depth in Chapter 9, but for now, start to let this shift take shape. Start to release your grip on the wagon and explore what your Health Zone might look and feel like.

Allow the idea of this new paradigm to take shape as we explore some of the other challenges we are up against in bringing them to life!

As we continue on our quest to shine light on the Elephant in the Gym, I'll introduce 10 principles – one per chapter. These grounding principles serve as the big message I hope you take away from each chapter.

Principle #1: Be You

You are unique – and so is your health! There isn't a single other person on this planet with the same genetics, interests, priorities and values as *you*. Stop trying to stick your awesome curvy round peg into a boring square hole and create a completely customized approach to your health that honors and evolves with *you* – so you can be happy and healthy for life!

CHAPTER 1 POINTS TO PRACTICE

★ *The struggle is real and you are not alone.* The majority of people struggle to create a healthy lifestyle and it's not *you* – it's the approach we've taken … until now!

★ *Health doesn't look like anything.* As you pursue your healthy lifestyle, bring your focus back to what *your* body can do and how it feels doing it!

★ *There is no perfect program, just the one that will work for you, right now.* As you pull together your unique plan, use a critical lens with a good dose of common sense. And whatever you do, be consistent. Give it time to take effect!

★ *Change is hard, but so is the struggle.* Reframe the work and connect to why it matters, so you can keep your priorities in check.

★ *Give yourself permission to be where you are.* It's okay if you aren't quite ready to make changes. You get to decide when and if change is on the horizon.

★ *Health is not a wagon you jump on and off.* It is a constantly evolving practice that is a reflection of your interests, priorities, and values.

Do this now: Celebrate your body (three to five minutes).

Think about what your body has enabled you to do in the past week alone. Make a list of all the various ways it has served you – from allowing you to hug or console a loved one, climb a set of stairs (or a mountain), fight off an illness, or heal a scrape. Your body is amazing – take a moment to celebrate it by writing a letter to your body to thank it for all it has done and continues to do. (P.S. I can feel you rolling your eyes, but stick with me. I've done this exercise with many of my clients and it is always PROFOUND. Give yourself a chance to experience this powerful exercise.)

In the next chapter, you'll learn why I used to believe that being a bully to myself was a good thing, and then what happened when I ousted that bully. You'll also learn why eating a donut doesn't make you a bad person. Are you ready to dig in?

The Elephant in Your Head

The Elephant in the Gym doesn't just refer to the challenges we face from cultural norms and ideals. Nor is it simply referring to the difficulty of trying to wade through the overload of information we're bombarded with, or the punitive relationship we often have with 'Hard Work.' It also refers to the *internal* struggle so many of us face – yet perhaps turn a blind eye to.

In the last chapter, I introduced the notion that what drives this formula is a 'Desire to Change,' and it is this desire that leads us to explore 'The Program' and commit to the 'Hard Work.' What drives that desire to change is multi-faceted and is rooted in your emotions, thoughts, and language.

I want to address this desire and help you shift from 'shoulding' to acceptance through self-compassion. And that shift starts in your mind. Your mindset and beliefs are at the *core* of this struggle and it is this work that is pivotal to your ability to achieve lasting success.

Open Your Mind(set)

I've spent periods of my life ignoring the Elephant – pretending he wasn't there and shrinking in his shadow. I've spent time being angry that he's there and also fruitlessly pushing him to *move out of my way*. I've also spent considerable time getting to *know* my Elephant, really looking at him, and gaining an intimate knowledge of who he is and why he sticks around.

Possibly my greatest sense of peace with the Elephant came fairly recently when I acknowledged my struggle on a very public stage. At the time, I was a well-established fitness professional with more than a decade of experience.

I had clients who looked up to me and the respect of other professionals in my industry. I was already becoming known as a trainer with a body positive approach, that is, encouraging my clients to embrace their bodies.

Yet I still struggled. My post-babies body had way more lumps, bumps and loose skin than I wanted, and as much as I worked to embrace it, I still felt that pull of 'not enough.'

However, I knew that the path to acceptance required me to share my struggle – to shine a light on the Elephant.

Inspired by another fitness leader, I took a picture of my torso in plank position. In this position, gravity does its thing, and my belly just hung there, like a momma cat. I first shared this picture within a fitness accountability group that I offer, and the response was unbelievable...

"I thought *I* was the only one."

"This could be *me*. Same shorts, same tank top, and same tummy!"

"Thank you."

The relatedness, the connection, and the strength I drew from that private post gave me inspiration to share it more broadly.

When I did, countless women (and even a few men) responded to my post. The comments ranged from applause for my brave stand to emotion-filled notes of gratitude. The resounding message was this: when they saw that I, a fit and healthy woman, also had loose skin, stretch marks, and cellulite, it helped them redefine their own expectations around their body. There was a palpable and collective sigh in my community.

With each share, comment, and conversation that followed, I felt an increased level of comfort in my own skin – like I had never experienced before!

Nothing had changed about my physical body before or after that picture, but something dramatically shifted. (Note: want to see that picture? Go to www. elephantinthegym.com/plankpicture). I gave myself permission not to be 'perfect' according to unrealistic ideals set by society, and in doing so I found a new level of acceptance and peace.

The ideals set by society aren't changing any time soon; but how I relate to those ideals (how I relate to the Elephant) is up to me. By sharing my struggle, and honoring my body just as it is, my vulnerability became my strength, and the Elephant and I developed a new relationship.

The shift that occurred was far more dramatic than losing 70 pounds. It was a shift in mindset that ultimately freed me to truly love and embrace my body, so I could stop wasting my energy on the struggle of fighting the Elephant and live my life to its fullest potential!

I always thought that when I finally looked a certain way, I would find peace, and I'd be able to give up the desire to change. It turns out peace starts on the inside and when you find it, everything else sorts itself out…

Lasting Change Starts in Your Mind

The mind?! Why do we have to start there, Gillian? I just want a plan!

I spent 25 years looking for that magic bullet – but there isn't one. As we discussed in Chapter 1, there are about a million plans and programs on the market. *Having a plan is not the answer.* The challenge we face isn't a question of *what* to do – it's the *doing* it. The oh-so-magical motivation we all seek. And that, my friends, starts in the *mind*.

Emotions, thoughts, and language are powerful motivators; but they can work for or against you. Tapping into strategies that harness this power enabled me to experience more success and freedom than I had in my entire life. Once I gained this clarity, I started sharing these strategies with clients, and the results were equally as profound for them.

Strategies like Mindfulness, Self-Compassion, and Growth Mindset, to name a few. We're going to spend the remainder of this chapter, and the next three chapters, exploring these ideas and strategies. As we explore, be open to what shows up. Some things will resonate with you and some may not. Pick up the things that do, and ditch the ones that don't. Honor your path and your journey.

Are You Shoulding Yourself?

Client: Hey Gillian, it's time! I'm ready to jump back on the wagon and lose this weight!

Me: I'm glad to hear you're ready to make your health a priority. Tell me more. Why is this important to you?

Client: Well none of my clothes fit, and I refuse to buy a bigger size. I just need to stop eating junk and get my butt to the gym.

Me: Tell me more about what you've done in the past. Do you enjoy going to the gym?

Client: Ugh, no! But it's the only thing that works. That, and I should really give up carbs. (Insert dramatic eye roll and shoulder slump).

Can you hear the "but...I don't want to"? I can too. It's a red flag that tells me I will need to help the client dig deeper and get more curious about their motivation. Because 'should' isn't coming from a place of lasting motivation. What I've learned from both personal and professional experience is that 'should' is coming from guilt and shame. And while guilt and shame can be great short-term motivators, long term they are often destructive to motivation *and* to sense of self. I'm not just saying this because I've noticed it anecdotally in my work with clients – there is actual research to prove it (go science![1])

What are guilt and shame (really), and why do they seem to show up when it comes to our health and fitness?

I once heard the difference between guilt and shame described very simply as this:

Guilt is feeling badly about something we did or didn't do.

Shame is feeling badly about *who we are* based on something we did or didn't do.

For example, a client comes to their session. The first thing they tell me is, "I'm feeling gross because I ate a donut. I wasn't planning on it, but I was tired and they were there. I should have stuck with the snacks I packed." This is guilt.

The client feels badly because they ate something that was not in line with their goals.

Shame looks a little different.

Client: "Ugh, I'm so bad! I ate a donut today. I just don't have any willpower! I suck at this, and it's only day two. I'm never going to be successful!" This is one variation of words I've heard from countless clients. This is shame. Instead of simply recognizing that eating the donut was a poor choice, the choice becomes a reflection of their poor character and their inability to be successful!

Objectively, we know that eating a donut doesn't make us a bad person, and while the words may be said with an eye roll and some levity, they indicate a level of frustration and disappointment that is fueled by guilt and shame. While guilt isn't as destructive as shame, neither are helpful to your ability to be successful.

I used to think that being hard on myself was a good thing – that it pushed me to dig deeper and work harder. But that's not actually the case for the majority of people – especially those who struggle. I learned this from exploring the work of Dr. Kristin Neff.

Dr. Kristin Neff is a self-compassion researcher, author, and associate professor at the University of Texas in Austin. According to Neff, we believe we need to be self-critical to be motivated, especially when it comes to self-improvement. However, research points to the opposite conclusion.

In her book *Self-Compassion: The Proven Power of Being Kind to Yourself*, Neff talks about the negative correlation between self-criticism and self-efficacy or self-confidence. She makes the connection between our level of self-confidence and the impact it has on our ability to reach our goals.

According to Dr. Neff, self-criticism undermines our belief in our *ability*, which means it may harm our ability to do our best.[2]

Think of your self-critic as a heckler. How well do you perform if you have someone leaning over your shoulder and critiquing your every move? What if this heckler was on high volume as you tackled a new task or skill (like developing new healthy habits)? What if this heckler was in your head? Yeah... let that land for a hot minute.

If it's so unhelpful, why do we do it?

In her TEDx Talk[3], Neff explains it this way... self-criticism taps into our fight or flight response, and this system initially evolved due to threats to our body. Think: there's a wild animal chasing me, I'm not fast enough to outrun this animal (functional self-criticism); therefore, I need to run ahead and climb that tree to safety (disaster averted). Since we generally no longer have to physically flee for our life, this system has since evolved to also include our self-concept and it can be triggered by mental and emotional stress. The major challenge with how this system has evolved is that it's now a fight-or-flight double whammy. Not only do we have self-critical thoughts, we make meaning out of the self-critical thoughts and then evaluate those thoughts and criticize ourselves for that too. "I'm not fast enough, I'm such a loser. I really shouldn't call myself a loser..." You get the idea...

In this all too common scenario, we are not only the attacked (receiving the criticism), we are also the attacker (we are internally generating the criticism).

Sigh. It doesn't really serve us, does it?

Fight, Flight, or Freeze is Messing with Your Motivation

Clinical psychologist, author and lecturer, Dr. Christopher Germer, is another leader in the conversation around self-compassion. In his book *The Mindful Path to Self-Compassion*, he gives a detailed explanation of how we react when our system is triggered by mental or emotional stress. Typically, when faced with stress (emotional or physical), the human response is to fight, flight, or freeze. When it comes to mental and emotional stress, "fight becomes self-criticism, flight becomes self-isolation, and freeze becomes self-absorption, getting locked into our own thoughts."[4]

So how does that undermine our motivation? Think about the last time you were under significant stress. How did you respond? Did your inner critic speak kindly to you, or was it overly critical of you and how you were handling the situation (fight/self-criticism)? Did you reach out for support or did you retreat in shame (flight/self-isolation)? Did you let it go or did you become excessively focused on the stressful situation (freeze/ self-absorption)? The result of all three of these responses is that the impact of the natural stress response is not only extended, but also magnified by our own internal response. Our brains become so preoccupied with managing this internal attack that our capability to make healthy choices or create new habits (a.k.a. motivation) goes out the window.

Let me clarify with a real-life scenario. You head home exhausted after a long day of solving problem after problem at work. On the way, you pick up your kids from after-school care. One is coming down with a cold and the other has a book report due the next day that you're *just* hearing about now. At home, it turns out that you forgot to pull the chicken out of the freezer for dinner and the fridge is... um, lacking in the food department. Your husband calls to say he has to stay late at the office. You think to yourself, "Why can't I ever seem to get things together?!"

You ignore your husband's subsequent text and also the girlfriend who calls (self-isolation) and you push through. You prepare dinner and get it on the table, all to the sound of your inner critic harping at you, "I need to do a better job of meal planning... this isn't a very healthy meal... all my friends seem to get healthy meals on the table, but I don't... I'm such a bad mom..." (double whammy of self-criticism and self-absorption).

After dinner, you step out of your head to help your kid get the book report finished, just in time to get both kids off to bed. And you collapse onto the couch. You don't drink alcohol, so you reach for the chocolate you have stashed in the cupboard. One little square should do it, right? Nope – the Whole. Damn. Bar.

Why? Because comfort. Because tired. Because it tasted good.

Why don't you crave kale when you're stressed or tired? (Self-criticism).

We don't tend to make great choices under stress – because fight or flight is all about survival. 'Just get through this.' The stress response requires a tremendous amount of energy and therefore is also tiring. When our energy lags, we are more likely to seek out quick energy bursts, most often from sugar or caffeine – although we know these aren't the best choices for our health. This leads to more guilt and shame. And around in a circle we go.

How do we break the cycle? Self-compassion.

The Self-Compassion Strategy

There is another instinctive response to stress called '*tend and befriend*,' which according to Dr. Neff is about tapping into our Mammalian Care Giving System. Here's the other neat thing about humans: during stressful times, we're wired to both care for others and to be cared for. This is the basis for why self-compassion is helpful during times of stress. Self-compassion is a strategy by which we tend to and befriend ourselves.

From a physiological standpoint (i.e., what's happening inside your body), what research has found is that self-compassion is correlated with a reduction in our cortisol (stress hormones) and an increase in our oxytocin (the 'feel good' hormone that makes us feel safe and comfortable).

Self-compassion is also strongly related to mental well-being, as well as to less depression, anxiety, stress and perfectionism. It is also related to happiness, greater motivation, and self-responsibility, making healthier lifestyle choices, and more connection with others. Simply put, self-compassion puts us in the optimal mind state to do our best![5]

The 3 Keys to Mastering Self-Compassion

Neff describes self-compassion as having three key components. The first is *treating yourself with kindness*. This means treating yourself like you would a good friend or loved one. When you find yourself feeling guilt and shame, or speaking unkindly to yourself, ask yourself, "What would I tell my best friend right now?" Try speaking to yourself from that space and see how it feels.

The second key component is *common humanity*. This is an understanding of how you are the same as others (as opposed to feeling self-critical and isolated in our suffering when things go wrong). This is really tough in the age of social media where everybody shares their highlight reel. It may feel like everyone has it all figured out... but as we've already explored... they don't. They're human too. When you struggle, recognize that you're not alone, and remember that you're human —struggle is part of our human experience.

The third key component is *mindfulness*. This is the practice of being in the present moment. One of the greatest abilities we have as humans is to be self-aware, but often what I've found, in both my personal and professional experience, is that we're so caught up in the 'busyness' of life, that we've lost some of our capability to be self-aware. Notice when you are being hard on yourself and remind yourself that one rough week or a choice that doesn't align with your goals is not the end of the world! Mindfulness meditation can be a powerful tool to support this key. Both Dr. Neff and Germer have meditations available on their websites that support the development of mindfulness and self-compassion.

That sounds nice Gillian, but what does that look like in real life? Let me share a personal story of self-compassion in action.

Recently, I overindulged in chocolate (*read: ate half a bag of dark chocolate chips*). I ate them without even thinking, and after the fact I had two choices: criticize myself for the 'totally off the wagon' choice or self-compassion.

It's still easy to get pulled into self-criticism, but this time I called upon self-compassion to explore what was going on. I started by offering myself some *kindness* – speaking to myself the way I would to a client or a dear friend. "It happens. So you ate some chocolate – it's okay, really!" Then I embraced my *common humanity:* I know I'm not the only woman on the planet who struggles with this! And finally, *mindfulness*. I explored what happened. In this case, my husband was away, and I'd been juggling the kids, my business, and life all on my own for the entire week. I was also feeling slightly overwhelmed and stressed about a deadline for this book (oh, the irony!).

So the kids were finally off to bed and I was melting into the couch and about to indulge in an episode or two of *Friends* and unwind. I wasn't hungry for the chocolate, but for the sweet escape it offered.

In this scenario, had I remained stuck in my self-critical pattern, I may have let this one choice cascade into additional less healthy choices as I continued to berate myself. But with *self-compassion,* I was able to redirect my thinking and reclaim my confidence in my ability to make choices that better suited me.

Self-Compassion Leads to Life-Changing Action

Hey Gillian, self-compassion sounds a lot like giving yourself excuses for not having any discipline.

Yeah, I hear you on that, but here's the thing: it's not.

Being kind to yourself isn't license to eat bonbons and never exercise again because "you're being self-compassionate." Self-compassion means that when your choices don't align with your vision for your health and fitness, you're not *unkind* to yourself about it. A self-compassionate approach means that you see every choice as an opportunity, but you also acknowledge that you're human, and that you *will* take missteps, steps backwards, and steps sideways as you move forward. Finally, and possibly most importantly, being self-compassionate means that you'll be *mindful* as you journey forward. You'll be aware and thoughtful about your choices and in doing so become empowered in your choices. Instead of mindlessly eating this or letting being busy side-track you from your commitments, you'll make conscious steps toward your goals.

Principle #2: Embrace Your Humanity

Your healthy lifestyle is not about being perfect, it's about taking care of your body, mind, and soul. As you shift your habits and do the work, there will be challenges. You will slip back into old patterns and old ways of being. And when you do, you'll likely be hard on yourself. *Notice* that. And then *reframe.* Speak to yourself as you would to a dear friend. Embrace a self-compassionate approach to shifting your habits and feeling empowered and inspired.

CHAPTER 2 POINTS TO PRACTICE

★ *Setting the stage for success starts in the mind.* It begins by becoming aware of, and turning the volume down on, your inner critic (a.k.a. that heckler in your head).

★ *The heckler is well versed in guilt and shame and it's messing with your motivation.* Guilt is feeling badly about your choices. Shame is feeling like a bad person for making those choices. Guilt and shame undermine your self-confidence and your ability to be successful.

★ *You can turn down the volume on the heckler by embracing self-compassion.* Self-compassion has three key components: kindness, common humanity, and mindfulness.

★ *Be kind to yourself.* When you struggle, speak to yourself the same way you would speak to a loved one when they struggle.

★ *Recognize that you are human and you're not alone.* All humans struggle – you're not a robot!

★ *Be mindful and move forward.* Just noticing these voices and becoming aware of your choices is a huge step toward success.

Do this now: Take a mindful pause with this Self-Compassion Meditation (One minute).

Sit comfortably, and if it feels good, close your eyes (if not, just move to a soft gaze). Bring your attention to your breath at either the nostrils or your belly. You may wish to place your hand on your belly to notice the rise and fall of breath. Take five breaths and simply notice. Any time you notice your mind drift (as it will) just come back to the breath. At the end of your five breaths you can complete your meditation. If you like, you can place your hands on your heart and repeat the following phrases commonly used in Self-Compassion Meditation: *May I be safe. May I be healthy. May I be happy. May I live with ease.*

"I've never been good at sports. I can't dance; I've got two left feet. I would try that, but I'm not a strong swimmer…" In the next chapter, learn not only why these statements are untrue, but also how it's the belief behind them that is really what is preventing you from engaging more in your life.

CHAPTER 3

I Think You Can; Do *You*?

When we met, Mary was 42 and she had two kids and a very full life. She worked full time as an accountant and her schedule was tight. When she phoned to inquire about my *Learn to Run* clinic, she told me that currently she didn't even walk on a regular basis, but in college she had been an avid runner. Her best friend wanted to run a 10K to celebrate her 40th birthday and she wanted Mary to be by her side at the finish line. Mary said she was concerned about whether she'd be able to commit to the schedule and actually run again after all these years.

"I get that all the time," I told her. "I'll tell you what... I want you to trust the process. I've helped literally hundreds of people just like you get to the start line. Just show up to our sessions each week, commit to completing at least 80 percent of the homework runs, and believe that you can do this, okay?"

Mary trusted me enough to show up to each Thursday run session, ready to give it her all. She had a great attitude and was always encouraging to others around her. In fact, she took my advice to believe in herself to another level! She made use of the clinic's Facebook group and started organizing weekly homework sessions with her best friend and some of the other participants. She not only completed more than 80 percent of her homework sessions, she also helped others do the same!

I was fortunate to be at the finish line when Mary and her best friend crossed that line with their interlocked hands raised up high! I caught up with them after their triumphant finish, and as I walked toward them, I noticed a tear in Mary's eye.

"Are you okay, Mary?"

With a proud smile on her face she said, "I did it, Gillian! I made it happen!"

Not everyone who starts *Learn to Run* completes their race. Injuries happen, work and life get in the way, and other commitments take precedence.

What was the difference between those who didn't complete and Mary?

Mindset.

Choosing a Motivational Mindset

Carol Dweck is one of the world's leading researchers in the field of motivation. In her book *Mindset*, she talks about the two kinds of mindset – fixed and growth. When you have a *fixed mindset*, you believe your qualities are set in stone – the concept that basically 'you are who you are.' This can relate to your personality, intelligence, athleticism, etc. Fixed mindsets are generally cultivated through experience – something happens in our lives and we derive meaning from it. We determine or decide something about ourselves from that experience.

A simple example is someone who does poorly in a school subject and creates a fixed mindset about his or her ability regarding that subject. It becomes something you believe, and then it can also be something that those around you believe. But where a fixed mindset really takes hold is in how it transforms the way you *show up*. It becomes pervasive in your life – in how you speak and in your behaviors. You find the studying difficult, and as a result, you don't study as much or you study with less focus. You aren't successful partly because your behaviors become aligned with your fixed mindset, so any potential growth is stunted.

Conversely, a *growth mindset* is based on the belief that your basic qualities are things you can change or improve through effort. While we all have different talents, interests or temperaments, everyone can change and grow through consistent practice. There are many examples of this in sport – let's take Canadian hockey legend Wayne Gretzky. Gretzky holds or shares 61 records, including six all-star records and nine MVP records. What you might be surprised to learn is that he was not considered a naturally gifted player. What made Gretzky "the great one" was his tremendous work ethic and his passion for the sport of hockey. He is a wonderful example of growth mindset at work – with emphasis on the word *work*.

People with a growth mindset are committed to their growth. They don't quit when they hit a roadblock; they simply look for an alternate route. They are committed to their goals but flexible about the process of getting there.

Let's circle back to Mary. She saw a possibility for herself with running – to reclaim her college love of the sport and to support her friend. But she didn't just *hope* for it; she put the time into making it happen. She showed up each week to the clinic and also completed the majority of her homework runs. But her journey wasn't without its bumps! Our clinic started in February and ran through to April, a tremendously busy time for an accountant! But she saw that challenge in advance and planned for it. She also had a few hiccups that she couldn't have planned for, like being hit with the flu in week five. But she didn't see her challenges as insurmountable roadblocks – just minor detours that required creativity.

When it comes to creating a sustainable healthy lifestyle, this is what I've come to recognize: people who are successful not only release their *fixed mindset*, but also develop a *growth mindset* – and they're willing to put in the work required.

Hone a Growth Mindset and Transform Your Life!

You are not born with a growth mindset; you develop it and nurture it.

I still remember lacing up my shoes for my very first run that summer in Port Moody. I didn't own proper running shoes, just a clunky old pair of Nike cross-trainers that I'd had since high school. I was dressed in a ratty cotton T-shirt and Russell Athletics shorts that had UVIC stamped across the rear. I pulled on my REM concert hat and hit the road. We lived on a hill and the only way out was to go down (and then go back up). Once I was off, I was committed – one foot in front of the other. Running when I could, walking when I couldn't. With each running session I gained confidence. My new friends at work asked me how it was going and they were very supportive of my efforts. I felt proud of my body for perhaps the first time in my life!

With time and practice, I improved my strength and stamina, and before I knew it, I was running a 6K loop near my home. Fast forward 18 months and I was in my first half marathon (21.1K)!

When I first started running in my worn-out Nikes, if you'd told me I would be running a half marathon just 18 months later, I would have laughed, or stared in disbelief. But with consistency and practice, I honed my growth mindset and I came to believe that anything I set my mind to was possible.

I experienced success on my own terms and I realized that the factor limiting me the most was not my body – it was strong and capable. What was holding me back was my old mindset – that I wasn't good enough. And once I really let that go, I felt unstoppable! Not just in my pursuit of physical challenges, but in life as well!

Each of us is capable of so much more than what we believe. And changing our beliefs starts with creating a healthy and productive mindset – a *growth* mindset.

Creating Your Growth Mindset

How do you develop and nurture a growth mindset? There isn't a singular method to adhere to, but you can foster a growth mindset by taking these three steps of inquiry:

1. **Explore your thoughts through journaling.** Spend some time to do a free flow journal entry to explore your thoughts and feelings. Writing can help you gain clarity and insight. Below are some questions to consider, and as you explore the answers it's important to leave judgment or criticism at the door. There's a Maya Angelou quote I love, "I did then what I knew how to do. Now that I know better, I do better." The last thing you need to do now is let your self-critic bring up guilt or shame about past efforts or failures. As the saying goes, "It is what it is." Instead, explore the ideas below with self-compassion, and consider how you might shift your thinking as you approach your health and fitness with a new lens and a new mindset.
   - Take some time and journal about areas where you struggle. What mindset do you bring to the practice?

- Also look at an area of your life where you've been very successful. Think back to an accomplishment that you're proud of. How did you achieve it? Did you have a growth mindset? How did that growth mindset enable you to be successful? Looking at your past successes is a powerful way to highlight your capabilities. It has been my experience that most people are far more capable, strong, determined, and motivated than they give themselves credit for.

- Consider your relationship with health and fitness. When you've had periods of time where it was 'working,' what mindset did you have? Alternately, during periods where your fitness was difficult to maintain and you weren't successful, what fixed mindset or limiting beliefs did you have?

2. **Practice mindfulness.** The application of these insights can be profoundly affected through *mindfulness*. As we explored in the previous chapter: in its simplest terms, mindfulness is the act of being in the present moment. This is very much *a practice*, so be patient with yourself. Start by simply noticing when you're reinforcing a limiting belief or fixed mindset. Reframe the fixed mindset into a growth mindset. Remember Mary? Think about the mindset she brought to her pursuit of running. Some days it was simply about getting out of her head, lacing up her shoes, and getting into motion.

3. **Don't think – just do.** There's a reason the Nike slogan 'Just Do It' is so wildly successful. It's powerful. It's one thing to set an *intention* – to say you're going to do something – but it's another to *take action*. Taking action and following through (sometimes in spite of your thoughts and feelings about it) often has the most profound impact on your belief about your capabilities. Show yourself you can and you'll start to be a believer.

As you work to develop your growth mindset through processing, mindfulness, and action, be patient with yourself. Remember this is a *practice*. A practice that takes persistence, consistency, and above all else, patience.

Principle #3: Show Up

Trust the process and take action! You've been up against a lot – but don't give away your power! Shift your thinking and decide you *can*. Go in with a mindset that you will succeed and then put the work in to make it happen! Find your grit, determination, and perseverance. Decide you're worth it, and start living into your full potential!

CHAPTER 3 POINTS TO PRACTICE:

★ *"Whether you think you can or whether you think you can't, you're right."* This quote from Henry Ford speaks to mindset beautifully. The mindset we bring to everything we do has a dramatic impact on our ability to be successful.

★ *In areas where we struggle, a fixed mindset may be holding us back.* A fixed mindset assumes we are who we are and there is nothing we can do to change that.

★ *Successful people hone their growth mindset.* A growth mindset is based on the belief that while we do have innate capabilities and talents, much of our capacity is developed through work.

★ *Successful people aren't 'lucky'; they work hard to achieve success.* They believe they can and then put in the work to make it happen.

★ *Growth mindset isn't innate; it's developed.* Develop your growth mindset through awareness, mindfulness and taking action.

Do this now: Take ONE step (Two minutes).

Do something *right now* that will move you forward towards greater health. Go have a glass of water. Register for a fitness class. Put on your shoes and get out the door for a walk. Order that book you've been meaning to read. Call a friend to coordinate a weekend activity. Big or small – the believing is in the doing.

You are both your greatest fan and your strongest critic. In the next chapter, learn why this life lesson is so profoundly true and also what you can do to quiet the critic and amplify the fan.

CHAPTER 4

The Words that Shape Your World

You talk to yourself. Don't worry, I do too. In fact, we all do (phew! right?).

The idea of this internal dialogue dates back to Socrates and Plato.[6] It has since been studied by many psychologists and is commonly referred to as 'self-talk.' It includes the things we say to ourselves both internally and out loud.

So why do we do it? Psychologists have posited that self-talk provides a variety of instructional and motivational functions, including but not limited to: problem solving, planning, memory, task switching, self-control, and self-regulation. It is also believed to affect focus, confidence, effort regulation, cognitive, and emotional control, and automatic execution. Essentially, it allows us to express our emotions, impressions, biases, and associations. And as we do this, it also enables us to redefine new experiences that are part of our past, which may, in turn, help us to process, as well as direct our behavior.[7]

Bottom line? We talk to ourselves for a variety of reasons.

So how does it impact us day-to-day? Self-talk is typically categorized as positive or negative. Positive includes the things you say to yourself that are encouraging or generally have an encouraging tone, such as, "I've got this," or "I'm doing really well." Conversely, negative self-talk may reflect anger, frustration, or discouragement. Examples in this case might include, "You can't do this," or "This is awful!"[8]

It's not a huge leap to consider that speaking positively or negatively to ourselves has an impact on our performance and our overall experience. This has been most widely studied in the realm of sports psychology, but it has logical implications for health and wellness, which is what we will discuss here.

While much of our self-talk is seemingly automatic and subconscious, through practice we can also have some control over it. The sports psychology theory that resonates most deeply for me is called *dual-process theory*. Within that model, there are essentially two systems of self-talk, and these two systems work in conjunction to interpret input from stimuli. In other words, we take information from our physical experiences engaging with the world and translate them into our inner dialogue. These two systems are named System 1 and System 2 (fancy, I know!). System 1 self-talk is fast, effortless, and emotionally charged – it's our 'gut instinct' or 'intuition.' It is self-talk that expresses our experiences, beliefs, and bodily reactions to the outside world translated into language. System 2 self-talk is slower, effortful, and consciously monitored. This self-talk is generated from consideration and planning, and it is more likely to lead to logical, instructional, task-focused, or motivational self-talk.

Let's explore this with an example from sport. You are playing tennis and miss a shot. System 1 triggers an automatic response of frustration that may sound like you berating yourself, "I'm no good at this!" System 2 evaluates these feelings and emotions and draws in the data from the situation (including the fact that you missed the shot) to develop a response based on intention and logic. This might look like instructional self-talk ("keep your eye on the ball"), calming self-talk ("it's just a game for fun"), or motivational self-talk ("I'll get the next shot").

The good news for us is that System 2 self-talk utilizes input from System 1 self-talk. Meaning, you can consciously counteract the more instinctive way you speak to yourself. So while we may not have overt control over System 1 self-talk, we do have significant capability to control our System 2 self-talk.

How do we do it?

Just like everything else, it takes *practice*. The research indicates that self-talk that is *practiced* has a stronger performance-enhancing effect than self-talk that is not.

But before you start becoming the world's loudest internal cheerleader, you need to know this: research has also found that in cases where the positive self-talk practiced was 'dissonant' with regard to the beliefs of the individual, the self-talk *damaged* performance. In other words, there needs to be at least a *kernel* of truth in what you're saying in order for it to be effective. So think, genuine heartfelt supporter, not syrupy inauthentic cheerleader.

The Voices in My Head

For years I told myself I was a slow runner.

I berated myself during training runs. I would even go as far as bullying myself as I struggled to run up hills. "You'll never be skinny if you don't push harder." Ouch.

Thankfully, that inner bully didn't stop me, and I experienced success training for and completing numerous running events and triathlons. However, in spite of my success, there was always a 'but' when I shared my accomplishments. I'd proudly tell people about the half marathon I was training for, but I would quickly discount my accomplishment by declaring that I wasn't fast. And my experiences validated my self-talk; I was often in the back third of the pack, and once I even finished dead last! So my experience validated my self-talk, and my self-talk reinforced my experience. It was a vicious cycle that continued until about four years ago.

I'd come far enough along my own path to realize that being a 'slow runner' didn't mean anything. It just was. I had embraced my 'back of the pack' status and even celebrated it.

But secretly I also wanted to be faster.

So I trained to become faster, but I didn't see marked changes. I would do the requisite speed work and drills to improve technical ability and speed, but I seemed to be stuck at one slow, steady speed.

Then in 2014, I was introduced to Carol Dweck's book *Mindset,* and the concept of *Fixed Mindset* and *Growth Mindset* struck me. I suddenly realized that "I'm a slow runner" was a serious fixed mindset that was holding me back!

I started to listen in on my internal dialogue, and I noticed that in workouts and even while out for a fun social run, I made unhelpful (and often unkind) comments that involved comparison at best and shame at worst.

Once I realized what I was doing, it was like someone had flipped a switch. Instead of holding onto my fixed mindset, I decided to shift to a growth mindset empowered by self-talk. Doing that meant creating a new definition of myself, and most importantly, changing the associated language. Instead of calling myself 'a dedicated back-of-the-pack runner,' I created a mantra: "I am faster than I think; I am stronger than I think."

Then I went into my training with that mantra and that attitude. My mindset was brought to life by *language* and reinforced by *behavior*. And guess what happened! In my very first race after my 'mindset shift,' I knocked more than six minutes off my previous year's time! I clocked my fastest 10K time ever! I was in my mid–thirties and I was faster than when I was at 20!

I need to be clear about this. It wasn't easy; the training was tough. Before the shift I had been complacent about my place in the pack, and it was reflected in my effort. Using my mantra didn't magically 'give' me results. Changing my self-talk helped me to shift my mindset, and it was that shift in mindset that enabled me to stop making excuses for myself and work hard for the results.

Does this success mean I *never* have that innate and automatic "I'm a slow runner" self-talk creep in? Not at all. My 'System 1' self-talk is still pretty strong; it will likely be with me for life. But I've made a concerted effort to support and reinforce my 'System 2' self-talk – and that has made all the difference.

Changing the Voices in Our Heads

The first step in this process is to become *aware* of your self-talk. Often we say things and we're not really aware of it; it's a habit. Once we're aware, then we can make gentle shifts where necessary.

When it comes to negative self-talk, I've found that there are a few different ways to make the mental shift. One great way is to notice your negative thoughts and ask yourself, "Does this thought provide value? Is it kind? Is it helpful? Is it moving me forward or pulling me back?" If it's pulling you back, examine it. Is it based on fact or is it an assumption? Is it based on an old limiting belief or fixed mindset? Think back to that first key of self-compassion and consider this, "Am I speaking to myself the way I would speak to someone I love?"

Simply being aware can go a long way to helping you retrain your mind and your self-talk behaviors. And you may also need a more physical reminder. I once had a friend who wore an elastic band around his wrist when he was shifting thought habits, and he would gently snap it each time he had an unhelpful thought. The idea is to simply bring your awareness to the moment and give you an opportunity to refocus your thoughts and language. This is the concept of a *touchstone* – something physical that you use to bring your awareness to something. It's a useful practice when you are working on mindfulness. Your touchstone might be an elastic, a necklace, or something small that you carry in your pocket, like a smooth rock.

Being aware is a great start, but what can we do to be more proactive? To help us develop and increase our positive self-talk, one of the most commonly used, and extremely effective, tools is a mantra. Mantras are words or phrases you use that promote positive feelings and thoughts. I like to think of them as language that supports helpful thoughts and a growth mindset. Simply put, mantras enable you to practice your System 2 self-talk.

Creating a powerful mantra can start with looking at the negative thoughts you have, and then looking at how you can eliminate a frequent negative thought by using a mantra that counters it (in a way that resonates with you). One client I worked with had two consistent negative self-talk phrases, "I'm inconsistent" and "I have no self-control." It especially impacted her ability to make healthy food choices. As we worked together, she created a mantra that completely inspired her, "I am a nutritional badass." For her, being a 'badass' meant she was completely *unstoppable* when it came to her commitments, no matter what. Using this mantra, she was able to shift her negative self-talk and replace it with this mantra that better matched the vision she had for her healthy life. Was it perfect for her from then on? Nope. She still struggles from time to time (she's human), but overall her attitude and her outcomes went through a major shift towards creating a healthier relationship with food.

Create a Mantra to Live By!

Create a mantra for your health and fitness, and make sure it is coming from a place of growth and possibility. Here is a simple method to use:

1. Take a piece of paper, and on the left side, write down the negative self-talk that is holding you back. (You might want to refer back to your journaling from the last chapter where you explored your limiting beliefs and fixed mindset.)

2. On the right side, write down a present-tense, positive version of the self-talk.

3. Then look at how you can string those positive statements together to create a mantra.

TIP: Make sure your mantra is in the present tense and uses only positive words. Remember that in order for it to effectively impact your performance, it needs to hold a kernel of truth for you – you have to believe it on some level!

MANTRAS THAT MOTIVATE!

Looking for some inspiration? Try on some of these...

★ I am daring and adventurous.

★ I am fierce and unstoppable.

★ I am calm and focused.

★ I am enough.

★ My body is strong and capable.

★ I choose *progress* over *perfect*.

★ Don't think, just do.

★ I can and I will.

★ Every move is a good move.

Example 1: Black and white labeling.

One client came to me struggling with her relationship with food. She had strong labeling and self-talk around 'good' and 'bad' foods. When she chose the 'bad' foods, she would criticize herself for her bad choices, and this self-talk would often cascade and shape the rest of her day. She knew this was counterproductive to her success, and she wanted to shift her self-talk and shift her mindset.

At the core of this type of self-talk is a philosophy (her beliefs were shaping her self-talk). We started an inquiry together by exploring the idea of 'good' and 'bad.' What did that mean to her? Why did she feel that one choice had to impact the next?

She explained that after years of dieting, she viewed foods that were on her diet plan as good and foods that were *not* on her plan as *bad*. When she made one bad choice, her instincts (her System 1 self-talk) told her that she had failed. And then the negative self-talk ensued. This magnified her feelings of frustration and often destroyed her motivation. The resolution she often came up with was the decision to 'start fresh' tomorrow, which led to more "bad" choices and overeating for the remainder of the day.

I challenged her notion that our bodies are that discrete, and asked her to consider the idea that each of her food choices was independent of the next one. And also that she could have something 'off plan' and then the very next choice could be 'on plan.' For her, it was an 'aha' moment.

I encouraged her to embrace a compassionate voice when she was struggling, and additionally to consider a new mantra to reinforce her positive System 2 self-talk. Instead of the negative self-talk "I might as well start fresh tomorrow," she was able to realize that she could reframe around her clean slate thinking. She developed the mantra *"Every choice is a clean slate."*

Example 2: Breaking the negative self-talk loop.

Often when clients come to me, they've tried and failed many times. One such client had been very successful with a more extreme approach. She'd lost more than 70 pounds and was feeling very happy. Then she moved, changed jobs, and struggled in her personal life. Not surprisingly, with so many changes happening all at the same time, her routines were destroyed. She regained much of the weight she had lost, and she was very upset with herself – so upset that every step forward felt arduous.

Her negative self-talk was punitive, angry, and unhelpful, and it was destroying her confidence and her ability to move forward. She was stuck in a negative feedback loop of self-talk and also in a health rut.

I asked her, "What would you say to your sister if she was struggling in this way?" Immediately she shared that she would tell her sister that it was okay, and that she could start again and repeat what she had done before! I encouraged her to find that kind and self-compassionate voice when she was talking to *herself* and to create a mantra that would help her to find her patience and her confidence.

I shared with her the Maya Angelou quote that I shared with you earlier in the book, *"I did then what I knew how to do. Now that I know better, I do better."* It resonated with her and it became her mantra. Each week, instead of trying to make sweeping changes, she focused on small shifts that she could sustain – even when life got messy. Most importantly, the changes she made were all grounded by her mantra. That helped her release the stress response of fight (self-criticism) and freeze (self-absorption), and refocus on moving forward – her way!

Example 3: The all-or-nothing trap.

Sometimes that inner critic just has "I'm too busy" *on repeat*. Clients often come to me with the belief that if they can't do things exactly as written in their program, they may as well not bother.

Somewhere along the way, we decided that health and fitness is all or nothing. But that's simply not true! Any choice you make that moves you towards better health and fitness is *a great choice*. Many of my clients utilize video-based fitness paired with simple nutrition guidelines. The series that many of my clients begin with includes short daily workouts and a portion-based approach to nutrition.

When one of my clients purchased the program, she let me know that she was going to purchase *now* so she could read up and get ready, but she wouldn't start until the *next month* because life this month was too hectic. When I pressed further, I found out that she had one commitment per week in the evening that would interfere with her workout time, and she had a family social event every weekend for the next three weeks. So I asked, "Could you commit to just two workouts this week? Is that possible?" And the response was, "Yeah, I could actually do three, maybe even four... but that's not what I'm supposed to do, so shouldn't I wait until I can do it properly?"

I asked her, "Do you think doing three or four workouts this week would benefit your health?" She smiled. "Well, of course!" So I then asked her, "What if you follow the nutrition guide as best you can, do you think you might make some better choices overall?" She chuckled, "Well, of course!"

I introduced her to one of my favorite mantras: *"Something is better than nothing,"* and she got started straight away. Was it perfect? No, but it was definitely progress.

Taking Your Mantra on the Road

Once you've developed a mantra that speaks to you, put your mantra into practice – because the power of a mantra comes from *repetition*. Write it on Post-it Notes and put them in places where you'll see them frequently. You may wish to use an app or a free design site to create an image with words, and then use that image as your wallpaper on your desktop or smart phone. And make sure to repeat your mantra in your head or out loud every time you think of it. It's also helpful to create habits regarding when you repeat it, and make sure you repeat it every time you notice yourself having a counterproductive or negative thought.

Principle #4: Unlock Your Potential

You are both your loudest critic and your biggest cheerleader. Stop looking outward to people or things; instead, look inward and become aware of the words you choose to speak to yourself – because your words work! Speak with kindness and intention. If the inner dialogue isn't helpful, turn it around with the power of positive self-talk. Develop a mantra that speaks to you, inspires you, and motivates you to take action.

CHAPTER 4 POINTS TO PRACTICE

★ *You talk to yourself (we all do), but* how *you speak to yourself is what matters most.* The way you speak to yourself can have a profound effect on your mental health and your capability to be successful.

★ *Self*-talk can be both positive (I've got this!) and negative (I'll never get this).

★ *Some self-talk is automatic and instinctual, and other self-talk is more thoughtful and intentional.* We don't have a lot of control over our automatic response, but we can develop and nurture self-talk to counter the impact of the more automatic system.

★ *The practice of self-talk can dramatically influence your performance, but only if you believe it.* Find that kernel of truth and then be your own raving fan!

★ *Using a mantra is one way to develop your positive and intentional self-talk.* Develop one that speaks to you and put it on repeat! The power is in the practice.

Do this now: Get moving with a mantra (One minute).

Take one of the mantras shared in this chapter and try it on! Repeat it 10 times and notice how the shape of your day changes! Love it? Embrace it! Not so much? Hey, it was worth a try!

Flip the page to learn the secret to lasting success with your health (hint: it's not hitting the gym every morning at 6 a.m.).

(I heard that sigh of relief.)

CHAPTER 5

Rewire Your Brain

Our brains are brilliant. Our brains are capable of wiring and rewiring, which means we are capable of learning, changing, and evolving. And we're doing it all the time. Whether it's learning a new skill, or learning about a new friend, our brains are at work storing information and developing new connections. But we're up against some challenges when it comes to making this rewiring happen – especially when it comes to health.

I see this show up a lot in my work with clients. They have a clear and grounded idea of what they want for their life. They have realistic goals and a plan that is functional for their body, their commitments, and their priorities. But for some reason *it just doesn't happen*. They feel stuck, like *really* stuck. Why is that?

Part of the reason we struggle is because the neural pathways of old habits are so engrained that they are like well-trodden 'auto-pilot' routes in your brain. To take an alternate path would be like taking a *brand new* route you've never driven before.

Which is easier? Yeah – the familiar one. At least it is *short term*. With time and practice, the new route will *also* be easy to travel. But practice requires effort. And therein lies the rub. In order to develop the new neural pathway – the new habit – we need to do the work.

How do you bridge the gap between the familiar and the novel? By discovering what's in it for *you*.

What if the autopilot route is overly congested and not really pleasant to drive? What if driving that route puts you in a crummy mood *every time* you drive it? What if the new route ultimately gets you to your destination more efficiently and it's a more pleasant drive that makes you feel great? There's value in that. That *value* is the *magical motivation* we all seek. Knowing what's in it for *you* can make all the difference in your ability to muster the energy to do the work required to bridge that gap.

Great. Be clear on what's in it for you. Use that dangling carrot to find the energy to commit to the effort. Practice, and you'll rewire your brain and establish the new habit. Got it? Simple. Except... not. There are a few other challenges we face in our efforts to rewire our brain and lay down new habits.

Challenge #1: You belong in struggle.

Just when you thought there was only one elephant, there may actually be a herd of elephants holding you back! As we discussed in Chapter 1, the struggle for health is far more common than not! So it's familiar lunchroom banter to discuss the latest and greatest diet, weight loss gimmick, or fitness program. People love commiserating over their struggle. It bonds us – it's the "oh hey, I'm not alone" that provides connection. So if we don't have this to commiserate over, what happens?

We innately want to belong. It's a fundamental human need.

According to social psychologists Roy Baumeister and Mark Leary, we are "naturally driven toward establishing and sustaining belongingness." Furthermore, humans are "at least as reluctant to *break* social bonds as they are eager to *form* them in the first place."[9] In other words, it's hard to create bonds and it's hard to break them. So if we bond over our common struggle regarding health, sometimes that means we avoid change. Because if we do break our bond with our sisters in the health struggle, the lack of belongingness (in an ironic twist) can cause a variety of not-so-awesome effects, including a decrease in our levels of happiness and health! Sigh.

What does that mean? It means getting off the 'health struggle bus' is hard. Because in addition to the effort of changing habits and forming new ones, we also have the threat to our sense of belonging and connection – because change may require breaking social bonds and forming new ones.

I hear about this struggle a lot. Clients tell me that they really want to make changes, but it's hard because their family and friends aren't on board. And I get it, because family and friends can be our biggest supporters *and* our biggest saboteurs. Maybe *you're* ready, but they *aren't*. But if your bond and connection is at least partially built on this common struggle, what happens when you make changes? How does that impact your relationships? How do those important people in your life respond?

In *The Dance of Intimacy*, Dr. Harriet Lerner discusses the idea of a "change back reaction." This is how I would summarize it: Humans don't like change. Change is hard. We like routine and stability – homeostasis (as in "we're wired that way"). When we make changes, it's because the 'cost' of staying the same is greater than the 'cost' of the struggle to change. But just because that cost-benefit evaluation makes sense for us, it doesn't mean it makes sense to the rest of the people in our life! Bummer.

So when we change, but those around us don't, they may react in a way that isn't helpful or supportive – either passively or overtly requesting that we 'change back.' Which makes change (that is already hard) harder.

So if your close friends and family aren't 'on board' with your health changes – what then? What do you do?

There are three strategies that I've used personally and also recommended to my clients. Note: If you try on any of these strategies, just make sure you are gentle with yourself and with your friends and family.

Strategy #1: Find your tribe and love them.

Author and motivational speaker Jim Rohn famously said that we are the average of the five people we spend the most time with. Why? Because, like it or not, our habits, behaviors, and attitudes are influenced by others.

While it will require work to develop this new belonging, it's very helpful to build connections with people who *support* you – fitness friends you can count on or a health community that aligns with your philosophy. Surround yourself with people who lift you up and encourage you to be your best. Spending the majority of your time with these people (either in person or online) can go a long way to having the social acceptance, love, and belonging you need to push through the struggle of getting to autopilot on that new route!

I see the value of this strategy daily in my virtual groups. I have clients who have never met – from all over North America – but who have formed incredible bonds. These women not only lift one another up in their efforts to be healthy and well; they have connections that go beyond fitness. Some of them have become so close that they've traveled to see one another for weekend getaways.

Strategy #2: Lead by example.

This can work really well – sometimes. By virtue of you improving yourself, others around you often step up – cool. But it doesn't always go this way. Remember that they might not be ready yet. But when they are, if you've led by example without putting pressure on them, they'll often become your biggest supporters and allies!

When I was in my early days at Simon Fraser University, studying kinesiology and still working to develop a healthy relationship with food, my dad and I joined a popular weight loss program together. At the time, I was still living at home, and doing the program with my dad was a great support. But my mom wasn't on board; she just wasn't ready. She did her best to support us, but it wasn't easy. She wasn't *unsupportive*, but she didn't go out of her way to make it easy for us either. Both Dad and I were conscious of not putting pressure on her to join us (we knew from past experience that this strategy didn't work for Mom). Instead, we did our thing and gave her space. We knew that when and if she was ready, she would join. It was over a year before she eventually joined us at meetings. Working as a trio was so helpful and it created a great support structure.

Strategy #3: Speak your truth.

Have an honest, open, and non-judgmental dialogue where you share that you are making some changes and invite others to join you. If you take this step, it's really important to also acknowledge that they may not want to make changes – and that's okay. And it really *does* need to be okay – because most people can smell a lack of authenticity from a mile away. Make a request that they support you – and give them concrete examples of what that would look like for you. I know this might *sound* simple, but I realize that it may not be easy. Be gentle with yourself, and remind yourself why having the conversation is worth it!

I know firsthand that this isn't easy. I've had more than one of these conversations in my lifetime, once with a good friend and once with family. Neither conversation was easy, but I'm absolutely grateful I had them.

Challenge #2: The struggle serves you.

What if you don't want to get off the struggle bus? In Chapter 1, I shared the story of a client who admitted that she really just didn't want to change – not yet.

Sometimes you need to stay on the struggle bus, because getting off would require exploring a new place that you've never visited before, and you're simply not ready to go there. This is a totally fair reason not to change!

Vulnerability researcher and author Dr. Brené Brown talks about the fact that we're wired for struggle – and that humans are simply created this way. We're built to struggle and to be challenged by life; it's just what we do. So if you stopped struggling with your health, what other struggles in your life might come to the forefront?

I long considered my weight to be my Achilles heel – the 'thing' that held me back in my life and in my work. And when I gave that up, I had to acknowledge and own that it wasn't about the weight. As Geneen Roth so eloquently puts it in her book *Women, Food and God:* "It's not about the weight, it was NEVER about the weight." So if it's not about the weight, what the H-E-double hockey sticks is it about?

That was harder to look at.

There's a beautiful quote from Thich Nhat Hahn:

"People have a hard time letting go of suffering. Out of a fear of the unknown, they prefer suffering that is familiar."

I stayed on that struggle bus for a long time, because while it was destructive in so many ways, it was also safe and familiar. It was easier to blame my lack of success or any failure I had on my fat. And a heck of a lot *harder* to blame my innate capabilities, work ethic, or talent. Yeah. That was a juicy aha moment for me.

Once I stopped blaming everything on my fat, and once I owned my capabilities, work ethic, and talent, successes, and failures... Boom! Talk about a shift!

Letting it go was hard. I'd carried that blame since I was five years old – when I was too fat to keep up with the big kids. Or when I was too fat to be liked by that boy I had my eye on. Or when I was cast as the courageous lion instead of Dorothy in the school production of the Wizard of Oz. I could go on, but you get it.

It's important to acknowledge that the blame – my 'not good enough' narrative – also served me, because it fueled my fire. "Oh yeah, Fat, f*cking watch me! Watch me try out for the rowing team. Watch me learn to run all by myself. Watch me do Ironman."

Narratives (the stories we tell ourselves) aren't all bad, unless we allow them to drive the bus without our awareness. Kind of like driving a bus without your glasses on. You sort of see where you're going, but it's a whole lotta dodgy. And the really cool thing about narrative? Once you can see it, you can't unsee it, and the whole world just sharpens up as if you were wearing magic glasses.

Does knowing this stop me from having my narrative drive? Nope. I've had it nearly my whole life, and it's likely to stick around forever. But my awareness of it is profoundly more acute, and I can notice when it's helpful and when it's unhelpful.

Challenge #3: You may not be negative, but your brain is.

If I ask you what you did really well today, how long is the list?

What about the list of things you *didn't* do well, or *should* have done, but *didn't*? How long is that list?

I bet your second list is twice as long.

One of the other areas I see my clients struggle with is the tendency to focus on what they *aren't* doing (or aren't doing *well*). When I connect with them about how they are doing, the initial reaction is to tell me what they *didn't* do. But when I press and ask them more questions, what I often hear from them is that they took some great steps forward and made some awesome choices that really aligned with their goals. But it took me asking, and sometimes really pressing, for them to really see that!

And the big bummer of it all? That focus on what they didn't do well? It is actually what's preventing them from being successful – oh, the irony!

But it's not their fault (not really)! It's how our brains are wired. We're wired to focus on the faults so we can improve. There's even a name for this brain feature: *negativity bias*. It's the tendency for us to weigh more heavily the negative or perceived negative rather than the positive. In other words, we focus on what we *didn't* do well, not on what we *did* well. This was extremely helpful from an evolutionary perspective, and also to the young brain as it is learning to survive. If I touch a hot stove, it will really hurt and I'll get burned. If I put my fingers in the dog's mouth, it might bite me, and that won't feel good. Our brains actually have specialized circuits that immediately register negative experiences in our emotional memory. In contrast, positive experiences must be held much longer in awareness for the circuitry to transfer from short-term to long-term memory – with the only exception being if the positive experience is extremely novel or intense. Psychologist Dr. Rick Hansen uses this analogy: "The brain is like Velcro for negative experiences and like Teflon for positives ones."[10] The challenge is this: while this feature is helpful to the developing brain, as we evolve into the adult brain, it is much less helpful. And yet it persists!

How your negative brain sidelines your success

Ultimately, what this means to us as adults is that it's easier for our brains to focus on the negative experiences and their associated emotions. When it comes to our habits or choices around health and fitness, two of the most frequent negative emotions are guilt and shame. These two emotions are powerfully correlated with our ability to be motivated – but not in our favor! That means we end up in an extremely unhelpful feedback loop of unhelpful habits!

Remember that feature of our brains called neuroplasticity? It happens through practice – repeating the new pattern consistently and training those neural pathways to fire. Unfortunately, due to negativity bias, instead of reinforcing the thought and behavioral patterns we wish to take hold, we reinforce the old ones that aren't serving us.

A winning strategy to rewire your brain

As with so many things we've discussed, often the most important step you can take is to gain awareness.[11] Just *knowing* that you're wired to focus on the negative can have a tremendous impact on your ability to view it with perspective. Once we're aware of it, we can look for ways to give the negativity bias less power. The more we focus on our negativity bias, the more power we give it. By simply gaining mindfulness around it, we can unhitch a lot of its power.

The other strategy that I often employ with clients is to encourage them to keep a list of wins or successes. When clients get started with this strategy, I encourage them to make note of *all* their successes or wins, no matter how small they might seem.

- Walked past the 'treat' table at work and ate an apple. Win.
- Took my gym clothes with me to work. Win.
- Drank a glass of water before my Friday night wine. Win.

These might seem like little things, but small things done consistently can have a lot of impact.

The bonus? Not only have we found a strategy to sidestep the negativity bias; we've found a way to reinforce the thoughts and behaviors we wish to cultivate. And we've reinforced our belief in our ability to be successful, which builds confidence and self-esteem – thus creating a positive domino effect in the direction we wish to go!

Challenge #4: Your Mental Mirror Is Eating Your Mental Real Estate

We've already identified in the last chapter that you talk to yourself (as we all do). And doing so is completely normal and healthy. But one aspect of self-talk that we haven't yet discussed is self-objectification. After years of cultural programming, you are constantly monitoring your physical appearance as a third–party viewer. This is referred to by psychologists as 'body monitoring.' Author and researcher Renee Engeln refers to it as the 'mental mirror.' It's the internal dialogue that continues after reviewing your reflection in the mirror, and it keeps tabs on how you look as you go about your day.[12]

Is my hair staying the way I want it? Are these pants too tight? Is my muffin top hanging over? Does this shirt look good? Did I put on enough makeup? Or too much? Is this shirt too revealing? Is this too sexy? Not sexy enough?

This constant barrage of internal dialogue is familiar to many people, and it's yet another challenge we face when it comes to rewiring the brain – because all this body monitoring is taking up mental real estate! Have you ever lost focus in a meeting or conversation because the volume of your internal dialogue was too high? Yeah, me too!

Does this mean you're vain or a narcissist? Not at all. The roots of body objectification are a result of living in an objectifying cultural environment. It is a psychological strategy that allows people to anticipate how they will be viewed and treated by others, and to make adjustments where they deem necessary. In essence, it gives us more control.[13]

Your mental mirror is messing with your mojo.

According to psychologists Frederickson and Roberts, the third person perspective on the self leads women "to place greater value on how they look to others rather than how they feel or what they can do." This may contribute to various mental health consequences – including body shame, appearance anxiety, safety anxiety, reduced concentration or 'flow' experiences when it comes to mental and physical tasks, and diminished awareness of internal bodily states such as satiety, hunger, fatigue, and various emotions.

Chronic body monitoring also leads to decreased motivation. Simply put, the productive and creative state of mind required for motivation is not compatible with the self-consciousness of body monitoring. Further to this point, according to research out of Yale University, chronic body monitoring also results in decreased levels of self-efficacy (our belief in our own capability).[14]

This is a major issue when it comes to creating a lasting healthy lifestyle – which requires both motivation and self-efficacy. Layer this with body shame, anxiety, reduced concentration, and diminished awareness of our bodily states, and we have a huge obstacle to our capability to form new health habits and mindfully make healthy choices.

Turning down the volume on the mental mirror.

Much like changing the aesthetic body ideals we strive for, changing the cultural conversation that leads to objectification – sexual or otherwise – in an effort to prevent body objectification from developing will be a long and difficult battle. We can certainly affect change by speaking up, by not buying into this cultural dialogue, and by mindfully choosing how and where we invest our energy.[15] However, this isn't a book about activism; this is a book about *you*. And I want to give you some practical strategies to take action now!

Much like Challenge #3 (You may not be negative, but your brain is), part of the solution is increased awareness – like simply becoming mindful of the way you are speaking to yourself and then shifting your internal dialogue. *How do you do this?*

I have found the practice of meditation to be particularly helpful in this area. One of the teachers from whom I've gained tremendous value is Sharon Salzberg. She is one of the leaders who brought meditation to the mainstream in North America and is one of the cofounders of the Insight Meditation Institute.

In meditation, the goal isn't to rid your brain of thoughts (which is simply not possible); the goal is to be more mindful of your *attention*. This is often achieved through focus on the breath, either at the nostrils or the belly.

One of the most profound learnings I've experienced from Sharon's teachings is that the most important moment in meditation is when you notice you've fallen away from the breath. And you simply begin again. And again. And again.[16] As it relates to body monitoring, I find this practice really helpful. When you notice your attention is focused on body monitoring, simply return your focus to the task at hand or the person you are with. Again. And again.

My exploration of meditation has been a tremendous gift to my ongoing learning. What I've discovered is that the practice of meditation – much like all areas of health, will be as unique as each person. So if you've tried to practice meditation but didn't have much luck, I encourage you to embrace the 'begin again' lesson of meditation and simply begin again. There are many wonderful resources to support you if you choose to explore meditation. Two of the teachers I've most valued besides Sharon Salzberg are Dr. Kristin Neff and Tara Brach. If you find the softer, more traditional voices in meditation less inspiring, or if you're just generally skeptical of the whole thing, you might particularly enjoy Dan Harris and Jeffrey Warren's new book *Meditation for Fidgety Skeptics*. There are also some useful apps to explore, including Insight Timer, Calm, Buddhify, and Smiling Mind. And you can find some additional book titles and links to the apps in Appendix C.

Change Is Not for the Faint of Heart

Change will involve a ton of struggle. It's not as simple as plugging the coordinates into the GPS and taking the new route. You may find yourself on some bumpy back roads with a lot of potholes. And you may or may not have the support crew you need. You might even have a heckler in the car trying to steer you in the wrong direction, and you'll have to manage that. You might run out of gas, or you might have to spend a night in a motel in the middle of nowhere. You might even get trapped in the moment, where all you'll see is the dingy motel, the lack of progress you're making, and all the wrong turns you took. You might feel 'stuck,' but with patience you will find your way back on the road, and realize the pit-stop was exactly what you needed. Your windshield might get clouded and you might question the whole damn trip. You might wonder why the heck you didn't just take your old route – because it would have been so much quicker and easier. But then you'll notice the view. And you'll stop. And you'll breathe it in. And you'll be so glad you did.

Principle #5: Practice Patience and Perseverance

Understand and accept that you are wired for struggle and that change is not easy. Find the people you need to support you through the struggle. Be willing to explore your relationship with struggle; become aware of it and make peace with it. Don't let the challenges you face stop you from taking action in your life. Lean into change and practice patience and perseverance.

CHAPTER 5 POINTS TO PRACTICE:

★ *Habits are hardwired in your brain like autopilot routes.* Creating a new autopilot route takes work, so figure out what's in it for you to take the trip.

★ *You might be ready for change, but those around you might not.* Find the support you need and give those around you the space and grace they need to travel their own path.

★ *Sometimes the struggle you know is better than the one you don't.* Give yourself permission to take the time you need to make the shift.

★ *Your brain is wired to find faults, and it's not helping you.* Shift your negativity bias by focusing on your wins and watch them grow!

★ *The mirror in your mind is eating up your mental real estate.* Reclaim your mind and your motivation by practicing mindfulness.

Do this now: Make a Wins list (Two minutes).

In a note on your phone or on a scrap of paper, make a list of all the things you've done in the last 24 hours to support your health and fitness. I'll get you started: you're reading this book (way to go!).

You can be healthy and never hit the gym, or drink green smoothies, or eliminate sugar (true story). It's time to redefine Health – Super You style.

CHAPTER 6

Health and Fitness Are Not Married

Throughout this book you may have noticed that I regularly reference both *health* and *fitness*. That is because I think *both* words are at the foundation of your overall health and well-being. However, what I've found is that many people use these two terms interchangeably and this misconception can trip you up.

In my time as a trainer, I've met many people who are *fit* but not *healthy*. They may have 'healthy' body composition and be able to run long distances, or lift heavy weights, or be active recreational athletes – but they don't have a healthy relationship with food or they don't get enough sleep. Are they fit? Absolutely, but they're *not* physically healthy.

I think we can all think of an example or two. That co-worker who is uber thin and looks fantastic by the 'fashion standards,' but who subsists on Twinkies, red vines, and coffee. Or the athlete who has gotten so lean that she's missing her period and losing hair by the handful. Sure, their physique might look great by the standards set by the media, but looks can be deceiving.

The 3 Elements of Physical Health

So, how do we define physical health? There are essentially three elements to consider:

1. Fitness – the capability of your body to do the physical things you ask of it.

2.   Nutrition – ensuring your body has the nourishment it needs to perform those tasks.

3.   Sleep – allowing adequate rest and recovery so as to be physically and mentally well.

There are *guidelines* given for each of these three elements, but please remember that a *guideline* is not a steadfast rule. The word 'guide' is defined by Oxford as "a thing that helps someone to form an opinion or make a decision or calculation." So as you review the guidelines that I mention in this book, please remember that they need to be applied with consideration for your specific interests, priorities, and values.

What you really need to know about 'Fitness' (no gym required)

As a personal trainer, I am passionate about helping people discover a way to be fit and healthy that truly *works for them*. But what I so often find is that people have a lot of misconceptions that tend to cause them to stall or stagnate.

So here's what you really need to know about fitness and how your body works! Bear with me, this first part is a little dry, but it's important…

There are two ways we develop our fitness:

- *Physical activity* is the movement of our body that gets us through our daily lives. Whether that's running after the kids or running to the store for groceries, or just running, it all counts toward our health.
- *Exercise* is movement that is much more intentional and it has an objective. It's what we typically think of when we think 'fitness.'

Both *physical activity* as described above and our intentional *exercise* contribute to our overall level of physical fitness, and *both* contribute to our overall health. In fact, there is increasing research that points to the idea that the antidote to a sedentary lifestyle is *not* simply a daily bout of exercise. Your daily 30-minute sweat or five-mile run doesn't undo the impact that a full day of being sedentary has on your health.[17] It's just not that simple.

Our bodies were designed to move. The whole notion of 'fitness' is actually a relatively new one. The 'fitness industry' itself wasn't really born until the 60s and 70s when we started to understand the impact that a sedentary lifestyle has on our health. Previously, more people had physical jobs or were generally more active, whether walking or doing chores. But our lives have become more automated – from automobiles to washing machines and freezers and dishwashers – and the result is that even the simple tasks of transportation and housekeeping that once kept us active no longer do. So we sought out exercise to fill that void.

That is why we have things like "Physical Activity Guidelines," based on research and developed by experts in medicine and physiology, to guide our level of activity and keep us moving as a culture.

It's important to understand that when we talk about those general recommendations referenced in Chapter 1 (the ones that the majority of North Americans are overwhelmingly not achieving), those guidelines are specific to the development and maintenance of *general* physical fitness for overall health and well-being. They aren't designed to ensure that we are in peak physical condition or that we will be proficient at a sport. That's different, and we'll get into that shortly.

The general guidelines are meant to help otherwise healthy adults understand what their body's needs are regarding physical movement – in order to ensure a healthy heart and lungs, bones, and muscles, and to prevent lifestyle related diseases like certain cancers, heart disease, diabetes, and stroke.

These guidelines aim to address the following five components of physical fitness.

The 5 Components of Physical Fitness

1. Cardiorespiratory endurance: the ability of your heart, lungs, and muscles to work together and keep your body active over long periods of time (think walking, running, cycling, or swimming).

2. Muscular strength: the ability of your body to lift heavy things (think a dumbbell, your groceries, or your kid).

3. Muscular endurance: the ability of your muscles to repeatedly con-
    tract, whether that's lifting heavy things or performing a movement
    pattern (think running, walking, tennis, or shoveling a wheelbarrow
    of dirt).

4. Flexibility: the ability to easily move your joints in their full range of
    motion (think stretching, yoga, reaching the top shelf, or reaching
    down to tie your shoes).

5. Body composition: technically speaking, the optimal percentage of
    muscle, fat, bone, and water in your body. Keep in mind that what is
    optimal regarding muscle and fat will vary significantly according to
    one's age, gender, genetics, and interests (to name just a few contrib-
    utors).

THE GENERAL GUIDELINES FOR ADULTS[18] ARE AS FOLLOWS:

★ Avoid inactivity by keeping in mind that any activity is better
   than none (hey, that sounds familiar!).

★ Depending on your desired intensity, choose one of the following
   approaches:

   ★ 150 minutes (two hours and 30 minutes) each week of mod-
      erate-intense aerobic physical activity (such as brisk walking
      or tennis).

   ★ 75 minutes (one hour and 15 minutes) each week of vigor-
      ous-intensity aerobic physical activity (such as fitness classes,
      jogging, or swimming laps).

   ★ An equivalent combination of moderate and vigorous-inten-
      sity aerobic physical activity.

   ★ Note: minutes can be completed in episodes of 10 minutes
      or greater and ideally should be spread throughout the week.

The guidelines go on to suggest that for even greater health benefits,
adults can do one of the following:

★ Increase moderate-intensity aerobic physical activity to 300 minutes (five hours) each week.

★ Increase vigorous-intensity aerobic physical activity to 150 minutes (two hours and 30 minutes) each week.

★ Doing more will lead to even greater health benefits.

The guidelines also recommend that adults do muscle-strengthening activities (such as lifting weights or using resistance bands) that are moderate or high intensity and that involve all major muscle groups on two or more days a week.

And here's where it gets to be fun (Oh phew! Yes, this was getting a little dry, Gillian). How you achieve these guidelines is *completely up to you*. *You* decide what you want to do, what intensity level works for you, and what will realistically work for your life and schedule. Yay!

For a list of 99 activities to explore visit www.elephantinthegym.com/resources for the free download!

I Can Read Your Mind

Some of you may feel somewhat overwhelmed by these guidelines. Hey, I get it! And it's okay! Remember the mantra I shared: "Something is always better than nothing." These guidelines are simply something to work towards. It's not about going from zero to hero; it's about you improving your overall health and discovering your Health Zone – in a way that works for you!

Others will say, "But Gillian, I want more!"

Cool! When it comes to general health and well-being, these are just *the basic guidelines*. If they inspire you to build to more specific or more ambitious fitness outcomes – that's great!

Remember the Health Zone concept and how your zone will evolve and change with you? Instead of viewing health as an on-off switch or being on or off the wagon, consider that every individual is at a different place on a giant continuum of physical health. Where they are on this continuum will depend on a variety of factors, including but not limited to their priorities, interests, and values. But the overall goal is to find and maintain a place on the continuum that feels right for you!

Let me explain by sharing a client story.

Jane came to me with a keen interest in improving her overall health. She was basically pretty sedentary, so our initial objective was to simply get her moving more. We didn't even talk about the guidelines or the Health Zone; instead we focused on what she could do each day to move a little more. My goal was simply to move her further along the continuum.

For Jane, that was daily 10-minute walks during her lunch break and using a Fitbit tracker to measure her steps taken. By using the tracker, she became more aware of her overall level of (in)activity and this motivated her to do more. As Jane continued and was successful in increasing her activity, she felt inspired to join a Zumba class with a friend. That was a big step from being sedentary, but she was ready to take it because she had developed a base of movement first!

As she leaned in with more intentional exercises, she and I started to consider the five components of fitness to ensure that she was improving her overall fitness. As Jane continued, she was inspired to work up to being able to try the more intense boot camp-style class offered at the studio. We came up with a weekly schedule that involved more intentional fitness designed to improve her cardiovascular capability as well as her muscular strength and endurance so she could feel confident about trying out the boot camp class!

She had shifted from a general interest in moving her body for health benefits to the more specific interest of developing cardiorespiratory fitness as well as muscular strength and endurance so as to be able to do a specific class (outcome). She was definitely moving along the continuum.

Had I started Jane with the suggestion to go to Zumba three days per week, she probably would have become discouraged. It's essential to start where you are and go from there.

When you learn to swim, you don't start by jumping in the deep end and doing a 1000m swim! You start in the shallow end and possibly take some lessons. You learn how to float and then try some rudimentary strokes – hopefully with the guidance of a qualified instructor. With time, you build confidence as well as the physical fitness capacity to be able to swim one 25m length, then two. And with time you reach 1000m.

The take-home message: when it comes to fitness, successful individuals start with building the foundation of physical health by moving their body more, with the ultimate vision of achieving or exceeding the general health guide-lines. Through this process, they may become inspired to develop their physical fitness with a more specific objective. Awesome! I love seeing people grow and evolve this way.

Build Your Foundation First

When I first started running, I did not have a master plan to complete an Ironman. I started by running three days per week because I was inspired by my work colleagues to run – just for fun. The goal of Ironman came later, once I had established the habit of running – but that too, took time to develop. I had to start where I was and lean in.

When I first got started, I followed a progressive walk-to-run program that one of my friends had suggested. The program alternated intervals of running with walking, and I slowly built up my cardiorespiratory endurance. I also worked on my flexibility by doing stretches after each run. Once I was comfortable running 5K I maintained that level of fitness through my first semester at Simon Fraser University. Unfortunately, even though I had followed a progres-sive plan, my knees started bothering me, and my first injury felt like such a letdown! It was frustrating to have come so far and then have to stop – when for the first time I didn't want to!

With help from my physiotherapist friends, I realized that I had some imbal-ances in my strength and flexibility. I started adding workouts in the gym on my non-run days in order to develop my muscular strength and endurance. With patience (and perseverance), I was able to rebuild my running ability and come back stronger!

At that point, I was exercising five days per week for 30 to 60 minutes. I continued with this for about a year, and then I caught the triathlon bug! I layered in swimming, and I used my gym cross-training time to incorporate the bike. Then, once the weather permitted, I added a ride or two outdoors.

After 12 weeks of training, I completed my first triathlon, and a year later, I ran my first half marathon. Then I completed my first standard-distance triathlon, and later that year a half Ironman. The following August, I ran across the line at Ironman Canada!

Obviously, none of this happened overnight, and it wasn't without its challenges. I developed a few more injuries beyond my knee issues, but with each injury I learned more about my body and its capabilities. I learned what my body needed to stay healthy and happy while continuing to be challenged!

When people decide they want to do something, they often look to their peers and role models for someone to emulate. This is logical, and it is certainly a strategy that is employed when people decide they're ready to get healthy and fit. They look to the healthiest and fittest people they know. Of course, the problem with this is that healthy and fit people did not *start* where they are now.

I didn't start by running half marathons or running an Ironman! I started at the foundation level with a walk-to-run program three days a week – simply with the intention of being more physically active. Then, with time and consistency, I gradually built my fitness to the level where I could successfully complete a half marathon, and then a triathlon, and then an Ironman.

Since that athletic peak, I've had many ebbs and flows in my fitness. I restarted the process of running after having my two sons, and since then I've had years where I've trained to complete half marathons and triathlons, and also years where I've run and trained simply because I enjoy it!

Honor where you are! Don't rush it! You can't 'cram' fitness. If you do, what generally ends up happening is that you overwhelm your body (and your mind) by doing too much, too soon. Remember back to Chapter 1 and the problems with 'The Program?' I want you to be successful – so start where you are and build from there. Here are some tips based on where you might be starting from.

I'm stepping off the couch:

Be proud of your decision to start. That is often the hardest part! Now that you've made the decision to start, keep these ideas in mind and lean in:

- Start with small manageable increases in your physical activity: park further away, walk to complete an errand, take the stairs instead of the elevator.

- Squeeze your activity in when you have 10 minute intervals (heck, I'll take five minutes!).

- Try a steps tracker. There are so many devices on the market now. Fitbit, Garmin, and Apple watches all have features to do this. Or an old fashioned cheap pedometer you strap to your waistband works too! For many people, having a visual of how many steps you have (or haven't) taken is helpful for motivation. Devices like Fitbit take things a bit further and incorporate social engagement by encouraging friends to find one another on the app and challenge one another. As long as this doesn't trigger you to be competitive in an unhelpful way, this can be a really fun and engaging feature.

- Be creative! Use the stairs in your home to sneak in a quick burst of activity, use breaks at work to do a couple of strength-based exercises, or have a living room dance party with your kids. You might even consider challenging work colleagues to walk over to your desk instead of calling, or to use the stairs instead of the elevator.

- Keep it fun. At this stage on the continuum of physical health, it's all about enjoyment. If you don't enjoy it, you won't do it. Tap into what works for your life! Release the 'shitty shoulds.' Own your place on the continuum and be proud.

- Also focus on the other benefits of movement. There are many other reasons to move beyond just physical health, including but not limited to decreased rates of depression and anxiety, and management of stress. For example, there is a growing body of research that points to the huge *mental health* benefits provided by regular exercise – so much so that in Britain, exercise is utilized as a first-line treatment for depression. The benefits are both immediate (during and after a bout of exercise) and long term.[19]

Example: Sarah

When Sarah and I met for the first time, I knew she was going to be successful.

A busy self-employed mom of two, Sarah had spent many years on and off 'the wagon.' She was tired of the start/stop nature of her relationship with fitness and food, and was ready to make a shift. She also had issues with her back and she was working with a physiotherapist to resolve them. At 38, she was tired of having back issues, and she wanted to be stronger, fitter, and healthier.

Although her back was a big part of her push to fitness, she also wanted to be a better role model for her kids.

Sarah wanted to get back to the gym, but her body wasn't ready. So initially we focused on creating strategies to complete the rehabilitation exercises prescribed by her physiotherapist. For this, we utilized the strategy of Habit Pairing. Each morning after she brushed her teeth, she immediately did her physiotherapy exercises. She used the established 'cue' of brushing her teeth to trigger the new habit of her physio exercises.

She and I connected weekly by email, and we had a monthly 30-minute call. Sarah had a great sense of humor, and even when she found herself struggling after a holiday or a couple of busy weeks where some of her routines did a backslide, she was able to refocus, reframe and reclaim "October Sarah" (a.k.a. the Sarah who was 'rocking it'). Habit layering, habit pairing, focusing on the wins, and creating small sustainable shifts all added up to a big win in the long run – going skiing with her family over the Christmas holiday with no back pain! Hello real life victory! (I may have shed a tear when she sent me the picture of herself on the ski lift.)

I'm ready to start exercising:

- Find something you love (yes, this is a trend). There are so many ways to exercise, so explore the options and find something you can truly enjoy. Here's a list to get you started:
  - Dance inspired fitness like Zumba or Bellyfit
  - Gym-based strength training workouts
  - Workouts at home using videos
  - Walking, hiking or running
  - Road or mountain biking
  - Swimming
  - Sports leagues like soccer or ultimate frisbee
  - Yoga
  - Pilates
  - High Intensity Interval Training (HIIT) classes like spinning, kick-boxing, or Tabata.
  - Strength-based fitness classes like kettlebell, Barre or boot camp

Don't forget to visit www.elephantinthegym.com/resources to download the list of 99 Activities to get you inspired to move!

- Start with two to three days per week for 20-30 minutes. This is a great way to start, and if you do more, awesome! Try to space your days out so you can recover in between (both mentally and physically). Building new habits can be hard, so be patient with yourself.
- Rest! Rest is an essential element of a good exercise program. As you progress, make sure you include at least one day per week of active recovery (where you do lighter activities only, like gentle walking or yoga).

Example: Mike

Mike was 39 and feeling tired, old and unhealthy. He had two young boys and he was a busy professional. Over the years, he'd had on-and-off success with fitness and struggled with consistency. His weight had always been an issue and had become an even bigger challenge in the last year or so because a back injury had sidelined him. He'd gotten the all-clear to get moving again, and with just nine months to his 40th birthday he decided he wanted to lose 40 pounds as a present to himself. As you know, I don't particularly love weight-focused goals but this one was catchy, and what I knew about Mike was that his deeper reason for doing it was to be a great role model for his boys.

What I haven't mentioned about Mike is that he was married to a personal trainer. He had all the tools available to him to be successful, but until he connected with his deeper why (his sons), nothing had really stuck.

Mike got started with a home-based workout program and basic healthy nutrition principles. He focused on moving a little each day using video-based workouts – starting with a Tai Chi based program and progressing slowly to more challenging programs. When Mike turned 40, not only had he lost more than 40 pounds, he had also gained back his confidence, his pride, and his sparkle. And I can say that because Mike is my husband.

Having an at-home personal trainer, or a personal chef or assistant to slap food out of your hand, doesn't make a bit of difference. *You* have to decide that you're ready to do it. Mike is now the fittest and healthiest that I've ever known him. There have been bumps along the way – injuries, illness, stressful periods at work, but five years later he's still connected to his why, doing the work, and having fun doing it!

I've got a goal and I'm ready to smash it!

This is all about having a plan that you feel super pumped about. To help ensure that you have that plan, you may choose to work with a qualified fitness professional. For tips on how to find a qualified fitness professional, you can refer to Appendix A.

The 5 Principles You Need to Know to Smash Your Goals.

Whether you work with a fitness professional or not, I want to empower you with a better understanding of how your body works and how it responds to exercise. I want to remove some of the mystery of 'The Program' so you can evaluate your options with a critical eye. The following are five widely recognized[20] principles of fitness that *everyone* should understand. They are based in exercise physiology (a.k.a., the science of how your body responds to exercise), and an understanding of these principles can empower you to make choices for yourself in your personal fitness approach!

1. Specificity: your body responds specifically to the exercise demands you impose upon it, i.e., if you want to improve at running, you need to run. Sure, other cardio-type activities will help your cardiorespiratory capability, but if you want to run, you need to practice running! The same applies to all other exercises or skills within an exercise form. For example, in swimming, if you wish to improve your front crawl, you need to practice it to improve the specifics of that stroke.

2. Overload: in order to develop any of the four key areas of physical fitness (cardiorespiratory, muscular strength, muscular endurance, and flexibility), you need to *challenge* those particular systems. Simply put, you don't get better by doing the same things over and over at the same intensity. You improve by pushing the limit (just slightly). Within each of the components, this looks somewhat different:
   • Cardiorespiratory overload: pushing your intensity (how hard) and/or your duration (how long)
   • Muscular strength overload: lifting heavier
   • Muscular endurance overload: completing more repetitions
   • Flexibility: deeper or longer stretching

3. Progression: results take time (a.k.a., no zero-to-hero). Increase your general enjoyment (and decrease your injury risk) by gradually building your overload. For example, if you want to perform a push-up from your toes, start by learning the basic form and using a modified version while you build the necessary strength. Work on the range of motion first, and then as you build core and chest strength, start with a decreased range of motion from your toes until you have the strength to complete it!

4. Diminishing Returns: we all have an innate capacity (you can thank your genes). When we initially start challenging our body through overload and progression, the response by the body (the return) is often quite significant. Over time, the return on the same level of

overload and progression (investment) diminishes as we near that capacity. This is not to say we can't continue to improve, just that the rate of improvement will be slower – and this is where patience and perseverance really come into play!

5. Reversibility: if you don't use it, you lose it! If you don't continue to challenge your body, it's capability to perform will diminish. So if you've had a period away from any activity, it's important to reintroduce it gradually! The body will experience 'deconditioning' (loss of capacity) in as little as two weeks. So if you've taken some time off (for illness, injury, or life!) get back into your activities slowly and methodically. Yes, you'll need to 'backtrack' a bit, but instead of looking at it as a failure, view it as a 'cha-cha' – two steps forward, one step back. Overall you're still moving forward!

Rest Is Part of the Program

The biggest mistake I see people make in fitness is not taking rest. And by rest, I don't mean taking a day off and binge watching a Netflix series. I mean taking a day where you allow your body to recover.

Science lesson: during exercise your muscle fibers are breaking down. This breakdown signals to the body that it needs to become stronger, and it becomes stronger through rest (with proper nutrition being essential to ensure the appropriate building blocks are available). We don't get stronger without adequate rest. This is especially important with more intense exercise types like HIIT (High Intensity Interval Training), hard running, spinning, intense weight lifting, etc. These strategies can be very helpful to challenge the body and build cardiorespiratory gains as well as muscular endurance, but they are also harder on the body (more output). High intensity exercise is stress on the body. And when the body is under stress, we see an increase in the hormone *cortisol*. Without adequate rest and recovery, over time these levels of cortisol can be counterproductive to good health outcomes, especially the maintenance of a healthy weight.

This topic could become another entire chapter if I got into the details, but for now please just know this: *rest is important*. It is as important, if not more so, than the exercise sessions themselves. So make sure you're taking rest, especially if you're incorporating HIIT or other high intensity exercise. These sessions are generally short and shouldn't be done with more frequency than one to three times per week (depending on the intensity and one's individual tolerance). Remember that our bodies get stronger with rest. Work hard when it's time to work hard; rest when it's time to rest. The guideline of 24-48 hours between exercise sessions of similar types is a helpful one to remember.

Do You Have an Off-Season?

Whether you're an avid exerciser hitting the gym or a runner training for events, you are an athlete, and you should have an off-season! Periodization is a methodology used by athletes that incorporates all five of the above principles in order to build up to a peak or several peak events. They will incorporate periods of preparation, building, tapering, and also rest, throughout their training cycle. The training cycle may be months, or it may be a bigger snapshot of the entire year. I believe that periodization is important to consider for *all* athletes (and it often is not). If athletes don't consider this, the body makes its own off-season through injury or illness (a symptom of overtraining). Prevent this by taking measured recovery periods and allowing the body to periodize to peak performance!

What is your Fitness Personality?

Not only does your *body* respond differently to different types of training, so does your *mind and spirit!* Fitness isn't just about the physical body; it's also very much about our mind and spirit! So when you're considering what approach to take toward fitness, it's important to factor these in. That might involve some mindful trial and error, including exploring new types of activities, and the factors that influence the enjoyment of an activity. As you try things on, consider how they make you feel. Even if it was a hurdle to get going, once you did it, was it satisfying? Here are some factors to consider:

- Surroundings. Where do you enjoy exercising most? Some locations to consider: at home, at a gym, in a studio, at the recreation or community center, outdoors, etc.

- Social. Do you prefer to go solo or with friends? Do you enjoy one-on-one, small groups, or big groups?
- Style. Do you enjoy intense exercise, or do you prefer lower intensities? Not everyone enjoys high intensity (think bootcamp, circuit training, kickboxing, running), while others thrive on it. This isn't just a reflection of your fitness level, but also personal preferences and genetics. Yes, you read that correctly! Your genetics may predispose you to liking (or not liking) certain types of exercise.[21] So honor your personal preferences and keep exercise enjoyable! And remember that, just like most things with health, your style will evolve!

My Most Important Fitness Tip

Be consistent. You can be successful with just about anything – if you do it with consistency. So the 'trick' is to explore what you can do *consistently* by factoring in your personality and your priorities. We'll be exploring this idea in depth in Chapter 9, but for now, as you explore new activities and approaches, consider whether it works for your personality and your priorities (a.k.a., real life) in a way that will enable you to be consistent!

Example: Beth

I will never forget the moment I watched Beth cross the finish line at her first marathon! My eyes welled up and my heart was bursting with pride and joy. I'd always known she could do it, but now I knew she believed it too.

Beth came to me after a good couple of years being consistent with a generally healthy lifestyle. She'd improved her fitness and settled into a healthy body composition through modifications to her nutrition and going to the gym consistently to participate in bootcamp-style classes. She had also been running for two years, starting with a learn-to-run program and then progressing to a half marathon. When she came to me, her goal was to tackle the marathon. Due to her many accomplishments over the last few years, she had developed a lot of confidence in her capabilities. But when it came to this goal, Beth was nervous. She decided her best bet was to join my Run Strong Training Clinic, as this would give her the training and the community that she needed.

Together we mapped out a training program that worked for her busy life and her body. I factored in the five core components and ensured that the program was balanced and that it incorporated rest and recovery.

Her journey to the marathon wasn't without challenges. She worked full time and her shifts meant she couldn't always attend group runs, but she put in the running time in other ways. During her peak training, she also got married to her long-time partner. She planned a wedding, worked full time and trained for a marathon – hello strategic planning! But she found a way to make it all work and I will never forget the day she crossed that finish line. I know she won't either.

You Are a Work of Art

What I hope you've noticed throughout this chapter is one extremely important and common theme: there is actually quite a lot of science to creating a healthy lifestyle. But don't let it overwhelm you or sideline you! Because all that science isn't absolutely conclusive – we are constantly learning more in this ever–evolving field. At the end of the day, we return to the theme of this book: "You do *you*."

Health is a science; how we apply it in our lives is an art.

Remember that you are the artist. You decide what brush strokes you apply. You determine what color palate to use. And you create the composition. And just like any good artist, your style will evolve as you do. Remember that the most successful artists *own* whatever direction they go in. They stand proudly in their decisions and don't let popular opinion or critics sway their art. And much like all art, there is no such thing as perfection when it comes to your fitness. There are always things you'd like to change or a different approach you wish you'd taken. At some point you will let it rest, and then you'll know that what *is*, at this moment, is *perfection*. Flaws and all.

Principle #6: Explore the Science, Practice the Art

Health is a science and fitness is a science, but how you apply them to your life is an art. Remember that health and fitness are two distinct things, and every move is a good move when it comes to your health! There is no one right way to be fit, just the one that works for you, in your life, right now. Start where you are and find the practice of health and fitness that works for you!

CHAPTER 6 POINTS TO PRACTICE

★ *Fitness is part of your health, but it's not the whole picture.* Nutrition and sleep are also important factors that need to be considered.

★ *You don't have to do formal exercise to be healthy.* Regular physical activity is essential to your health – but it can be achieved in a multitude of ways from walking and gardening to taking the stairs!

★ *Start where you are and lean in.* For overall health and wellness, aim to achieve a minimum of 150 minutes of moderate to intensity physical activity per week.

★ *If you have more specific fitness related goals, keep the 5 Principles of Fitness in mind:* Specificity, Overload, Progression, Diminishing Returns and Reversibility.

★ *Rest or active recovery is essential to your body's ability to adapt.* Make sure your approach includes rest days and periods.

★ *Keep in mind that we all have a unique fitness personality.* Keep exploring until you find the complement of activities that works best for your body, mind, and spirit!

Do This Now: Take a movement minute (One minute).

Every minute counts! Even if you're already exercising regularly, our generally sedentary lifestyle is not great for health. So wherever you are, stand up and move for one minute. March on the spot, do a few stretches, do some jumping jacks or go up and down a flight of stairs.

In the next chapter, I'm going to break down the topic everyone dreads: nutrition. But know this: your healthy diet can include both chocolate and kale — or neither! In fact, I don't have one single rule you need to follow! I'm crazy that way. Are you ready?

CHAPTER 7

Flying the White Flag and Ending Your Battle with Food

When I was young, *fat* was the enemy – low fat *everything* was all the rage. As the trend caught fire, I once overheard someone suggest that a candy was healthy because it was 'low fat.' *Sigh.* Then there was the dawn of 'bacon and cheese with every meal and skip the carbs' (they're evil, don't you know). Oh, that low-carb trend. And it's still going strong, friends, with a few modifications (less bacon and cheese, and more coconut oil and avocado). No wonder people are confused.

The pendulum swing that is the diet industry is dumbfounding. It's gotten to the point where it's hard to know right from wrong and healthy from not. It all adds up to a lot of confusion, and for some, complete complacency.

I get it; my head was spinning too – until I flew the white flag and ended my battle with food.

Sign the Peace Treaty

We tend to overcomplicate nutrition. You don't have to love broccoli or give up meat – necessarily. Nor do you have to swear off carbs or fat – necessarily. Eating healthy doesn't have to be boring and it doesn't mean the end of all yummy things; healthy eating should be varied, interesting and delicious. It should inspire your eyes and your palate! It should be livable and sustainable. And what that looks like is completely up to you.

My goal in this chapter is to give you some basic information to help you wade through the possibilities and find the path that works for you. And to help you end the battle with food and sign a life-long peace treaty.

As a personal trainer, my scope of practice is to recommend that my clients make use of the available national food guidelines. In Canada, this means *Canada's Food Guide,* and in the US, the equivalent is the *Choose My Plate* guidelines by the USDA. In both cases, they offer good basic guidelines for the generally healthy population.

These nutrition guides are meant to *help* you form your own ideas and make your own decisions about what may or may not work for your body. Shocker alert: once again, the common denominator is you! You decide what will and won't work for you.

> You might wish to explore the *Choose My Plate* guidelines or *Canada's Food Guide* using the links provided in the book resources available at www.elephantinthegym.com/resources

When it comes to nutrition, I always invite my clients to be curious. What the heck does it mean "to be curious"? It means: be open to trying on new strategies and approaches that feel right for you and see how your body responds. That said, I also believe it is essential that at the root of each of these strategies and approaches are two very important foundations: scientific grounding and common sense.

Science Is Not a Fan of Your Fad Diet

Very few programs out there are based on true scientific method. Much of the information on the Internet is based on quasi-science at best, or anecdotal evidence at worst (a.k.a., it worked for this woman on the internet… apparently). In my opinion that's not enough. In all cases, I highly recommend becoming educated about the approach before jumping in feet first. Here are some questions you may wish to consider before you leap:

1.   What does the research say? *Was* there research? Who funded it? How many people were studied? And are they a similar 'population' to you?

2.   Who is recommending this approach? What are their credentials? What do those credentials mean?

3.   What is the potential cost to the approach? Is it safe? Are there risks? Are you comfortable with those risks?

4.   What would your doctor say? Would they be in support of this approach? Do you value their opinion?

Give the Common Sense Side-Eye to that Extreme Diet

I know this seems like a no-brainer, but as the saying goes, "Common sense isn't always common practice."[22] Here are my common sense questions to help you evaluate any nutrition approach:

1.   Does it work within the structures of your life? (i.e., Will you have the time, finances, and energy to follow the practices recommended?)

2.   Does it require you to eat in an entirely different way than your family? Are you okay with that?

3.   Does it make eating out impossible? Are you okay with that?

4.   Is it extreme? How far away from the guidelines (Canadian or US) does it take you? Does that feel right for you?

5.   Is this approach sustainable long term? Could you eat this way for the rest of your life?

6.   Does it feel right for you? What does your gut instinct say?

If you can get through these two series of questions, you'll likely have a generally good read on whether the approach is something you want to explore. Once you've decided to give it a whirl, I think it's important to set a timeline to evaluate the efficacy of the program for you. As with any program, you need to give yourself a reasonable amount of time to learn the approach, to lean in, and to adjust your habits. So my general recommendation is to stick with something for two to three months before evaluating it. That said, if at any point the cost (health-wise, energy-wise, cost-wise, time-wise) outweighs the benefit of the program, cut your losses and call it a learning experience!

6 Ways To Track Progress (That Don't Include Your Scale!)

I get it. It's helpful to have a method to monitor your progress with whatever approach you choose – so you can tell if it's 'working.' The challenge is that the most common method used (the scale) is limiting because, as we've already discussed, body composition is not the whole picture when it comes to health! For my full opinion on scales, read the sidebar, but suffice it to say that I don't think it should be your end-all-be-all. Especially since there are many other (more objective) ways to measure progress!

Having *a* method to monitor how you're doing can be a wonderful way to gain objective feedback about whether the strategies you've employed are working, or not. Depending on your overall goals, your method of monitoring will look different.

Some of the most objective and important measures of overall health are blood pressure, blood glucose, and blood cholesterol. Obviously, these aren't all things you can monitor on your own. Work with your family physician to monitor these metrics at an interval you and your doctor agree on.

If your goals are around making some shifts in your body composition and you want a physical measure, try using one article of clothing that you can try on one or two times per month. You might also consider taking pictures. Not for some dramatic before and after purpose, but because we can often see results in pictures before we notice changes in the mirror or in measurements. This can be incredibly motivating.

You might also consider tracking. Not in an obsessive over-the-top way (more on my resistance to that later), but in a more qualitative way. Instead of track-ing every morsel of food and evaluating your macros and calories, keep a simple calendar where you track what you ate, your hydration, your energy levels (you could use a scale of 1 to 10), and sleep. You might also consider noting how you are feeling before and after meals and snacks. You can find the simple tracker I use with my clients for this purpose, in the resources download, available at elephantinthegym.com/resources.

SMASH YOUR SCALE (IF YOU WANT TO)

Used objectively, a scale can be one measure of progress. Unfortunately, most often *objective* is not the adjective I'd use to describe how most people relate to their scale. If stepping on the scale to monitor your 'progress' with your healthy lifestyle is making you feel: crummy, unsuccessful, frustrated, elated, happy, triumphant, upset, smug, or any other emotion, I would advise you to get rid of it. Because here's the thing: the number on the scale doesn't define you. Nor should it define your day. Let me paint a picture: You've been kicking butt at your workouts, eating well, and drinking your water. You've been loving your healthy lifestyle. You just woke up after a great 8-hour sleep and you step on the scale. Say what? Yup. You've gained! WTF? (Seriously)! Your mood has gone from content and proud to frustrated and defeated (and a little h-angry because you haven't even had breakfast yet).

So you decide to screw it. Hit the drive-thru wherever and get the (fill in the blank) pastry and a double mocha for breakfast. Lunch is much the same (insert emotional eating indulgence of choice) because "it doesn't matter anyway." But then you feel the guilt. So you hit the gym after work and "make your fat cry." Dinner is okay (you decided something green should be on your plate), but overall you end up feeling crummy. You go to bed with the resolve to "start fresh tomorrow" (but not before you hit the hidden chips in the snack cupboard… because well, you "start fresh" tomorrow, right?).

Sound familiar? Perhaps my story is the extreme version – but variations of this are all too common and this is exactly why I wrote this book. Because this is the relationship so many people have with their weight.

Up to the point where the scale got involved, things were awesome.

Consider this: *you* rocking your healthy lifestyle has very little to do with your weight. The scale is NOT an accurate reflection of: your overall health, level of cardiovascular fitness, muscular strength, endurance, or flexibility. Nor is it a measure of your determination, commitment, or dedication. It is not a reflection of *you;* it is a reflection of the relationship your physical mass has with gravity. We've just been taught that it means *more* (and that bit of social programming is the basis of almost the entire first half of this book!).

Yes, body composition is a component of health that we can't ignore completely, but determining what body composition is healthy for *you* is up to *you*. It might be *one* of the metrics you discuss with your family physician. Ultimately, though, remember that the scale is just *one* metric; and if your relationship with it isn't healthy, take a break from it (and maybe even break up permanently). Instead, work with another metric (or two) that leaves you feeling motivated and inspired.

And, if you read this and thought: I have no idea what you're talking about, Gillian (and you're not just pulling a head-in-the-sand moment), then totally cool. If you've got a healthy relationship with your scale and you find it to be a helpful tool, carry on! You do you!

4 Questions To Evaluate Your Level of Awesome

When it comes time to evaluate and monitor your progress, make sure you consider these questions to help you evaluate whether your program is working for you!

1. How are you generally feeling? Do you feel well overall? How is your energy when you eat this way?

2. Is this way of eating sustainable? Do you feel like you could actually (be honest) continue eating this way for the rest of your life?

3. Do you enjoy eating this way? If eating this way is making you miserable, it's unlikely that you'll continue long term, even if the results please you.

4. Do you want to continue? Or are there things you would like to tweak about the approach to make it suit you better?

Once you have the answers to these questions, continue to be curious. You may decide to drop the approach altogether, or like most things, you'll take the parts that work for you, and discard the pieces that don't! I want to empower you to create your very own personalized plan that suits *you* exactly!

10 Tips To Help You Eat Whatever You Want... And Be Healthy

I'm often asked for meal plans and menus. My answer is always "No." Because *I* can't tell you what to eat – you need to find the way to eat that works best for *your body*! There is no broad brush '*right way*.'

Furthermore, simply providing you with a meal plan or menu doesn't really teach you anything! As the adage goes, "Give a man a fish, and you feed him for a day. Teach a man to fish, and you feed him for a lifetime."

I don't want to give you a fish. I want to teach you to fish.

So instead of a menu, meal plans, and grocery lists, I will give you the simple tips I share with my clients. You won't find any hard and fast rules, just simple strategies I've discovered through my own personal experience and my work with clients that have helped me and my clients find a peaceful and enjoyable relationship with food. Try them on and see if they feel right for you!

1. No food is off limits.

Unless you have diagnosed dietary restrictions or allergies, no food group or food should be 'off limits' entirely. The moment you have a black and white rule like this, what most people do is run in the opposite direction right to the food. Or they do what I call the pendulum swing. Maybe this sounds familiar: you eliminate a specific food for a period of time in an effort to 'get on track,' and then when the period of time is over you swing to the other end of the pendulum and eat *the entire kitchen*. This is counterproductive to your healthy relationship with food. Instead, consider creating sustainable guidelines around certain foods.

For example, I love good chocolate. Really love it. But if it's in my house, it calls to me from the cupboard and before I know it, it's gone. So instead of making myself crazy, I just don't keep chocolate in the house. If I want some, I either need to plan for it, or I need to go and get it myself! This is helpful for two reasons: if I have to plan for it, I'm less likely to be eating it for emotional/ stress/boredom reasons, and if I have to go out and get it and am willing to do that, then I must really want it. So I can go to the store, buy a small amount, eat it, savor it, and move past it.

2. Drink up.

Your body is composed of 60-70 percent water by mass. That's a lot of water. You also lose water through breathing, sweating, and elimination. So if you don't replace those fluids, you could find yourself feeling dehydrated. What does dehydration feel like? For one, it often feels like a mid-afternoon slump. If you're genuinely tired and need sleep, that's one thing (refer to the next chapter), but if you're well rested and have been eating for energy, then the culprit may well be dehydration.

So how much should you drink? There are a few different guidelines that are floated about. One of the general guidelines provided by many in the field is to aim for the equivalent of half your body weight (in pounds) in ounces each day. Another popular guideline is to drink eight 8-ounce glasses per day. Neither are well founded in research.

Regardless of the guidelines, the bottom line is this: You need to consume enough so that you avoid the symptoms of dehydration, including but not limited to thirst, dry lips and mouth, flushed skin, tiredness, and headache.

TMI tip? If your urine is a clear light yellow, it's usually a good indication you're hitting the mark! Keep in mind that certain vitamins and medications can change the color of your urine as well.

If you need a more concrete number to work with, according to the Dietitians of Canada, healthy women living in a temperate climate should aim to have about nine 8-ounce glasses per day, and men 12.[23]

This might seem like a daunting number, but keep in mind that this general recommendation considers all fluid. If your diet is rich in veggies and fruit, that water content counts. If you consume smoothies, juices, and soups, that hydration also counts. The majority should be coming from water, but generally speaking, all hydrating beverages count. Even caffeinated ones (up to a max of 400 mg of caffeine, or about four cups of coffee per day[24]). What?! Yup, coffee lovers rejoice! The reason you've likely been told to limit caffeinated coffee and teas is because of the mild diuretic effect of caffeine. The what? Essentially, caffeine makes you pee. But in generally healthy people, moderate consumption of caffeinated beverages shouldn't cause dehydration.[25] So yeah, coffee anyone?!

As with all things, the amount you need is going to vary from person to person, and these are by no means hard and fast rules (by now, I'm sure it's become clear to you that I don't roll that way). But it's a great place to start. Evaluate how much fluid you should be getting in theory, then take a look at how much you're actually getting – all things considered. Then work up to your quota by using this simple hydration hack:

1.   Find a bottle or glass that you like drinking out of and measure it.

2.   Figure out how many of those you need per day to top up your hydration.

3.   Bonus tracking tip: put that number of elastic bands around the bottle or glass, and each time you fill it, take off an elastic band.

Tip: don't jump up your level too quickly. Your body will take time to adjust to a new level of hydration. If you don't want to end up in the bathroom all day, start by increasing it by about four to eight ounces per day until you're there! Why? Think of that plant you forget to water. What happens to the water when you finally do add some? It runs right through or pools on the top! That's because the soil is so dry it has a hard time absorbing the water. Your body is the same – give your cells time to adjust to increased hydration!

3. Eat foods your grandparents would recognize.

I'm guessing your grandparents wouldn't recognize the majority of the overly processed sugar-laden junk that lines our grocery aisles. I'm not suggesting you need to set up a homestead and raise chickens (unless you want to), but I am suggesting that we would benefit from eating more whole foods and less processed ones.

Does that mean you can't ever have a bag of chips or your favorite fast food meal? Nope – refer back to #1! That said, I think we can likely all agree that our bodies generally appreciate it when the majority of our foods contain more whole, natural ingredients that come from the earth.

One way to simplify this is to look at the list of ingredients. Make it a habit to check out a product before you buy it. Can you recognize most things on the label? Or are there a lot of chemicals listed? Are the ingredients as close to their whole form as possible (e.g., whole grains vs. processed bleached flours)?

This might feel cumbersome when you first start. But if you're like most people, you generally stick to the same products and brands. So start with one or two products each week. Continue this process until you're aware of what is in *all* of your go-to foods!

4. Eat your veggies.

Yeah, yeah, I've heard this a million times, Gillian. Since I was a kid.

Yup. Because it's true. But here's the twist...

I don't want you to force feed yourself or ignore your gag reflex. We all have a few things that just don't appeal to our taste buds, and that's okay. And I want to remind you of this very important fact: you are an ever-evolving human. You might actually like the foods you didn't like as a kid, as a teen – or heck, even last week. This week, you might even love the food you hated last week!

But you won't know unless you try! I know you picky eaters out there are shaking your head right now, but I want you to consider this: your dislike of specific vegetables (or vegetables in general) is a thought habit that is generated from a fixed belief you developed as a kid. You decided you didn't like them and so your approach to eating them has been tainted by this. You whined and complained as a kid, and like most parents, yours didn't want the fight so they likely gave up serving them. So you developed a narrow palate that didn't enjoy variety. And before you go there – no, I am not blaming your parents. I get the struggle; I'm a mom.

Learning to love veggies is about first changing your mindset into a growth mindset, and then finding the vegetables you like and learning new and exciting ways to prepare them. If you don't like a certain veggie, try it in several different ways before you completely give up on it. If you get to a certain point and you've tried it various ways – hey, you tried. Maybe take a break and try again in a few years.

You might surprise yourself. I did.

I was five years old when the eggplant fiasco happened.

My dad had been away all week, and to celebrate his return, my mom cooked a beautiful eggplant parmesan.

She was so excited about the dish that my eight-year-old sister and I dove right in. Within seconds, we were groaning and complaining. To our five- and eight-year-old palettes, it was terrible. (I need to preface this all by saying that my mom is an extraordinary cook. So I have no doubt that it was fabulous, but we didn't like it, and that's an understatement.) From that day forward, I decided that eggplant was not for me, and for most of my life I've avoided eggplant. When I did try it, I didn't enjoy it.

That changed when I was at an event recently and the main course was a roasted half eggplant. When I saw the menu, my heart sank a little, but I generally loved the food at this restaurant and I trusted the chef. And am I glad I did! When it arrived at the table, I was immediately pleasantly surprised. It looked amazing! Then as I cut into it, the aroma of herbs and garlic made my childhood experience come back and I felt somewhat hesitant. But the moment I took my first bite, my resistance disappeared. Gone was the rubbery, slimy texture of my memory. This eggplant was buttery and smooth, and it had a beautiful bouquet of flavors. A true gourmet experience! So... it turns out I do like eggplant, depending on how it's prepared.

The moral of the story? Be open. Aim to eat a variety of different veggies, and make veggies a substantial component of your nutrition. Find ways of preparing veggies that you can enjoy, and don't give up on a veggie until you've tried it in different ways. You might find that you don't like certain veggies raw but really enjoy them cooked, or vice versa. Bottom line? Keep trying! Your body will thank you!

Some ideas to spice up your veggies:

- Experiment with different cooking methods: sauté, steam, roast, stir fry.
- Try different herbs and seasonings. Some of my favorites include: fresh-squeezed lemon, all-purpose herb seasonings (no salt), tamari, minced garlic, or the classic salt and pepper.
- For raw veggies, play with healthy spreads and dips, like tzatziki made with Greek yogurt, or hummus.

5. Lose your portion distortion.

Portions are huge – literally. Our plates are getting bigger and we're filling them with more and more food. Most restaurants serve portions that are better suited to two or three people than to one, and we eat them. Common sense can really come into play here. Take a look at the Choose your Plate or Canada's Food Guide 'serving size' recommendations. These are great general guidelines to follow to ensure your plates are not only portioned, but balanced!

Don't carry a measuring cup and spoons around with you? Me neither! Here are some handy visual references you can use:

- 1 C = baseball or tennis ball (fruit, leafy vegetables, milk, flaked cereals)
- 1/2 C = your clenched fist (grains like pasta, rice, oats; beans and lentils; cooked vegetables)
- 1T = your thumb (nut butter or hard cheese)
- 1t = your index fingertip, knuckle to end (oils or butter)
- 3oz = the palm of your hand or a deck of cards (meat)
- 1oz (dense food) = a small palmful (whole nuts)

Use these guidelines mindfully, but don't get too caught up in them. There is mounting research indicating that it is far more important to focus on the *quality* of nutrients rather than the *quantity*. One long-term study of over 100,000 men and women found that people who consumed a greater proportion of vegetables, nuts, fruits, and whole grains were more likely to maintain a healthy weight than their counterparts who consumed a higher proportion of more highly processed, sugary and high fat foods.[26] Yes, quantity matters (obviously), but if you focus on quality first (see Point 3), the quantity will often work itself out. Why? What the study proposed was that the higher fiber and slower digestion of these foods increases satiety (fullness), which makes you less likely to over eat (quantity). Seems logical to me.

6. Embrace staples.

Eating *staples* is a great way to take some of the thinking out of the process. But don't fret: 'staples' doesn't mean that you keep serving the exact same things all the time! I've got some great examples to help you keep things interesting, and you can change up your staples weekly, monthly, with the seasons, or when you find you're bored!

I like to make use of staples because they're a convenient way to take the decision making out of eating. That doesn't mean I don't listen to what I need and want, but generally speaking, I don't have to put a lot of thought into my choices. This is extremely helpful to maintaining healthy choices because making decisions actually requires a lot of thought. If you're trying to make some shifts in your nutrition, too much thought is exhausting. Instead of a one-way ticket to overwhelm, try this strategy:

Hold a few things status quo and uncomplicate your life. To keep things interesting (a.k.a., prevent boredom), have two or three of each that you love – for breakfasts, lunches, and snacks – and rotate through them daily or weekly. Then for dinner, add a little more variety by having eight to 10 staple meals that you can rotate through.

Bottom line? Find a way to 'staple eat' that works for you. Bonus? Grocery shopping is easy-peasy because you know what to grab!

Below, I've listed some of my favorite staples for breakfast, lunch, dinner, and snacks:

- Breakfast ideas:
  - Smoothie: 1C frozen fruit, 1C unsweetened almond milk, 1C spinach, 1-2t nut butter and 3/4C Greek yogurt or a good quality protein powder.
  - Veggie scramble: 1C of veggies of your choice, sautéed with seasonings of your choice in 1t oil with two eggs scrambled in. Add 2T goat or cheddar cheese for some extra flavor.
  - Yogurt parfait: layer up 3/4C Greek Yogurt with 1/4C granola and 1C fruit.

- Lunch staple ideas:
  - Sandwich: kind of a classic, but a good old-fashioned sandwich can be a great go-to. Whole grain wrap or bread, topped with lean protein, hummus or nut butter, and served with a healthy side of veggies!
  - Big salad: 1-2C of a greens mix, and mixed raw veggies of your choice (chopped), topped with a serving of lean protein (tuna or chicken breast are my go-to's).
  - Soups: I love cooking up a big batch of soup, full of veggies, early in the week and using this for lunch all week!

- Dinner staple ideas:
  - Tacos hard or soft, or fajitas. With turkey/ beef/ chicken/ fish, and with peppers/ lettuce/ slaw/ tomato. Also salsa/ guacamole/ Greek yogurt or sour cream. So many options! Have fun!
  - Chilis and stews: there are a ton of healthy recipes out there for stews and chilis that are packed with veggies and healthy proteins. Vegan too! Lentil and chickpea curry is a current household fave!
  - Bowls: hot or cold! Take a base of rice/quinoa, or some whole grain noodles (hot or cold), and layer on veggies (cooked or raw), seeds and nuts, protein (stir fried tofu or chopped chicken), and a sauce that inspires! My kids especially love this one because it can be build-your-own, which gives them the opportunity to build it to their liking (*read*: no complaining).

- Snack staple ideas:
  - Fruit and a palmful of nuts or one to two teaspoons of nut butter.
  - Yogurt and fruit.
  - Veggies and hummus or a healthy dip made with Greek yogurt.

Want some more ideas and recipes? The internet can be a fabulous resource! In Appendix C, you'll find links to some of my fave sites for recipes and so much more!

7. The power is in the prep.

Preparation is essential to success, but you need to find *your* way of doing it. For some people this looks like spending half a day on the weekend planning, shopping, and preparing food for the week. That's not my jam, but it works well for them (cool). If you gain joy from that process, fill your boots. I prefer to spend about 15-20 minutes writing out a menu plan for the week and then creating my grocery list for the week. This is not a complicated process. Since I embrace staples, I use a fairly small rotation of staple foods for most breakfasts, lunches, and snacks. This means I only really plan dinners. Here's how I do it:

- Look at the week ahead and keep your weekly schedule in mind as you plan. Consider things like evening commitments, your general mood (ex. Friday nights are not complicated at my house), and what you might feel like eating based on the season or family preferences.

- I try to find a balance of meals cooked from scratch and those that I take from my freezer. I scratch cook when I have less on the schedule and also on weekends, and freezer meals are saved for those nights when we have a revolving door of activities!

- I cook one big-batch recipe per week (ex. spaghetti sauce, soups, chili's) and we freeze what is left after dinner. I also do this with dressings or sauces, which gives me a stock in the fridge to keep my salads interesting. Most of my recipes for big-batch make two to three family meals, which means I'm ahead by one or two meals for one night of cooking (winning).

- I try one new recipe per week. Either I get creative, or I use something I've found online. Want some inspiration? You might wish to start with my *Top 10 SuperYum Recipes*. This free download is available in the book resources at www.elephantinthegym.com/resources.

Don't like planning by the week? That's okay too! Everyone will have a different approach to planning. The trick is to find the way that works for *you*. I have some clients that love the routine of planning and picking up groceries every few days.

Just remember that every good plan also has a back up plan! Have a few 'always on hand' meals you can source from your pantry or freezer and make in 15-20 minutes. The guideline I like to use for these meals (and all meals) is to make sure they contain three food groups (a starch, a veggie, and a protein source).

I make sure the ingredients for at least 1-2 of these meals are on hand pretty much at all times so I can quickly make something healthy in a jam (read: I only meal planned until Wednesday, and it's Thursday at 5pm):

- Whole grain pasta with a jar of marinara mixed with cooked ground meat of choice, or canned beans or lentils.

- Scrambled eggs with sautéed frozen kale or spinach mixed in, topped with cheese, and whole grain toast with nut butter.

- Breakfast for dinner! Whole grain pancakes or waffles topped with Greek yogurt and berries.

- Stir fry using frozen stir fry veggies with frozen shrimp or chicken on top of brown rice.

- Quesadillas or tortilla pizza. Go traditional with a whole grain tortilla stuffed with cheese (keep some shredded in the freezer) and beans, and serve with some cut veggies (or frozen mixed veggies), or lay it flat and top it like a pizza! Use about 1T of tomato paste sprinkled with salt, pepper, basil and oregano to really bring out the pizza flavor!

8. Put down your nutrition tracker.

What?! Why? Yes, you read that correctly! I don't recommend using detailed nutrition tracking long term. What!? Yes, you read that correctly. I don't think it's a great long-term habit. I think tracking is great short term – it can provide some useful feedback and insights, and it can provide awesome awareness. But both personally and professionally, I've seen how tracking can become counter productive to nutrition goals when we become consumed by the tracking of food. Why? Because when you're so focused on the *tracking*, you become less focused on your *body*. You lose sight of the natural signals your body is giving you for hunger and thirst. When we lose sight of those, it's really hard to make great choices.

But as noted, there is some value in tracking – mostly because tracking increases awareness. So – what I recommend to my clients is *periodic* tracking. Do it on a regular basis – either scheduled (such as a few days or one week per month) OR when you feel like you could use a check-in. Use it as follows:

- To increase awareness about what is going into your body (and reduce mindless eating).
- To gain insight into your nutrition habits (you may also wish to track activity to help you notice potential correlations – such as a spike in eating when you watch TV or after harder exercise sessions).
- To have a look at your portions and nutritional balance – are you getting enough vegetables, fruits, healthy fats, whole grains, and proteins?

But most importantly – once you've gained this awareness, I suggest you walk away from your tracker. Listen to your body's cues and eat to nourish your body!

If you are going to track, try using the tracker that I use with clients: it will bring your focus more toward overall health and well-being and away from the nitty gritty details. You can download it for free at www.elephantinthegym.com/resources.

9. It's a treat, not a cheat.

Enjoying a glass of wine with a friend, or giggling while eating a cookie with your kid isn't cheating. It's a treat – a food that is less about its nutritional value and more about the joy it brings! Food isn't just about nourishing our body, it's also about nourishing our soul!

As discussed in Chapter 4, our words shape the lens through which we view our world. They have impact.

When we label something as a *cheat*, the implication is that we've been bad or wrong, or that we've 'fallen off the wagon.' But we haven't. We've just had a treat.

And here's some life-changing news: treats can be part of your healthy nutrition!

Food is woven into the fabric of many or our cultural traditions. We celebrate birthdays with cake, Christmas with a turkey dinner, Hannukah with latkes, Easter with chocolate, summer BBQs with burgers, girls' night with wine… food is part of the fabric of celebration in our society, to completely divorce the two is not only impossible – it's a complete buzz kill.

The solution? Reframe.

Remember that one treat doesn't undo all the great nutrition you've provided for your body. One day doesn't undo the other 364 days of the year. Breathe and keep your perspective. Aim to have 80 percent of your nutrition choices honor your body's nutritional needs, and 20 percent of the time just relax and enjoy your food! Remember that you can choose to stop and savor chocolate or chips, and your very next choice might be broccoli or a spinach-packed smoothie. Both choices are part of you living a healthy and fulfilling life!

10. Listen to your body.

Your body will generally give you feedback if there are foods it doesn't like or if it's hungry or full. Pay attention. Sometimes that means slowing down. Breathe for a minute instead of rushing through the day (I know, very funny, right?!). But seriously, it's important. At a retreat I led recently, we sat down and had a mindful meal. Participants were instructed to eat *mindfully* – from the foods they selected at the buffet style spread, to where they sat (alone or with people), to the pace at which they ate, and the amount they ate. No one talked, and there were no distractions. What we all found (myself included) was that we therefore honored our needs much better than we typically do. If we didn't like the taste of something, we listened and didn't continue to eat it. We noticed textures, flavors, and tastes more than we typically do. And we slowed down – a lot. Every single participant commented on what a powerful practice it was. As best as you can, slow down when you eat. Consider what your body needs and what you genuinely want. Honor your body's cues and signals, and be mindful throughout the process.

Example: Jessica

Jessica had done every program under the sun when we met. She'd cleansed, dieted, detoxed, wrapped – and she was done with it all. In fact, she'd spent a year devoted to loving her body – no change required (amen!). Over the years of being involved in diet culture and programs, she had developed a strong black-and-white diet mentality. When we connected, she'd swung from her overly restrictive dieting approach to overeating. She was really happy, but she didn't feel like her outside matched her inside. She was ready to love herself into a body that felt like a better match. Her goals were to reframe her relationship with food, shed some weight, and keep the body love and appreciation she had developed.

I knew it would be important for Jessica to have a new lens through which to view food, so I encouraged her to utilize a portion system that I use with some of my clients. It's not restrictive; it's just a simple way to view the portions and balance of macronutrients without being overly complex or rigid. We used this as a tool, not a rule. If some days she was 'over' in her portions, I encouraged her not to stress about it.

The primary goal was to be more mindful of her overall intake and her body's needs. One of the questions that guided her practice was one that I've borrowed from Geneen Roth, author of *Women, Food and God* and a leader in the discussion of our relationship with food.

Jessica began using the question, "What am I hungry for?" and acknowledged that oftentimes she ate when she wasn't actually hungry. Exploring that through journaling, and through participation in our retreat, was a powerful catalyst for her. Throughout our work together, I encouraged her to listen to her body, become more mindful with her eating, and recognize that weight loss was simply a byproduct of having a healthy relationship with food.

Jessica found a way of healthy eating that felt good for her body and that worked with her life, and she naturally settled into her healthy weight. In this process she realized it wasn't about the weight or the food; it was about her relationship with herself. For her, it was a powerful moment when that finally sunk in. Jessica is now continuing this process and becoming even more connected to her body and her needs. Having fully embraced the 'mindful meal' at our retreat, she also decided to incorporate a mindful meal each week, with the goal of becoming more mindful at all meals and snacks in the future.

Principle #7: Reclaim Your Relationship with Food

Nutrition science is genuinely complex, but your relationship with food doesn't have to be! Ditch the diet and reclaim your gut instincts. Remember that your approach to nutrition will be as unique as your priorities, individual needs, goals, and tastes! Food should be enjoyed, and any approach to nutrition that is going to yield long-term results needs to be something you can maintain long term. There is no one right way to eat – just the one that works for you and your body!

CHAPTER 7 POINTS TO PRACTICE

★ *There is no one right way to eat – just the way that works for you.* To investigate any approach, evaluate its scientific grounding and common sense.

★ *Track your progress without losing track of what matters – how you feel!* Consider moving away from a focus on calories and macros, and towards other metrics that are better indicators of health, such as blood work or blood pressure.

★ *Consider ditching your scale – it's not the only way to measure shifts in your body composition.* Try using a specific article of clothing every few weeks or taking pictures once per month.

★ *Get back to the basics:* hydrate, eat food your grandparents would recognize including lots of veggies, mind your portion sizes, embrace your own way to meal plan and prepare food, and utilize strategies like staples and big batch cooking to simplify things.

★ *Get rid of the rules and embrace the guidelines that work for you.* Remember that your body is your most important guide of all!

Do this now: Drink up (One minute).

Go have a glass of water.

You're welcome.

It's time to talk about the unsung hero – the super champ of health, the master of vitality! But first, a nap (just kidding… well, only sort of!) It's time to find out why getting your zzz's is pivotal to feeling fabulous and optimizing your hormones so you can achieve your healthy weight!

CHAPTER 8

Your Health Lies Between the Sheets

Get your mind out of the gutter – I'm talking about sleep! It is truly the unsung hero when it comes to your health. It's incredibly undervalued in our society and absolutely essential to good overall physical and mental health. We all know how we feel after a great night's sleep, or even more so how we feel after a crappy one. It's the difference between feeling energized, alert and engaged, and feeling foggy, groggy and sluggish. According to the Center for Disease Control and Prevention (CDC), one-third of Americans don't get the recommended seven hour minimum per night,[27] and the same can be said of Canadians.[28] We know we don't feel our best when we aren't well rested, but are there consequences beyond feeling crummy?

The answer is a resounding yes! Both poor *quantity* (less than seven hours) and poor *quality* of sleep are correlated with a number of health outcomes including type 2 diabetes, cardiovascular disease, depression, and reduced well-being, to name just a few.[29]

How it does this is the content for another entire book. If you're curious, you might want to check out Arianna Huffington's book *The Sleep Revolution: Transforming Your Life, One Night at a Time.* For our purposes, we'll just focus on this: good quantity and quality of sleep is essential to good health. Not just for the prevention of disease, but also to ensure that we feel energized, alert, and engaged with life!

So, what can you do to improve your sleep quantity and quality?

Counting Sheep and Getting (enough) Sleep

When it comes to the quantity of sleep, the general recommendation for adults is a range of seven to nine hours per 24-hour period. Generally, we assume that these hours should be in sequence, a.k.a. at night, but there is some new and conflicting research showing that naps might also be an acceptable way to gain this quota (yay, naps!). But it's not conclusive, so your best bet is probably to aim for the seven- to nine-hour range at night.

If you find napping is a helpful habit for you, remember that only *you* will be able to best know what your optimal range will be, and how you can best achieve it. And it will change along with all the various other health factors. Sick? You'll need more. Your body needs extra rest to fight off those bugs! Training for something? You're also likely to need more.

Sleep is when our body recharges and recovers, and it is essential to success when it comes to health and fitness. It is important for optimal hormonal functioning and it helps your body do what it needs to do to respond to the demands you impose upon it. This can really come into effect when you glide past the status of physical activity and into fitness – where you're training for something specific. As you train more, you will need more sleep. Anyone who has ever trained for a long-distance event (running, cycling, triathlon) will understand this effect. Train hard = need naps. Not into training hard? Just recall the last time you spent a day outside being physical – whether it was doing yardwork or going for a long walk or hike – I bet you slept like a log that night!

Sleep is also when your brain lays down neural pathways and stores memory.[30] So if you're working on new habits or new learning, sleep is of utmost importance (yup, my mom was right!). Here's where it gets ironic. Often times my clients will decide to tackle the physical activity piece first thing. I love an early morning sweat for many reasons, but if that schedule means you're sacrificing sleep, I don't recommend it. Either find a way to go to bed earlier or you'll need to find another window for exercise.

Shortchanging your body on sleep hampers success. Without adequate sleep, you won't have the energy and vitality you need to make great choices and develop healthy habits. Furthermore, there is evidence that lack of quality sleep can put you at a hormonal disadvantage for the maintenance of a healthy weight, among many other things.[31] Are you kidding? Nope. According to a review of 18 studies of sleep and appetite, six hours or less of shuteye actually bumps up the production of the hunger hormone grehlin and also limits leptin, which helps to cue your body that you are *full,* and helps to manage your overall intake.[32] It's not just that you're tired and you're grabbing that quick fix of sugar; there is a hormonal shift that is magnifying that challenge!

Bottom line: sleep is important. Aim to get between seven and nine hours per night. Find your 'magic' number that helps you feel your best, so you can make great choices that align with your goals and have the energy and vitality to execute them!

Tip: Change your mindset about sleep. As a society, we tend to place a weird value on cutting sleep, bragging about how we only got x hours of sleep last night – like somehow it's a badge of honor. Sleep is essential if we want to be healthy and well. Reframe and change your language around sleep, and encourage others to do the same!

8 Tips for Quality Pillow Time

But Gillian, I'm in bed for nine hours every night and I can't sleep. Or once I'm asleep I can't stay asleep, and that's frustrating!

There are so many factors at play when it comes to good quality sleep, but here are some general tips that can be helpful:

1. Have a consistent bedtime and wake-up time. Our bodies were actually designed to follow the light – winding down with sundown and waking up with the sunrise. Obviously, that's often not possible in our current society, but do your best to be consistent with what time you go to sleep and wake up. Yeah, I know this puts a dent on your weekend, but just do your best with it. Hack: try setting a 'go to bed' alarm on your phone to remind you when it's time to wind down and get to bed! I find when I abide by my 'go to bed' alarm, waking up is much easier.

2.   Be more physically active. Shocker, I know. But this is really important. Think about how kids or puppies sleep after a really busy day. Apply the same logic to yourself!

3.   Avoid large meals before bedtime. I know this isn't always doable, but do your best. Digestion is actually stimulating for the body and it's also hard work. If you're digesting, the body can't get into a deep sleep until its work is done!

4.   Avoid caffeine and alcohol close to bedtime. And what is 'close' really depends on the person. I've found (through very frustrating experimentation) that I can't have any caffeine past about 3:00 p.m. without taking a hit on my sleep quality. I'll be able to get to sleep, but I likely won't stay asleep. The same goes for alcohol.

5.   Avoid nicotine. I feel like this is just a good general health tip, but with regards to sleep, it's especially important. Talk to your doctor and kick that habit to the curb![33]

6.   Make sure your bedroom is quiet, dark, relaxing, and at a comfortable temperature. Dark makes a *big* difference, and you can buy blackout curtains at very little cost if you need them to make your room dark.

7.   Remove electronic devices, such as TVs, computers, and smart phones, from the bedroom. Not only will the incessant binging disturb your rest or sleep; screens are stimulating! So be mindful of your screen use within the few hours before bed and of course once you're off to la-la land.

8.   Try doing a progressive muscle relaxation or a calming meditation before bed. The internet is full of great resources and apps. (One of my favorite apps is called "Calm." It even has a section called "7 days of sleep" – a series of meditations to help you develop better sleep.) For simple progressive body relaxation, follow the instructions in the box below.

SIMPLE PROGRESSIVE MUSCLE RELAXATION

I often use this simple technique at the end of a yoga class, or any time I need to wind myself down. It's a great strategy.

★ Find a comfortable position lying on your bed. You may wish to be on your back with pillows under your head and under your knees for support.

★ Ensure that the room is a comfortable temperature and that it is quiet and dark.

★ Close your eyes and focus on your breath. Take five slow, easy breaths in and out. It may be helpful to notice your breath either at your nostrils or at your belly, and you may choose to place your hand gently on your belly.

★ With every breath, notice your body relaxing and melting into the bed.

★ Starting at your toes, notice your body. Notice each body part, and intentionally create tension in that area and then release it. Travel up the body as slowly as you can, developing tension and releasing it. As you release, allow your body to melt into the bed. Body parts you may wish to include: feet, ankles, lower leg, knees, thighs, hips, internal organs, belly, low back, ribs, arms, hands, fingers, shoulders, neck, tongue, jaw, ears, face, scalp, mouth, and eyes.

Don't rush this exercise; take as much time as you need, and remember that there is no wrong way to meditate or relax. Turn your mind off and enjoy. To download this progressive muscle relaxation as an audio file, please visit www.elephantinthegym.com/resources. This is an issue out of my wheelhouse and if you are really struggling, I highly recommend speaking with either your family physician or exploring your sleep issue with a naturopathic doctor.

Principle #8: Yawn Your Way to Success

Sleep is the unsung hero of health. It is truly essential and should never be under-valued. Approach sleep with a positive attitude and make seven to nine hours of sleep per night a priority. Maybe even inspire others around you to do the same. Give your body, mind, and spirit the advantage of being optimally rested and recovered so you can get out there and be your best!

CHAPTER 8 POINTS TO PRACTICE

★ *Reframe your mindset about sleep.* It's not a luxury – and lack of sleep is not a badge of honor!

★ *A good sleep doesn't just feel amazing; it's essential to your health!* Good quality and quantity of sleep decreases your risks of certain diseases, supports good metabolism, and improves memory.

★ *Research indicates that most people benefit from seven to nine hours per 24-hour period.* Yup, that can include naps!

★ *Quantity matters, but so does quality!* Work to improve your sleep quality by considering your sleep environment (cool and dark is best), having a great bedtime routine (including a consistent bedtime), and avoiding screens and stimulants (caffeine and nicotine).

★ *Set the stage for great slumber.* Try using meditation, gentle yoga or a progressive relaxation exercise as part of your bedtime routine.

Do this now: Set a go-to-bed alarm (One minute).

When I talk to clients about what stops them from getting enough sleep, it's always not getting to bed on time. This little hack has helped a lot of people. So try it now! Get your phone, and set and label an alarm to signal you to go to bed. You might even set two alarms: get ready for bed and go to bed. Alarms are great triggers to help initiate a routine and build a habit! Have a great sleep!

It's time to put all this theory into practice! Are you ready? Awesome! Let's do it!

CHAPTER 9

A Winning Practice
(Designed for You)

We have uncovered the Elephant in the Gym and taken a good look at the misconceptions and challenges that are tripping us up and holding us back. We have explored not only what health and fitness means – but also what it means *to us*, and now it's time to pull all these pieces together and put them into a practice. A practice that is not only going to *work* for you – it is also going to inspire and empower you to create and maintain your healthy lifestyle!

In the next two chapters, we're going to help you to create a vision and a plan to implement *your* healthy lifestyle. I invite you to bring to the table everything you've learned thus far – both from this book and from all your own experience. As you develop *your custom plan*, trust that *you* are your very best advocate. You know your body best! So listen to it, own it, and honor it. Trust your instincts about what will (and will not) work for your body and your life!

To guide this process, if you haven't already, I encourage you to download my free handbook: *Unleash the Elephant: Defining Your Practice.* You can access this free tool at www.elephantinthegym.com/resources.

First, before we dig into creating a vision and developing a *practice* that inspires you, we must begin by exploring what living a healthy lifestyle means to *you*. Instead of that desired lifestyle outcome being hinged upon an unrealistic aesthetic or a specific result, I invite you to explore *what being healthy would mean for your life*… what difference would it make to your life, your relationships and your overall happiness and fulfillment?

Define Health on Your Terms

Having a clear idea of what health means for *you* is going to guide your entire practice. This is not about getting stuck in analysis paralysis; it's about gaining more clarity around why it really matters to you.

This is a great time to circle back to the notes you made in Chapter 1 when we first explored *your definition of health*. Some of the questions you might revisit:

- What does health mean to you?
- How would your body feel? What could it do?
- What would being healthy mean for you and your life?
- How would you feel – physically, mentally, spiritually?

As you consider health on your own terms, ask yourself what optimal health and fitness would look like for you, keeping in mind all your individual interests, priorities and values. Start to explore your working definition of health and fitness and why it matters to you. Remember that this isn't an on-and-off switch but rather an ever-changing and evolving relationship with your health.

Action Step: Take some time and journal about the questions above. Once you feel somewhat grounded in your ideas, continue on and we'll deepen the conversation.

For this action step, you may find it helpful to break 'health' down into the three elements I discussed back in Chapter 1:

- Physical: this is the health of your physical body, and the three primary components to consider are: movement (physical activity and/or fitness), nutrition and sleep.
- Mental: your emotional, social, and psychological well-being. Practices may include: mindfulness, stress management, personal or professional development, and working with a coach or counselor.
- Spiritual: your connection to a higher power or belief system. It may be defined by your religious faith and/or your personal values, beliefs, principles, and morals. Practices may include: self-compassion, prayer, devotions or meditation, relaxation, gratitude practices, journaling, going to church, or connecting with loved ones and nature.

Please remember that these are not concrete definitions but flexible concepts. Don't get too attached to getting it perfect; remember that just like your healthy lifestyle, your definition of health will continue to evolve. Explore your personal definition of these elements in the handbook.

Your Customized Practice Starts with a Vision

Now that you've explored how you wish to define optimal health for yourself, we can begin to look realistically at the bigger picture. We started with specifically looking at your health, because I'm assuming that is why you picked up this book. But ultimately your life isn't broken into silos. All the various commitments and priorities in your life fit together into a beautiful (sometimes complex) puzzle. Which is why, when you're creating a vision for your health and fitness, I also encourage you to consider your vision for all areas of your life. We need to bring all the pieces of the puzzle together so as to see the complete picture!

The 5 Pillars of Your Healthy Life(style).

Here are the five key areas to consider as you explore your vision: work/business, family (immediate, extended, and the family you choose, a.k.a. close friends), community (volunteer, church, 'extended' friendships, etc.), personal development (schooling/coursework/reading), and of course, health and wellness. These are not listed in any particular order – we're not talking about priorities (yet).

Creating a vision for your life starts with being clear and grounded in your current situation. To help with this, I've developed a simple process called a Compassionate Audit that I use personally and with my clients. This audit isn't about highlighting the things you're doing wrong (I'm not looking to reinforce your negativity bias!); it's about taking the 'pulse' on your current level of satisfaction. This boils down to two questions:

- Are you happy?
- Do you feel fulfilled?

If the honest answer to either of these questions is No, then we can explore further. And we can dig a bit deeper with this question:

- If nothing changed, would that be okay?

If the answer is a straight up YES, awesome! Take a moment to ask yourself:

- What has me feeling happy and fulfilled in this area?
- What practices, habits, and routines are important for me to continue?

If the answer is NO (even just a little), you've identified something that is *also* really awesome – an opportunity for growth! Does this mean you need to make dramatic changes? Not necessarily, and maybe not at all. In fact, sometimes the biggest shifts come from our feelings and attitudes.

I would encourage you to explore what it might look like to cultivate true acceptance and gratitude.

Sometimes true peace and joy come not from changing our situation, but changing how we *relate* to it. In *The Book of Joy*, the Dalai Lama and Archbishop Desmond Tutu talk a lot about acceptance and gratitude as *pillars of joy*. They phrase it this way, "acceptance is not fighting reality, gratitude is embracing that reality."

Consider how you relate to this area of your life. Could you accept things as they are? Could you embrace things as they are?

As you begin to explore your vision, consider these questions:

- What would true acceptance look like?
- How would it feel to be grateful for your struggle?
- What would it look like to be happy and fulfilled?
- Don't get into logistics, but consider what might need to change to move the needle towards greater happiness and fulfillment.
- This isn't about setting goals. It's about really exploring what makes you happy and fulfilled. Not driven from a place of should (guilt and shame), but driven from a place of 'what lights you up?'

As you explore, think about painting a picture of your life. What will it look like and feel like? Try to use all of your senses to create this vision for your life!

Action Step: For each of the 5 Pillars, complete a Compassionate Audit and explore your vision.

- Work/Business
    - Are you happy and fulfilled? (If the answer is yes, obviously carry on to the next pillar.)
    - No? Ask yourself:
        - Do I wish to accept what is or make changes?
        - What does a fulfilling work life look like for me?
        - Do I need work to fill my bucket/light me up, or am I okay with things as they are? That is, do I live to work (it's my vocation) or work to live (to have the money I need and to live a life that lights me up)? (Generally there should be some 'balance' here, but this is a really important question.)

- Family (immediate, extended, and the family you choose, a.k.a. close friends)
    - Are you happy and fulfilled?
    - No? Explore these questions:
        - Do I wish to accept what is or make changes?
        - What would a happy and fulfilling family life look like for me?
        - What would my relationships look like?

- Community (volunteer, church, 'extended' friendships, etc.)
    - Are you happy and fulfilled?
    - No? Explore these questions:
        - Do I wish to accept what is or make changes?
        - What community involvement would fill me up?
        - What inspires me to be *more* or *less* involved in my community?

- Personal Development (schooling/coursework/reading)
    - Are you happy and fulfilled?
    - No? Consider these questions:
        - Do I wish to accept what is or make changes?
        - Is there an area of growth I wish to pursue for personal or professional development?

- How would growth in this area contribute to my happiness and fulfillment?

- Health (physical, mental, spiritual)
  - Are you happy and fulfilled?
  - Yes! (*Sometimes I hear this from clients: "Now that I've really explored this with you, I'm actually feeling really great about my choices and my overall health!" That's wonderful!*)
  - No? Dig deeper and ask yourself:
    - Do I wish to accept what is or make changes?
    - What will my living a healthy lifestyle look like (not just physically, but also mentally, emotionally, and spiritually)?
    - How will I feel in my body?
    - How will I feel mentally/emotionally?
    - What about my spiritual health?
    - Are my intentions to be physically active for health, or do I have more specific fitness outcomes I wish to achieve?

Note: You may find it helpful to complete a Compassionate Audit on an annual basis. It can be a great way to start the vision process and help you gain clarity.

Explore Your Vision

There are several ways you can do this. I highly recommend starting with some *thinking* before you get to the serious work of writing it down. Consider your answers to the Compassionate Audit as you go on a walk or get your body moving. If you like to meditate, you may wish to meditate on your answers before you launch into *doing!*

Once you're ready, you may want to consider one of the following approaches to help you solidify your vision:

1. Pen to paper: my personal fave is pen to paper. I simply explore each of the five categories listed above, and I tend to use bullets or create a 'word cloud.' With the word cloud, I take a big piece of paper and list each area. Then around each area I note the vision(s) I have.

2.   Visual vision board: this is the classic when it comes to visioning. My only caution with this visual approach is to be mindful of the physical image you are connecting with. If you're too drawn to a specific aesthetic, try using words and add some of your own notes in a hybrid visual/word format!

3.   Virtual vision board: in the age of Pinterest, you might also wish to create a visual and informational vision board that links in the ideas and areas you wish to explore. This can be really helpful as you explore new ideas that you want to 'try on' – especially around health and personal development!

4.   Slide presentation: this more 'high tech' option was used by one of my clients and I thought it was brilliant! She created a slide deck that layered in imagery, words, and mantras set to music so she could play it any time she needed to be reminded or inspired. Google slides, Haiku, and Prezi are also great tools.

Whatever approach you use, it's important to turn off the inner critic and the logistics manager. *Visioning* isn't about determining if it's possible or how you'll do it, just jot down the first ideas that come to mind and don't judge them. Vision isn't about analyzing the details and tasks that will be required; it's about letting your mind wander to *your big dreams* – where nothing is impossible!

The other distinction I want to make here is with *language*. This is not goal setting (more on that later); this is about who you *wish* to become. If you say, "I want to run 5K" that statement begs me to ask, "Do you...?" Instead, shift your language so it is action-oriented:

"I will run a 5K" Much better, but it leaves me wondering, "Then what?" It's a nice *goal*, but what happens after you achieve it? How can we make it more visionary?

"I am a runner." YES! This is inspired! It leaves me feeling hopeful and excited! Notice there aren't any logistics here. Not how you'll accomplish it, just what the *vision* is. (Don't worry, we'll get to the *how*, but for now, just focus on the *who* you want to be, *how* you want to feel, and *what* your life will look like!)

Here are some more examples:

From wishy-washy hope...	→	From so-so goal...	→	To empowered visionary statement!
I want to hike more.	→	I will go for more hikes.	→	I am an avid hiker.
I'd love to walk on my lunch break.	→	I will walk during my lunch break.	→	I am a dedicated lunch time walker.
I want to get more sleep.	→	I will get seven hours of sleep every night.	→	I get to bed on time so I can wake up rested and energized.

Do you see the difference? Your vision can't just be covert goals; it needs to be visionary and inspiring. Circle back to your answers and make sure you didn't just put down *goals* under each area.

My Vision Story.

I created my first vision on a napkin, sitting with girlfriends as I was nearing the end of my university career.

Spring exams were over and we were relishing the newfound free time. One of our friends was returning after a semester away and we all gathered over brunch to connect and celebrate the end of term. That brunch became an afternoon coffee as we excitedly looked toward our futures with anticipation and hopefulness. By the end of the afternoon, we each had a tattered napkin with our vision for the next one, three, and five years. Each of our visions was different, and all were inspiring.

Three years later, one of my girlfriends mailed me my vision on that tattered napkin. When I looked at it, I saw that not only had I brought nearly all of my vision to life, in many cases I had gone above and beyond what I had visualized. What is interesting about this story is that I gave her the napkin after that brunch and I hadn't seen it since; I hadn't referred to it or used it as my guide. It seemed that the simple act of *declaring* my vision had a profound impact on the choices I made and the path I took – more so than I could ever have imagined.

Since that spring day, I've continued to create a vision for my life each and every year. These days, I tend to envision one or two years at a time, and while I've upgraded from tattered napkins, I still keep the process relatively simple. I generally start with taking some time to reflect, either on a walk or run, or after a meditation. Then I sit down with an 8.5 x 11 sheet of white paper and colored pens. I divide the page into the different areas of my life and explore what comes up. My only rule is no judgment, if it's there for me, I write it down. This is my opportunity to dream big! This sheet of paper lives in my office, but I don't refer to it. Creating a vision isn't about the tangibles of how; it's about the process of dreaming, and exploring our desires! I find the process extremely helpful to my growth and development as a person and as a business owner.

Give Failure a Hug, Not the Finger

You have a vision. You're energized. You're motivated. You're ready to go! And then life happens. Kids are pulling you in 20 directions. Work is a big old ball of stress and you Just. Don't. Have. Time. Oh boy, here we go again!

Let's be real – we are not robots. Life happens; life can go sideways. So sometimes we have to change our vision and change our plans. And sometimes we need to redefine success to include failure. Because failure and success are not black and white: success doesn't make us good, and failure doesn't make us bad. Together they make us human.

Redefine Success and Failure.

You're feeling excited about your new walking regime, and you commit to walking five mornings per week for 30 minutes, Monday to Friday. Then the very first week you get called into work early on Friday morning and miss your morning walk. If you're like many people, you'll view this missed walk as a big red 'F' for the week. You'll feel frustrated that so quickly into your new regime you're already failing, and maybe you'll even make it mean something about your capability to be successful (insert nasty self-talk here).

But if you take a step back, you can recognize that the one missed walk doesn't negate the other four you *did* take! Overall you still achieved 120 minutes of physical activity! Sure, you didn't get that 150 minutes, but you achieved 120 minutes more than you did the week prior! And that's a wonderful thing.

Then if you take *another* step back, you may be able to look objectively at that Friday morning meeting and explore how you might have prevented it from cutting into your walk time. Maybe you could have walked during lunchtime, or shifted your Friday walk to Saturday or Sunday.

We need to *shift* our perspective on *failure*.

Remember this wisdom from a Chinese proverb, *"Failure is not falling down, but refusing to get back up."*

I once heard someone reference the idea of *failing forward*. Taking our missteps and looking at them as an opportunity for learning, growth, and evolution is a foundation for reframing our relationship with failure and success.

One of the best ways I've discovered to do this is to view your health as *a practice*. When you make a choice that doesn't align with your definition and practice of health, acknowledge it, own it, and move on.

This is powerful. Clients tell me all the time what a difference this alone has made regarding their nutrition and health habits. One client recently relayed to me that she made the mistake of stopping at the grocery store while she was hungry (pro tip: never grocery shop hungry, and definitely not hangry). She picked up some cookies as a treat and ate three of them in sequence as she drove home. When she got home, she felt that pang of guilt; she knew she had made a poor choice. But then she reframed. She reminded herself that she was human. She found her self-compassion, owned the choice, made a healthy dinner, and moved on.

This is not usually how it goes for most people who struggle with their nutrition and health. For many, this is how the story would have gone: stopped at the grocery store hungry, bought cookies, ate three in the car on the way home, decided to 'throw in the towel and start fresh tomorrow' and continued to overeat foods that weren't in line with my goals for the remainder of the night.

It's like you're a mind reader. I know, I hear that a lot. I *get it* because I do it too. But finding my self-compassion, embracing my humanity, and owning my choices, especially the ones I didn't feel great about, has had a profound impact. Owning the choice gives me the opportunity to learn. It's like my client's mantra, "Every choice is a clean slate." Yes! Beautiful! Every choice is a clean slate, but before you wipe it clean, learn from the chalk marks. Learn from the misstep. Embrace the failure and start with a clean slate.

The Power of Your Health Zone

What might have happened if you'd defined your new walking regime as a 30-minute walk three to five mornings per week? How might that have shifted things? All of a sudden, that Friday morning meeting wouldn't have thrown a wrench in things at all! You still would have been well within the goal you had set for yourself. That is the power of your Health Zone.

I first introduced the idea of your Health Zone in Chapter 1. To jog your memory, the Health Zone is a way of looking at your practice of health as *a range*. Instead of having hard and fast rules to abide by, or quotas to meet, you approach your health as a range. This range gives you a healthy amount of flexibility while still bringing your definition of health to life!

At one end of the zone, we have your lower limits – the habits you'll maintain no matter what (you can think of these as non-negotiable habits – you do them no matter what). At the other end, we have your upper limits (this is what you would do in your ideal world – where your life is running smoothly).

In the past, when you've set health and fitness goals, you've likely done a great job of setting those upper limits. This time I invite you to also explore those lower limits – your non-negotiables.

Defining your Non-negotiables.

When I met Andy, she was struggling with a common complaint: when stress hit, she dropped everything. She'd be cruising along, feeling fantastic about her choices, and then a kid would get sick, a work deadline would get bumped up, and all while her husband was out of town for work! She always found that as soon as life got complicated, her commitment to her health was the very first thing that got dropped. She'd skip spin class, eat takeout every night, and squeak by on five hours of sleep. Then she'd be tired, stressed and feeling depleted.

Sound familiar? I bet. It happens to me too – this is so common and so human! When we enter periods of stress from work or life, we naturally drop the things that are 'nonessential.' In fact, health *isn't* one of those, but if our health habits aren't firmly ingrained, they will be the first to go.

This is where the power of the Health Zone can really become powerful. Because your non-negotiables become essential habits that are not dropped – no matter what!

Non-negotiables are habits you do almost without thinking. They're the habits you maintain even when life is nuts and time is limited. Think brushing your teeth. You don't question it, you just do it. If you can firmly establish your non-negotiable health habits, this can go a long way to helping you have a sustainable practice of health.

Important tip: Remember that your non-negotiables are *not* what you'd 'ideally' like to be doing (that's the other end of your Health Zone!). They are what you'll do without fail - the minimum. And (surprise) they will be different for every person. And they will change and evolve right along with you. Your non-negotiables are a reflection of your current priorities and commitments. Here are some examples I've seen work really well for clients, and they also include a reference to the upper limit or 'optimal' habit. What you'll notice about each of these non-negotiables is that in each case the shift is reasonably significant and relative to the client's 'optimal.' It is important to make the non-negotiable so easy you can't possibly do anything but succeed!

- Drinking six glasses of water per day: one first thing (1), and one with each meal (3) and snack (2). (Optimal: eight to 10 glasses per day)
- Taking a certain number of steps on an activity tracker like a Fitbit or Garmin. (Optimal: more specific fitness activities)
- Exercising three days per week. (Optimal: five to six days per week)
- Eating a minimum of three servings of veggies per day by having one with lunch and two with dinner. (Optimal: four to six servings per day)

I explored the idea of non-negotiables with Andy and she loved the concept. She immediately found peace in knowing that she could release some of her all-or-nothing thinking and embrace a something-is-better-than-nothing attitude! She created the non-negotiables of *a daily steps goal* and being *a hydration boss* – no matter what. And you know what? I'm happy to report that the next time life hit, Andy rocked those non-negotiables, and as soon as things settled, she resumed her typical ongoing practices of getting to her favorite spin class three times a week, cooking meals at home five nights a week, and getting seven hours a night of that blissful, recuperative sleep! She was elated, and I was thrilled to see her redefining health and fitness – her way!

Action Step: Explore your non-negotiables.

Make your non-negotiables simple and super easy for you to make happen, and meanwhile, keep your optimal habits in mind as something that challenges you out of your comfort zone – just slightly. Set yourself up for success!

Seeing the brick wall before you hit it.

Even with your non-negotiables in place, you will inevitably face challenges. If you can see them coming and prepare for them (possibly even prepare an alternate route), you will be more able to pass through them with ease, grace and health!

Each of us typically has a few common threads that run through our experience when it comes to our challenges. If we look back with an objective eye, we can usually see what our downfall was. I know that periods of stress typically trigger me to overeat (and not kale).

Knowing this about myself has enabled me to develop strategies to better manage myself in times of stress. I have developed other tactics and acquired more tools to support myself. For example, I know that during times of emotional stress I'm a talker; I need a good ear. So I have my list of go-to friends and colleagues I can lean on. Does it always save me from eating pickles and chocolate? Nope. But it does some of the time and I call that a win.

Action Step: Start by taking a look at your past experiences relating to your health. Name three things that have prevented you from being successful in the past. The more honest and vulnerable you are, the greater the opportunity for awareness and growth.

Once you have clarity around what tripped you up or held you back, explore how you can handle it differently next time. Sometimes the simple act of awareness is enough to shift the outcome, and sometimes we need to be proactive. What could you do to set yourself up for success next time?

Principle #9: Own It

Your health, your fitness, your life. Create a vision for your life that genuinely inspires you. Define your unique practice of a healthy lifestyle and then own it. Keep your eyes in your own lane, and don't let the gloss and glamour of quick fixes and fads take you off your own awesome course. Don't fear failure, embrace it as an opportunity to learn more about what works (and doesn't) for you and your life. Be open to the evolution of your health, wellness, and life!

CHAPTER 9 POINTS TO PRACTICE

★ *Your health isn't a stand-alone silo.* All areas of our life piece together into a sometimes complicated puzzle. Explore the big picture before you try to put the pieces together.

★ *In order to know where we're headed, we need to (honestly) evaluate where we are.* Start this process by completing a Compassionate Audit in all 5 Pillars (health, family, community, work, personal/ professional development).

★ *Consider if you are happy and fulfilled in each area of your life.* If the answer is no, consider that acceptance is a viable option.

★ *Success isn't perfection – failure is part of the process.* Embrace failure as part of learning what doesn't work for you, and as with meditation, begin again.

★ *Embrace flexibility with your own unique Health Zone.* Explore the idea of non-negotiables and upper limits and find the range of healthy habits that work for you and your life!

Do This Now: Try it on (Two minutes).

Decide on one non-negotiable you can try on for the next week. Keep it small. Hydration and servings of veggies are both great places to start. Remember to keep in mind where you're starting and consider how you'll make it happen. Share it with a friend and challenge them to join you!

I'm going to knock your socks off in the next chapter (assuming you're wearing some). I'm going to explain why I don't want you to set goals. Possibly ever again. Because I think they may be one of the other major things tripping you up. Are you ready to get over that final health hurdle?

CHAPTER 10

Don't Set Goals — Define Your Practice

Don't set goals? What the WHAT?

If you're looking to create sustainable changes to your health and wellness, I *don't* want you to set goals.

Don't get me wrong – goals have a place. There's a decent amount of science to support the creation of goals. But in my nearly 20 years of experience working with clients, I would say that goals are massively overrated when it comes to creating a healthy lifestyle. *Especially for those who have struggled to be consistent in the past.*

Why?

Because goals are outcome based and they are often focused on a singular end result. As we discussed in Chapter 1, when it comes to health and fitness, all too often the 'end result' or desired outcome isn't connected to true health and fitness.

Goals are part of the problem.

If you've felt frustrated and challenged by creating a healthy lifestyle; if you've had an on again/off again relationship with healthy habits; if you've been consistently inconsistent… I want you to abandon the notion that there is an end result or a desired outcome.

But Gillian…? Don't I need goals?

No, you don't. What you need is to be focused on *the process*. Instead of focusing on concrete *goals*, bring your vision to life by focusing on *the practice of health and fitness*.

The Process is the Point

"I reached my weight goal!" Alice shared.

I thought we were about to celebrate her success. Then she said, "I feel disappointed. I thought it would feel different getting back to my pre-baby weight."

Someone in the group asked her, "Why are you disappointed?"

"All this time working out and eating well, I kept looking so forward to the day I would be *here*. But now I'm *here* and I feel nothing. I thought something would happen when I got here."

She continued, "Like there should be something more. But it's just me, wearing my pre-pregnancy pants again. And I don't feel any different about my body than I did before I began."

Someone in the group asked her, "What were you expecting?"

She replied, "I don't know... balloons and confetti!?"

We all had a good laugh – not because it was funny (though it was), but at the familiar absurdity of the situation. We could all relate. We'd all had that experience of achieving a goal and then feeling kind of... underwhelmed.

In health and fitness, there seems to be this pre-occupation with "getting there." As if something magical exists in this place where we achieve our ideal size and physique. And even if you can get past the typical preoccupation with the aesthetic, and focus on fitness and overall health, this deflation effect can still exist. When we finally find our consistency with exercise, when we run that 5K race or complete a fitness challenge... now what?!

There is no dramatic shift in how you feel about your body (or your life) when you get 'there.' There is no change in your relationships with others, or with your life. There's just you on the other side of your goal.

Here is the take home message I want you to hear:

Bringing your vision to life by developing a practice of health and fitness isn't about getting 'there.' *This isn't goal setting in disguise.* There is nothing magical on the *other* side of your vision. The *magic* is in the process and practice of bringing your vision to life. It's about who you become in the process and what you learn about yourself, your relationships, and your life along the way.

Create a bold vision for your health and your life, and connect to that vision deeply and profoundly. Focus on the process of realizing your vision through daily practice – because no one else will do it for you. You bring it to life through your consistent commitment and perseverance. You do it by staying *in* the process and absorbing the many lessons that growth and evolution have to offer.

Don't Set Goals; Develop Your S.U.P.E.R. Practice

With your definition of health, your unique vision, and an awareness of your individual challenges front of mind, I invite you use this 5-Step S.U.P.E.R. Process to develop your practice. You can do this in a journal or on a big piece of paper, or on a white board, or in the Handbook (go to www.elephantinth-egym.com/resources to download it if you haven't already).

Throughout this process, remember that your practice of health will always be evolving. So nothing you map out is set in stone. Feel free to be creative and to be open to trying new and different approaches.

Step 1: Develop Your STRATEGIC PLAN.

Habits and routines are the cornerstones of a sustainable healthy lifestyle. In order to create habits and routines that work, you'll need to take into consideration where you are starting from, the overall direction you wish to go (your definition of health and your vision), and what reasonable steps you need to take to travel along that path. Getting started with your practice requires a strategic plan.

As you develop your plan, keep in mind the questions below (without getting into analysis paralysis). This process starts by further clarifying your overall vision (including each of the 5 Pillars) and answering the 5 W's in the order I have listed below. I know it's not the typical Who, What, When, Where and Why – but trust me, I put them in this order on purpose.

- *Why* does this matter? What is the deeper and more profound reason behind this vision? What is driving this desire to change? (Check in that guilt and shame aren't driving your vision.)
- *Who* do you need in your court? Who will be your champions (family, friends, colleagues)? Who will be your supports? Your supports will vary depending on the pillar, but may include mentors, your boss, a spiritual leader or pastor, health professionals like a personal trainer, or health coach, or dietitian, etc.
- *Where* will you get the information you need, and who will you get the information from? Are they qualified? Does their philosophy resonate with you? Make sure that your source is credible (and not just based on Facebook likes or Google analytics). What is their education, and why should you trust their information? Is it based on valid, unbiased research? And *where* will you take action? What is your fitness personality? Do you prefer activities at home/in the gym/at the recreation center/outdoors?
- *What* specifically will you do? What tools do you need? What knowledge or information do you need to be successful? If you're not sure what tools you need, it's time to do some research. Be curious. Ask people you trust for their ideas and input.
- *When* will you make it happen? When can you schedule in the things you need to do to be successful (grocery shopping, meal planning, time for fitness, and activity). The more specific you can be with scheduling, the more successful you will be.

Action Step: In a journal or your Handbook, complete Step 1 of Defining Your Practice.

- Explore your answers to the 5 W's.
- Map out your strategic plan to bring your vision of health to life. Keep in mind all of the 5 Pillars (work, health and wellness, family, community, personal and professional development).

STEP 2: Identify Your UNIQUE PRIORITIES.

In Step 1, we already examined the 'why' of your practice. Your 'why' will bring meaning to your practice and help you determine where it stands in your list of priorities (i.e., how does it stack up against all the other commitments in your life?).

Now I want you to get really honest about how the pillars of your life stack up. Once you decide what the priorities are, you need to dig into logistics. This comes down to one question: *what actually needs to happen so you can make this a priority?*

You'll need to be realistic about what is possible in your life, and then create boundaries around what is and is not going to work! This involves a really honest (and sometimes vulnerable) look at your life.

Life is a perpetual game of give and take, ebb and flow. When I think of priorities, I envision that baby toy with the hammer and pegs (the baby version of Whac-A-Mole!). If you hammer one peg down, the others go up, and vice versa. Instead of randomly pounding out which one is up or down, and letting the urgencies of life dictate the priorities, I invite you to take a good look at the five key areas of your vision and choose which pegs you wish to hammer down in order to bring the others to the forefront.

Have you ever noticed that when you're stressed at work and not setting good boundaries with your time and commitments, it's difficult to have the time and energy you need to devote to your family or your health? Yeah, me too! But it doesn't have to be that way!

What would happen if you started by creating better boundaries with work? How could this impact your family or your health?

Identify Your Catalysts for Change

Consider that shifts in one pillar can *positively* impact others. They can have a domino effect, or as I like to call it, a healthy snowball. And it all starts with one shift.

Let's look at an example...

Sandy came to me for health coaching. She was working 60+ hours per week as a lawyer, and her family and health were feeling the strain. She was also desperately missing her community connections that were part of her volunteer work. We discussed the challenges she was up against, and when it came to creating her practice, a light bulb appeared. She had previously realized that she needed to create better boundaries at work – but she had failed to see how that was the key to *all* the shifts she wanted to make!

She started by setting an alarm at work to ensure she would leave on time, and she made this non-negotiable. No matter what, she left each day at 6:30 p.m. (which was better than 7 p.m. or later). This meant she had time to get home, make dinner and sit down with her family. Eventually she started leaving at 6 p.m. After some time being consistent with this, she felt like she could commit to an evening activity two nights per week, and she started attending a dance class. (Previously she had felt this wasn't possible because of the 'mom guilt' she would feel if she left so quickly after arriving home. Now that she came home earlier, it worked.

By shifting *one habit* (leaving work on time), a whole sequence of other healthy habits was triggered, creating a healthy snowball! For Sandy, shifting the habit of her work hours was a 'catalyst' habit.

In Sandy's case, she needed to shift her habits and routines in the work pillar of her life in order to affect change in her health and wellness pillar. But the concept works *within* a pillar too. Think about how you feel when you get enough sleep. You're rested, energized, and capable of making better nutrition choices. Adequate quality sleep is often a catalyst habit.

To identify your catalyst habit or habits, begin by being curious. Peel back the layers. Start with an area of struggle or something you wish to change. Consider what you would need to shift to make that change happen. And then keep going until you get to the core!

Action Step: In your journal or Handbook, complete Step 2.

Look back at your strategic plan and consider your priorities. To begin, ask these questions to clarify:

- If you gave it your focus and attention, which pillar of your life (work, family, community, personal development, health) would *most* benefit from making shifts in your habits and routines?
- Which pillar could potentially impact others as those shifts were made? In other words, is there a catalyst habit you could start with? – one that would naturally/organically impact others?
- Are there habits or routines you could employ that would create a snowball effect on others?

Take an honest look and rank your priorities. Keep in mind potential *catalyst habits*, and use a highlighter or a system of stars or circling to highlight the top priorities. Remember that it can't *all* be a priority; choose one or two things from each Pillar that are a priority for you this year. Then consider how you might order these priorities by numbering them one to 10. Then you'll need to take a good solid look at the *how.*

Once you determine your highest priority, take a deeper dive with these questions:

- What needs to happen so you can make your top priority be a top priority in action?
- What do you need to say 'no' to, so you can say 'yes' to your priorities and yourself?

Consider that sometimes the most important first step is to create the space and time required to take action.

STEP 3: Clarify Your Plan with PERSPECTIVE.

You need a strategic plan. You need to define your priorities. You also need to maintain your *perspective*. It's time to circle back through your strategic plan with this filter:

What is actually going to work for my life?

Sure, you may wish to go for an hour-long walk on the beach each day for your physical and mental health, but perhaps that's not feasible with a full-time job, two kids busy with activities, and your once-a-week volunteer commitment.

But perhaps a 30-minute walk three or four days per week is feasible, if you get up early before the house wakes up.

This is where we embrace and clarify the concept of your Health Zone. Keeping in mind your components of health (movement, nutrition, sleep), explore the lower and upper limits of your Zone. Incorporate the ideas you developed in Chapter 9 around your lower limits or non-negotiables.

As you explore the health habits that define your Health Zone, incorporate your personal definition of health (body, mind and spirit), your strategic plan, and what you learned in Chapters 6 through 8 about health. Keep the following important points in mind:

- Movement includes both physical activity and exercise. The general guideline for health is to work towards a weekly total of 150 minutes accumulated in increments of 10 minutes or more.
    - How will you increase the overall activity of your life? Be specific!
    - If exercising is part of your plan, what specifically will you do?
    - Remember to let joy lead!

- Nutrition is not just about nourishing your physical body but also balancing that with nourishing your soul. Not all food is fuel!
    - What nutrition habits do you wish to develop? (Revisit the guidelines listed in Chapter 7 for inspiration.)
    - What nutrition habits do you wish to eliminate?

- Sleep is essential to good health. Aim to get between seven and nine hours per 24-hour period.
    - What sleep habits do you wish to develop? (Revisit the tips on sleep quality and quantity in Chapter 8.)

Action Step: In your journal or Handbook, complete Step 3.

For each area of your health priorities, identify the habits you wish to focus on. Once you've determined those habits, clarify them with an upper limit (optimal) and lower limit (non-negotiable) to give yourself flexibility.

As you explore, keep in mind your current life priorities and commitments.

Once you've completed this, ask yourself these questions to gain clarity:

- Does my Health Zone fit with my current priorities, commitments and interests?
  - Do my upper limits stretch and challenge me slightly out of my comfort zone?
  - Do my lower limits seem reasonable if I was in the middle of a busy chaotic week?

- Am I comfortable with the upper and lower limits I've defined?
  - If yes (be honest) – awesome!
  - If no – how can you scale your lower and upper limits accordingly?

STEP 4: Evaluate Your ENVIRONMENT.

Have you ever considered how much your environment impacts your choices?

Our environment dramatically impacts our ability to shift, change, and evolve. The people, places, and things we surround ourselves with impact our mood and motivation significantly. Some of this we can control, some we can't. Let's break this down...

Consider all the various environments at play in your life. Environments aren't just where you spend your time; it's the other people and things in these environments that either distract you or support you.

People: this is anyone you spend a decent amount of time with who has the capacity to either distract or support you. Keep in mind that this isn't just the people you spend time with physically! Because we spend so much of our time connected to our devices, we are also impacted by our virtual connections.

Places: this is anywhere you spend a significant amount of time each week. And it's not just the obvious places like work and home. Think about places you go to once per week – like to a kid's activity or a place where you volunteer.

Things: these are the things in your life that either distract or support you. Some are obvious, like screens (TV, iPhones, tablets, etc.). But you also might consider things like the PJs you put on after work, the magazines you read, or your home gym. How do these things make you feel?

Also consider that some people, places, and/or things could be neutral. That's okay too!

One of the ways my mom expresses her love is through food. Whenever she hosts gatherings, the food is thoughtfully prepared, and beautifully presented. She's an incredible cook and host. This has always been the case, and as such, I associate my mom's house with amazing food – and it's easy to get caught up in the delicious bounty and overeat! The behavior associated with this environment isn't necessarily conducive to my optimal nutrition.

I used to get really stressed out about it, but with time I've recognized that I'm only there a handful of times a year, and the overall impact on my nutrition and health isn't huge. This is a case of five days out of 365! This perspective allows me to be objective and remember the bigger picture.

Also, when I know I'm going to be there, I take steps to not overeat. Yes, I indulge, but instead of a cheat and overeat mentality, I enjoy a treat and savor it mindset. Also, when I'm visiting there, I make an effort to get a daily dose of physical activity by packing my running shoes and my yoga mat. Sometimes I'll even get the whole family involved in some activity by suggesting a walk to the local park. Movement is a catalyst habit for me – and taking time to move daily goes a long way to supporting my intention not to overeat the treats!

This step is all about exploring how your environments affect you and also what you can do about it. If you start to realize that every time you walk past your colleague's desk on the way to the copier, you have a candy – change your route. If you notice that every time you're with a certain relative, you use food to manage stress – explore other stress management strategies and employ them mindfully. If you find yourself feeling down about your body every time you read a magazine – stop buying them.

We have far more control over our environments than most of us think. Don't be a victim of your environment – be aware and make powerful choices.

Action Step: In your journal or Handbook, complete Step 4.

Make a list! Be as specific as you can.

- People: anyone you spend a decent amount of time with. For example: spouse, partner, kids, friends, work colleagues, kids' friends' parents, relatives, virtual friends (such as those in Facebook groups you frequent), etc.
- Places: anywhere you spend a significant amount of time each week. For example: work, home, gym, recreation center, community hall, the homes of others in your life, etc.
- Things: what are the things that impact your choices, habits, and routines? For example: screens, clothing, books, magazines, exercise equipment, etc.

Once you've made your list, ask yourself these questions:

- Which of these environments support you? How might you increase the amount of influence they have on your life?
- Which of these environments distract you? What steps can you take to set yourself up for success?
  - Can you decrease or eliminate your exposure?
  - Can you manage your exposure?

STEP 5: Develop Your ROUTINES.

Your health isn't impacted by the grand gestures you make towards it once per week; it's about the seemingly small things you do daily that add up…!

In Step 3, you identified what health habits define the upper and lower limits of your Health Zone. Routines are what bring those habits to life day to day!

Think of Routines as the daily and weekly practices you will employ to create lasting healthy habits.

When you're looking at your Routines, I invite you to consider each of the following areas: Physical Health (physical activity or exercise, nutrition and sleep), Mental Health, and Spiritual Health.

To get your creative juices flowing, I'll give you a short list of the routines I've found particularly helpful, both in my personal life and with clients:

- *Physical Health*
  - Movement Routines:
    - Take five minutes on Sunday night to schedule your workouts for the week.
    - Use an alarm to take a walking break every hour on the hour.
    - Develop a daily lunchtime walking routine with work colleagues.
    - Put on exercise clothing as soon as you get home from work (instead of jumping straight into your PJs – no, I'm not spying on you, I do it too!).
  - Nutrition Routines:
    - Meal plan once per week or every few days.
    - Grocery shopping once a week (amp it up by making a list beforehand).
    - Have at least one serving of veggies with lunch and with dinner.
    - Drink a glass of water first thing every morning.
    - Have a cup of tea each night before bedtime to stave off mindless snacking.
  - Sleep Routines:
    - Use a bedtime alarm to get you to bed at a suitable time.
    - Get up at the same time each day (even Saturday and Sunday).
    - Have a bedtime ritual like a meditation or a bath.

- *Mental Health:*
  - Write down your daily or weekly wins.
  - Do a progressive muscle relaxation exercise each night before bed (circle back to Chapter 8 for a refresher).
  - Have one *mindful* snack or meal per day, or perhaps once per week.
  - Listen to podcasts or audiobooks during your drive to work.
  - Speak with a counselor or coach on a regular basis (routinely, not once in a while).

- *Spiritual Health:*
  - Have a midday five-minute meditation practice using an app like *Calm* or *Insight Timer.*
  - Go to church each week, or benefit from prayer or daily devotions.
  - Practice gratitude daily or weekly.
  - Journal daily or weekly.
  - Spend time in nature every Sunday, on your own or with close friends or family.

Get Out of Your Routine Rut

You might start to notice that you have routines in your life that aren't particularly helpful. What I've found most helpful both personally and professionally is to *crowd out* the unhelpful routines and habits by implementing helpful ones. This not only brings the focus onto the *positive,* it is typically very effective.

However, if you find that one routine is particularly resistant to being 'crowded out,' it might be worth exploring how you could change that routine by using one of these tactics:

- **Unhinge it:** just as we connect habits through habit pairing, sometimes we need to take action to *unhinge* habits. This is best used when you have two (or more) habits that are connected. Think glass of wine while you make dinner, snacking while watching TV, or getting a treat with your afternoon coffee. Since this habit pair has been linked in the neural pathways in your brain, you have to take action to 'rewire' and unhinge the habits. Step one is *noticing* the pairing. Step two is coming up with a strategy to disconnect them. For example, waiting to have a glass of wine until it's dinnertime OR swapping your wine with sparkling water. With TV, it can be helpful to have a 'no screens' rule while you eat. Play around and get creative and 'consciously uncouple' those habits!
- **Peel it back:** this is habit layering in reverse. Just as we lean into some habits by layering them on piece by piece, we can also peel them back. I had a client who had a routine of unwinding after a tough day of work by having a cigarette and a glass of wine. She knew this was not a habit that connected to her vision and she wanted to make a change.

She also knew she really didn't need the cigarette because she could go for weeks without it when she was on vacation or around family. She started by cutting the cigarette (the habit she was most comfortable with eliminating) while still allowing the glass of wine. She felt stable with that shift. Eventually, she also transitioned away from the wine. She recognized that she wasn't drinking it for the enjoyment of the wine, but rather for stress decompression.

- **Swap it out:** how can you swap out the unhelpful routine by putting a new routine in its place? This starts by examining what is at the core of the habit – what is the reward you are seeking? In my client's case, she recognized the wine was a tool she was using to unwind. We explored other ways she could unwind – like taking a bath, reading a book, or taking a walk with her dog. She liked being physically active and knew that a 15-minute walk would also work well in her life. Walking would give her the same release, and the dog was happy about this routine too. Bonus: the dog quickly became conditioned to this new routine and was a GREAT accountability partner when she arrived home – it's pretty hard to settle onto the couch when the dog is bouncing with enthusiasm rearing to go for a walk. When my client started, she would only have the wine *after* she had gone for her 15-minute walk. Then she found (no surprise) that the 15-minute walk helped her clear her mind and decompress from her day, and often she ended up skipping the wine altogether. Slowly she released the crutch of the post-work wine wind-down and also added 75 minutes of walking to her week in five short bursts (movement win – and bonus win for the dog)!

Action Step: In your journal or Handbook, complete Step 5 and create a four-week plan!

This isn't about mapping it out forever – it's about setting yourself up for success one week at a time.

Remember back to the tool of habit layering? It's time to apply it! Instead of overhauling your whole approach at once, start with one small habit within the area you'd like to shift. Once you've succeeded with that habit, layer on another habit. This might happen in a week – or it might take more time.

As you develop your plan, keep your priorities in mind. Also consider the catalyst habits that you identified for yourself.

- Is there one health habit that could potentially shift others and cause a healthy snowball? Consider starting there and generating momentum from that habit.

What daily/weekly routines do you need to put into place in order to implement your Health Zone?

- Physical Health Routines
  - Movement (physical activity or exercise)
  - Nutrition
  - Sleep
- Mental Health Routines
- Spiritual Health Routines

What daily/weekly routines do you need to eliminate or minimize to support your strategies and bring your vision to life? Note what they are and how you'll do it (unhinge, peel back or swap).

- Physical Health Routines
  - Movement (physical activity and/or exercise)
  - Nutrition
  - Sleep
- Mental Health Routines
- Spiritual Health Routines

Mindfully Review

If you were working on an important project at work, you would take time to regularly evaluate your progress – and the same is true for your life! In your practice, include intervals of evaluation. It doesn't have to be heavy or overwhelming, just set aside time to mindfully reflect and consider what did and did not work for you. I recommend doing this more casually on a weekly basis and more formally on a monthly basis as you start to look towards the next month!

Action Step: spend some time on a regular basis to step back and objectively evaluate your progress with your practice. I highly recommend doing this as part of your routine, on a specific day/time that works for you. It could be Sunday evenings or Monday mornings, for example. Here are the three questions I encourage you to explore:

1. Count your wins! What worked?

2. Insights. Explore what didn't.

3. Evolution. What do you need to revamp or release? How will you do that?

Your Life on the Continuum

As we discussed, your vision for health and fitness is constantly evolving. Which means that you'll likely want to revisit this entire process on a regular basis. That might be quarterly, every six months, or annually. You'll find the rhythm that works best for you and your life. I especially recommend going through this process any time you experience a major change in any of the 5 Pillars – whether that's a major job change, a shift in your family structure or relationships, or a change in your health.

Start back with the Compassionate Audit, and then cycle through checking your vision, evaluating your Health Zone, and using the 5-step S.U.P.E.R. Process to develop your ongoing practice. Don't forget to schedule those weekly mindful reviews! Ongoing awareness and adjustments along the way are essential to making this a functional practice that works for your life!

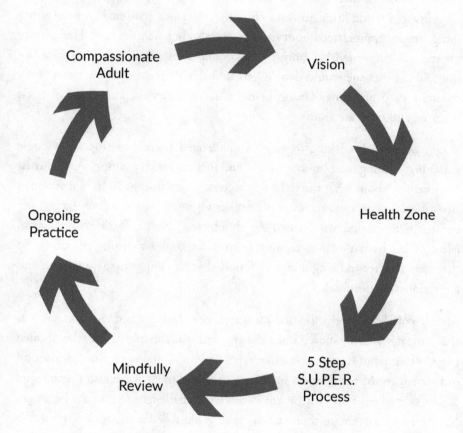

Don't Think, Just Do

Now it's time to take your practice and put it into action! Don't get stuck in analysis paralysis. At some point you need to stop visioning, exploring, reading and researching, and start **doing**.

Brenda came to me after she had tried everything, or rather, *researched* everything. Brenda loved to research and the science mattered to her (something I really appreciated about her). It was also her Achilles heel. Her affinity for research prevented her from doing the most important thing – taking action. Sometimes she would dabble here and dabble there, but she never really committed to anything. Unsurprisingly, her results were lackluster. She felt defeated and frustrated and overwhelmed.

When we started working together, I challenged Brenda to stop her Google searching, reading, and investigating – and just *start* taking action. And to trust her instincts about what the right first step was, and simply do it. Consistently. After a great session where we explored her vision, talked about obstacles, and defined her practice, we decided she should start with a focus on hydration. Most of her hydration was coming from coffee and a morning smoothie. So she used a water-tracking app and found that she enjoyed the analytics and appreciated the feedback.

After a couple of weeks focused on water, Brenda informed me that she was ready to start *moving* more. Since the app was really inspiring her, she decided to get a Fitbit and start tracking her steps. By joining (taking action), she found out that three of her friends, including one workmate, were also on the app! So she started engaging with them in fun daily challenges to increase her steps. She and her workmate then started taking daily walks at work – even five minutes out of the office if that was all the schedule allowed (way to apply that non-negotiable, Brenda)!

At our monthly check-in call, Brenda was elated. This was the first time she'd ever seen herself committed. She noticed her clothes were looser and she had more energy! Six months later, and Brenda is still going strong. She's even started going to yoga class once per week and is eating more veggies! She's feeling stronger, fitter, and healthier than she has in years. No goals required. No research required. Just a clarity of vision, a process-focused practice, intention, and action!

But I Like Goal Smashing!

Bottom line: if you find goals motivating and inspiring, and setting goals and creating plans to achieve them is your thing, rock it!

Let me be clear: I don't have a problem with goals.

Goals absolutely have their place. In fact, I am quite fond of them myself and I regularly set goals to smash! But becoming overly attached to our goals or 'getting there' is counterproductive to the desired outcome we want – which is *to be happy and fulfilled with our health and our life.*

What if you have more specific goals? No problem! This five-step S.U.P.E.R. process absolutely works to bring any goal to life. This approach is about reframing the process so you are connected to that goal on a much deeper level. That way, you can embrace the process and practice required to bring it to life.

The Practice of Smashing Goals

Mariah came to me because she wanted to complete her first triathlon. The race was in six months. When we met, she had no running experience, she could swim a little (to survive), and her bike was currently collecting dust in her garage. But she was already signed up (hello commitment) and was ready to take action. She was already content with her general health and was ready to tackle her more specific goal. She established her vision, and after a short conversation about potential challenges, we got to work creating a practice.

We looked at the strategic plan she would need, and we explored the 5 W's (Why, Who, Where, What, When). She knew her why – she loved a good challenge and found that events motivated her. Her best friend was also training for it and she was excited about them spending time together training. Mariah also knew that 'the who' would be important.

I connected her with a swim coach. We discussed her running program, and I directed her to a great local bike shop where she could get set up properly on her bike.

Together we mapped out a progressive, realistic plan to get her ready. Since her goal was completion, she planned to do two workouts in each sport each week. We mapped out the workouts, keeping in mind the 7 Principles of Fitness we discussed in Chapter 6. Since she'd be starting in the winter, we brainstormed ways to deal with cold and inclement weather. We also figured out how to keep up her training momentum when she was scheduled to be away on a work-related trip.

We talked about how she would make this a priority in her life. She knew it would be tricky with the work trip and with some long work days, but she wanted to go for it. That meant being flexible. On those two busy weeks, she got one workout in for each sport.

We also talked about environment. She felt pretty confident with her bestie by her side for support, but she knew that with so much of her time devoted to training, her husband might start feeling a bit neglected. She also had two small kids and a full-time job. That meant she needed to be strategic with scheduling. She decided she would swim when her kids were in their lessons, and then spend 15 minutes playing with them in the pool after the lessons! She also got her hubby on board to join her once a week at a spinning class, something that involved him in her goal and acted as a fun active date night. She knew it wouldn't all be seamless, but these strategies worked as a starting-off point.

Finally, we looked at her routines. She put in place a weekly day and time for scheduling everything, because her work wasn't traditional hours, she needed to be flexible each week. Having a routine made a big difference in helping her not to stress about the logistics but trust that she could figure them out. She also knew that with this increased training volume, she'd need to focus on sleep, so she put an alarm on her phone to remind her to get to bed.

Mariah's journey was not without hiccups. The flu took down her whole family just one month into training. Once everyone was healthy again, we adjusted the plan. She checked in with me monthly as part of her support structure, so we were able to evaluate progress, and adjust her course as needed. That also helped when she struggled with a knee injury. On my advice, she went to a physiotherapist for treatment and added a few extra stretches and exercises – and that did the trick.

I was there when Mariah crossed the finish line. With 100 meters to go, her two girls ran to their mom and together they ran across the line, hands held high. Her husband stood just at the finish line with a huge bouquet of flowers and a proud smile on his face. It was a beautiful (and teary) moment.

After I gave her a huge hug, and heard her 'race report,' I asked her, "So when's the next race?" I loved her response...

"This has been so much fun! Training with Mary (her bestie) and crossing this line goes down as one of my proudest accomplishments ever, but I'm not sure the pace of this type of training really works for my life, so I'm looking forward to simplifying things. I'm actually really enjoying the swimming, and I'm planning to keep that up two times a week when the kids swim. Maybe down the road I'll do another Tri, or maybe not, but I have *loved* this whole experience."

Goal-setting Caveat.

If you use the system of developing a practice for the achievement of a goal or goals, I have one caveat: before **you reach your goal, decide what is next.**

Why?

If you don't, you risk falling into the trap of letting that goal be *an end date.*

So if we're working to be *less attached* to end dates and desired outcomes, does that mean you have to keep doing an activity you don't love? No!

It means just before you reach your goal, you evaluate whether this is something you wish to continue or not. If not, it's time to try something else on! The big picture objective is to maintain a healthy lifestyle, to have fun along the way, and to be happy and fulfilled in your life.

Embrace the Effort

This will take effort – because change involves taking new routes and developing a new autopilot. It requires tapping into your bravery and stepping out of your comfort zone. But it's worth it (I promise) because that is where all the magic happens.

If you're not happy with your current health and fitness, or your life, that's uncomfortable. Instead of looking at the struggle of shifting your habits and creating new routines as this arduous thing you *have* to do (a chore) – look at it as something you *get* to do (an opportunity). And always remember, *you* get to choose whether the discomfort of this change is worth the effort to make it happen.

Choose your hard.

I have found that when the discomfort of staying the same outweighs the discomfort of change – that's where true transformation lies.

A word of caution. We all have a different *barometer* when it comes to our comfort with discomfort. So determine the level of discomfort you're willing to withstand and stretch yourself to there. As we say in yoga, "find your edge." It's not about extremes or pushing *past* your edge; it's about respecting the edge and also continuously challenging it so you can deepen your practice and grow towards your vision.

Decide Differently for Life

Over the last 10 Chapters, you've explored many ideas, theories, and strategies. You've read about health research and how it applies to your life. You became curious about what being in great health means, and what it means to you. Then you pulled all of it together and defined your personal practice of a healthy lifestyle – one that considers your broader vision, embraces failure as an opportunity, and (I hope) leaves you feeling inspired and ready for action.

At the end of the day, this book is about so much more than just your health; it's about you living an extraordinary life! Because when you are fit and healthy, you exude confidence and you're inspired in every area of your life. You are willing to rise to the challenges that come your way, and you foster and develop meaningful relationships. Simply put, you rise to new levels.

I wrote this book because I've seen, over and over again, what is possible when you let go of the struggle and difficulty, and develop an empowered relationship with your health and your life. It's transformative! I've seen it in myself, and I've seen it in so many of my clients.

Are you ready? You have the insight; you have the capacity; you have the vision and the process to bring it to life. It's time to put that practice into action. Believe in yourself.

We've talked about the power of mindset and the impact our thoughts and words make on our ability to be successful. Now is when this really comes into play.

Decide that you are worth the effort. Then put in the time and energy. If you have a vision that inspires you, a solid plan, and a redefined relationship with success and failure, I know you're going to be unstoppable.

And that unstoppable attitude will impact more than your relationship with health and fitness.

Thank you. For your vulnerability. For your willingness to explore and to be curious. For your grit and determination as you explored the tough stuff and worked through it. Bravo!

Your relationship with health and fitness is truly the tip of the iceberg, and while exploring all of this might not be easy, I promise you: it's worth it! And it all starts with you making a decision to do something different.

Principle #10: Unleash the Elephant

Release your attachment to reaching that oh-so-magical goal, and let the beauty of your vision guide your practice. Let it permeate your daily habits and infiltrate your routines. Allow your vision to come to life through a strategic plan that is grounded in perspective and connects with your unique priorities. Find magic in the minutiae of momentum, and be flexible to the nuances of life. Be bold and take action to make your vision your reality.

CHAPTER 10 POINTS TO PRACTICE

★ *Don't set goals; define your S.U.P.E.R. Practice!* This five-step process will help you bring your vision to life in a practical and functional way. It works for goals too – just make sure you're not too attached to that 'end result.' Focus on the *process* and the outcome will show up.

★ *Step 1: Your Strategic Plan brings clarity to your vision and defines your practice.* This is the Why, Who, Where, What and When of your practice.

★ *Step 2: Identify your Unique Priorities.* Consider what actions you can take that would create the greatest impact by creating a healthy snowball.

★ *Step 3: Clarify your plan with Perspective.* Bring the vision into focus in your life right now by defining your Health Zone.

★ *Step 4: Evaluate your Environment.* Identify the people, places and things that support or distract you. Explore strategies to manage these.

★ *Step 5: Develop a Routine.* Utilize catalyst habits and habit layering to develop NEW habits through routine, and release old routines by using unhinging, peeling back, or swapping. Create a one-month map to help you put these routines in place and set a date to mindfully review them.

★ *Take action and commit to the work.* Change isn't easy, but staying the same isn't either. Choose your hard.

Do This Now: Declare it! (Five minutes).

Call a friend, share it on social media, shout it from the rooftops – *how* you do it doesn't matter, but take this powerful step forward and declare your desire to make lasting change. Tell everyone you're ready to Unleash the Elephant and be happy and healthy for life! Want some props? Use the #unleashtheelephant and connect with this powerful community!

A FINAL INVITATION

Thank you for reading this book, for taking the time to explore these chapters and the ideas within them. I know not all of it was easy work (really, I do!). I hope you found value and gained new insights in the process.

As you embark on this exciting adventure, please know that you are not alone. I would like to invite you to join our dynamic online community – the SuperCrew.

The SuperCrew is a free source of support and encouragement. Connect with us, lean on us, and celebrate with us! Visit https://www.facebook.com/groups/superyousupercrew/ and join the SuperCrew.

I wish you all the very best with your Practice of Health. May it be fulfilling, and may it bring you happiness and joy! And may you be SuperYou!

ACKNOWLEDGEMENTS

When people ask me why I wrote this book, I often say I felt called to write it. After nearly 20 years working with clients and traveling my own bumpy road to creating a healthy lifestyle, I knew I had a unique perspective to offer. But as a first-time author I had literally no idea where to begin. Thankfully, I connected with Book Launchers. With the help of Julie Broad, Jaqueline Kyle, Alix Sloan, and the team at Book Launchers my book took shape from a diffuse idea to a clear vision with purpose. I can honestly say without a shadow of doubt that the current evolution of this book is possible because of their support.

This book contains my own story – but also the stories or composites of the many clients I've had the opportunity to work with over the course of my career. I would not be the coach I am without their trust, faith, and vulnerability.

This book would also not be possible without the brain picking, feedback, and support of an incredible number of people – my 'Elephant in the Gym' support tribe!

For everyone in my life who regularly asked with genuine excitement how my book was coming – thank you. Your enthusiasm contributed to the well of energy I needed to make this book come to life. There are too many of you to list but please know I deeply appreciate each and every one of you. There are a specific few that I would like to call out for their contributions to me and this process. I'd like to thank my trail running mates, Krista Bryce, Sandra Johnstone, Erin Dahle, Dana Ellis, Suzanne Armour, Peggy Peppard, Karen Dibblee, Teresa Rock-Prince, and Tracy Hedberg. This book literally took shape on the trails. Our moving meditations and many conversations helped me solidify my message and stay true to my purpose. I'd also like to thank two brilliant librarians and dear friends, Dominique Sullivan and Jennifer Lunny, who were always willing ears and sounding boards as I developed my voice and found grounding in the process. My early readers, Audra Alderson, Krista Bryce, and Kate Fisher – thank you for your enthusiasm and honesty. You helped me hone my voice and clarify my vision. My most sincere and heart-felt gratitude to Patricia Chuey, Brenda Adams, Kathy Kutzer, and Jennifer Jasinski. I'm deeply honored to have had your professional eyes on these pages prior to publishing. Thank you for your feedback and insights as well as your mentorship, guidance, and support.

Thank you doesn't feel enough when it comes to my wonderful husband, Mike. I cannot possibly count the hours I said I was "just going down to write for a few minutes" after the kids went to bed on a Saturday night, and disappeared for hours. Your calm, quiet patience, and your willingness to listen to my constant ramblings and out loud brainstorming sessions is truly a testament to your love. I'm not sure every man would have put up with me. I appreciate you more than words can say.

Being a mom and writing a book involves sacrifice. And often the sacrifices were made by my children. I'm deeply proud of and grateful for my incredibly resilient kids, Connor and Chase, for their willingness to watch a show (or three) so I could sneak in one more bit of writing when 'writing between the school bells' morphed into more. And more importantly for being patient when mommy was thinking and needed to write something down before she could answer their question. But mostly for their genuine and insatiable curiosity in all things. Thank you for being my inspiration.

So much of what is between these pages was developed through my own experience and growth. I am abundantly clear that every experience I had – 'good' and 'bad' informed my story and shaped my philosophy. I would like to thank my parents, Karen and Tim Stiles, as well as my sister, Joanna Drake. You were always a soft place to land and a constant source of love and encouragement. I won the family lottery being born into this family – I don't take that for granted.

And finally, dear reader – I thank you. Bravo for your willingness to explore. To consider a different perspective and challenge the current paradigm. To step out of the box and do the work to develop your very own unique definition and practice of a healthy lifestyle. My hat is off to you.

APPENDIX A

How to Find the Right Fitness Professional for You

Finding the right fitness professional is like finding the right hairdresser. It's about finding someone who has the right skill set and personality to suit *you*. Whether you're hiring a personal trainer or attending a fitness class with an instructor, first and foremost you need to feel comfortable with the person. They should empower and inspire you in a way that makes you feel like the extraordinary person you are. It's also important that they're qualified in their craft. You need to be confident that the recommendations they're giving you are based on science and best practices. If you're feeling nervous about asking them straight up, you may wish to look at their website or that of the facility. Most trainers will list their credentials for this reason. And if not, don't be shy. Whenever I get asked, I'm proud to share this type of information with potential clients. And a wee bit impressed that they're asking – because it shows me that they value the investment they are making in their body by employing my services!

When it comes to a professional's qualifications and credentials, here is what I think you should be considering:

Credentials and Experience

Credentials and experience are huge when it comes to finding a qualified fitness professional. There is a wide range of options for becoming a credentialed fitness professional, and unfortunately very little governance of this field. This means that as a consumer you need to be savvy. At a bare minimum, you want to find a fitness professional who is registered or certified through a regional or national governing body. Please keep in mind that not all certification processes are equal. Some are as little as a one–day or weekend course, and some involve extensive coursework and practicum hours. As with any designation, continuing education and experience also play a huge role in the quality of the practitioner. Not all designating bodies require the same degree of continuing education. When you're hiring a fitness professional, don't just ask if they are certified, also look to ensure they are maintaining that certification through ongoing continuing education. Also ask about their experience working with clients similar to you.

Some of the governing bodies to look for are listed below.

In Canada:

- CanFitPro (Canadian Association of Fitness Professionals)
- National Fitness Leadership Alliance (NFLA), regional including:
    - British Columbia Parks and Recreation Association (BCRPA)
    - Alberta Fitness Leadership Certification Association (AFLCA)
    - Saskatchewan Parks and Recreation Association (SPRA)
    - Manitoba Fitness Council (MFC)
    - Ontario Fitness Council (OFC)
    - Nova Scotia Fitness Association (NSFA)
    - Fitness New Brunswick (FNB)
- Certified Personal Trainers Network (CPTN)
- Canadian Society of Exercise Physiology (CSEP)

In the United States:

- American Council on Exercise (ACE)
- National Strength and Conditioning Association (NSCA)
- National Academy of Sports Medicine (NASM)
- American College of Sports Medicine (ACSM)
- National Federation of Personal Trainers (NFPT)

In Europe:

- European Register of Exercise Professionals (EREPS)
- EuropeActive (formerly the European Health and Fitness Association)

Depending on what you're looking for, you may also wish to look for a personal trainer who holds a degree in human kinetics, physical education or kinesiology. This is especially important if you have health conditions or are looking for support around injury rehabilitation, or if you are working with a chronic health condition such as osteoporosis, arthritis, diabetes, or high blood pressure.

Do they have valid first aid/CPR qualifications and insurance?

Hopefully these will not have to be used, but if they do, you want them to have the appropriate training and coverage. Also, if they have these, it shows due diligence on their part.

Do they have testimonials or references available?

If they have clients that you can relate to and who have had a great experience with them, the likelihood is that you'll also have a positive experience. Look for testimonials on their website, or reviews on Google or their Facebook page – or even better, ask around. Find others you know and trust who can give a personal reference.

Bottom line? Listen to your gut instinct. If the advice they give feels right for you, and they motivate and inspire you to be SUPERYOU – then you've probably found the right person!

Tools of the Practice

Throughout the book, I've mentioned strategies and tactics I utilize in my personal practice as well as in my work with clients. Here's a helpful list to turn to when you need to refocus and refine your practice for a healthy lifestyle.

Mantras or Positive Affirmations: both are mindfulness tools that can be useful in daily life or in meditation. Mantras are traditionally words, sounds, or invocations used in a spiritual practice. In contemporary society, the word is often used interchangeably with 'positive affirmations.' Positive affirmations are words or phrases that set intention and promote positive feelings and thoughts. They can be particularly helpful when you have a negative thought habit you would like to extinguish, or you want to bring your attention to your intentions around your health and fitness. For example, if you had a negative self-talk or thought habit around your relationship with food or fitness, you might choose to reframe it with a mantra.

Mindful Meals: bringing awareness to our nutrition choices and habits is a powerful tool for initiating change, and for reconnecting to our bodies. One of my favorite strategies around this is to become more mindful during meals and snacks by minimizing distractions. Start by choosing one meal or snack and eliminating all distractions. No screens, no conversation, no books or magazines. Just you, your body, and the food. Notice how you feel before, during and after the meal or snack. Take your time. You may choose to journal after this process.

Non-negotiables: this strategy is particularly helpful as you enter into periods of major stress or busyness. Non-negotiables are the habits you'll maintain no matter what. As with brushing your teeth, you'll do them without much thought. Typically, it's best if they are significantly scaled down versions of your regular habits. For example, if you typically eat five servings of veggies per day, the non-negotiable might be three servings (one at each meal). Or if you typically walk three days per week, the non-negotiable might be 5000 steps on your tracker daily.

Wins List: this strategy is really helpful to reduce the impact of our built-in negativity bias. The objective of this strategy is to become more mindful of your choices and bring increased awareness to all the ways you are *successful* in pursuit of your goals and the manifestation of your vision. An example of a 'win' would be, "I walked by the treat table and didn't stop. I wasn't hungry," or "I didn't have time for the gym, so I did a 10-minute walk because that is what I had time for." When I use this strategy with clients, I typically recommend that they do this daily and record wins as they notice them, and also that they review them at the end of each day as well as at the end of each week.

Catalyst Habit: this is a habit that triggers a domino effect with respect to other habits. In other words, they create a 'healthy snowball' habit. Discovering them involves looking at an area of struggle and 'peeling back the layers' until you can see *the core*. For example, you get home with the intention of making a healthy meal, but you look in the fridge and you don't know what to do, or you don't really have the right ingredients. You know meal planning and prep would help you with this problem, but you don't ever seem to find the time or you simply don't enjoy it! Peeling back the layers comes down to exploring how you can create more time in your life to set yourself up for success – which may mean saying no to some commitments, or reconsidering your work hours. Once you create the time, it's about prioritizing this habit to set yourself up for success – perhaps by scheduling meal planning as a routine activity in your week. Or perhaps by identifying the fact that you don't *like* planning (at least not every night), and therefore making the decision to utilize one of the various home delivery services that delivers all the ingredients you need and a recipe in a box. Dealing with your areas of struggle can take some time because it requires being *curious*. But once you identify a catalyst habit, you can sometimes create profound shifts.

Habit Crowding: crowd out the undesirable habit by focusing on habits you wish to *increase* – and this will naturally *decrease* the undesirable habit. Similarly, crowd out unhealthy food choices by focusing on the habits you want to develop, such as drinking a healthy amount of water or eating enough fruits and veggies!

Habit Layering: break the habit into more manageable pieces and add the pieces in one layer at a time. For example, you: want to work on your desk posture by incorporating desk stretches. Start by setting your timer to complete one posture exercise once per day for a week. Once you've established that, then move up to two times per day. Continue until you achieve your goal of one stretch per hour for the duration of your work day!

Peeling Back Habits: this is Habit Layering in reverse. Just as we lean into some habits by layering them on piece by piece, we can also peel them back. For example, you have an unhelpful habit of letting your Friday night treat meal lead into more than a few glasses of wine. Start by setting a limit on the number of glasses you can have, and then each week cut that back until you get to the number you're comfortable with as an ongoing practice.

Habit Pairing: pair a new habit with an old and established habit. For example, if you want to do something DAILY, connect it with something else you do daily. The OLD habit acts as a trigger for the new one, until it's established! For example, repeat a mantra or a stretch every time you brush your teeth.

Unhinging Habits: this is Habit Pairing in reverse! It can be used to disconnect or 'unhinge' two or more habits. For example, you'd like to eliminate screens from the bedroom to improve your sleep quality and quantity. But evening screen time in bed is a habit pair. Start by *limiting* your time – it may be helpful to use a timer or set an alarm. Finally, use an alarm for your 'device cut-off time,' then leave your device charging elsewhere and head to bed!

Habit Swapping: when you have a habit that is unhelpful but is well established, the first step to making a change is to examine what is at the core of the habit – what is the reward you are seeking? For example, the glass of wine to unwind after work or the mindless snacking when bored, tired, or (fill in the blank emotion). Looking at your core needs in the moment can help you find a suitable substitute to swap.

Helpful Resources

As we've journeyed through this conversation, there may have been some areas where you found yourself really intrigued and perhaps even thought to yourself, "I'd like to learn more!" Cool! I love that curiosity! Here is a list of resources that may be helpful.

Websites:

http://self-compassion.org This is the website of Dr. Kristin Neff. If you're looking to explore the idea of self-compassion, she is a fabulous resource for books and audio. Her website also has some free guided meditations and self-compassion exercises you might enjoy.

https://chrisgermer.com Dr. Christopher Germer is the other leader in the area of self-compassion. His website also has some wonderful resources, including a considerable number of guided meditations.

http://www.rickhanson.net If you're ready to geek out on super cool brain science, Dr. Rick Hanson is your guy. He has a ton of resources, blogs, and educational videos on his site.

http://www.sparkinglife.org This not-for-profit organization, spear-headed by Dr. John Ratey, is moving the conversation forward around the benefits of exercise when it comes to brain health. On the website, there's great information regarding the impact of exercise on depression, anxiety, addiction, stress, ADD, and ADHD.

http://www.geneenroth.com Geneen Roth's *Women, Food and God* was one of the first books I read that really opened my eyes to the deeper nuances of our relationship with food. Her work still stands out as game changing, and her website has a series of free videos that you might wish to explore.

https://brenebrown.com I love all things Brené! Dr. Brown's work around vulnerability and embracing our imperfections has truly transformed my view of the world and the work I do. Her website is a wonderful resource, and I find that her weekly 'dose of daring' is a lovely reminder for us to Dare Greatly!

https://www.sharonsalzberg.com Sharon is a fantastic teacher. Her 28-day Real Happiness Meditation Challenge runs every February and is a wonderful introduction to meditation.

https://www.tarabrach.com Tara Brach's website is an incredible resource for guided meditations. I find her voice particularly soothing and I enjoy how she pulls in her vast knowledge from multiple areas of mindfulness and Buddhist philosophy.

http://www.10percenthappier.com Dan Harris is a news anchor turned meditation evangelist (in a good way). With humor and a thoughtful journalistic approach, he brings mindfulness meditation out of the realm of 'woo woo' and to a broader audience. His website has some excellent podcasts and downloads.

http://ohsheglows.com I love Angela Liddon's vegan recipes. They're fresh, relatively fast, and always a hit! Her cookbooks are also great!

http://janetandgreta.com/recipes Janet and Greta are the creators of the Looneyspoons Cookbook series, and their recipes are simple, family friendly, and easy to follow (and funny)!

http://www.superyou.ca Oh hey! That's me! I have a blog that includes a ton of yummy recipes, fitness tips, and videos. I also have a few free programs that might interest you, and I also work virtually with clients throughout North America. Heck, you might even consider joining the Super You SuperCrew – if you're looking for a tribe that follows the Super You Philosophy described in this book! To join visit facebook.com/groups/superyousupercrew.

Documentaries:

Embrace. "*Embrace* follows body image activist Taryn Brumfitt's crusade as she explores the global issue of body loathing, inspiring us to change the way we feel about ourselves and think about our bodies."

The Illusionists. "Sex sells. What sells even more? Insecurity. Multibillion-dollar industries saturate our lives with images of unattainable beauty, exporting body hatred from New York to Beirut to Tokyo. Their target? Women, and increasingly men and children. *The Illusionists* turns the mirror on the media, exposing the absurd, shocking, and sometimes humorous images that seek to enslave us."

Miss Representation. "Explores the under representation of women in positions of power and influence in America, and challenges the media's limited portrayal of what it means to be a powerful woman."

Books:

Beauty Sick: How the Cultural Obsession with Appearance Hurts Girls and Women. Renee Engeln, PhD

The Gifts of Imperfection. Brené Brown

Self-Compassion, Step by Step. Kristin Neff

Self-Compassion: The Proven Power of Being Kind to Yourself. Kristin Neff

The Mindful Path to Self-Compassion. Christopher Germer

Real Happiness: The Power of Meditation. Sharon Salzberg

Meditation for Fidgety Skeptics. Dan Harris and Jeff Warren

Radical Self-Acceptance. Tara Brach

Women, Food and God. Geneen Roth

Thrive: The Third Metric to Redefining Success and Creating a Happier Life. Arianna Huffington

The Sleep Revolution: Transforming Your Life One Night at a Time. Arianna Huffington

The Book of Joy: Lasting Happiness in a Changing World. His Holiness the Dalai Lama and Archbishop Desmond Tutu with Douglas Abrams

Spark: The Revolutionary New Science of Exercise and the Brain. John J. Ratey, MD

Apps:

Water Tracking: Plant Nanny or Gulp

Meditation: Calm, Buddhify, Smiling Mind, Insight Timer or 10% Happier

Spotify: Music to move you. Follow me at GillianGoerzen for playlists to inspire you to move!

APPENDIX D

The BE SUPER YOU Principles

At the end of each chapter, I shared a principle with you. These principles are short summaries or take-homes from each chapter, but they are so much more than that. I see them as the guideposts – leading you on a beautiful journey – and I encourage you to refer to them often. That's why they're included in the companion handbook to this book, *Unleash the Elephant: Defining Your Practice* (if you haven't yet, download it for free at www.elephantinthegym.com/resources). You can use this stand-alone page of the handbook as a reminder. Feel free to post it on your fridge or at your desk at work. However you use it, I hope you let the principles sink in and direct your own unique practice of a healthy lifestyle that you will love.

Be You. *You are unique – and so is your health!* There isn't a single other person on this planet with the same genetics, interests, priorities, and values as *you*. Stop trying to stick your awesome curvy round peg into a boring square hole, and create a completely customized approach to your health that honors *you* and evolves with *you* – so you can be happy and healthy for life!

Embrace Your Humanity. *Your healthy lifestyle is not about being perfect; it's about taking care of your body, mind, and soul.* As you shift your habits and do the work, there will be challenges. You will slip back into old patterns and old ways of being. And when you do, you'll likely be hard on yourself. *Notice* that. And then *reframe*. Speak to yourself as you would to a dear friend. Embrace a self-compassionate approach to shifting your habits and feeling empowered and inspired.

Show Up. *Trust the process and take action!* You've been up against a lot – but don't give away your power! Shift your thinking and decide you *can*. Go in with a mindset that you will succeed and then put the work in to make it happen! Find your grit, determination, and perseverance. Decide you're worth it, and start living into your full potential!

Unlock Your Potential. *You are both your loudest critic and your biggest cheerleader.* Stop looking outward to people or things; instead, look inward and become aware of the words you choose to speak to yourself – because your words work! Speak with kindness and intention. If the inner dialogue isn't helpful, turn it around with the power of positive self-talk. Develop a mantra that speaks to you, inspires you and motivates you to take action.

Practice Patience and Perseverance. *Understand and accept that you are wired for struggle and that change is not easy.* Find the people you need to support you through the struggle. Be willing to explore your relationship with struggle, become aware of it and make peace with it. Don't let the challenges you face stop you from taking action in your life. Lean into change and practice patience and perseverance.

Explore the Science, Practice the Art. *Health is a science and fitness is a science, but how you apply them to your life is an art.* Remember that health and fitness are two distinct things, and every move is a good move when it comes to your health! There is no one right way to be fit, just the one that works for you, in your life, right now. Start where you are and find the practice of health and fitness that works for you!

Reclaim Your Relationship with Food. *Nutrition science is genuinely complex, but your relationship with food doesn't have to be!* Ditch the diet and reclaim your gut instincts. Remember that your approach to nutrition will be as unique as your priorities, individual needs, goals, and tastes! Food should be enjoyed, and any approach to nutrition that is going to yield long–term results needs to be something you can maintain long term. There is no one right way to eat – just the one that works for you and your body!

Yawn Your Way to Success. *Sleep is the unsung hero of health.* It is truly essential and should never be undervalued. Approach sleep with a positive attitude and make seven to nine hours of sleep per night a priority. Maybe even inspire others around you to do the same. Give your body, mind, and spirit the advantage of being optimally rested and recovered so you can get out there and be your best!

Own It. *Your health, your fitness, your life.* Create a vision for your life that genuinely inspires you. Define your unique practice of a healthy lifestyle and then own it. Keep your eyes in your own lane, and don't let the gloss and glamour of quick fixes and fads take you off your own awesome course. Don't fear failure, embrace it as an opportunity to learn more about what works (and doesn't) for you and your life. Be open to the evolution of your health, wellness, and life!

Unleash the Elephant. *Release your attachment to reaching that oh–so–magical goal, and let the beauty of your vision guide your practice.* Let it permeate your daily habits and infiltrate your routines. Allow your vision to come to life through a strategic plan that is grounded in perspective and connects with your unique priorities. Find magic in the minutiae of momentum and be flexible to the nuances of life. Be bold and take action to make your vision your reality.

ABOUT THE AUTHOR
Gillian Goerzen

Health and Fitness Coach Gillian Goerzen wants you to ditch your diet and quit doing workouts you dread. With a degree in Kinesiology and over 20 years of health coaching experience, Gillian's personalized lifestyle strategies have helped hundreds of clients redefine what fitness means to them, and get lasting results they never dreamed possible - free from diets, programs, systems, pills and products. From hating her body at the age of 5, it took more than 20 years, an eating disorder, an Ironman, and becoming a mom to finally uncover the kinder, more compassionate approach to health and fitness that she teaches today.

Gillian lives on Vancouver Island with her husband Mike and two children Connor and Chase. She teaches running clinics, fitness and yoga locally in her hometown of Nanaimo, BC and coaches clients from all over North America through her business Super You.

References

1   http://journals.plos.org/plosone/article?id=10.1371/journal.pone.0070048
     http://www.scapps.org/jems/index.php/1/article/view/1688
     https://pdfs.semanticscholar.org/5c03/cfbc761031787464c1291bb23f2f5f9a90fe.pdf
     http://www.scapps.org/jems/index.php/1/article/view/1688
2   Self-Compassion:The Proven Power of Being Kind to Yourself, Kristin Neff, PhD, p162-164
3   https://www.youtube.com/watch?v=IvtZBUSplr4
4   Mindful Path to Self-Compassion p. 85
5   https://www.youtube.com/watch?v=IvtZBUSplr4
6   Schwartz, R.M. Cogn Ther Res (1986) 10: 591. https://doi.org/10.1007/BF01173748
7   Van Raalte, J.L. Psych of Sport and Ex 22: 139 (2015) https://doi.org/10.1016/j.psychsport.2015.08.004
8   https://www.sciencedirect.com/science/article/pii/S1469029215000874
9   Baumeister R. F., & Leary M. R. (1995). The need to belong: Desire for interpersonal attachments as a fundamental human motivation. Psychological Bulletin, 117, 497-529.
10   http://www.rickhanson.net/how-your-brain-makes-you-easily-intimidated/
11   http://www.rickhanson.net/how-your-brain-makes-you-easily-intimidated/
12   Renee Engeln, Beauty Sick, Chapter 5
13   https://kar.kent.ac.uk/33425/1/ENCY.OBJTHEORY.CASH.pdf
14   Gapinski, K. D., Brownell, K. D., & LaFrance, M.(2003). Body objectification and "fat talk": Effects on emotion, motivation, and cognitive performance. Sex Roles: A Journal of Research, 48(9/10), 377.
15   http://psycnet.apa.org/record/2010-13678-009
16   https://www.sharonsalzberg.com/realhappinessblognyimcpower-and-blessing-beginning-again/
17   https://www.ncbi.nlm.nih.gov/pmc/articles/PMC3404815/
18   https://health.gov/paguidelines/guidelines/adults.aspx
19   http://www.sparkinglife.org/why-exercise-works/depression/
20   ACE Essentials of Exercise Science for Fitness Professionals p243
21   https://www.ncbi.nlm.nih.gov/pmc/articles/PMC1762341/
22   Brendan Burchard
23   http://www.unlockfood.ca/en/Articles/Water/Facts-on-Fluids-How-to-Stay-Hydrated.aspx
24   Government of Canada (2013). Health Canada reminds Canadians to manage their caffeine consumption. Available online: http://healthycanadians.gc.ca/recall-alert-rappel-avis/hc-sc/2013/34021a-eng.php.
25   Grandjean AC, et al. (2000). The effect of caffeinated, non-caffeinated, caloric, and non-caloric beverages on hydration. Journal of the American College of Nutrition, 19(5): 591-600.

26   http://www.nejm.org/doi/full/10.1056/NEJMoa1014296?query=TOC&#t=articleTop

27   https://www.cdc.gov/media/releases/2016/p0215-enough-sleep.html

28   https://www.statcan.gc.ca/pub/82-003-x/2017009/article/54857-eng.htm

29   https://www.nhlbi.nih.gov/health/health-topics/topics/sdd/why

30   http://healthysleep.med.harvard.edu/healthy/matters/benefits-of-sleep/learning-memory

31   https://www.medscape.org/viewarticle/502825

32   http://jandonline.org/article/S2212-2672%2812%2901344-5/fulltext

33   https://www.cdc.gov/features/dssleep/index.html, https://www.cdc.gov/sleep/about_
      sleep/sleep_hygiene.html